Pelican Books

The Political Thoug

Stuart R. Schram was born in Minnesota, U.S.A., in 1924. He took his B.A. at the University of Minnesota in 1944, followed by a Ph.D. in political science at Columbia University in 1954. From 1954 to 1967 he carried out research at the Centre d'Étude des Relations Internationales of the Fondation Nationale des Sciences Politiques in Paris, where, with Hélène Carrère d'Encausse, he was responsible for the Soviet and Chinese Section. He is now Professor of Politics (with reference to China) in the University of London and Head of the Contemporary China Institute of the School of Oriental and African Studies. In his research he is chiefly interested in the role of ideology in politics, especially in Communist countries, and in the history of Leninist theories together with their application by the Communist movement in Asia.

Professor Schram has also published *Marxism and Asia* (with Hélène Carrère d'Encausse), and *Mao Tse-tung* (a Pelican in the Political Leaders of the Twentieth Century series, 1966, revised in 1969).

Apart from his research, Professor Schram is interested in music, poetry, the theatre and nature.

STUART R. SCHRAM

The Political Thought of Mao Tse-tung

ENLARGED AND REVISED EDITION

Penguin Books Ltd, Harmondsworth, Middlesex, England
Penguin Books Australia Ltd, Ringwood, Victoria, Australia

First published in the U.S.A. by Frederick A. Praeger 1963
Published in Pelican Books 1969
Reprinted 1971

Made and printed in Great Britain by
C. Nicholls & Company Ltd
Set in Monotype Times

Contents

Preface to the Revised Edition

In the five years since this book first appeared, Mao Tse-tung and China have been constantly and increasingly in the public eye. 'Mao Tse-tung's thought' in particular has become a familiar notion not only in China but throughout the world. The sense in which this term is used is, however, rather different from what is meant by 'the political thought of Mao Tse-tung' in the title of this book. My concern in this volume was to present Mao's political thinking as it has grown and developed in the course of the past half century. I endeavoured to show how Marxism had been shaped both by Mao's own personality and by the situation of China in the early twentieth century, and how Mao had modified his views in the course of the revolutionary struggle in the light of experience and of changing conditions. 'Mao Tse-tung's thought' as used today in Peking refers to a body of ideas which are presumed to have sprung full-blown from Mao's brain sometime around 1920, and to have been handed down ever since as absolutely immutable and universally valid truths.

Although some attention is given in the present edition to Mao Tse-tung's thought in this new sense, and more generally to the ideas which have been put forward in Mao's name in the course of the 'Great Proletarian Cultural Revolution', the emphasis remains on the genesis and development of Mao's thought and on the variations in his theories and policies in the course of the successive phases of his struggle, first to achieve power and then to transform the face of China.

In addition to the up-dating both of the selection of texts and of the introduction to take account of the developments of the last five years, substantial changes have been made in this edition in the portions of the book dealing with earlier periods. These are inspired both by the new facts and documents which have come to light in the course of the last five years, and by the new ideas and insights which I have derived from my own research over this period. The introduction has been very extensively revised with the aim of showing more clearly the relation between the development of Mao's political thought and his revolutionary experience, as I have had the occasion to study it in preparing my biography of Mao Tse-tung. These changes and additions are particularly important in the portions of the introduction dealing with the late 1920s and early 1930s, and with the early years of the Chinese People's Republic.

As regards the texts, Chapters VI and VII, containing materials relevant to internal developments in China since 1949, have been completely recast and greatly amplified. A number of additions have also been made to Chapter V on Mao's military principles, a subject which was rather neglected in the first edition of this book. Chapters VIII, IX and X have been less extensively modified, but a few texts have been added to each in order to bring them up to date.

In order to make it easier for readers familiar with the original edition to locate a particular item in the present edition, a comparative table listing all the texts in both editions appears at the end of the volume. An index is also included in this edition for the first time in order to make it easier to locate material on particular topics. The bibliography and chronology have likewise been brought up to date.

I am conscious of the fact that despite these additions and improvements, this book still constitutes only a provisional and inadequate account of a very complex subject. The information which has become available in the course of the Cultural Revolution calls into question much that we have thought in the past, both about Mao Tse-tung's career and about his ideas and strategy. It is still too early to arrive at any considered judgement as to how much of the material contained in Red Guard newspapers and similar sources is authentic or substantially authentic, and how much is merely fabrication in order to serve immediate political aims, but it is already plain that both our knowledge of the facts and our understanding of them leave much to be desired. In addition to these difficulties which must be faced by anyone working on the subject, I am acutely aware of the gaps and deficiencies in my own interpretation of Mao's life and thought. In undertaking the present revision, I have been actuated not by the ambition of producing a definitive study, but simply by the hope that an expanded and up-dated version of this book might be of some use until such time as I or someone else can produce a better one.

In the course of the past five years, I have benefited from conversations with many people working on contemporary China, which have greatly contributed to deepening my own understanding of the subject. A list, which could only be incomplete, would be unfair to those who were omitted. I have therefore left the *Acknowledgements* as they stood in the first edition, merely inserting notes in the body of the book to thank those who have supplied me with the Chinese texts of certain of Mao's writings. I am none the less grateful for this counsel and stimulus without which the present book would be even more imperfect than it is.

Acknowledgements

I should first of all like to express my gratitude to the Rockefeller Foundation for assuring me of the leisure to undertake the research that has made this book possible. Needless to say, the Foundation is in no way responsible either for Mao's own views or for my interpretation of them. I should also like to thank the East Asian Research Center of Harvard University and its Director, John K. Fairbank, for the hospitality extended to me during the past year, which has provided me with a pleasant and stimulating environment for my research.

Thanks are due to Mr Edgar Snow and Mrs Helen Foster Snow for their kind permission to reproduce passages from the original manuscript of Mr Snow's interviews with Mao Tse-tung in 1936, and to Mr Boyd Compton and to the University of Washington Press for authorization to reprint, with a few minor textual changes, extracts from Mao's speeches of 1 and 8 February 1942, as translated by Mr Compton from the original Chinese text and published in *Mao's China*.

In view of the documentary character of this volume, special importance attaches to the assistance of the librarians of the Chinese collections at Harvard University, Columbia University, and the Library of Congress, and above all to that of Mr Eugene Wu, Curator of the East Asian Collections of the Hoover Institution and Library in Stanford, California. The majority of the original texts used as a basis for this volume were obtained from this source, and the unfailing courtesy and helpfulness of Mr Wu and his staff greatly facilitated my exploration of this unique collection.

Mr S. T. Leong made the original drafts of the English versions of that part of the materials in Chapters I–V which had never before been translated from the Chinese. I revised these after comparison with my own French translations; the new translations in the remaining chapters are entirely my own.

M. Jean Touchard, the director of the collection in which the French version of this volume is appearing, and Mrs Jean Steinberg, who has edited the English text, have both gone over the manuscript with care and made useful suggestions for achieving greater clarity and readability.

My interpretation of Mao Tse-tung's thought has been enriched by conversations with many specialists both in France and in the United States. My greatest debt in this respect is unquestionably to Benjamin Schwartz, but I doubt that either he or any of my other interlocutors would agree completely with the use I have made of the ideas they have suggested to me. In any case, the reader should not hold them responsible for any errors of fact or interpretation of which I may be found guilty.

Introduction

Ideas grow out of history; they also shape history. We may consider how the interaction of a tradition or traditions and a historical situation in the mind of an individual produces his ideas. We may also treat a man's thought as a key to understanding his acts and intentions. This second approach is particularly important when we are dealing with a Leninist revolutionary such as Mao Tse-tung, who conceives of his own thought as an instrument for the transformation of society. With such a figure, we must consider not only how the situation in China in the early twentieth century and the intellectual currents abroad at the time combined with the bent of Mao's personality to produce his thought; we must also consider how Mao, and the political apparatus directed by him, employ his thought as a guide in their efforts to change the face of China.

But the problem does not stop there. Mao Tse-tung today rules over one fourth of all humanity. The shadow of his power is cast over all of Asia, and his ideological influence is felt from India to Albania, from Africa to Latin America. Thus, no examination of his thought would be complete without an analysis of the potential appeal his peculiar brand of Communism exerts on the peoples of other underdeveloped countries seeking a model for the rapid transformation of their own societies.

These, then, are the three questions with which I shall deal in this introduction: What are the origins of Mao's thought? Where is it going? What is likely to be its impact on the world at large?

1. The Formation of Mao Tse-tung's Thought

The thought of Mao bears the imprint of the historical situation in which he grew up, of the intellectual currents to which he was exposed, and also of his own very strong personality. The markedly individual bent of Mao's personality is undeniable. And yet there are many traits that may strike the Western reader as unique which Mao in fact shares with other Chinese of his generation. Let us therefore examine China's political and intellectual climate at the beginning of the twentieth century before considering what is original in Mao's response to the problems of his time.

a. China in transition. The process that has been going on in China for a century or more has been variously called 'modernization' and 'Westernization'. Neither of these terms is quite appropriate. China has not been simply modernized, for though the Chinese empire in the eighteenth and nineteenth centuries was not the timeless and immutable entity it appeared to European observers, change would not have taken place either at the same time or in the same way had it not been for the impact of the West. On the other hand, China has not been simply Westernized, for though she has absorbed ideas and techniques from the West, these imported elements have not brusquely supplanted traditional modes of thought and behaviour, but have been incorporated into a living fabric that contains not only much that is Western, but also much that is Chinese. This is true even today, after China has been reshaped for nearly two decades by professed adherents of that most radical of Westernizing ideologies – Marxism-Leninism.

How shall we designate this process if we reject both 'modernization' and 'Westernization' as too one-sided? It might be defined as follows: the process of adaptation to the modern world, and more specifically to Western pressures, by the selective adoption of certain Western ideas, institutions, and techniques, and the critical re-examination of China's own tradition. This process constitutes the basic framework essential to an understanding of Mao's development. In place of this long, cumbersome definition, I shall use such terms as 'the transformation of China', 'adaptation to modern conditions', and even 'modernization' or 'Westernization'. However, it should be understood that all these are merely shorthand expressions for a very complex phenomenon.

When the 'Western barbarians' began their incursions, with the Opium War in 1840, and when the military superiority of the West had been convincingly demonstrated, the Chinese ruling élite sought to arm itself with similarly potent weapons in order to meet the invaders on equal terms. It never occurred to the imperial officials who controlled the state that it might also be appropriate to study the principles guiding the European society and economy for an explanation of Western dynamism. The superiority of their own culture and social system was simply taken for granted.

Three of the reasons for this complacent attitude deserve mention:

1. China had never belonged to a system of states dealing with one another on a basis of equality, but had been for several millennia virtually a universe unto herself, in contact only with less powerful peoples whose rulers were regarded as naturally tributary to the only genuine Son of Heaven, the Chinese emperor.

2. Except for the introduction of Buddhism from India early in the Christian Era, the Chinese had been in contact largely with peoples not only less powerful but culturally inferior, so that they tended to identify their own civilization with civilization as such.

3. The ruling group had a vested interest in preserving the traditional principles of society and government, which were the basis of its own power. Whether one defines the locus of power in the empire as the emperor and his bureaucracy, as does Karl A. Wittfogel,[1] or as the landlord class, as do Marxist writers (including Mao), there is no doubt that the position of those in power, whoever they were, was buttressed by Confucian principles of subordination to authority.

The first two of the above points explain the natural tendency of the Chinese élite to regard all foreigners as inferior barbarians and to attempt to force the Europeans into the same tributary status as any nomadic people or savage tribe. The third point explains in part the reluctance of the ruling group to envisage any significant modifications in the existing system even when their ingrained belief in China's superiority had been severely shaken by events.

Little by little, the Chinese ruling élite was driven to understand that arms could not be borrowed from the West without creating the industrial basis for their production, and that modern industry could not be established without smuggling in not only Western technical knowledge, but a host of ideas and attitudes subversive of the existing political and intellectual system. One generation, that of Tseng Kuo-fan, to which Mary Wright has devoted a brilliant and provocative study,[2] preferred to forgo such strengthening of the country as could only be bought at the cost of inroads on what they regarded as its *raison d'être*. Later generations of mandarins and intellectuals were more audacious. But on the one hand, the degree of acceptance of Western techniques and ideas necessary to modernize the Chinese economy and create a new basis for Chinese power was probably incompatible with the maintenance of the existing political system; on the other hand, the reaction of the Empress Dowager and her supporters to the attempts of the reformers of 1898 to turn China into a modern state organized along Western lines showed that those who held power were not then prepared for the experiment of pouring the new wine of industrialization and modernization into the old bottles of the traditional social and political forms. To be sure, in the early years of the twentieth century the court accepted reforms such as the abolition of the old examination system and the creation of a kind of parliament, but it was too late to save the dynasty, which collapsed in 1911 under the double weight of its own incompetence and the shock of repeated military defeats at the hands of the West and of Japan.

Meanwhile, there were emerging intellectual currents and political forces which were prepared to sacrifice not only the existing political system but much or even all of China's traditional culture in order to save the country. Initially, these men were radical reformists; later, more and more of them were revolutionists. Intellectually, they were no longer 'culturalists' but nationalists.

This latter transition has been subtly and penetratingly chronicled by Joseph Levenson.[3] It means that the central value these thinkers wished to preserve was not the Chinese 'way', but the entity of China, defined as a people, a state, or a combination of the two.

After 1898 at the latest, virtually everyone who was to have an impact on the future China may be said to have been 'nationalist' as opposed to 'culturalist'. But within this broad limit existed the greatest possible variety of attitudes. As regards the Western powers, some were violently hostile, others basically friendly – though few went so far as T'an Ssu-t'ung, who actually affirmed that, by invading and subjugating China the foreign powers, hastening the collapse of what was rotten in the existing society, had done its people a service for which they were not properly grateful.[4] Some, although they had dethroned traditional Chinese culture as the supreme *value*, still thought that a revitalized tradition could serve as the *instrument* for saving the Chinese nation. Others, such as Ch'en Tu-hsiu, maintained precisely the opposite: China's misfortunes, they thought, resulted largely from her own weaknesses and could best be cured by learning from the West. Still others discovered in the theory of imperialism a new basis for opposing the West politically, at the same time injecting into their society something of the Promethean attitude of the West toward the transformation of nature and society.

Perhaps one might call the attempt to revitalize tradition in order to strengthen the nation 'tradition-oriented nationalism', the tendency to blame China's weakness largely on herself and to propose learning from the West as a panacea 'radical Westernization', and the various currents that attributed China's misfortunes to the 'imperialists' and proposed turning the tables on the West by the radical transformation of Chinese society so as to create a dynamism equivalent to that of the West, 'revolutionary nationalism'.

The first two decades of the twentieth century were the years during which tradition-oriented nationalism lost ground without disappearing altogether and radical Westernization had its brief heyday, while revolutionary nationalism was already coming to the fore. Politically, they witnessed the fall of the monarchy, the failure of Yüan Shih-k'ai's attempt at restoration, and the emergence of the 'warlords' as the real holders of power in China – a predominance they were to maintain to some extent until 1949.

This was the situation in which Mao Tse-tung grew to maturity and apart from which it is impossible to interpret his mind and thought. There is also a more precise, highly significant context – the 'May 4th Movement'. In the narrowest sense, the May 4th Movement was a movement of Chinese students initiated on 4 May 1919, against the decision of the Paris Peace Conference to cede the former German concessions in Shantung to Japan rather than return them to China. But as Chow Tse-tsung has shown in his monumental study of the subject,[5] the street demonstrations and strikes taking place in Peking and elsewhere during May and June, 1919, were merely one in a series of climaxes in a period of exceedingly rapid political and cultural change that extended from the founding of the iconoclastic and Westernizing magazine *New Youth*, in 1915, to the founding of the Chinese Communist Party in 1921. These dates coincide with the most critical years in the life of Mao Tse-tung, who began his real political activity in 1915, while still a student in Changsha, participated in the May 4th Movement in 1919, was converted to Marxism during the following winter, and participated in the First Congress of the Chinese Communist Party in July 1921.

b. Mao Tse-tung during the May 4th period. The general outlines of Mao's biography are well known, although certain periods and episodes remain obscure.[1] He was born in Hunan in 1893 into the family of a formerly poor peasant who had gradually risen to the status first of middle peasant and then rich peasant

1. The basic sources are, first of all, Mao's autobiography, as told to Edgar Snow and published in *Red Star over China*; the books of the two Hsiao brothers, Hsiao San (or Emi Siao, as he himself transcribes it) and Hsiao Hsü-tung (Siao-Yü); and finally, Li Jui's biography (in Chinese) of the young Mao. This last work, completely hagiographic in character, provides important information from sources not otherwise available, including Mao's notes from his years at the Normal School in Changsha. (For titles and other bibliographical information regarding these works, see the bibliography at the end of this volume.) The first serious and properly-documented biography was that of Jerome Ch'ên (*Mao and the Chinese Revolution*, Oxford, 1965). I have also made my own attempt to trace the pattern of his life and political action in *Mao Tse-tung* (Pelican Books, 1966; revised edition, Pelican Books, Allen Lane, The Penguin Press, and Simon & Schuster, New York, 1967; second revised edition, Pelican Books, 1969).

and grain merchant. He thus found himself in an intermediate and somewhat contradictory social position: On the one hand, he was materially better off than many of his neighbours, who often did not have enough to eat; but on the other hand, his father's lack of respect for education that did not serve purely utilitarian purposes and Mao's poor clothes and lack of social polish placed him in a position distinctly inferior to that of the landowners' sons who were his fellow students in primary and middle school.[6] This early experience may well have engendered in him an ambiguous attitude toward social problems – the rebellious attitude of one who had been treated as an inferior on the one hand, a feeling of solidarity with those who, like his father, possessed a certain amount of power on the other hand, despite his hostile relations with his father. A large number of examples could be cited to illustrate this. One will suffice. In 1905, during a famine, Mao's father indulged in a practice that had caused much resentment among the poor peasants in the past: He continued to ship grain to the cities although his less fortunate neighbours did not have enough food. Thereupon the poor peasants seized one of the grain shipments. 'I did not sympathize with him,' said Mao in 1936. 'At the same time, I thought the villagers' method was wrong also.'[7]

The various indications of Mao's hostility to his father and his own statements on the 'dialectical struggles' in his family, in which he sided with his mother and brother against the paternal 'ruling power', might lead some to a psychoanalytic explanation of his revolutionary attitudes. But conflict between father and son is a universal phenomenon, especially in a country like the old China, where the power of the family and of the elders over the individual was so strong. And yet, all rebellious sons do not become revolutionaries, even in the Orient.

Like most young Chinese of his generation, Mao was exposed to a variety of modernizing and/or Westernizing influences. When he was thirteen or fourteen, he read *Warnings to the Seemingly Prosperous Age*, by the comprador Cheng Kuan-ying, and was, he says, deeply influenced by it. This was a plea for greater freedom for private enterprise, but it also contained denunciations of various social abuses and an indictment of the foreigners' treatment of the Chinese in Shanghai.[8] Two years later, while a student at the higher primary school, he read and reread a volume of Liang Ch'i-ch'ao's periodical *Hsin-min ts'ung-pao* and a book about K'ang Yu-wei and the reform movement. The two great reformers K'ang and Liang became his models and remained so until they were displaced by Ch'en Tu-hsiu and Hu Shih in 1915–17. In 1912, he spent six months at the library in Changsha reading on his own; he devoured a number of Western books in translation: *The Wealth of Nations*, *The Origin of Species*, and works by Mill, Spencer, Rousseau, and Montesquieu. But all this progressive literature seems to have marked him less than the tales of Japan's might he heard from one of his teachers at the higher primary school, a returned student, or the book he read about Napoleon, Peter the Great, and other 'great heroes of the world'. And he seems to have been less influenced by Cheng Kuan-ying's plea for modernization and social reform than by a pamphlet he read at the same time, which began with the words, 'Alas, China will be subjugated,' and which lamented the loss of Korea, Indochina, and Burma.[9]

Indeed, if one were to characterize Mao's mind and personality on the eve of the May 4th period, the two most deeply etched traits appear to have been an emphasis on military strength and heroism and a vigorous nationalism. Mao may well have learned something of the importance of military power from the six months he spent in the anti-Manchu army after the revolution of October 1911, as Hsiao San affirms.[10] But his concept of the hero was drawn from Chinese history and popular fiction. Among the emperors, he was particularly fascinated by Ch'in Shih Huang-ti, who unified the empire, and Han Wu-ti (the 'Martial Emperor'), who extended it and fought against the Huns. (Neither of these rulers was particularly liberal in his internal policy, but it would be unfair to conclude from Mao's admiration for them that he necessarily approved the former's burning of the books or the latter's use of slave labour.[1]) The warrior-statesmen of the *Romance of the Three Kingdoms* and the heroic bandits of *Water*

1. These are the only two emperors mentioned by Mao in his autobiography, in addition to the legendary figures Yao and Shun. (Snow, op. cit., p. 121.)

Margin (translated by Pearl Buck under the title *All Men Are Brothers*), who struck at the rich and helped the poor and righteous, were also close and familiar figures to him, as to all young Chinese.

But if these were the figures that peopled Mao's imagination, we are fortunately not obliged to restrict ourselves to speculations about his sensibilities. The article he wrote in 1917, which includes the passages that constitute the first selection in this anthology, provides us with a solid basis for analysing the form and content of Mao's thought in the first years of the May 4th period.

This text is of interest both for what it reveals of Mao's mind and as a point on the trajectory that carried him from a Chinese intellectual world to the adoption of Marxism-Leninism as his basic world view. It also reveals something of the sources of his ideas.

Of the basic traits revealed in this article, two have already been mentioned above: nationalism and the martial spirit. Another theme emphasized by him is that of the importance of conscious action and individual initiative as opposed to a mere mechanical execution of orders. All three of these themes run through all of Mao's life and thought. The first two have survived undiluted to the present day. The third patently contradicts the emphasis on organization that Mao also exhibited even before he had thoroughly assimilated the Leninist principles of democratic centralism. For half a century, Mao has been torn by the conflict between an ideal of spontaneity and the will to impose the discipline necessary for effective action. This contradiction obviously still persists in the China of the Red Guards.

What conclusions can we draw from the 1917 article regarding the extent to which Mao Tse-tung might have been regarded at the time as 'progressive' or 'revolutionary' as compared with his contemporaries? At first glance, his thought appears conservative rather than revolutionary, Chinese and traditional rather than Westernized. The text is studded with references to the Chinese classics and most of the individuals for whom he expresses admiration are figures from China's past or present. One is particularly struck by the reference to Tseng Kuo-fan, the governor general who crushed the Taiping rebellion. Today, Tseng is considered an arch-reactionary villain and a tool of the foreign imperialists, but then Mao designated him by a highly honorific title, 'Wen-cheng', under which he was canonized after his death. Evidence from persons who knew Mao in Peking in 1918 indicates that he not only admired Tseng but actually identified with him. Clearly he saw in Tseng Kuo-fan not only an eminent Hunanese like himself – though that factor was certainly important – but a statesman who knew how to exercise power.

It would, however, be altogether too one-sided to suggest that the Mao Tse-tung of 'A study of physical culture' was entirely uninfluenced by modern and progressive ideas. Mao wrote this article during an era of transition and upheaval. Even the most radical and advanced thinkers, those who could and did read Western writings in the original and wished to imitate the West, were still marked by the Chinese tradition and the Chinese vocabulary.

At least three major influences are clearly discernible in the 1917 article. The first is that of the philosopher-patriots of the early seventeenth century, who, stigmatizing the mystical tendencies that, in their view, had weakened China and made possible the Manchu conquest, advocated increased emphasis on the martial virtues and on practical activity as a means of redressing the situation.[1] The second is the emphasis on strengthening the country militarily and opposing foreign incursions, which Mao seems to have absorbed particularly from Liang Ch'i-ch'ao but which was almost universal among Chinese writers at the time, whether reformists or revolutionaries.[2] The third is the magazine

1. Of the early Ch'ing philosophers, two of the most important, Yen Yüan and Ku Yen-wu, are mentioned in the extracts from Mao's 1917 article on physical culture. Mao also attended meetings of a Changsha society that read the works of a third, Wang Fu-chih. For a good brief summary of the political thought of these men, see H. G. Creel, *Chinese Thought from Confucius to Mao Tse-tung*, University of Chicago, 1953, Chapter 11, also John K. Fairbank and Ssu-yü Teng, *China's Response to the West. A Documentary Survey*, Harvard University, Cambridge, Mass., 1954, pp. 7–11. I have endeavoured to trace the influence of these men on Mao Tse-tung in more detail in the introduction to the French translation of the 1917 article (Mao Ze-dong, *Une Etude de l'éducation physique*, Mouton, Paris, 1962).

2. On the nationalism of Liang Ch'i-ch'ao, and his emphasis on military values, see Joseph Levenson, *Liang Ch'i-ch'ao and the Mind of Modern*

Hsin ch'ing-nien (*New Youth*), from which Mao drew an emphasis on strength and courage that reinforced the influence of Yen Yüan and Liang Ch'i-ch'ao, and the individualism that constituted the most modern and Western trait in his personality at the time.

Before saying more about the *New Youth* magazine in general, its place in the May 4th Movement, and its influence on Mao Tse-tung, a word is in order about one of its contributors who had a very close relationship with Mao Tse-tung indeed – his teacher of philosophy in Changsha and future father-in-law, Yang Ch'ang-chi. Mao had entered the Normal School in Changsha in 1913, but it was only later that he came under the influence of Professor Yang, who taught the upper classes. Yang was a disciple of T. H. Green, but his ethical ideas had such unexpected antecedents as Samuel Smiles, whom he had learned to appreciate while studying in England. (He had also studied in Germany and Japan.)[1] At the same time, he remained deeply rooted in Chinese culture.[2] His influence is no doubt reflected in Mao's emphasis on conscious action, which had, in Mao's case as in Yang's, both Chinese and Western antecedents. Thus Mao justified the importance of subjective factors by a quotation from the Confucian *Analects*, 'What the superior man seeks is in himself.'

It is possible that Mao also learned from his teacher the practice of cold baths as an aid in strengthening the will, of which Yang Ch'ang-chi was an enthusiastic partisan.[3] Despite the emphasis on the importance of the body in 'A study of physical culture', Mao also absorbed from his teacher, especially during

China, Harvard University, Cambridge, Mass., 1959, Chapter 4. Mao may well have had his attention drawn to the Japanese military ethic, *bushido*, by Liang's article 'China's bushido' (ibid., p. 118).

1. See Yang Ch'ang-chi, *Hsi-yang lun-li chu-i shu-p'ing* (*An Exposition and Critique of Western Ethical Theories*), The Commercial Press, Shanghai, 1923, regarding T. H. Green; his article in *Hsin ch'ing-nien*, II, nos. 4 and 5, praises Smiles.

2. See the quotation in *Mao Tse-tung*, p. 35. (Here and throughout this introduction, I cite from the hardback edition, in which the pagination of the U.K. and U.S. editions is identical.)

3. See Mao's praise of this practice in the extract from his 1917 article given below p. 157.

1917–18, his last year in Changsha, a powerful dose of idealism.

Under the influence of Yang Ch'ang-chi, Mao wrote an essay entitled 'The power of the mind', for which he received a mark of 100. In his autobiography he states frankly: 'I was then an idealist.' [11] This idealism of Mao's is clearly a stumbling block to his biographers in Peking. Li Jui cites a whole paragraph of the autobiography praising Yang Ch'ang-chi, but omits the final sentence containing Mao's confession of idealism.[12] Instead, he professes to discover, in Mao's marginal notes on his copy of a textbook,[1] 'a precocious *penchant* for dialectical materialism'.[13]

In fact, on the basis of the excerpts from Mao's annotations which Li Jui himself cites, it is clear that whatever 'dialectical' component may have existed in Mao's thought in 1918 came rather from the heterodox currents in traditional Chinese thought than from Marx:

> I say: the concept is reality, the finite is the infinite, the temporal is the intemporal, imagination is thought, I am the universe, life is death, death is life, the present is the past and the future, the past and the future are the present, the small is the great, the *yin* is the *yang*, the high is the low, the impure is the pure, the thick is the thin, the substance is the words, that which is multiple is one, that which is changing is eternal.[14]

On the other hand, if one takes this passage together with the contrasting but in some sense complementary views of the article on physical culture, one can speak of a certain inclination toward a dialectical understanding of the relations between body and mind, thought and action. Although this dialectic may be Chinese in origin, Mao turned it to uses that strongly suggest Western influence. This is the case, in particular, of a passage in Mao's notes on Paulsen's book that extends this dialectic to the relation between man and nature:

> Although we are determined by nature, we are also a part of nature. Hence, if nature has the power to determine us, we also have the power to determine nature; although our power is slight, one could not say that it is without influence on nature.[15]

1. The book in question was a translation of *System der Ethik* by Friedrich Paulsen, a second-rank German neo-Kantian.

There is, perhaps, in these few sentences something of the activism of the revolutionary who wishes to transform the world. It is certain in any case that this idea of shaping nature contrasts with the tendency of traditional Chinese thought to advocate above all the adaptation of man to nature. These conceptions no doubt reflect the influence of the Western scientific and activist ideas expressed in *Hsin ch'ing-nien*, and which Mao was at last beginning to assimilate.

There is undoubtedly a relationship between the acceptance of Western, or partially Western, ideas regarding the relationship between man and nature and the acceptance of social change. Indeed, it may be suggested that Mao's advocacy of social transformation was inspired as much by a concern for modernization and efficiency as by a thirst for justice. In any case, his annotations to Paulsen's book, made during the winter of 1917–18, show the beginnings of an interest in social change that is completely absent from the article on physical culture written the previous winter. For example, he wrote:

> We must develop our physical and mental capacities to the fullest extent.... Wherever there is repression of the individual, wherever there are acts contrary to the nature of the individual, there can be no greater crime. That is why our country's three bonds must go, and constitute, with religion, capitalists, and autocracy the four evil demons of the empire.[16]

This is the first reference to capitalists, or to social categories or structures in any form, which I have been able to discover in the writings of Mao – if we assume that the citations given by Li Jui are authentic. The 'three bonds' rejected by Mao – between prince and subject, father and son, husband and wife – constitute the very heart of Confucian morality. And yet, even as he was assimilating Western ideas of individualism and of the relation between man and nature, Mao energetically clung to his deep emotional roots in Chinese culture, and especially its legends of military valour. Reading a passage of Paulsen maintaining that history was simply the record of the struggle between good and evil, Mao wrote in the margin:

> When we read history, we always praise the time of the Warring

States, the time of the struggle between Liu Pang and Hsiang Yü, the time of Han Wu-ti's battles with the Huns, the time of the battles between the Three Kingdoms – the periods when the situation is continually changing, and when talents are continually emerging. Those are the times that people like to read about.[17]

In the spring of 1918, when he received his diploma from the Normal School in Changsha, Mao's ideas, like those of his whole generation, were thus a patchwork of Chinese and Western concepts and influences. Far from claiming for himself, as does Li Jui, any precocious penchant for dialectical materialism, Mao in his autobiography has characterized his mind at the time of his graduation as 'a curious mixture of ideas of liberalism, democratic reformism, and utopian socialism'. 'I had', he added, 'somewhat vague passions about nineteenth century democracy, utopianism, and old-fashioned liberalism, and I was definitely anti-militarist and anti-imperialist.'[18]

The fact that he was torn between so many influences, diverse and in many cases contradictory, did not prevent Mao Tse-tung, during his last years in Changsha, from taking the lead in founding a student organization – the Hsin Min Hsüeh Hui, or New People's Study Society – which apparently had a relatively clear orientation derived essentially from *Hsin ch'ing-nien*.[19] Its practical effects were in any case decidedly radical, for many of the friends who came under Mao's influence in this context later followed him into the Chinese Communist Party.

In the fall of 1918, Mao Tse-tung went to Peking, where for the first time he entered into personal contact with the leading protagonists of the new intellectual currents that were shortly to be projected by the May 4th Movement into still greater prominence. By a fortunate coincidence, his professor of ethics, Yang Ch'ang-chi, with whom he had established close personal relations and who had served as the intermediary in persuading the editors of *Hsin ch'ing-nien* to publish his article on physical culture,[20] had just left the Normal School in Changsha for a chair at Peking University and was thus able to help Mao find a place in the capital. Thanks to an introduction from Yang, Mao secured a position as a librarian's assistant under the direction of Li Ta-chao, the man who, perhaps better than any other, represented the combination of the most radical Western ideas with Chinese nationalism.

The group around the review *Hsin ch'ing-nien* was a heterogeneous one. One fundamental cleavage that was to develop rapidly during 1919 under the impact of the May 4th Movement was that between the partisans of Western democracy and those who turned to more radical solutions, and in particular to Leninism. This cleavage was symbolized by the personalities of two contributors to the magazine, Hu Shih, the Deweyan pragmatist, and Ch'en Tu-hsiu, who was to become the first Secretary General of the Chinese Communist Party. But there was another, equally important division, which was illustrated by the characters of the two founders of the Chinese Communist Party, Ch'en Tu-hsiu and Li Ta-chao. Without doing too much violence to the truth, one can say that the former was above all a Westernizer, who turned to communism as the most efficient method for modernizing Chinese society, whereas the latter was a nationalist, who saw in the Leninist theory of imperialism a justification for his chauvinistic views. Mao owes something to both, but more to Li than to Ch'en.

In fact, Li Ta-chao joined the editorial board of *Hsin ch'ing-nien* only in the fall of 1918, and one of the factors that had hitherto kept him apart from the group around Ch'en Tu-hsiu and Hu Shih was precisely the issue of nationalism. Ch'en was a 'radical Westernizer' in the early years of the May 4th period, who tended to blame all of China's misfortunes on her own faults and weaknesses.[1] Li, on the other hand, under the impact of Japan's twenty-one demands, had, in 1915, written essays glorifying the Chinese people, 'which had stood in a superior position for four thousand years', and crying out for 'national revenge'.[2]

1. He exhibited this attitude as late as the fall of 1918 in his famous article 'The von Ketteler monument'. See Benjamin I. Schwartz, *Chinese Communism and the Rise of Mao*, Harvard University, Cambridge, Mass., 1951, pp. 14–15. (Extracts in H. Carrère d'Encausse and S. Schram, *Marxism and Asia*, Allen Lane, The Penguin Press, 1969, Text VI 4.)

2. The translation of the Chinese term *min-tsu* (people) and of the related term *Han-tsu* (Chinese people), is one of the knottiest problems in any attempt to render the exact nuances of this material in English. The nearest equivalent is 'people', but this word often leads to confusion because of its

It was not until 1920 that Ch'en Tu-hsiu finally embraced Marxism, but when he did, he took over and made his own all its basic analytical concepts, especially as regards the role of the various classes. Li Ta-chao, on the other hand, began by embracing the Bolshevik revolution and never really disciplined himself to reason in Marxist categories, nor did he divest himself of his nationalism.[21] To affirm that Mao Tse-tung's development was shaped by both these men, but more by Li than by Ch'en, is in fact another way of stating the basic thesis of this whole volume, namely that while Mao is a genuine communist revolutionary, and while the categories in which he reasons are Marxist categories, the deepest springs of his personality are, to a large extent, to be found in the Chinese tradition, and China's glory is at least as important to him as is world revolution.

According to Mao's own account, his position at the university library was so low that people avoided him. Nonetheless, he did establish personal contacts with a certain number of prominent figures in the intellectual world of the time, including both Li and Ch'en.[22] We may judge something of the nature of their influence at the time from their writings during the winter which Mao spent in Peking.

Ch'en Tu-hsiu had as yet shown no interest either in Marxism or in the Russian revolution. From him Mao no doubt absorbed the cult of 'Mr Democracy' and 'Mr Science', the two great figures in Ch'en's thought prior to his conversion to Leninism.

---

dual meaning – it may refer to one people as opposed to another, or to 'people' as opposed to 'rulers'. The Chinese term has only the first connotation. Moreover, it also has overtones of 'race' and 'nation', which are not conveyed by the word 'people', and are better rendered by the German *Volk*. For lack of a better word, I shall use the term 'people' when a noun is required and 'national' when the Chinese term has an adjectival force – for 'popular' corresponds, of course, to the other meaning of 'people'.

These essays are reprinted in the volume of Li Ta-chao's writings published in Peking (*Li Ta-chao hsüan-chi*, Jen-min Ch'u-pan-she, 1959, pp. 8–27). My attention was first called to them, when I was preparing the first edition of this book, by the then unpublished doctoral dissertation of Maurice Meisner, 'Li Ta-chao and the origins of Chinese Marxism', University of Chicago, 1962. This stimulating and perceptive study has since been revised by its author and published under the same title (Harvard University, Cambridge, Mass., 1967).

'Mr Science' especially, as a fighter against superstition and backwardness, left an indelible impression on Mao. Ch'en, like Mao, was also a proponent of physical strength and had praised the Japanese Fukuzawa Yukichi for his doctrine of the savage or 'beastly' nature (*shou-hsing chu-i*) in an article that Mao had probably read while in Changsha.[23]

Li Ta-chao, despite his commitment to Chinese nationalism, was far from ignorant of the West. Even after his imagination had been fired by the Russian revolution, he continued to be attached to parliamentary democracy. But, characteristically, he was less interested in science and logic than in currents such as Bergson's theory of free will, which was grist to the mill of his optimistic and activist temperament. He also admired Condorcet.[24] But two themes of particular importance emerge from his writings during the winter of 1918–19: revolution and the peasantry.

It was in July 1918 that Li Ta-chao had first expressed his enthusiasm for the Russian revolution, which he found superior to the French revolution of 1789 because it was internationalist. Li maintained that Russia was destined to play a great role as a mediator between East and West – and he also held that China was to have a pre-eminent part in the great synthesis. Secondly, he advanced the view that precisely because Russia was culturally backward, she had 'great surplus energy' for future progress. From this statement, it is not far to the conclusion that since China is even more backward, she must have even more 'surplus energy'. This clearly foreshadowed the thesis that China can progress faster because she is 'poor' and 'blank' advanced by Mao Tse-tung in 1956.[25]

A few months later, shortly after Mao's arrival in Peking, Li Ta-chao published his celebrated article 'The victory of Bolshevism', maintaining that it was not the Allies who had triumphed over the Central Powers, but the people of all countries who had triumphed over militarism and autocracy. More particularly, the victory was the victory of bolshevism, which was not merely the affair of the Russians, but 'the victory of the spirit of all mankind'.[26] At the same time, it should be emphasized that this enthusiasm for the Russian revolution did not yet imply on Li's part acceptance of its doctrinal basis. As late as the spring of

1919, when he had learned something of the Marxist theory of history, he still rejected the deterministic elements in Marx's thought, which he interpreted in a narrow and undialectical fashion.[1]

Mao Tse-tung himself dates his conversion to Marxism from the beginning of 1920. At the same time he says that 'under Li Ta-chao' in 1918–19, he had rapidly developed toward Marxism.[27] Taken together, these two statements tend to support my view that in Mao's case, as in that of Li Ta-chao, the impulse to revolution came before the commitment to Marxism as an intellectual system, and this impulse was to a considerable extent transmitted to Mao by Li. The same conclusion is also borne out by Mao's writings of the May 4th period, which are characterized by much fervour but show little knowledge of Marxism. But before considering these, a word is in order regarding another theme, the importance of the peasantry.

In February 1919, Li published an article entitled 'Youth and the villages' in a Peking newspaper. As Meisner argues convincingly, the views expressed in this text are astonishingly similar to those of the early Russian populists. There is not only the theme of 'going to the people', but the idea that the country is a more wholesome place than the city, which is a den of iniquity. But in this text there is more than an echo of the past; there is also a prophecy for the future: 'Our China is a rural nation,' writes Li, 'and a majority of the labouring class is composed of these peasants. If they are not liberated, then our whole nation will not be liberated.'[28]

As he emphasized in a speech of 1942,[2] Mao Tse-tung during his school years had cut his emotional ties with the countryside of his youth and regarded workers and peasants as dirty and physical labour as degrading. It was only five or six years later that he really rediscovered the peasantry, but Li Ta-chao in 1919 may well have started him on the road to that rediscovery. Li also probably communicated to Mao a 'populism' of a still broader kind,

1. Li Ta-chao, 'Wo ti Ma-k'e-ssu-chu-i kuan' ('My Marxist viewpoint'), *Hsin ch'ing-nien*, VI, No. 5. For an analysis of this article see Meisner, op. cit., pp. 90–95, and Schwartz, op. cit., pp. 13–17.

2. See Text VII E3.

namely the conception that the whole nation, with the exception of a few exploiters, is made up of working people who should all be conscious of their solidarity against the monarchs, aristocrats, militarists, and capitalists.[29]

His mind filled with the impressions gained in Peking, and in particular with the teachings of Li and Ch'en, Mao Tse-tung set off in the spring of 1919 to accompany some of his friends who were going to embark at Shanghai for work and study in France. 'Study hard in order to save the country,' he called out to them as the boat left the dock. Then he returned to Changsha, where he found himself plunged almost immediately into the political activity that sprang up following the May 4th demonstrations in Peking.

The energy displayed by Mao during the ensuing months was prodigious. He was once more active in the Hsin Min Hsüeh Hui; he organized a movement against the local warlord; he edited several journals, which were closed one after the other by the police, and when he no longer had a forum of his own he contributed numerous articles to the leading Changsha newspaper, *Ta-kung pao*. These writings of the latter half of 1919 are the first known to have been published by Mao Tse-tung following the article on physical culture. Unfortunately, we do not possess the full and authentic texts of any of these materials, but only extracts and summaries from secondary sources published since 1949 in Peking.[1] Indeed, with the exception of four articles contributed to the magazine *Hsiang-tao* in 1923 (two of which have furnished extracts for this anthology), and of resolutions presented to the Kuomintang apparatus in February 1924, I have not been able to locate any writings by Mao between 1917 and 1926 in their authentic form. Much of what follows, dealing with the intervening years, is therefore groping in the dark.

It is worth pointing out that, although a certain degree of scepticism is in order about the way in which communist historians present the *substance* of Mao's ideas of 1919, the *importance* of his role as a student leader during this period is by no means a recent

1. An extract from Mao's manifesto on taking over the direction of *Hsin Hunan* appeared in *Hsin ch'ing-nien*, VII, no. 1, but it is too short to give much of an idea of his thought. However, his vigorous and defiant temperament emerges clearly from it.

invention. One example will suffice. Summing up the experience of the May 4th movement in May 1920, Lo Chia-lun, now a dignitary of the government on Taiwan and then a partisan of the 'new tide' that had begun with the Russian revolution, wrote: 'If everyone will read an article of Mr Mao Tse-tung, entitled "The great union of the popular masses of the whole country" [*sic*], they will certainly have a better understanding of this point [the utility of the students' and merchants' struggles during the past year].'[1] This clearly shows not only that Mao's article, published in Hunan, was appreciated in intellectual circles as far away as Peking, but that it was so well known there that Lo did not even think it necessary to identify it further. (It is true that the precise footnoting of references is not a part of the Chinese tradition.)

There is no doubt that the most important and systematic exposition of Mao's ideas in 1919 is contained in a three-part article that appeared in nos. 2, 3, and 4 of *Hsiang-chiang p'ing-lun*, the review he edited during July and August of that year, entitled 'The great union of the popular masses'. This article was praised by the Peking weekly *Mei-chou p'ing-lun* as a remarkable contribution.[30] Such a reaction is not surprising, for Li Ta-chao was one of the editors, and on the basis of the extracts available to us,[2] this text appears to incorporate many of Li's favourite ideas: the historic greatness of the Chinese people, the affirmation that they and the people of the whole world should unite against the tiny minority of 'aristocrats and capitalists', the emphasis on consciousness and will. There is a new element: the idea of separate organizations for workers, peasants, etc. Li Jui attempts to force this into the mould of the 'united front' of later years.[31] Such an interpretation is hardly admissible, for even in the account which he himself gives of the article, there is no reference either to the leading role of the proletariat or to the existence of political parties of any kind, let alone of a communist party.[3] The

1. Lo Chia-lun, 'The victories and defeats of our student movement during the past year and the orientation that should be adopted in the future', *Hsin Ch'ao*, II, no. 4, May 1920, p. 849.

2. See Texts I A and IV A, pp. 162–4, 239–41.

3. For an analysis of the content of this article and Li Jui's methods in dealing with it, see the introduction to Chapter IV and the note at the end of the bibliography.

idea that the workers and the peasants are separate and distinct groups may reflect to some extent the reading of Marxist literature in which Mao had been engaged off and on since the previous winter, and he does state that the form of struggle he recommends was invented by Marx. But the experience of the May 4th Movement, in which the organized action of the students had been supported by separate but parallel organized action by the workers and businessmen (but not by the peasants) was probably equally important.

Here again, Mao Tse-tung claims less for himself than does Li Jui. He dates his conversion to Marxism only from the winter of 1919–20, following a second visit to Peking, during which he read the *Communist Manifesto* for the first time, and a trip to Shanghai to discuss the Marxist books he had read with Ch'en Tu-hsiu. 'Ch'en's own assertions of belief . . . deeply impressed me at what was probably a critical period in my life,' he told Edgar Snow. Modestly, he only claimed that, from the summer of 1920, he had been a Marxist 'in theory, and to some extent in action'.[32] In any case, he considered himself henceforth as a Marxist, and it is a fact that the first text from his pen that has something of a Marxist ring about it was written in November 1920.

This was an article on the occasion of the first anniversary of the Workers' Association; in contrast to the writings of the summer of 1919, Mao here for the first time places the accent on the leading role of the workers. He also puts forward ideas on the importance of organization that may be regarded as very close to the Leninist conception of democratic centralism. He proposed that the labour unions should have democratically formed executive organs entrusted with full powers, for if authority were too much divided, the result would be unsatisfactory.[33] Some of these conceptions may have grown out of Mao's activities as a labour organizer, which had begun in early 1920, and which were to continue for several years. But perhaps there was in his personality a kind of 'natural Leninism', analogous to the 'natural morality' of the theologians: i.e., a certain intuitive understanding of the importance of organization that is one of the reasons for his emergence as the leader of the Chinese Communist Party.

Another interesting aspect of this article was that it referred exclusively to the workers, making no mention of uniting with the peasants or with any other class. This was to some extent natural, since Mao was addressing himself to the workers. But it is also possible that it reflected a tendency to apply to China the classical Marxist schema of a social revolution led by the proletariat rather than the Leninist schema of a national revolution in the dependent countries carried out by an alliance of the workers, the peasants, and the bourgeois revolutionaries.

The documentation to support this hypothesis just formulated is sketchy but suggestive. Before presenting it, it is perhaps appropriate to summarize the essence of the Leninist position, and what distinguishes it from the so-called 'orthodox Marxist' approach, which emphasizes economic determinism and regards only Europe as ripe for revolution.

c. The Leninist theory of revolution in the underdeveloped countries. It is a paradox that has been frequently pointed out that Marxism, which grew out of the analysis of the historical development of the most advanced capitalist countries of the West, has hitherto inspired successful revolutions only in relatively backward countries such as Russia or Yugoslavia, and in very backward countries such as China and Vietnam.

Several different issues are involved in any theory of the revolution in underdeveloped and/or dependent countries. The first is that of the place of these countries in the overall strategy of world revolution, which is intimately bound up with Lenin's theory of imperialism. The phenomenon of the politico-economic domination of Europe and America over the underdeveloped countries – referred to as 'imperialism' by both its critics and its protagonists – thrust itself increasingly on the attention of all socialist politicians and thinkers in the early twentieth century. Eduard Bernstein regarded colonization as a service rendered by the civilized peoples; Karl Kautsky considered it the negation of a civilizing mission; but nearly all saw the colonial peoples as passive objects.[1] Even an extreme revolutionary such as Rosa Luxemburg

1. See the extract from their debate on these issues at the 1967 Congress of the Socialist International in *Marxism and Asia*, Text I 9.

was convinced that resistance on the part of the colonial peoples was impossible and that the world could be saved only by the European proletariat.[1] Lenin was one of the few to break out of this Europocentrism and to suggest that Asia could play an active role in world revolution. He advanced such views shortly after Russia's defeat by Japan and developed these systematically in his well-known work on imperialism. According to him, it was the profits from the exploitation of Asia and Africa that enabled the bourgeoisie of the capitalist countries to corrupt part of their own working class; by cutting off this possibility, a revolution in the colonies would contribute to the outbreak of revolution in the mother country.

The problem at issue here is not Lenin's fidelity to Marx but Mao's fidelity to the ideas of Lenin and his successors. Although there is some basis in Marx for Bernstein's attitude regarding the benefits conferred on the underdeveloped peoples by colonization, there is also a basis for Lenin's theory that revolutions in dependent countries are not only progressive, but may even contribute to revolution in the mother country. Marx advanced the first thesis with regard to India, and the second with regard to Ireland and to China herself.[34]

The thesis that revolutions in colonial countries are both possible and desirable and may serve to hasten revolution in Europe and thus advance world revolution has been an essential article of faith of Leninism since 1916 at least and has never been called into question by anyone – though there have been ample variations and divergences regarding the relative importance assigned to the European proletariat and the peoples of Asia and Africa in the strategy of the world revolution as a whole. The other issues of what kind of 'revolution' is to occur in the underdeveloped countries, and who is to lead it, are much more obscure, and even today no absolutely clear-cut, definitive, and universally valid answer to these problems has been propounded either by Moscow or by Peking. Certain general principles have, to be sure, remained fixed. These include the propositions that – as in the more highly developed capitalist countries – there will

1. See her pamphlet of 1916, 'The crisis of social democracy'; extracts in *Marxism and Asia*, Text II 7.

be two stages to the revolution, a bourgeois-democratic and a socialist stage, but that, because of the factors of backwardness and dependence, the roles of the various classes will be somewhat different. In essence, this means that because of backwardness, the peasantry will play a greater part, and because of common hostility to foreign domination, the bourgeoisie of the colonial countries will play a more progressive role than its European counterpart. All these ideas have precedents in Marx.[35] But is the bourgeois revolution to be left to the bourgeoisie, with the support of the proletariat – i.e., of the communists – or should the whole two-stage process be carried out under the *leadership* of the proletariat? Lenin changed his views repeatedly on these two points, as he adapted his tactics to the revolutionary situation first in Russia, then in the world as a whole. Lenin's thinking on these questions is best represented by his views at the Second Congress of the International in July 1920.[36] This presentation is the most coherent and exhaustive treatment of the problems of revolution in the underdeveloped countries to be found anywhere in Lenin's writings and speeches; and it laid down the Comintern line in force on the eve of the founding of the Chinese Communist Party in 1921 – that is, precisely at the moment when we are attempting to evaluate the position of Mao Tse-tung.

Three basic tendencies collided at the Second Comintern Congress: an extreme 'Occidental' tendency, represented by the Italian delegate Serrati; an extreme 'Oriental' tendency, represented by M. N. Roy, the Indian communist who was later to play a role in China; and between the two, the position of Lenin.[1] The first, who made light of the importance of the underdeveloped countries and wanted nothing to do with the bourgeoisie in any form, rallied no support at all. Following the dimming of hopes for an early revolution in Europe, all eyes were fixed on Asia, and no position minimizing Asia was likely to be taken seriously by the delegates. The debate was therefore between Lenin, who was the official *rapporteur* on the 'national and colonial question', and Roy, who had submitted theses of his own on this subject. The two men differed first of all on the respective importance of

1. For a summary of these discussions, with extracts from the debates of the congress, see *Marxism and Asia*.

proletarian revolution in Europe and revolutionary upheaval in the colonies. Roy made of the latter a condition *sine qua non* of the former. This was too much for Lenin, who was willing to give equal weight to Europe and Asia, but unwilling to reverse the established position of the Second International and make of the European workers mere passive objects awaiting the initiative from the East, which would make possible their own victory. On this point, the position of Lenin was clearly endorsed by the Congress, but this did not check the tendency of Asian communists to regard their countries as the true home of revolution in the twentieth century – a tendency that finds its apotheosis in the attitude of Communist China today.

The second point at issue between Lenin and Roy concerned relations with bourgeois revolutionaries. In his original theses Lenin spoke of collaboration with 'bourgeois-democratic' movements. As a concession to Roy he agreed to change this to 'national-revolutionary' movements, but he made quite clear in his interventions that he regarded this as a mere verbal modification, and that in his eyes the two terms meant the same thing. For his part, Roy demanded that the proletariat – i.e., the communists – assert its hegemony over the revolutionary movement from beginning to end. Lenin admitted that this was highly desirable. But, as a realist and as the leader of the Soviet state interested in weakening the European 'imperialists', he was prepared under certain circumstances to turn over the leadership of the revolution in the colonies to the bourgeoisie, until such time as the communists should be in a position to take charge themselves. This debate between Lenin and Roy offers curious parallels with that between the Soviets and Mao Tse-tung. At the time, the Comintern Congress adopted both sets of theses, undisturbed by the contradictions between them.

On one point at least, Lenin and Roy were agreed: In countries where the communists *did* succeed in establishing their predominance, they could lead the peasant masses to socialism without passing through a capitalist stage of development.[37] The line of the International in 1920 regarding revolution in the underdeveloped countries can be summed up in a few simple propositions: This revolution will not be exclusively social, as in Europe, but above all *national*; it will not be the work of the proletariat alone, nor even of a coalition of the proletariat and the peasantry, at least not in all cases; where an indigenous bourgeoisie exists, and where elements of it are prepared to fight against foreign domination, the communists should form an alliance with them and even allow them to lead the revolution during its first phase. This was the line on the eve of the foundation of the Chinese Communist Party. Let us see how Mao and his comrades applied it.

d. From sectarianism to collaboration with the Kuomintang. In using the phrase 'how Mao and his comrades applied it', I do not mean to suggest that Mao Tse-tung played a leading role in the Chinese Communist Party in its early years, or that he was responsible for its theoretical position. But it is interesting, as a background for evaluating Mao's ideas at the time, to consider the position of the Party. In the 'First decision as to the objects of the Communist Party of China', adopted at the First Congress in July 1921, one finds the following passage: 'Towards the existing political parties, an attitude of independence, aggression, and exclusion should be adopted.... Our party should stand up on behalf of the proletariat, and should allow no relationship with the other parties or groups.'[38]

It is clear that this narrow and sectarian insistence on the proletariat as the only revolutionary force, and the absence, in the documents of the First Congress, of any reference to national as opposed to social revolution, reflect either complete ignorance of the decisions of the Second Comintern Congress or a refusal to accept the positions adopted there. The latter hypothesis seems more probable, for according to Ch'en Kung-po a manifesto attacking Sun Yat-sen as no better than the northern warlords was drafted but not adopted, because of a division of opinion.[39]

Which side was Mao on? The little evidence available suggests that he was probably on the side of the majority. In his letters to his friend Ts'ai Ho-sen,[1] Mao analyses the problems of world revolution exclusively in terms of 'capitalists' and 'proletarians'. There is not a hint here that the situation in China might be any different from that in France, where Ts'ai was living. This im-

1. See Text VI A 1.

pression is reinforced by Ts'ai's letters calling for a 'dictatorship of the proletariat' in China modelled on Russia's and showing no concern whatever with the complex and contradictory character of Chinese society. To this Mao replied that he 'agreed with every word'.[40]

There is no doubt that Ts'ai's influence on Mao was strong and that Ts'ai Ho-sen's passionate revolutionary temperament was very much in tune with Mao's. As the correspondence of the winter of 1920–21 indicates, their ideas were, at that time, very much in harmony. But in Mao's case, revolutionary passion and the tendency to see the world in black and white – capitalists and proletarians – conflicted with another equally strong passion – nationalism. And so, when he once more emerges into view, in 1923, after an interval of two years for which we have no really significant texts, it is as an enthusiastic partisan of the alliance with the Kuomintang. Indeed, he does not merely advocate alliance with the bourgeoisie; he actually sees the merchants as the leading force in the national revolution.[1]

Although this is very unlike either the earlier or the later Mao, it was in harmony with the official policy of the International, imposed on the Chinese Communist Party in August 1922; beginning in 1924, this policy was implemented on a large scale by having communists enter the Kuomintang as individual members and by having a number of prominent communists, including Mao, sit in the executive organs of the Kuomintang.[2] It was also in line with the thinking of Mao's master Li Ta-chao, who as early as January 1920 had put forward the idea that the Chinese as a whole constituted a 'proletarian nation', part of the world proletariat. To be sure, he did not believe that the Chinese should submit to the leadership of the more privileged among these 'proletarians'; on the contrary, he advocated an immediate struggle for socialism, in alliance with the world proletariat. But toward the end of 1922, he wrote that the organization, by the

1. See Text III A.

2. It is not possible here to go into the intricacies of Moscow-Chinese C.P.-Kuomintang relations during 1923–7. For an account of this period, see Conrad Brandt, *Stalin's Failure in China: 1924–1927*, Harvard University Press, Cambridge, Mass., 1958, and also *Mao Tse-tung*, Chapters 4 and 5.

whole Chinese people, of a 'democratic united front' constituted a part of the world revolution.[41] To postulate that the Chinese *people* was in fact a revolutionary *class* oppressed by the imperialists enabled both Li and Mao to be simultaneously revolutionaries and nationalists. In other words, it enabled them to be revolutionary nationalists, which is what they were and what Mao has remained.

Ch'en Tu-hsiu accepted the new orientation of collaboration with the Kuomintang when it was forced on him by Moscow, but he accepted it with resignation rather than with enthusiasm. Although sincerely concerned with China's fate, he had always remained a Westernizer at heart and could not share the nationalist *mystique* of Li and Mao. This in itself was probably enough to disqualify him as the leader of the Chinese revolution, even had he not been made the scapegoat for Stalin's failures.

Li Ta-chao's evolution from 1920 down to his execution in 1927 appears to be in a relatively straight line.[1] Lecturing to a students' organization in Peking in May 1924, he carried his ideas of China as an oppressed proletarian nation to new heights of intensity and fury. The Europeans, he said, regard the world as exclusively a white man's world, in which they themselves constitute the upper classes and the coloured peoples the lower classes. Thus the race question on a world scale becomes a class question. The Chinese people must be prepared to enter into a class struggle with the other races of the world and once more demonstrate their national peculiarities.[42]

There is no evidence as to whether Mao Tse-tung, despite his nationalism and his feeling for China's past glory, ever expressed himself in quite such un-Marxist terms at this period. The articles of 1923, while furiously antiforeign, do not altogether neglect class analysis; the merchants are warned that they must unite with the workers and peasants if they wish their revolution to succeed.[2] But it does appear that, like Li Ta-chao, he went through a kind of ultranationalist phase.

1. For some qualification of this rather sweeping statement, which none the less appears to me basically true, see the introduction to *Marxism and Asia*.

2. See Texts IX A and III A.

It is clear, in any case, that his utterances during 1924 and 1925 are not in keeping with the image of Chairman Mao it is now desired to give in Peking; there can be no other explanation for the fact that his works for these years are never cited. We are told by the editors of the *Selected Works* that at the First Congress of the Kuomintang in January 1924, Mao 'played a great role in launching the Kuomintang on the revolutionary path'.[43] And yet neither they nor anyone else writing in Peking offers the slightest hint as to what he may have said on this occasion.

On the basis of what he wrote in 1923, and of what we know of his actions during the succeeding two years, it is possible to guess the nature of Mao's deviation: on the one hand, excessive zeal in cooperating with the Kuomintang; on the other, underestimation of the revolutionary force of the peasantry. It is true that Li Jui describes in detail how a miners' strike, organized by Mao at Shuikoushan in 1922, led in turn, early in 1923, to the organization of a peasants' association in the surrounding countryside.[44] But Mao himself told Edgar Snow that he only became conscious of the revolutionary potential of the peasantry at the time of the incident of 30 May 1925,[45] and, barring strong evidence to the contrary, this must be taken as the earliest possible date.

During 1924, Mao Tse-tung worked with Hu Han-min in the Kuomintang's Shanghai bureau, earning the derisive epithet 'Hu Han-min's secretary'.[46] Since Hu, though now a member of the right wing of the Kuomintang, was one of the first Chinese to have grasped the Marxist view of history, there may have been some advantage to this situation, though no influence can be readily traced. But the basically revolutionary bent of Mao's personality could not be permanently suppressed. However close his collaboration with the Kuomintang bureaucracy during 1924–5, he never doubted that the future belonged to the Communist Party, which would one day take over the Kuomintang from within. This was, of course, the intention of Stalin and every other communist. The problem was simply when and how.

In this respect, Mao could scarcely have been more prudent and patient than Stalin himself, who was to show himself ready to risk the annihilation of the whole urban labour movement in the vain hope of conciliating Chiang Kai-shek. In any case, whether it be for the reasons of health, alleged at the time, or because his situation had become uncomfortable as a result of the accusations of class collaborationism thrown at him by some of his Party comrades, Mao Tse-tung returned to his home in Hunan late in 1924. There he discovered the revolutionary potential of the peasantry and in the following spring began to organize peasant associations. It is curious that, although of peasant origin, he had been so long in rediscovering the peasantry. As early as 1922, the Chinese Communist Party had stated in a manifesto adopted by its Second Congress: 'Three hundred million Chinese peasants are the most important factors of our revolutionary movement. ... It is to be believed that the Chinese revolution will quickly succeed when the majority of the peasants ally with the workers.'[47]

No doubt the explanation for Mao's belated awareness is to be found above all in the psychological reaction of a young intellectual against the 'unrefined' world of his youth, reinforced by the Marxist hostility to 'rural idiocy'. His attitude cannot be attributed to the mere fact that he was involved in the official policy of collaboration with the Kuomintang, for in this early period the party of Sun Yat-sen took the lead in efforts to tap the revolutionary potential of the peasantry. At the very beginning of its reorganization in early 1924, following Sun Yat-sen's decision to cooperate with the communists and accept Soviet aid, the Kuomintang set up a Peasant Department, and this department shortly proceeded to establish an institute for training agitators to work among the peasantry. To be sure, much of this activity was actually carried out by young communists who were members of both parties, and who made use of the Kuomintang apparatus as the most effective channel for reaching the masses.[1] But if the work of this peasant-oriented minority was approved and encouraged by the Comintern, many of the leading members of the Chinese Communist Party showed a tendency, rooted in an orthodox interpretation of Marxism, to minimize

1. The most celebrated of these pioneers was P'eng P'ai, the first head of the Kuomintang Peasant Department, who later founded the first peasant soviet at Hailufeng. See Eto Shinkichi's articles on P'eng in *China Quarterly*, no. 8, 1961, pp. 161–83, and no. 9, 1962, pp. 149–81.

the importance of the rural areas. Mao was thus in good company in neglecting the countryside himself. In any case, when he did at last turn to the peasantry, he threw himself into this new activity with characteristic energy, and soon made up for lost time.

e. Mao's writings in 1926 and 1927, and the problem of a peasant-based revolution. Mao Tse-tung spent only a few months organizing the peasantry in Hunan in 1925; then, pursued by the local warlord, he took refuge in Canton. But from a series of posts in the Kuomintang apparatus he continued to acquire knowledge and experience of the peasant movement. On his return from Hunan in the autumn of 1925, he began to play a role in the Kuomintang Peasant Movement Training Institute, of which he formally headed the Sixth Session the following summer. He likewise assumed the editorship of a new magazine created by the Kuomintang in December 1925, *Cheng-chih chou-pao* (*The Political Weekly*). The fact that he was entrusted with this responsibility serves to emphasize that, although Mao had henceforth espoused the cause of the peasantry as the principal force in the Chinese revolution, this by no means implied that he had turned against the bourgeoisie or against the leader of the Kuomintang, Chiang Kai-shek. A passage from his editorial in the first issue of the magazine shows him going rather to the opposite extreme:

Why are we publishing *Cheng-chih chou-pao*? To serve the revolution. Why do we want revolution? In order to achieve the liberation of the Chinese people, in order to realize people's rule, in order to bring economic well-being to the people.

For the sake of the revolution, we have offended our various enemies – the imperialists of the whole world, the big and small militarists throughout the country, the comprador class and the village bullies and bad gentry everywhere, and all the reactionary political factions such as the Anfu Clique ... etc. These enemies ... have foreign and Chinese navies, armies, and police; they have vast international propaganda organs (such as the Reuter Agency); they have the newspapers and schools of the whole country ...

... The propaganda organs of the reactionaries in Peking, Tientsin, Shanghai, Hankow etc. are anxiously creating a disturbance, and are making use of their poisonous tongues to curse and calumniate us as best they can.... Expressions such as 'civil disorder', 'communism', etc. are spread about everywhere. It seems that Kwangtung has really become a hell.

We can no longer remain indifferent to this. We intend to counter-attack. 'To counter-attack counter-revolutionary propaganda, so as to demolish counter-revolutionary propaganda' – such is the task of *Cheng-chih chou-pao*.

Our method for counter-attacking the enemy by no means involves the extensive use of polemics; it consists simply in faithfully reporting the facts about our revolutionary work. The enemy says: 'Kwangtung is communist.' We say: 'Please look at the facts.'...[48]

If it was natural enough at the time for Mao to deny that the base in Kwangtung was run on communist lines, one is struck by the extremely broad definition of the revolutionary forces implicit in his enumeration of the enemies of the revolution. To be sure, one must take into account the audience to which this was addressed. But Mao's speeches to the Second Kuomintang Congress in January 1926, in which he played a prominent part, likewise illustrate his tendency at that time to seek the widest possible united front in order to pursue the aim of China's national liberation. Thus, he even went so far as to urge leniency for the most extreme rightist faction in the Kuomintang, on the grounds that these comrades might still return to the revolutionary path.[1]

It is in this context that one must interpret the two articles Mao wrote in January and February 1926, of which the second constitutes the first item in the current canon of the *Selected Works*.[2]

1. On this point, and on Mao's role at the Second Kuomintang Congress in general, see *Mao Tse-tung*, pp. 76–8.

2. Text III C includes the portion of Mao's February 1926 article, entitled 'Analysis of all the classes in Chinese society', dealing with the big and middle bourgeoisie, as well as the conclusion. The part of this article dealing with the proletariat constitutes Text IV C. As for the peasantry, I have preferred to reproduce the main passages from the article Mao published one month earlier, devoted exclusively to the classes in the countryside, and which sets forth his position at somewhat greater length (Text IV B). Regarding the changes made by Mao in preparing his writings for the current edition, and the manner in which the variants are indicated in the present anthology, see the special note that follows this introduction.

This article, entitled 'Analysis of all the classes in Chinese society', is now presented in Peking as a brilliant example of Chairman Mao's revolutionary intransigence at this period. In fact, when he wrote that the world situation was characterized by the final struggle between the forces of revolution and counter-revolution, he saw as the bearer of the 'red banner of revolution' in China none other than Chiang Kai-shek. (The reference to the hegemony of the proletariat in the revolutionary struggle, reproduced in the little red book of *Quotations from Chairman Mao Tse-tung*,[1] was added in 1951.) There is nothing particularly reprehensible about this, if one regards Mao as a man subject to error, who acquired an understanding of the revolutionary process only gradually, and not as a semi-divine being who possessed from the very beginning a clear and infallible vision of the road to victory, which only the treachery of Ch'en Tu-hsiu and others prevented him from putting into practice. After all, nearly a year later Stalin himself, when he made his famous remark at the Seventh Comintern Plenum, 'In China armed revolution is fighting against armed counter-revolution,' was likewise referring to Chiang's army and not to the Chinese Communist Party (which had in any case no armed forces of its own at the time) as the vanguard of the revolution.[49]

Apart from the question of Mao's tactical line in 1926, the articles of January and February 1926 confirm that his grasp of Marxist theory at the time was extremely deficient. This is strikingly evident, first of all, in his classifying the whole of the Chinese population according to income, with no distinction between urban and rural categories, and no attention to the role of the people concerned either in the social structure or in the economy. In the original version of his February 1926 article this tendency manifests itself in such astonishing statements as that dividing society into upper, middle, and lower groups, or that classifying the landlords as part of the bourgeoisie – but the approach is clear even in the revised version in the current edition of the *Selected Works*.

1. Compare the text given in *Quotations from Chairman Mao Tse-tung*, Corgi and Frederick A. Praeger, 1967, p. 8, with the end of the article in Text III C below.

The phrase 'the big landowners *are* the big bourgeoisie' raises a significant point regarding the importance of semantic factors in the assimilation of Western ideas by non-Western peoples. The Chinese expressions coined to translate 'bourgeoisie' and 'proletariat' mean literally 'propertied classes' and 'propertyless classes'. To Mao Tse-tung, who was able to read no language other than Chinese, it may have seemed perfectly logical to write: 'The big landowners are the big propertied class.' At the same time, it is clear that not only the concepts but the basic structure of Leninist thinking were somewhat vague in his mind. Another illustration of this is Mao's affirmation, 'The attitude of the various classes in China toward the national revolution is more or less identical with the attitude of the various classes of Western Europe toward the social revolution.' This was Trotsky's position, not Lenin's, but it would be absurd to explain Mao's attitude by 'Trotskyite' influences. Basically, the roots of his position are to be found in his revolutionary temperament, expressed in the lines that follow the sentence just cited: 'Today's revolution is one, its goals and its techniques are everywhere similar, the goal being to overthrow world capitalist imperialism, and the technique being the union of the exploited peoples and classes to wage war.'

As the reference to 'war' suggests, and as we know from his earlier writings, especially the article on physical culture, Mao was a fighter, and a fighter requires enemies. There was, to be sure, the external enemy, foreign imperialism, but an internal enemy was required as well. Later he was to define this enemy in proper Leninist terms as the landlords and the 'compradors'. For the moment, he denounced the great majority of the bourgeoisie as false or uncertain friends. But at the same time, his populist and nationalist *mystique* required that the overwhelming majority of the Chinese people be fighting on the side of the revolution. Mao solved this problem by a simple feat of arithmetic: Of China's 400 millions, not more than five million were counter-revolutionaries or waverers. Hence his battle cry: '395 millions, unite!'

If one were to judge the importance of the various social groups essentially on numerical grounds, then obviously the peasantry constituted the greater part of these 395 millions. To be sure, there is a paragraph in the article of February 1926, explaining in Marxist terms why the proletariat, despite its small size, was the 'major force' in the Chinese revolution.[1] But this is hardly more than a formal precaution. In fact, Mao first wrote an article dealing exclusively with the peasantry,[2] and then derived from this, by analogy, his analysis of what he regarded as the corresponding classes in the cities. And in his article on the peasantry there is not even so much as a mention of the workers, though he says that 'we' (obviously the Kuomintang) are to organize them. At the same time, Mao praises the rural vagrants, or *éléments déclassés*, who were later to play such a large role in his first Red Army detachments.

In his autobiography, Mao claims that Ch'en Tu-hsiu opposed the publication of his article on the classes of Chinese society because it called for 'a radical land policy and vigorous organization of the peasantry, under the Communist Party'.[50] Nothing of the kind is stated or implied, even in the revised version of 1951. On the other hand, the earlier article on the peasantry *does* end with the statement that the peasants should 'struggle' against the landlords and 'overthrow them altogether' in special circumstances, where they are particularly reactionary and evil.[3] In making the statement regarding Ch'en's attitude in 1926 Mao perhaps confused these two articles. But Ch'en's principal objection to both articles was probably that they were simply too crude.

Shortly after Mao wrote these two articles, Chiang Kai-shek carried out his *coup* of 20 March 1926, with the aim of limiting the influence of the communists and of forcing Stalin to accept a Northern Expedition for the re-unification of China. Although, at the end of March, Stalin energetically rejected every idea of 'military expeditions of an offensive character' on the part of the Kuomintang regime in Canton,[51] Mao at the same moment enthusiastically embraced Chiang's plan. One of his reasons for doing so was, as he put it in the course of a meeting of the Kuomintang Committee on the Peasant Movement on 30 March 1926, the 'close link between politics and the movements of the

1. But not, as in the current version, the 'leading force'. See Text IV C.
2. See Text IV B.
3. See Text IV B.

popular masses' – in other words, the likelihood that the Northern Expedition would set off an upsurge of the peasant movement in the areas in its path. In the light of this remarkably accurate prediction, Mao proposed that propaganda work should be undertaken immediately among the peasants of the regions in question.[52] Apart from his desire to exploit every opportunity for tapping the revolutionary energy of the peasants, Mao was undoubtedly encouraged to rally behind Chiang Kai-shek by the fact that he saw the technique of revolution as being essentially 'the union of the exploited peoples and classes to wage war'. If war is the form taken by the class struggle, then the army must be its instrument. Stalin saw the Chinese revolution in this light, and hence, despite the unpleasant events of 20 March 1926, he soon swung around to support the plans of Chiang Kai-shek, who possessed the only effective 'revolutionary' army in China. Mao, as we shall have occasion to consider further, sees not only the Chinese revolution but all revolutions in these terms; hence his immediate espousal of Chiang's projected Northern Expedition.

The *coup* of 20 March 1926 is one of the decisive events in a period of over a year, from the autumn of 1925 to the end of 1926, regarding which historians writing in Peking have outrageously distorted the chronology of Mao's activities in order to conceal the fact that he went on collaborating with Chiang Kai-shek longer than any other communist equally in view. The precise details do not concern us here,[1] but it is important to note the fact. Although all communists were theoretically barred from leading posts in the Kuomintang apparatus by the 're-organization' which Chiang imposed in May 1926, Mao served throughout the summer, until October, as principal of the Sixth Session of the Peasant Movement Training Institute. If this situation remained acceptable at the time to both Mao and Chiang, it was no doubt in large part because of the common bond of nationalism that united them.

At the same time, it should be emphasized that Mao's nationalism, which was a genuinely revolutionary nationalism,

1. I have endeavoured to set the facts straight in my account of Mao's life, *Mao Tse-tung*, pp. 74–84.

was an ambiguous factor in his relations with the Kuomintang. He had thrown himself wholeheartedly into the policy of co-operation with the Nationalists when it was first put forward in 1922–3 because he was convinced that these new allies shared the fundamental aim of re-establishing the dignity and independence of China and transforming her into a modern nation. He turned violently against Chiang Kai-shek when he became convinced that Chiang preferred to compromise with the foreigners rather than rely on the force of a peasant revolution which threatened the privileges of his supporters.

The great shift in Mao's attitude is already foreshadowed in the article he wrote in November 1926 regarding the peasant movements in areas near Shanghai, where he had just gone as head of the newly-created Peasant Department of the Chinese Communist Party. It is not clear, incidentally, whether this organization ever really existed except on paper; in any case, Mao carried out his activities, until the summer of 1927, primarily within the apparatus of the so-called 'Left' Kuomintang régime which set itself up in January 1927 in Wuhan, in opposition to Chiang Kai-shek in Nanchang. It was as a representative of the Left Kuomintang, as well as of the Chinese Communist Party, that Mao carried out, in early 1927, his celebrated investigation into the peasant movement in Hunan, which can be taken as the symbolic starting-point of his evolution toward a genuinely original position regarding the revolutionary way applicable in China.

The articles of November 1926 and February 1927 are no subtler as regards analysis than Mao's previous writings, but they amplify the brief reference to struggle at the end of his January 1926 article, until it becomes a passionate plea in favour of exploiting the potential of revolutionary violence that had revealed itself in the countryside. The brief extracts regarding the sufferings of the peasants in Kiangsu and Chekiang[1] show that, even before he again came into direct contact with them during his visit to Hunan in early 1927, Mao was increasingly aware of the importance of the peasant uprisings and identified himself wholeheartedly with them. He felt, however, that the peasant movement lacked organization. In Hunan he was to

1. See Text IV D.

discover that it had a very effective organization indeed – but a purely peasant organization. What was a Marxist – and Mao considered himself a Marxist – to do in such circumstances? This is the central issue in the controversy raging around Mao's Hunan Report.[1] In order to clarify it, two basic questions must be put: To what extent does Mao's conception of the role of the peasantry differ from that of Lenin? What are the origins of these deviations, if any?

There is not the slightest doubt that Lenin had gone very far in sketching the role of the peasantry in the underdeveloped countries. On the other hand, can one claim that Lenin anticipated *all* the theories and actions of Mao Tse-tung? In dealing with this question, one must distinguish between the idea that the peasantry must constitute the chief *force* of the Asian revolution, and the idea that the Communist Party, which directs this revolution, can *issue* exclusively from the peasantry. The first notion is indeed of Leninist origin. The second most emphatically is not. At the Second Congress of the International, Lenin talked at great length of the formation of 'peasant soviets' and of the role of the peasantry as the essential force in the national revolution in the underdeveloped countries. But all of this was said under the clear proviso that the 'proletariat' – that is to say, the indigenous communist movement if one existed, or the emissaries of the International if it did not – would guide these rural masses. At the Baku Congress of the 'peoples of the East' in 1920 there were even references to the 'dictatorship of the poorest peasantry' – but one can hardly regard opinions advanced for demagogic purposes at a congress attended by a majority of non-communist Muslims as serious doctrinal innovations.

More significant are Lenin's recently-published jottings, during the Second Comintern Congress, according to which it would be necessary to 'adapt' the composition of the Communist Party itself to conditions in the peasant countries of the East. While it is difficult to be absolutely categorical about the interpretation of

1. The literature on this controversy is exceedingly voluminous. For a brief statement of the two major positions, see Karl A. Wittfogel, 'The legend of "Maoism"', and Benjamin Schwartz, 'The legend of the "legend of Maoism"', in *China Quarterly*, nos. 1 and 2, 1960.

these very concise notes, it seems virtually certain that Lenin was envisaging the admission of a substantial number of peasants into a Communist Party under proletarian leadership, and not the formation of an exclusively peasant party calling itself communist.[1]

All Marxists, beginning with Marx himself, have looked on the peasantry as an extremely important revolutionary force. None has ever recognized that the peasants were capable of independent revolutionary action. For Lenin, as for Trotsky and all their contemporaries, the peasants were fated to fall under the influence either of the proletariat or of the bourgeoisie, the only two classes capable of establishing their domination over society as a whole. It is hard to deny that in the Hunan Report, Mao attributed to the peasants a degree of initiative[2] going well beyond Lenin's theoretical formulations, and well beyond what Stalin was disposed to accord them at the time.[3] But we must still ask ourselves: Is this a manifestation of heresy, or simply of immaturity? And what is the place of this important moment in Mao's intellectual development?

1. Lenin's notes are to be found in the fifth Russian edition of his works (*Polnoe Sobranie Sochinenii*, Vol. 41, p. 457). For a translation of the relevant passage, see the introduction to *Marxism and Asia*.

2. Karl A. Wittfogel has stated that the famous sentence attributing seventy per cent of the accomplishments of the Chinese revolution to the peasantry and only thirty per cent to the city-dwellers plus the army was eliminated by Mao in revising his text in 1951, because it did not give sufficient credit to the peasantry (*China Quarterly*, no. 2, 1960, p. 20). But in rewriting the Hunan Report for the current edition of his works, Mao made no less than ten significant changes bearing directly on the role of the various classes in the revolution, all of which have the effect of attenuating the merit attributed to the peasantry in general and to the poor peasantry in particular (see Text IV E). It is hard to believe that Mao made ten changes calculated to diminish the role of the peasantry, and only one in the opposite direction; it seems more logical to conclude that Mao, re-reading this text in 1951, found that the seventy per cent formula manifested the inordinate enthusiasm for the peasantry that had gripped him in 1927.

3. In his speech to the Seventh Plenum of the Executive Committee of the Comintern, Stalin justified the policy of cooperation with the Kuomintang by the necessity of supplying the cadres without which the amorphous 'ocean' of the peasant masses was incapable of acting alone (*Works*, VIII, pp. 386–7).

If it were a question of a deliberate and carefully weighed ideological utterance by a master of Marxism-Leninism, making no mention of working-class leadership but referring, on the contrary, to 'the leadership of the poor peasants', then one could unhesitatingly reply: 'heresy'. But Mao's mastery of Leninism was far from complete, and his Hunan Report was not written in a quiet study but in the white heat of passion. For fifteen years, Mao had lived in cities and had, by his own admission, learned to despise the dirty and uncultivated life of the villages. Now, in contact with the peasants who had risen against the domination of the landlords, he suddenly re-established a link with the world of his youth. Under this stress, his Marxist veneer cracked, revealing the basic personality traits of the young revolutionary, admirer of violence in the service of justice, which we have encountered in his previous writings:

> A revolution is not the same as inviting people to dinner or writing an essay or painting a picture or embroidering a flower; it cannot be anything so refined, so calm and gentle, or so 'mild, kind, courteous, restrained, and magnanimous'. A revolution is ... an act of violence whereby one class overthrows the authority of another. [53]

Another trait of Mao's personality that appears in striking fashion in the Hunan Report is his detestation of the restraints placed on the individual by the institutions and ideas of the old Confucian society. The emphasis which he places in this context on the emancipation of women is particularly characteristic. Mao's concern with equality of the sexes and with freedom of choice in marriage goes back much earlier, as is indicated by his articles of 1919 regarding the suicide of a young girl of Changsha who had been compelled by her parents to marry against her will.[1] He no longer advocates sexual freedom, as he did in 1919 and 1927, and a passage regarding this was removed from the Hunan Report in 1951; the climate in today's China is a stern and puritanical one. But the restraints on love and sex are new and different ones, imposed in the interest of revolutionary discipline and economic efficiency; Mao's hatred of the older limitations placed on the freedom of the individual by religion and family ties has by no

1. See Text VI C1.

means diminished and is probably one of the reasons for the experiment of the communes.

The Hunan Report is neither 'orthodox' nor 'heretical' Leninism; it is essentially a-Marxist. But at the same time it reveals vividly Mao's 'natural Leninism', which was to enable him, once he had directed his revolutionary enthusiasm into the proper ideological and organizational channels, to become the leader of the Chinese revolution. This 'natural Leninism' manifests itself not only in the concern with organization, which marked Mao's thought as early as 1920, but in the firm grasp of the principle that political struggle is the key to economic struggle. The proposition that politics always takes priority over economics in periods of revolution is in fact the very heart of Leninism. Not to know this, Lenin wrote, is 'to forget the ABC of Marxism'.[54]

The fact that Mao Tse-tung, amidst the excitement caused by his exposure to the revolution in the countryside, was unable to cast his reflections in proper Marxist form certainly did not disqualify him as a future theoretician. His master, Li Ta-chao, when he turned his attention to the peasantry once more in 1926, wrote an article in praise of the peasants' associations known as the Red Spears that makes no mention whatever of working-class leadership; on the contrary, it calls on the peasants to 'rely on their own strength' to overthrow the imperialists and militarists.[55]

Following his investigation of the peasant movement in Hunan, Mao returned to Wuhan, where he participated in various discussions regarding the agrarian policy of the Left Kuomintang government. It was there that he first began to develop ideas regarding land reform more radical than the line of the International. Whereas Stalin's position, as late as September 1927, was that only the land of the big landlords should be confiscated, Mao came forward in April with the view that not only all landlords – large, medium, and small – but likewise all rich peasants were 'uniformly counter-revolutionary' and should be deprived of their land. He appears to have propounded a similar line at the Fifth Congress of the Chinese Communist Party, held in Wuhan in late April and early May, and this may have been the reason why he was deprived of his post as head of the Communist Party's Peasant Department. But he remained a leading member of the Executive Committee of the All-China Peasant Association, and in this capacity, as a disciplined communist, he faithfully carried out Stalin's orders to 'restrain' the peasants in order to avoid a break with the Left Kuomintang.[1]

f. The road to power. The road that led Mao Tse-tung first to unchallenged predominance in the Chinese Communist Party, and then to the conquest of all China, was a long and tortuous one. We cannot follow it here in all its twists and turns. To be sure, theory cannot be separated from action in studying the mind of a revolutionary. But we are concerned not with the history of the Chinese Communist Party, but with the broad outlines of Mao's concept of revolution. We shall therefore concentrate primarily, in the following account of the years 1927–49, on those periods and episodes that best illustrate the basic traits of his mentality, or mark decisive stages in his elaboration of a model for revolution in an agrarian society.

The first and one of the most important of such episodes was the so-called 'Autumn Harvest Uprising' of September 1927. This undertaking, together with the Nanchang Uprising of 1 August 1927, marked the first attempt by the Chinese communists to reply to the violent repression being exercised against them by Nationalist generals of all hues, by revolutionary violence substantially under their own control. Mao was closely involved in laying the overall plans in Wuhan in late July and early August; he was then sent to Hunan as Special Commissioner to supervise their execution in his home province. (The uprising had originally been planned for four provinces, but attempts were finally made only in two, Hunan and Hupei.) Following his arrival in Hunan, Mao repudiated certain of the ideas which he had previously accepted, and became involved in an extremely sharp controversy with the Central Committee regarding important issues of theory and tactics.

Although the International continued to insist that the pro-

1. For a detailed account of Mao's attitude during the spring and early summer of 1927, with quotations from his writings and speeches on the peasant question, see *Mao Tse-tung*, pp. 89–104 *passim*.

jected insurrection should be carried out under the flag of the Kuomintang (even though only an insignificant minority of Left Kuomintang leaders were still prepared to cooperate with the communists), Mao declared that this banner was henceforth 'nothing but a black flag' which should be left to the militarists, while the communists should 'immediately and resolutely raise the red flag'. Although Stalin had as yet authorized only preliminary propaganda to familiarize the masses with the idea of soviets, and forbade the actual formation of soviets in China until the next revolutionary upsurge, six months or a year hence, Mao called for the immediate formation of soviets. And although the International and the Central Committee still advocated confiscating only the land of the large landlords, Mao proposed confiscating all land, even that of the smallest peasant proprietor, and dividing it up again. Mao's espousal of a radical line on these three points, several weeks in advance of Moscow and the Central Committee, is interesting as a manifestation of his tendency to swing from one extreme to another. He had been one of the most zealous partisans of the alliance with the Kuomintang in 1923–4; now he was one of the first to advocate a complete break. But it is of smaller lasting significance than the other key issue in his polemics with the Central Committee, namely the respective role of organized military force on the one hand and spontaneous mass violence on the other in carrying out a revolutionary uprising. Although he defended himself against the charge of 'military adventurism', protesting that, in his plans for the insurrection in Hunan, the four 'regiments' at his disposal figured only as 'auxiliary forces' to 'make up for the insufficient force of the workers and peasants', it was quite clear from the tactical plan itself that in fact he had already come to the conclusion that only a revolutionary army, acting on behalf of the masses, could effectively resist the onslaughts of the anti-communist generals and open the way to the victory of the revolution.[1]

1. I have put forward my own interpretation of Mao's attitude at the time of the Autumn Harvest Uprising in my article 'On the nature of Mao Tse-tung's "deviation" in 1927', *China Quarterly*, no. 18, 1964, and in the account of this episode in *Mao Tse-tung*, pp. 104–14. Recently, Roy Hofheinz has published a detailed monograph on the uprising, of which he

The fact that Mao had grasped the necessity for relying above all on a red army as the instrument for carrying out revolution in China by no means implies that the whole strategy which later carried him to victory had already sprung full-blown from his brain. On the contrary, although he had broken with orthodoxy on this one point, by demoting the masses from star billing to a supporting role in the revolutionary drama, in several other respects he still espoused views quite contrary to the methods he was ultimately to employ. This was the case of the relative importance of the cities and of the countryside, and of the time scale for the revolution.

Although the Autumn Harvest Uprising was to begin in the countryside, the forces originally deployed there were to converge rapidly on the Hunanese capital of Changsha and take the city in a combined operation involving a military siege from outside and a workers' insurrection within. Mao had shown himself even more inclined than the Central Committee to concentrate exclusively on this objective, rather than to scatter his resources in an effort to foster peasant uprisings throughout the province. This emphasis in Mao's strategic planning was closely linked to ideas regarding the speed with which victory could be achieved. The insistence on taking Changsha immediately reflected a conviction that the time was ripe for a nation-wide revolutionary upsurge for which the establishment of Soviet power in the Hunanese capital would give the signal. In Roy Hofheinz's apt phrase, Changsha would be the Petrograd of the Chinese October.

---

very kindly allowed me to see an earlier version in January 1966, when I was putting the final touches on my Mao biography. ('The Autumn Harvest Insurrection', *China Quarterly*, no. 32, 1967, pp. 37–87). This study is based on fuller research and more extensive documentation than my own brief account, and on points of fact must be regarded as more accurate. As for interpretation, however, I remain unconvinced that Mao's divergence from the Central Committee regarding the slogans for the insurrection was 'marginal' (op. cit., p. 64). These differences were, to be sure, as much a matter of words as of the substance of policy, but for a communist revolutionary words are important. In any case, we are agreed that the most important point in Mao's conflict with the Central Committee, and the one which best foreshadows the original methods of revolution he was shortly to develop, is that regarding the role of organized military force.

When the attempt to take Changsha failed because of a combination of insufficient force and general military disorganization and incompetence, and Mao retreated with the few broken remnants of his 'army' of four regiments to the Chingkangshan, he was obliged to re-examine all his assumptions about the pattern of revolution in China. His first discovery was the concept of base areas. Instead of attempting a general offensive immediately, the revolutionary forces would entrench themselves in a limited area from which they could wage guerrilla warfare against the white armies, and within which they could carry out experiments in agrarian reform and the mobilization of the masses. But for several years, Mao continued to view these activities as merely a holding operation which would enable the communists to conserve their own forces and prepare themselves for the nationwide revolutionary high tide which alone could sweep them to victory.

In order that Mao could move on to the conception of a revolution which would expand and develop gradually in the countryside, so that the taking of the cities would be, not the signal for the decisive offensive, but simply the consecration of a victory already won, it was necessary for him to strengthen his conviction that the peasantry was capable of being, not merely the leading force, but virtually the sole force, in the revolutionary process. In the course of the years 1927–37, he set about creating an organization composed of peasants and rural vagabonds which none the less called itself the party of the proletariat, and proposed to play the role attributed by Lenin to the proletariat and its party as the guiding force of the bourgeois-democratic revolution.

Karl A. Wittfogel points out that Stalin and his spokesmen eventually gave their full approval to this strategy – as indeed they did. It would have been strange had they repudiated a revolutionary authority that was soon to rule over millions of people in Kiangsi at a time when victories were scarce. But it is equally true that the Central Committee under Li Li-san, and later Wang Ming, undoubtedly enjoyed the support of Moscow in its efforts to promote a more familiar strategy based on the urban proletariat and the reconquest of the cities. In a resolution of August

1931, the Executive Committee of the Comintern affirmed the orthodox position in language of thc utmost clarity:

> The hegemony of the proletariat and the victorious development of the revolution can be assured only on the condition that the Chinese Communist Party become a proletarian party not only as regards the political line, but also as regards its composition and the role of the workers in all its leading organs.[56]

There is no doubt that Mao carried his indifference to the workers and to the cities far beyond anything Lenin's disciples, sitting in Moscow, would have considered admissible. (Needless to say, this neglect was only provisional; Mao had no intention of remaining indefinitely in the wilderness, nor was he indifferent to the question of whether his party *represented* the proletariat, even though it might not have been recruited from the real urban proletariat.) In the Hunan Report, he had expressed his preoccupation with the peasantry in terms that, whether or not 'heretical', omitted the formulas regarding 'proletarian hegemony' that any good Leninist is expected to use. There were two good reasons for not continuing in the same vein. On the one hand, he actually *was* a Leninist, or at least an apprentice Leninist, and though he had momentarily forgotten it in the excitement of his discovery of the agrarian revolution, he naturally wanted to justify his actions in terms of his theoretical convictions. And secondly, he was obliged to do this if he wished to maintain his position in the eyes of Moscow and of the leaders of the Chinese Communist Party, who were disturbed by the purely peasant base of his movement. So the more unconventional he became in behaviour, the more impeccably orthodox he became in words. A passage from a report of April 1929 to the Central Committee illustrates the skill with which Mao infused new content into orthodox formulas. 'Proletarian leadership,' he observed, 'is the sole key to the victory of the revolution'; and he paid lip service to the necessity for preparing the reconquest of the cities. But at the same time he added that if there should be any Party members who feared that the revolution might suffer because the power of the peasants might become such as to overwhelm the leadership of the workers, these comrades were in error. 'The revolution in semi-colonial China will fail only if the peasant struggle is deprived of the leadership of the workers; it will never suffer just because the peasant struggle develops in such a way that the peasants become more powerful than the workers.'[57]

The dubitative expression 'if there should be any Party members' can only have been ironic, for Mao knew very well that Li Li-san had such ideas. Mao's reply to Li, and indirectly to Stalin, was impeccably orthodox, but the reality it pretended to express was not. Although Schwartz perhaps goes too far in stating that the only claim of Mao and his colleagues to the title of 'vanguard of the proletariat' was their subjective conviction, it is true that as a result of the severe losses caused by war and repression, the percentage of workers among the cadres of the Party soon fell to homeopathic levels. Thus Schwartz is quite justified in writing that 'the experience of Chinese communism . . . casts a doubt on the whole organic conception of the relation of party to class.'[58] This is the basic question raised not only by Mao's thought, but by that of Lenin and by the whole history of communism for the past half century.

A decisive turning-point in Mao's elaboration of a strategy for the conquest of power by protracted guerrilla warfare from gradually expanding rural bases was the unsuccessful attempt to take several major cities in Central China, including Wuhan and Changsha, ordered by Li Li-san in the summer of 1930. This action was regarded as premature and adventurist by Stalin – though in typical fashion he refrained from open criticism of Li Li-san's deviations until they had led to failure.[1] But it was in

1. In his book *Power Relations Within the Chinese Communist Movement, 1930–1934. A Study of Documents*, University of Washington, Seattle, Wash., 1961, Hsiao Tso-liang has endeavoured to demonstrate not only that Moscow did not agree with Li Li-san but that, in fact, Mao's line was essentially that of Moscow. Such equating of Mao's strategy with that of the Comintern cannot possibly be defended. According to Hsiao Tso-liang, the key document proving the identity of the two lines is a Comintern instruction of 23 July 1930 which says that for the moment the Red Army should be strengthened in the rural districts, and the cities should be taken only 'in the future'. He suggests that this meant that the cities should be attacked only in the *distant* future, as actually turned out to be the case. In fact, if we look at the text of this document, we find that it places extremely strong

keeping with the general thrust of Comintern thinking, which involved taking major cities as soon as the Red Army had been sufficiently strengthened, in order to re-establish a link with the Communist Party's proletarian base. Its collapse led Mao to abandon at last his hopes for early victory. As late as January 1930 he had anticipated a 'revolutionary high tide' in the near future, and in the light of this prospect he believed it possible to conquer very rapidly the whole of Kiangsi province, including the major cities. Now he abandoned all such prospects of early and easy victory, and settled down to a long struggle in the outlying areas.

If the winter of 1930–31 thus marks an important stage in the development of Mao's thinking, it also marks the beginning of a period for which it is singularly difficult to know what he did think. For in the summer of 1931, leading figures of the Central Committee, dominated since Li Li-san's failure and disgrace by the 'Returned Student' group trained in Moscow, began to move from their underground hiding place in Shanghai to the base in Kiangsi, where a Chinese Soviet Republic was proclaimed on the symbolic date of 7 November 1931. The result was that Mao could no longer pay lip service to orthodoxy and in fact do what he liked, but was increasingly subjected to the control of the Central Committee and in due course became little more than a figurehead, even though he retained the ceremonial dignity of Chairman of the Republic. The situation was such that even when we discover a contemporary text by Mao, it is hard to

---

emphasis on working-class leadership over the peasantry and deplores the lack of contact between workers and peasants resulting from the communists' isolation from the cities; that it calls for general strikes in all of China, or at least in a number of major centres – a tactic that was totally foreign to Mao's thinking – and that it affirms that the decisive battle will occur 'in the very near future'. It is hard to see this as a description of Mao's strategy and as proof that the latter was laid down in Moscow. The Chinese text of this directive is in *Shih hua*, 30 October 1930; a Russian text – dated June 1930, but otherwise virtually identical – is in *Strategia i Taktika Kominterna v natsional'no-kolonial'noi Revoliutsii na primere Kitaia*, Moscow, 1934, pp. 272–81. For a further discussion of this question, see *Mao Tse-tung*, pp. 130–35, and also James Harrison's articles, *China Quarterly*, nos. 14 and 15, 1963.

judge whether this represents what he really thought or what he was obliged to say by the circumstances in which he found himself. It is for this reason that his writings and speeches of the years 1931–4 are sparsely represented in this anthology.[1]

One key area of disagreement between Mao and the Returned Student leadership (supported by Chou En-lai and possibly also by Chu Te) concerned military strategy. Opinions are divided as to whether Mao has made an original contribution in this domain. I shall not attempt to offer an answer to this question here, since it is clearly a matter for specialists.[2] But whether or not Mao's ideas were altogether novel, there is no doubt that by the early 1930s he had come to have strongly-held opinions in this domain. This is not surprising, for although without professional military training (save for his brief experience as a soldier in 1911–12), we have seen that he had always taken the strongest interest in war and strategy. In any case, the issues which divided him from the Central Committee were not narrowly technical, but had important political implications.

'The Red Army fights not merely for the sake of fighting, but exclusively to agitate among the masses, to organize them, to arm them, and to help them establish political power,' Mao had written in 1929.[3] In the course of the ensuing years, he had come to attach greater importance to military operations, but the concept of guerrilla warfare as a process of mass mobilization remained primary. The majority of the Central Committee, on the other hand, tended to regard the Chinese Soviet Republic as a full-fledged state endowed with a powerful army which ought to be capable of meeting the enemy head on, instead of applying the

1. For a summary attempt to suggest which of the policies of the Kiangsi Soviet Republic were really Mao's and which were not, see *Mao Tse-tung*, pp. 151–63. When my Mao biography was in preparation, there appeared two studies dealing with the Kiangsi period: Shanti Swarup's *The Chinese Communist Movement*, Oxford University, 1966, and John Rue's *Mao Tse-tung in Opposition*, Stanford University, Stanford, Calif., 1966. Unfortunately neither of them has produced a satisfactory solution to the problems raised by the history of this period; for all its faults, Hsiao Tso-liang's book remains probably the most useful work on the subject.

2. For indications regarding some of the literature on the subject, see the corresponding paragraph of the bibliography at the end of this volume.

3. See Text V D.

flexible tactics developed by Mao Tse-tung and Chu Te in the early days of the Chingkangshan, which involved 'luring the enemy deep' into the base area so as to fight in the most favourable political conditions, with the support of a fully mobilized population. Here was indeed a crucial dilemma. This policy of 'luring the enemy deep' appeared to set limits to the expansion of the base areas, for how could one create a stable and large-scale political organization – a state within a state – if this so-called 'Soviet Republic' could not even defend its citizens against constant incursions by enemy armies bent on destruction and reprisals? On the other hand, the attempt to follow a 'forward and offensive' military line, and to meet the enemy in pitched battles beyond the frontiers of the Soviet area, imposed by the Returned Students with the support of the Comintern, was to prove beyond the capacity of the Red Army, even though it had by now attained a nominal strength of several hundred thousand. These tactics only hastened a defeat which was probably inevitable in any case, culminating in the abandonment of the base in Kiangsi and the Long March to the north-west.

In fact, there was probably no escape from this dilemma in the political context of the early 1930s. Only the persistent Japanese aggression, by its effects in mobilizing the population so that henceforth the communists could appeal not only to the land hunger of the peasantry but to the overriding imperative of national salvation, created the conditions in which Mao could develop and apply the tactics that finally led to victory.

This road to power involved collaboration with the 'national' bourgeoisie on a more durable basis than Lenin or Stalin ever envisaged. It is true that, in its broadest outlines, Mao's position on cooperation with the bourgeoisie before World War II paralleled that of Moscow: 'united front from below' before the Seventh Comintern Congress in 1935, 'united front from above' thereafter. And within these limits there were a succession of adaptations to changing circumstances. And yet it is true, as Boyd Compton has written, that 'the general policy of the United Front was not channelled to the Chinese Communist Party from a Comintern source, but grew as a response to national conditions'.[59]

Signs of a certain degree of autonomy and flexibility on the part of the Chinese communists first became noticeable in 1933. Their line, following the Japanese attack in 1931,[1] had been identical with that of the Comintern, confirmed in a resolution of the Executive Committee of September 1932.[60] Resistance was possible only on the part of the masses, under the leadership of the Communist Party; before Japan could be effectively fought, the Soviet régime had to overturn the Kuomintang government and take power in all China. The same position was laid down once more in the declaration of war against Japan issued by the Chinese Soviet Government in April 1932.[61] But in the declaration of 10 January 1933, signed by Mao, Hsiang Ying, Chang Kuo-t'ao, and Chu Te, a new note is discernible. Under certain conditions (cessation of the attacks against the Soviet regions, granting of democratic rights such as freedom of speech, association, etc., and arming of the masses against Japan), the Red Army would conclude an agreement with 'any armed force' – that is to say, evidently, with any dissident commander who is prepared to deal with the communists.[62] Technically, this is still the united front from below, for no overtures are made to the Kuomintang government; on the contrary, it is still affirmed that the latter is the running dog of the Japanese imperialists and must be overthrown at the same time as the Japanese imperialists.[2] But by proposing to deal with regularly constituted military units, without expecting them to rally to communism, the first step was taken toward a united front from above.

The same line is reaffirmed in even stronger terms in the proclamation of 15 July 1934, which, while continuing the attacks on the Kuomintang, evokes the possibility of an understanding not merely with any given armed force, but with all the armed forces in China, to fight Japan.[3] The problem remains obscure, however, for when Ts'ai T'ing-k'ai's 19th Route Army in Fukien revolted

1. See Text III F.

2. These denunciatory passages were deleted in a rewritten version published in 1937, so as to give the impression that the offer to unite with 'any armed force' might have been directed also to Chiang Kai-shek. (See *Bor'ba za edinyi natsional'nyi antiiaponskii front v Kitae*, Moscow, 1937, p. 103; *Chiu-kuo shih-pao*, no. 1, Paris, 18 September 1937.)

3. See Text III G.

against Chiang Kai-shek in late 1933, the Red Army failed to honour the agreement concluded with Ts'ai on 26 October 1933 and stood idly by while his forces were crushed by Nanking. Mao may have supported this short-sighted policy.[63]

If the Chinese Communist Party – over which Mao finally obtained control in January 1935 – was moving toward a united anti-Japanese front with the Kuomintang before this was acceptable to Moscow, Mao, on the other hand, showed some reticence about coming to terms with Chiang Kai-shek himself. In December 1935, after the Seventh Comintern Congress, he still treated Chiang as the representative of the landlords and compradores, and not of the national bourgeoisie.[1] By 1936, when Edgar Snow visited him in Pao An, Mao had begun to envisage a broader union and had given up the claim to hegemony over the united front, which he had maintained in December 1935.[64] On 25 August 1936, this attitude was given official expression in a letter of the Central Committee of the Chinese Communist Party to the Kuomintang calling for a united front and a 'united democratic Chinese republic',[65] but Mao showed no great enthusiasm for collaboration with Chiang Kai-shek until after the Sian incident of December 1936. Indeed, available evidence indicates that his attitude toward Chiang at that time was more hostile than that of Moscow.[66]

The reasons are not too elusive: The rulers of the Soviet state were concerned not only with world revolution, but also with security on their own frontiers at a time when the situation in Europe appeared particularly alarming. Mao, on the other hand, had not forgotten the years of bitter struggle for survival against Chiang's encirclement campaigns. He was quite prepared to embrace the abstraction called the 'national bourgeoisie', but less inclined to pin this label on Chiang and thus make him respectable. But soon Mao bowed to the inevitable, and eventually went so far as to predict a 'brilliant future' for Chiang and for the Kuomintang.[2] The 'left' period in international communist strategy inaugurated by the Nazi-Soviet Pact in August 1939 once more encouraged him to take a firmer line; the wartime

1. See Text III H and the introduction to Chapter III.
2. See Text III J.

coalition between the Soviet Union and the Western democracies created a situation in which he again took a conciliatory line in his report to the Seventh Party Congress in April 1945, symbolically entitled 'On coalition government'. But despite these fluctuations, the basic line of Mao's thought regarding relations with the bourgeoisie is remarkably consistent.

The key formula in his writings on this subject, beginning with the report delivered in December 1935, and culminating in 'On people's democratic dictatorship' in 1949, is that of the 'four-class bloc' composed of workers, peasants, petty bourgeoisie, and national bourgeoisie. This formula, like many others that Mao uses, was coined by Stalin. However, Stalin emphasized that the period of four-class collaboration was merely a moment in the development of the revolutionary struggle, soon to be superseded by a phase in which workers and peasants would find themselves in conflict with the whole of the bourgeoisie.[67]

Mao, on the other hand, grasped very early that the peculiar circumstances of a revolution in a dependent country made it possible for the communists to obtain the support of a fraction of the bourgeoisie on a long-term basis. There were modifications in the terms on which this alliance was offered, depending on the strength of the communist position at any given time, but the general pattern of the theory was clear.

According to Mao's theory, at some time between the October Revolution and the founding of the Chinese Communist Party in 1921 (he is vague and contradictory as to the precise date – perhaps because he realizes that such changes do not take place overnight), the leadership of the Chinese revolution passed from the hands of the bourgeoisie to those of the proletariat and its party. The bourgeois-democratic revolution thus ceases to be a democratic revolution of the old type and becomes a 'new-democratic revolution', an integral part of the world socialist revolution.[1]

As Wittfogel points out, this theory comes straight from Lenin, via Stalin. Indeed, the idea of the hegemony of the proletariat during the two stages of the revolution – 'bourgeois-democratic' and

1. See Text III K, and also 'On new democracy', in which these ideas are developed at greater length.

socialist – is the least original aspect of Mao's thought. What *is* original is the skill with which, since 1939 at least, Mao has navigated between the two extremes of sacrificing proletarian (i.e. communist) hegemony and excommunicating the bourgeoisie altogether.

The year 1939 may be regarded as marking a decisive transition in this respect because, while one can find statements in Mao's writings both before and after that date acknowledging the leading role of the bourgeoisie, after 1939 it is clear that these are mere verbal concessions; in fact, he envisages that the reality of power will rapidly fall to the communists. In October 1938, on the other hand, when he hailed the Kuomintang as the leader of China's national struggle,[1] he was probably at least partly sincere. The reason for the change in his position is not far to seek. The new international situation created by the outbreak of the Second World War undoubtedly played a role, as already suggested, but the decisive factor was simply the increase in Mao's own power. Following the conclusion of an agreement with the Kuomintang in September 1937 for the establishment of an anti-Japanese united front, elements of the Red Army (now theoretically subordinated to the Nanking government and rebaptized 'Eighth Route Army') began to spread out behind the Japanese lines and establish guerrilla bases from which grass-roots political control over the population was exercised. This process has been most ably chronicled by Chalmers Johnson in his path-breaking study *Peasant Nationalism and Communist Power*.[68] The maps on pages 118–19 of Johnson's book illustrate the dramatic change which took place between the middle of 1938 and the middle of 1939. They make clear at a glance why Mao could adopt, in his writings of the autumn and winter of 1939–40, a completely different attitude from that of the previous October.

To be sure, in the original version of 'On new democracy', written in January 1940, Mao included a sentence (now deleted) stating that, if the Chinese bourgeoisie (i.e. the Kuomintang) was capable of assuming the responsibility of driving out Japanese imperialism and introducing democratic government, 'no one will be able to refuse his admiration' (*sui yeh pu neng pu p'ei-fu*

1. See Text III J.

t'a).[1] But he immediately added that if the bourgeoisie failed in this task, the major part of the responsibility for the future of the nation would 'inevitably fall on the shoulders of the proletariat'. And in 'The Chinese revolution and the Chinese Communist Party', addressed not to the population at large but specifically to members of the Party, he made no bones about the fact that the new-democratic revolution would be 'led by the proletariat'.[2] In 1944–5, Mao once more put forward as a temporary tactical necessity the demand for a coalition government presided over by Chiang Kai-shek. But never again would he seriously envisage relinquishing for a long period the role of leader of the Chinese nation to his old rival.

Mao's road to power can thus be summed up as revolutionary warfare waged in the countryside, and supported by the population on the basis of the double appeal of nationalism and agrarian reform. The relative importance of these two themes in the overall process of mobilization of the peasantry to support the military effort of the Chinese communists is a much-debated subject. In my opinion, Chalmers Johnson goes too far in suggesting that the appeal to the land hunger of the peasantry was so far secondary to the call for national salvation as to be virtually insignificant in explaining Mao's success. It is true that the Chinese communists did not achieve victory during the Kiangsi period, and eventually suffered a serious defeat. But if the peasantry had been as totally uninterested in agrarian revolution as Johnson suggests, the Red Army would hardly have been able to survive from 1927 to 1934 and achieve the successes it did in the face of constant efforts by Chiang Kai-shek to suppress it. The fact remains that the nationalist appeal was indeed, as Johnson has argued, decisive. Mao came to power because, in the eyes of a great many Chinese, he had emerged as the incarnation of China's national destiny.

Revolution, as suggested at the beginning of this introduction, is not merely a matter of taking power; it also means using power to transform society. How Mao did this is the subject of the following section, dealing with the period since 1949. But certain

1. See the extracts (with variants) in *Marxism and Asia*, Text VIII 3.
2. See below, Text III K.

aspects of Mao's style of political work, as it developed in the course of the years of struggle to achieve power, are directly relevant to the way in which he envisaged his task after 1949.

One of the most important of these is the approach to relations between the Communist Party and the population known as the 'mass line', which Mao described as follows in a directive dated 1 June 1943:

> All correct leadership is necessarily from the masses, to the masses. This means: take the ideas of the masses (scattered and unsystematic ideas) and concentrate them (through study turn them into concentrated and systematic ideas), then go to the masses and propagate and explain these ideas until the masses embrace them as their own, hold fast to them and translate them into action, and test the correctness of these ideas in such action. Then once again concentrate ideas from the masses and once again go to the masses so that the ideas are persevered in and carried through. And so on, over and over again in an endless spiral, with the ideas becoming more correct, more vital and richer each time. Such is the Marxist-Leninist theory of knowledge, or methodology.[1]

To be sure, the Soviets too, in Stalin's day as in Lenin's, talked about going to the masses, but both in theory and in practice they attributed to the masses a much more passive role than Mao Tse-tung and the Chinese communists. This is partly a result of the historic circumstances under which the two parties came to power. Lenin and his comrades seized power in the cities with the support of a segment of the working class. The peasants who made up the vast majority of the Russian population they regarded as unspeakably backward and ignorant, to be taught and gradually led into the modern world, but not to be relied on as a positive force in the revolution. Mao and his comrades, on the other hand, were able to survive during ten years of civil war, and then to carry out the remarkable expansion of their control behind the Japanese lines just described, only because they genuinely moved among the peasant masses, in Mao's phrase, like a fish in the water.

1. See Text VI C 3. As pointed out by Mao himself, the stages in the mass line exactly parallel the stages in his epistemology, as set forth in 'On practice' (Text II D). This idea is developed by John Lewis in his study *Leadership in Communist China*, Cornell University, Ithaca, N.Y., 1963, p. 72.

Stalin, too, sometimes talked about learning from the masses – but the 'masses' in question turned out to be an élite group of Stakhanovites gathered together in Moscow.[1] The difference between Soviet and Chinese thinking and practice in this respect is symbolic of a more general distinction between an emphasis on organizational skill and technical knowledge, and an emphasis on the enthusiasm and creativity of the masses, regarding which I shall have more to say in connection with recent trends in Chinese communist ideology.

Another important point, which is linked to the mass line, is the emphasis on subjective attitudes as a primary political reality. Lenin opened the way to this development when he laid it down, in *What Is to Be Done*, that the intellectuals of bourgeois origin who constituted the leading cadres of the Communist Party knew more about the real will of the proletariat than the workers themselves. But he never explicitly took the further step of suggesting that, by changing their political attitudes, men could change their objective class essence. Mao, on the other hand, confronted on the Chingkangshan by a situation in which the backbone of his army was not made up of peasants, still less of workers, but rather of rural vagrants or *éléments déclassés*, wrote in November 1928: 'In these circumstances, the only method is to intensify political training, so as to effect a qualitative change in these elements.'[2] This spirit, which sees in the transformation of men's minds a method for turning any human material taken at random into the vanguard of the proletariat, runs through the whole history of the Chinese communist movement over the past forty years, and is obviously very much alive in the China of the Great 'Proletarian' Cultural Revolution.

In order to instil correct thoughts first into his army, then into the Communist Party, and finally into the whole of the Chinese people, Mao developed in the course of the struggle for power a series of methods which were to find further and more spectacular expression after 1949. The most important and concerted effort for applying these methods prior to the conquest of power was

1. In his speech of 17 November 1935 to the First All-Union Meeting of Stakhanovites, *Voprosy Leninizma*, Moscow, 1952, pp. 543–4.
2. See Text V B.

the 'Rectification Campaign' of 1942, which aimed not only to give basic training in Marxist-Leninist ideology to the very large number of people from all classes and political horizons who had joined the Party since the beginning of the Anti-Japanese war, but to indoctrinate them with an interpretation of Marxism specifically adapted to Chinese conditions.[1]

Mao had first called for the 'Sinification of Marxism' in his report of October 1938.[2] At that time, he had not suggested that he himself had already accomplished this feat, but by 1942 such a claim was already implicit in the way the Rectification Campaign was conducted. To be sure, writings by other Chinese communist leaders, including Liu Shao-ch'i (as well as by Lenin, Stalin and Dimitroff) were included in those to be studied during the campaign. But in January 1942, Mao himself ordered all cadres, and especially the Army, to take as their textbook a resolution he had written in December 1929 and to read it over and over again until they were thoroughly familiar with it.[3] This evolution culminated in 1945 when, at the Seventh Congress of the Chinese Communist Party, 'the thought of Mao Tse-tung' was officially consecrated as the sole guide in all the work of the Party.

Thus began the shift from the *adaptation* of Marxism to the language, mentality, and conditions of the Chinese people (Mao's original definition of Sinification) to the *replacement* of all other forms of Marxism (including that of Marx himself) by the infallible thought of the leader. We shall have occasion to return to this process, which has reached its logical term in the Great Proletarian Cultural Revolution.

Directly related to the emphasis on subjective attitudes as the decisive factor in determining the 'class nature' of an individual or of a political movement is another idea characteristic of Mao: that of the infinite capacity of subjective forces to change ob-

1. Boyd Compton, *Mao's China*, University of Washington, Seattle, Wash., 1952, contains an abundance of documentation regarding this campaign, together with a very useful and cogent introduction.

2. See Text II A.

3. Only a brief extract from this resolution is included in the current edition of the *Selected Works*. See the note to Text V D. Regarding the order to study this resolution, and the beginnings of the Mao cult, see *Mao Tse-tung*, pp. 215–16.

jective reality. This trait, too, appears very early in Mao's career; in 1930, he declared that, if Lin Piao was unduly pessimistic regarding the possibility of rapid victory in one or more provinces, this was because he 'over-estimated the importance of objective forces and under-estimated the importance of subjective forces'.[69] Neither Mao nor Lin has ever been guilty of this error in the course of recent efforts to change the face of China.

2. The Transformation of Chinese Society

When Mao Tse-tung came to power, it was widely suggested, first, that he would be a faithful puppet of Moscow, and secondly, that the evolution of communist China would necessarily be a copy of Russia's evolution. Today everyone recognizes that the first of these hypotheses was false, but there are those who still hold tenaciously to the second. The many singular traits which mark the language, imagery, and political methods of the Chinese communists, especially over the past decade, they regard as merely secondary and accidental – a national veneer on a reality essentially 'Stalinist'. Others go to the opposite extreme and regard the substance of today's China as purely Chinese, communism being merely a foreign veneer on a national reality.

Although these two viewpoints proceed from opposite assumptions, and are used to justify widely different political conclusions, there is in fact a certain formal similarity between them. Both take as their starting-point the permanence of a given metaphysical essence – 'communism' in the one case, 'Chinese culture' or 'the soul of China' in the other – and regard this immutable Platonic idea as the decisive factor in interpreting reality. Thus, even though the partisans of each of these extreme views are prepared to take into consideration both 'communist' and 'Chinese' factors in Mao's China, their evaluation of the relative weight of each phenomenon is governed in the last analysis not by the objective examination of the facts but by an *a priori* judgement as to which aspect of reality is primary.

Both of these approaches reflect, as already suggested, a certain political or emotional bias. The 'Stalinist' interpretation serves to attack and to view with alarm; the 'culturalist' interpretation serves to reassure, both regarding the possibility of cooperation on a basis of national interest, and regarding the persistence of a China which the authors of this tendency have loved in the past, despite its faults. But apart from this, these viewpoints also represent the path of least resistance. Chinese society and Chinese culture, after a century of rapid change in response to the Western impact, represent a bewildering patchwork of indigenous and foreign patterns and ideas. If one arbitrarily decrees that the decisive element is either 'the Chinese tradition' or 'Stalinist political methods', order immediately emerges from this chaos. The aspect of reality which one has chosen to regard as primary provides the logical structure with respect to which the facts can be arranged and comprehended.

It will already be apparent to the reader, on the basis of the first part of this introduction, that I do not accept either of the two approaches just mentioned. Neither communism nor the Chinese tradition is a veneer or epiphenomenon in China today. The persistence of characteristically Chinese patterns of thought and behaviour is massively obvious, both in Mao himself and in the country at large. At the same time, Mao and his comrades are deeply committed revolutionaries who have irremediably shattered the basis of the traditional order, introducing alien and dynamic elements which are henceforth a part of the very fabric of Chinese society. It has never been more difficult to sort out these various components than today, in the midst of the 'Great Proletarian Cultural Revolution'. And yet the attempt must be made, if we are to achieve any kind of serious understanding of the nature and meaning of one of the greatest revolutionary upheavals in history. The problem is less to evaluate the relative importance of the Chinese and communist factors in the composite entity 'Communist China' than to grasp how they interact, and in what direction the system as a whole is moving.

This is the perspective in which I shall now endeavour to interpret the development of Mao Tse-tung's thought since 1949. It is perhaps worth emphasizing at the outset a fact which is in any case obvious, namely that the mere effort to give full weight to both aspects of reality does not in itself guarantee that the result will be of any value. My interpretation of Mao's ideas and methods may well be more superficial and less instructive than those put forward by the partisans of the unilateral 'Stalinist' or 'Chinese' hypothesis. I remain convinced that my approach is the correct one; whether or not I have applied it fruitfully is another matter.

China in 1949 differed radically from Russia in 1917 in many vital respects, including historical situation, level of economic development, and the course taken by the revolution up to that point. Despite certain peculiarities Russia was a European country. It had been shaped by the Greek and Christian traditions; modern techniques had been introduced by Peter the Great. China, in contrast, was a closed cultural universe, as far removed as possible from the Promethean spirit of the West. The contacts in the nineteenth century with Western arms and Western ideas had produced the profound intellectual and political crisis discussed earlier. While the tsarist empire was extending itself victoriously across the Asiatic continent to Vladivostok, China had known the humiliation of defeat and the servitude of concessions and unequal treaties.

As for economic and social conditions, although the degree of Russia's industrialization had its limits in 1917, although Russia was sunk in poverty and ignorance, this situation had no common measure with that of China, which, even in 1949 (except in Manchuria), possessed little more than a few textile factories in the coastal cities, and where agricultural methods were more primitive than those of the European Middle Ages. Centuries of subjection to family elder, landowner, and bureaucrat had created in the Chinese peasantry habits of submission further reinforced by the influence of Confucianism, which made of obedience to authority the supreme moral value. The highly effective work of political mobilization carried out by the communists, especially since 1937, had begun to modify these attitudes, just as the land reform in areas occupied by the People's Liberation Army during the civil war had begun to change the structure of economic power. But neither psychological nor social transformation had as yet gone very far in 1949.

Equally profound were the differences in the patterns of the struggle for power in the two countries. Victory had been achieved very quickly in Russia, though several years of civil war were required to consolidate it. Mao and his comrades had come to power only after a 'protracted war' which had persisted, in varying forms, for over two decades. In Russia, victory had been achieved in the first instance in the cities, by an insurrection in which the workers played an important part, and had then spread outward to the countryside. In China, Mao had, in the currently fashionable phrase, surrounded the cities from the countryside, by a peasant-based guerrilla war; and when the People's Liberation Army had finally entered Peking and Shanghai, the workers had stood by with folded arms and played no part in his triumph.

Given all these differences, the methods chosen by Mao when he first began his effort to establish a socialist system were surprisingly close to those employed earlier in the Soviet Union and in the more recent past in the European 'people's democracies'. The reason is probably to be found less in submission to Soviet pressures than in the prestige which attached to the Soviet example at the time. For all of Mao's adult life, since before he joined the Communist Party in 1921, 'socialism' had been identified in his mind with the Russian revolution. He had differed with Stalin about the way in which victory could best be achieved in China, and had developed his own original road to power. But once power had been achieved, and he set about the task of making China 'rich and powerful', his natural reflex was to follow the Soviet example of planned economic development. There was, however, a certain originality in the ideas he put forward in 1949 regarding the *form* of the new state.

a. The bourgeoisie and the 'people'. As regards the role of the various classes in Chinese society, Mao Tse-tung, speaking with the uninhibited frankness which the possession of total power allowed him to exercise, in 1949 outlined a schema for their transformation under the leadership of the proletariat. In so doing, he transmuted into theory the long-term collaboration with the bourgeoisie that had hitherto been largely a pragmatic principle of action. The heart of this new formulation is the use of the term 'people'. Hitherto, there had been talk of a four-class bloc or united front, but the national bourgeoisie had not been considered as part of the 'masses of the people'. Mao Tse-tung's ideas on this subject crystallized gradually during the years 1945–9.[1] They were given an incisive and definitive formulation in 'On people's democratic dictatorship'.[2]

These theoretical innovations by Mao Tse-tung coincided chronologically with the development in Russia and Eastern Europe of the theory of 'people's democracy', but their content is substantially different. The Eastern European theories, while according a temporary place to private enterprise in the new social system, very soon came to reject even the slightest concession on the locus of political power. 'All the specific traits that characterize the people's democratic state [as distinguished from the Soviet state] pertain not to the class nature of the state – for this is identical in the two cases, i.e., the dictatorship of the working class – but exclusively to its form', wrote two Czech authors, making quite clear that this dictatorship was directed against the bourgeoisie.[70] Mao, on the other hand, included the national bourgeoisie not only among the 'people', but even among the 'dictators'.

All dictators were definitely *not* equal in Mao's theory. The real power belonged to the proletariat (that is to say, to its emanation, the Communist Party). The peasants came next in order of privilege, as the surest allies of the proletariat. As for the bourgeoisie, petty and national, it was stipulated that they were only admitted to the exclusive club of the 'people' on good behaviour and would be subject to remoulding – gently, if they showed the proper attitude, and by force, like the landlords and compradors, if they did not.

In view of all these restrictions, one might ask whether the inclusion of the bourgeoisie among the 'people' was of any real significance – especially since in the late 1950s it was proclaimed

1. See Text IX F and the introduction to Chapter IX, as well as the following items in *Selected Works*, IV: 'The Chiang Kai-shek Government is besieged by the whole people', pp. 135–40; 'On the question of the national bourgeoisie and the enlightened gentry', pp. 207–10; and his speech at a conference of cadres, pp. 234–8.

2. See Texts III L and VI A3.

in China that the people's dictatorship was, in its essence, identical with the dictatorship of the proletariat. It would seem, nonetheless, that the role assigned to the bourgeoisie was of some significance; it reflected the fact that Mao Tse-tung and his colleagues had been able to carry along with them a minority of the privileged classes in Chinese society. From another standpoint, the theory of the people's democratic dictatorship can be seen as a manifestation of the need of every ruling group to legitimize its power by affirming that it speaks in the name of the overwhelming mass of the population – a kind of equivalent, for an underdeveloped country in the twentieth century, of the theory of the General Will.

b. Revolution in the countryside. In the course of the first stage of the Chinese revolution – the stage of the struggle for power – Mao had first participated in the attempt to apply Soviet tactics based primarily on the cities, and only then turned to the peasants in the countryside as the force capable of overthrowing reactionary rule. Similarly, in his search for effective methods of transforming China into a modern and democratic society, he first experimented with the Soviet model, and then looked once more to the peasantry for the revolutionary impetus necessary to destroy the very roots of the old society and lay the foundations of a completely new order.

The theory of the people's dictatorship was enunciated at a time when Mao's government was following a very moderate economic policy. In the cities, the 'national' capitalists often remained as the salaried managers of their enterprises and even received part of the profits. In the countryside, after a brief period of terror marked by the liquidation of some of the landlords and the dividing up of the land, nothing was done for several years to hasten collectivization. On the whole, it was carried no further than the creation of 'mutual-aid teams' whose members retained complete ownership of their land.

Not only was individual ownership of land on the whole respected, but there was positive encouragement to the maintenance of a 'rich-peasant economy' as a necessary concession in the interests of agricultural productivity, though at the same time steps were taken to limit the political influence of the rich peasants by excluding them from the peasant associations. In the course of the 'Cultural Revolution', the policy of leniency toward rich peasants has been denounced as a plot by Liu Shao-ch'i, but Text VII B 4, included in this edition for the first time, shows irrefutably that Mao himself approved this course. Nevertheless, a comparison of Mao's speech of 6 June 1950 to the Third Plenum of the Central Committee with Liu's report on agrarian reform delivered a few days later does reveal significant differences. Liu placed great emphasis on doing things in an orderly manner, and not allowing the process of agrarian transformation to get out of hand. Still more important, perhaps, he declared that collectivization would be possible only some time in the future when the necessary industrial basis had been laid so as to permit the introduction of mechanized farming.

The difference in emphasis between Mao and Liu on this issue may, in fact, serve to characterize not only the divergent temperaments of the two men, but the peculiar values and methods that distinguish Mao's brand of communism in both style and substance from more orthodox Leninism and/or Stalinism. In a word, Mao tends to exalt the revolutionary will of human beings until it becomes not merely an important factor in history, but an all-powerful force capable of re-shaping the material environment in a completely arbitrary fashion. This attitude is obviously linked to Mao's guerrilla experience and to his conviction that men, not weapons, are the decisive factor in a revolutionary war. While this strain in Mao's personality had not disappeared in the early years of the Chinese People's Republic, it was not much in evidence. The reason is that, as already suggested, Mao showed himself prepared at that time to model his policies on Soviet experience. And the essence of the Soviet method of 'building socialism' is rationally-planned and bureaucratically-administered economic development. There has been, of course, a great deal of irrational violence in the history of the Soviet Union, especially during the Stalinist period, but this was directed toward maintaining the political control of the leader. It did not seriously affect the substance of economic policy, which remained rational and bureaucratic.

It is these basic principles which have been constantly called into question in China in recent years. The fundamental dividing line in this respect can be situated in 1955. Before that date, Mao's policies, despite certain original traits, showed a considerable family resemblance with those of Russia and the Eastern European countries. After that date, he moved toward what Benjamin Schwartz has called 'the generalization of the Yenan heritage'. By the heritage of Yenan is meant, of course, a spirit and approach rather than a precise model. Mao was not now fighting a guerrilla war, but endeavouring to carry out a radical transformation in the social and economic structure of China and in the mentality of its inhabitants. But he became convinced that the same qualities of steadfast and unflinching struggle were required, and that, as in the case of revolutionary war, the mobilization of the masses was not only politically desirable, but could multiply the effectiveness of instruments and techniques. In a word, political mobilization became not merely, as in the Stalinist precedent, a device for enforcing conformity, but the motor of technical progress itself.[1]

The first outward manifestation of this new strain in Mao's thinking – or rather of the resurgence of a very old and fundamental strain – was to be found in his decision, imposed at the end of July 1955 (apparently against the wishes of a majority of the Party leadership), to accelerate the movement towards agricultural collectivization. At the time it was commonly believed, both within the country and abroad, that China would continue to advance more slowly and prudently in this domain than the Soviets had done. Once the regime had been consolidated, and the economy had begun to recover from twenty-five years of civil war and foreign invasion, the first Five-Year Plan was announced early in 1953. It was, of course, clearly understood that this implied a new stage in the transition to a socialist economy, and indeed in early 1955 the degree of control exercised by the 'national bourgeoisie' over the industries it had formerly

1. For more reflections on this theme, see Benjamin Schwartz's paper in Tang Tsou and Ping-ti Ho (editors), *China in Crisis*, I, University of Chicago, 1968, as well as my comments and those of Donald Munro.

owned was sharply reduced, and a campaign launched against 'bourgeois' ideological influence, symbolized by the person of Hu Feng. (It has now been confirmed that Mao himself participated directly in the attacks on Hu Feng.[1]) Despite these signals of mounting radicalism, few people were prepared for the policy announced in Mao's speech of 31 July, which was to precipitate virtually the whole of the Chinese peasantry into cooperatives, involving the pooling of land and the collective organization of labour, within a very brief span of time.[2]

An important and suggestive aspect of Mao's July 1955 speech concerns the relation between collectivization and mechanization. We have seen that Liu Shao-ch'i had stated in 1950 that collectivization must await the time when there would be an abundance of agricultural machinery, and this was also the Soviet position. Indeed, it could not have been otherwise given the emphasis on technological factors in social change characteristic of Lenin and his successors. It is true that in fact there were very few tractors around when Stalin launched the collectivization drive in Russia in 1929, but he nevertheless justified this step by claiming that the industrial basis had already been laid. In 1955, at an even earlier stage in the Chinese revolution, Mao took the opposite position. The sentence in our extract refers explicitly only to the need to form semi-socialist cooperatives prior to mechanization, but passages not included in this volume make clear that in Mao's view full socialist collectivization should also be completed before agricultural machinery was available on a large scale. He summed up his views in the sentence: 'The country's economic conditions being what they are, the technical transformation will take somewhat longer than the social.'[3]

1. See the extract attributed to him in *Quotations from Chairman Mao Tse-tung*, p. 120. Compare Merle Goldman, *Literary Dissent in Communist China*, Harvard University, Cambridge, Mass., 1967, p. 149, who correctly ascribed the attacks on Hu Feng to Mao.

2. See below Text VII B 5. At the time, however, the cooperatives were still 'semi-socialist' in the sense that each member's share of the product depended partly on the amount of land he had contributed and not solely on his labour.

3. Text VII B 5, p. 346; see also paragraph 10 of the speech.

Mao's speech of 31 July 1955 marked a decisive turning point, but even more characteristic are perhaps the commentaries he wrote at the end of 1955 for the collection of documents entitled *Socialist Upsurge in China's Countryside*, at a time when the formation of cooperatives was proceeding still faster than Mao himself had predicted a few months earlier. These passages are significant in themselves, and illustrate the link between a radical political climate and its ideological expression. But they are doubly interesting today because, with the benefit of hindsight, we can see clearly foreshadowed in them certain of the basic themes of the current 'Great Proletarian Cultural Revolution'. For this reason, I have added in the present edition a large number of new texts drawn from this source. The extracts included in the first edition stressed Mao's belief in the omnipotence of subjective forces,[1] and also his use of the imagery of combat.[2] Those now added spell out that the struggle required in China was to be specifically class struggle.[3] They also emphasize, in a passage which appears strikingly prophetic, that opposition to Mao's policies within the Party was so widespread as to be almost universal.[4] To be sure, he continued to attribute to the Party at the time the decisive role in the economic, social and political transformation of China.[5] But the divorce between Mao and the Party apparatus, which lies at the basis of the Cultural Revolution, was clearly already developing.

Further light on the similarities and differences between Mao's vision of the revolutionary process at this time, and the conceptions he was to develop a few years later, is shed by his speech of 25 January 1956 before the Supreme State Council. On this occasion, Mao presented and defended the 'draft programme for agricultural development' which had been adopted by the Central Committee of the Chinese Communist Party two days earlier. His speech displays in full measure the chiliastic hope of very rapid progress in modernization which was to characterize

1. See the text now re-numbered VII C 2.
2. See the text now re-numbered VI C 9, of which the present edition contains a longer extract.
3. Text VII B 6.
4. See the new portions of Text VI C 9.
5. Text VI C 8.

his attitude throughout the whole of the next thirteen years. Thus, he went so far as to state: 'Within another period of roughly three years, the socialist revolution can be basically completed in the whole country.' This was a claim that the Soviet leaders had never dreamed of making at a comparable stage in their revolution. But at the same time, Mao displayed an emphasis on the economic aspect of revolution, and a respect for the role of technical competence in furthering modernization, which are wholly absent today. 'The aim of the socialist revolution,' he said (not merely one of the aims, but *the* aim), 'is to release the productive forces.' And he added that, in order to carry out the 'vast design' of 'transforming the backward economic, scientific, and cultural conditions in our country so as to attain rapidly an advanced level by world standards,' the 'factor which decides everything' was 'the need for cadres, the need for a sufficient number of scientific and technical specialists.'[71]

This period, at the end of 1955 and the beginning of 1956, thus looks backward at the early period of the Chinese People's Republic, when Mao had been prepared to follow the Soviet emphasis on techniques and rationality, as well as forward to the utopian visions of the 'Great Leap Forward' of 1958 – not to mention the Cultural Revolution. This is not surprising, for so profound a change could not take place over night. If Mao moved forward in the course of the ensuing two years to a much greater emphasis on zeal rather than technical competence, this was no doubt due in part to the opposition his policies encountered within the Party itself. In the spring of 1956, Mao's ambitious plan for agricultural development was quietly put aside and did not re-emerge for a year and a half,[1] and more generally the tempo of economic and social change was slowed down during the latter part of 1956. At the Eighth Congress of the Chinese Communist Party in September 1956, the decision of the previous congress in 1945, hailing Mao Tse-tung's thought as the guiding principle of all the Party's action, was set aside, and henceforth the Party rules referred only to Marxism-Leninism. This measure was no doubt inspired in part by Soviet objections to the exaggera-

1. See Franz Schurmann, *Ideology and Organization in Communist China*, University of California, Berkeley, Calif., 1966, pp. 143, 200.

tion of Mao's role, but it clearly reflected also a certain uneasiness within China about the Mao cult, in the light of the revelations of the Twentieth Congress of the C.P.S.U. about the consequences of similar tendencies in the Soviet Union.

Apart from the resentment Mao may have felt at this downgrading of his thought, and more generally at the resistance encountered within the Party by his radical policies, another factor inciting him to reassert his leadership in even more intransigent terms was no doubt the disillusionment engendered by the outcome of the 'Hundred Flowers' episode, which he had launched in the spring of 1956, and which attained its climax a year later. Mao's statements during the winter of 1955–6 regarding the pre-eminent importance of cadres and technical knowledge were rooted in the conviction that by now the vast majority of the population had been persuaded of the superiority of the socialist system and was basically loyal to the principles of the new regime. The political foundation having thus been laid, one could concentrate on techniques. But the reaction when the floodgates were opened to criticism early in 1957 soon convinced Mao that the political and ideological revolution was far from accomplished, and must be given first priority.

In order to understand the theoretical ideas which Mao put forward during the 'Hundred Flowers' period, it is necessary to go back and deal with the philosophical basis of his thought as formulated during the Yenan period, which we neglected in the first part of this introduction. For the doctrine of contradictions, which he had developed in 1937, was used by Mao as the central concept of his speech of 27 February 1957, which constitutes his most important single theoretical utterance since 1949.

c. Mao Tse-tung and contradictions. The idea that contradictions are universal and are the motor of all change is, of course, not original with Mao. It was stated by Hegel, developed by Engels in his *Dialectics of Nature*, and used extensively by Lenin. Certain distinctive traits should, however, be noted in Mao's handling of contradictions.

Although the word 'contradiction' figures in the titles of only two of Mao's works – the essay 'On contradiction', dating from

1937, and the speech of 1957 on contradictions among the people – the concept is central to all his thinking about the problems and categories of Marxist dialectics. Hitherto only three items of this nature dating from the Yenan period have been available to students of the question: 'On practice', 'On contradiction', and 'Dialectical materialism'.[1] There has been, moreover, a great deal of controversy regarding the dating of these writings and their place in Mao's intellectual development. It has been claimed, in particular, that given the extremely low level of mastery of Marxist philosophy demonstrated by Mao in his article of 1940 on dialectical materialism, he could not possibly have written anything so sophisticated as 'On contradiction' in 1937.[2] Karl A. Wittfogel, on the other hand, although he does not have a very high opinion of Mao's 'Dialectical materialism' – which he has shown to be in large part plagiarized from Chinese translations of Soviet philosophical writings[3] – nevertheless finds it entirely possible to accept the official dating of 'On contradiction'. More recently, John Rue injected a new idea into this discussion by suggesting that the article 'Dialectical materialism' published in Shanghai in 1940 and attributed to Mao was in fact a forgery, concocted by pro-Moscow elements in the Chinese Communist Party, possibly with the support of Stalin, in order to discredit Mao and his leadership.[4]

If the three items just mentioned were the only ones of which the text was available for research, other philosophical writings by Mao were known to exist. Thus Chang Ju-hsin, one of the earliest commentators on 'Mao Tse-tung's Thought' in Yenan

1. See respectively Texts II D, II E, and II C.

2. The principal advocate of the theory that Mao did not write 'On contradiction' in 1937 in anything even vaguely resembling its present form is Arthur A. Cohen (*The Communism of Mao Tse-tung*, University of Chicago, 1964, pp. 7–28 and 139–46). Dennis J. Doolin and Peter J. Golas have echoed Cohen's views in the commentary accompanying their translation of 'Dialectical materialism', *China Quarterly*, no. 19, 1964, pp. 38–46.

3. See K. A. Wittfogel and C. R. Chao, 'Some remarks on Mao's handling of concepts and problems of dialectics', *Studies in Soviet Thought*, III, 4, December 1963, pp. 251–77.

4. 'Is Mao Tse-tung's "Dialectical materialism" a forgery?', *Journal of Asian Studies*, XXVI, no. 3, 1967, pp. 464–8.

days, cited in 1942 a book by Mao entitled *Pien-cheng-fa wei-wu-lun chiang-shou t'i-kang* (*Lecture Notes on Dialectical Materialism*), which he presented as the most important source for the study of Mao's methodology. He drew particular attention to Part 11 of Chapter 2, entitled 'On practice'. Commenting on this in a review article on Mao's dialectics, I wrote in 1967: 'It would obviously be a decisive contribution to our knowledge of Mao's development as a dialectician if a copy of this book could be found, but to my knowledge none exists outside China.'[1] By a fortunate coincidence, at the very moment when the manuscript for this revised edition of the present book was in the hands of the printer, I came into possession of a substantial portion of Mao's lecture notes, as they were serialized in 1938 in the magazine *K'ang-chan ta-hsüeh*.[2]

The fragment of 'Dialectical materialism' from which I selected extracts for the first edition of this book (and which has been translated *in extenso* by Chao and by Doolin and Golas) corresponded to the first chapter of a larger work. This larger work turns out to have been precisely the course of lectures recommended by Chang Ju-hsin in 1942, and which were apparently circulating in their complete form in Army and Party circles at the time. The text of Chapter I in *K'ang-chan ta-hsüeh* is identical with that published in Shanghai in 1940. Thus this fragment is unquestionably authentic, but instead of an article written in 1940 it is the introductory portion of a course of lectures given much earlier. Assuming (as I think we can) that the '*Shih-chieh-lun*' ('On practice') which originally constituted Part 11 of Chapter 2 contained the text of the lectures out of which Mao

1. *China Quarterly*, no. 29, 1967, pp. 158–9. The curious reader who compares what I have just written with the text of my 1967 article will find two discrepancies, both of them resulting from mistakes. The reference in the article to Part II instead of Part 11 is one of a very large number of typographical errors. The mistranslation of the title of Mao's book is my own blunder, resulting from the fact that the words '*chiang-shou t'i-kang*' were not clearly separated from the rest as a sub-title as they are in the text now available to me.

2. This version appeared in the spring of 1938 in Canton. (For bibliographical details see the note at the beginning of Text II C.) The Chinese text was very kindly supplied to me by Miss Bernadette Li, who copied it from the original available in the Bureau of Information Collection in Taiwan.

ultimately elaborated the item of the same name in the current edition of the *Selected Works*, and that these lectures were delivered, as we are told in a note to the present canon, in July 1937, then Mao must have begun lecturing during the winter of 1936–7. Hence Chapter 1 of 'Dialectical materialism' must date from late 1936 or early 1937.

Of the 'three items' to which I referred above, 'Dialectical materialism' and 'On practice' thus turn out to be respectively the beginning and the end of a single whole. (At the beginning of Chapter 2 of his *Lecture Notes on Dialectical Materialism*, Mao enumerates the various points he proposes to discuss, the eleventh and last being practice.) Having finished his lectures on practice, Mao then proceeded, in August 1937, to lecture on contradiction. Whether this was presented at the time as point 12 of Chapter 2 of the course as a whole, or as a special independent series of lectures, does not much matter. Even if it was not formally part of the same work as Mao's other two philosophical writings, it belongs to a single intellectual enterprise, namely Mao's attempt to come to terms with the philosophical basis of Marxism from the time when he was first exposed to it in July 1936 until the Japanese attack of September 1937 turned his attention to more practical things.

If we consider these facts about the circumstances in which 'Dialectical materialism' was composed in conjunction with the substance of the portion of Chapter 2 now available, then we can find some comfort for all the different positions which have been advanced regarding Mao as a philosopher – save for Professor Rue's hypothesis that the whole thing is a plot. Mr Cohen's argument that 'On contradiction' could not have been written before Chapter 1 of 'Dialectical materialism' falls to the ground, since it was in fact written (or presented orally) afterward. On the other hand, it is undeniable that the content of Chapter 2 is even feebler than that of Chapter 1. In particular, the extraordinarily simplistic exposition of the 'reflection' theory as the beginning and end of Marxist epistemology is a far cry from the sophisticated presentation of 'On practice'. It is true that Mao had only begun his study of Marxist dialectics in the summer of 1936, and might therefore have learned a great deal, relatively speaking, in the weeks or months between his lectures on matter and his lectures on practice. But although Mao did certainly lecture on practice, and also most probably on contradiction, in 1937, Mr Cohen is clearly right in affirming that the text must have required very extensive revision indeed in order to bring it to its present level.[1]

The fact is that Mao Tse-tung, despite the extravagant claims made today regarding his earth-shaking contributions to Marxist dialectics, has little talent as an abstract thinker, and little interest in philosophy as such. During the Yenan period, he had sufficient leisure to devote himself to the study of Marxist philosophy, on the basis of translations from current Soviet writings and works by Chinese comrades better versed in the subject than he. Because pre-eminence as a theorist has traditionally been necessary to consecration as a leader in the communist world, Mao no doubt felt compelled to set himself up as an authority on dialectical materialism, and to lecture on the subject at the Anti-Japanese University. The result was mediocre, even as measured against the extraordinarily low level of Soviet theoretical writings of the period. But it was above all dull, both because it is difficult to interest students in a subject which the lecturer has not properly digested, and because Mao himself was not really very interested. And the lectures on contradiction are more readable today, and were probably more readable even in their original form than those on 'matter' or on 'movement', because they are devoted in large part to the application of a highly flexible conceptual tool to a series of concrete problems.

If it is true that Mao's theoretical framework contains little that is original, this does not imply that there is nothing original in the way he applies it to Chinese and Soviet reality. Consider, for example, his contention that in the Soviet Union there still exists a contradiction between the workers and the peasants, which will be solved only gradually during the process of development from socialism to communism.[2] To be sure, Stalin himself

1. For a fuller discussion of the content of the newly-discovered part of 'Dialectical materialism' and of the conclusions which can be drawn from it, see the introduction to the complete translation of this fragment which I propose to publish in a forthcoming issue of *China Quarterly*.

2. See Text VI B 1.

had pointed to the contradictions in Soviet society at an earlier date, especially when the conflicts regarding industrialization and the first Five-Year Plan were at their height. But in 1936, he affirmed that the frontier between the workers and the peasants was in the process of disappearing, and in the chapter on dialectical and historical materialism, which he wrote in 1938 for the *History of the Communist Party of the Soviet Union*, it was stated that there was perfect correspondence between the basis and the superstructure in the Soviet Union.[72] Other, lesser, ideologists deduced from Stalin's statements that there were absolutely no contradictions whatsoever in the Soviet Union. [73]

It is possible that Mao did not realize in August 1937, when he originally wrote his article on contradictions, that the Russian materials he had been reading in translation were obsolete or obsolescent and that it would no longer be permissible to speak of contradictions between the workers and the peasants in the Soviet Union. But certainly, when his article was first published in April 1952, Mao must have known that it was out of harmony with the Soviet ideological line. The sudden decision to publish it, after the corresponding volume of his works had already appeared, may have been related to the 'Five-Antis' campaign, which reached its peak almost at the same moment. This campaign, directed against certain alleged dishonest practices of the national bourgeoisie, marked a new stage in the 'remoulding' of this class, which Mao had announced in 1949 in his article 'On people's democratic dictatorship', and in this context the analyses of 1937 regarding contradictions within society were of obvious relevance. But at the same time, the publication of such a text could not fail to be noted in Moscow and constituted in fact a challenge to the Soviet position as the sole ideological authority within the communist world.[1] It is obviously impossible to determine whether Mao deliberately decided to lay down such a challenge, or whether he was primarily concerned with internal

1. Interestingly enough, whereas the Soviet philosophical journal *Voprosy Filosofii* devoted an article written by a Chinese to Mao's essay 'On practice' when it appeared in December 1950, 'On contradiction' was not even mentioned in its pages.

problems and simply chose to ignore the larger implications of his gesture.

In any case, Mao's accent on the role of contradiction and struggle in the development of socialist society corresponds to a characteristic turn of his mind, with its mixture of flexibility and combativeness. I suggested earlier that the 'dialectics' of the young Mao was above all an expression of currents in traditional Chinese thought. But if it owes something to *yin* and *yang*, his idea of the dialectical method is also concrete and pragmatic, as the curious paragraph of 'On contradiction' regarding Sung Chiang's three attacks on Chu village[1] indicates. A constant effort to remain close to the infinite complexity of reality has been one of the most striking traits of Mao's behaviour – at least until recently.

If we turn now to the way in which Mao has developed the idea of contradictions since he gave a new direction to Chinese internal policy in 1955, we find that he has applied it both to the struggle with nature and to the struggle between human beings. The idea of a 'war against nature' is a favourite one of Mao's, and can be traced back at least as far as 1938.[2] But in Mao's view, such a rapid and violent effort for the transformation of the natural environment can be carried out only if the masses are properly mobilized to support this policy, and if opposition from backward and reactionary elements is smashed. In other words, the resolution of economic contradictions and social contradictions is inextricably linked.

These two aspects of the revolutionary process are present together in Mao's speech of April 1956, on the 'ten great relationships'. This speech, which has never been published for general distribution, is one of the most important theoretical documents of the crucial period 1955–8, in which Mao was moving toward new and original solutions to the problems of the Chinese revolution.[3] Like the commentaries of late 1955 and the remarks

1. See Text II E, p. 197.

2. See Text IX C.

3. Heretofore, this speech has been known only from summaries given in other sources – primarily from the account given in 1958 by Liu Shao-ch'i. On this basis, Franz Schurmann elaborated an interesting and perceptive

of January 1956 regarding agricultural development discussed above, the 'ten great relationships' clearly belong to a transitional period. On the one hand Mao stresses, in language that would today be regarded as 'economist' if it were used by anyone else, that a positive and activist attitude on the part of the masses can only be ensured if the Party's policy gives due weight to individual preferences and interests, and to the people's concern with their standard of living. He also attaches great importance to learning from foreign countries, and especially from the Soviet Union. (See his discussion of point 4, 'The relation between the state, the production unit, and the individual producer', and point 10, 'Relations between China and other countries'.) But at the same time, he declares that the minimum of 400,000 new technical cadres needed for economic development do not necessarily require much formal schooling, but can easily be recruited from among workers trained on the job, thus anticipating recent educational policies. (See point 2, 'The relation between industry on the coast and in the interior'.) Most striking of all, he concludes his appraisal of the situation by pointing out the advantages China derives from being 'poor and blank' – an idea which he was to develop at greater length and in much more radical and intransigent form two years later, as we shall see below. In 1956, he mentioned first and at greater length the *disadvantages* for China arising out of her 'semi-colonial' past and economic backwardness, and only then suggested that her 'poverty and blankness' also had a positive side (see point 10); in 1958, he saw only the advantages in purity and revolutionary zeal to be derived from China's backwardness.

As regards the methods to be followed in developing the economy, the keynote of the 'ten great relations' is balance, especially between heavy industry and light industry, and between industry and agriculture. Mao does not hesitate to state very bluntly that 'certain socialist countries' have committed errors in

---

analysis (op. cit., pp. 77–85). Jerome Ch'en has now kindly communicated to me the Chinese text as issued in December 1966 by the Peking Institute of Economics 'for study but not for quotation'. A complete translation of this important document will be found in his book *Mao Tse-tung*, to be published in 1969 by Prentice-Hall in the 'Great Lives Observed' series.

this respect, which China has hitherto avoided and should continue to avoid. These consist in neglecting light industry, and especially agriculture, in favour of exclusive concentration on heavy industry. China, too, Mao declares, gives priority to heavy industry, but 'we pay more attention to light industry and agriculture'. Excessive stress on heavy industry in fact defeats its own purpose, for it disorganizes the economy and undermines the morale of the population because of the resulting lack of consumer goods. 'The experience of certain socialist countries shows,' he says, 'that if the collectivization of agriculture is carried out badly, one cannot increase production either.' (See the discussion of point 1.)

In the political sphere also, the position expounded by Mao in April 1956 was one of moderation and balance. Counter-revolutionaries must be combated; it was right to kill some of them in the first years of the Chinese People's Republic, and a few must still be killed. But the general policy toward counter-revolutionaries, even if they have committed crimes worthy of death, must be to give them the opportunity of reforming themselves through productive labour. 'A man's head is not like a scallion, which will grow again if you cut it off; if you cut it off wrongly, then even if you want to correct your error there is no way of doing it.' (Point 8, 'The relation between revolution and counter-revolution'.)

From a theoretical standpoint, the most important aspect of this speech is Mao's emphasis on the fact that contradictions pervade the whole of Chinese society. The 'ten great relations' about which he is talking, he states repeatedly, are in fact ten contradictions. This is, of course, entirely consistent with the idea put forward in 1937 in 'On contradiction', and re-stated here: 'Everywhere in the world there are contradictions. If there were no contradictions there would be no world.'

Mao's conviction that contradictions within society, and not merely between man and nature, still exist under socialism, sets his views apart from those of the Soviets. Another important text in this respect is the editorial of 5 April 1956, which constituted the Chinese contribution to the 'de-Stalinization' debate then going on in the wake of Khrushchev's secret speech to the

Twentieth Party Congress.[1] Some naïve ideas seem to suggest,' wrote the authors of the editorial – in which Mao himself had a hand – 'that contradictions no longer exist in a socialist society. To deny the existence of contradictions is to deny dialectics. The contradictions in various societies differ in character, as do the forms of their solution, but society at all times develops through continual contradictions.'

By 'at all times', the authors of this article really mean 'at *all* times', even after full communism has been achieved. Moreover, this refers not merely to contradictions between man and nature, or between the productive forces and the relations of production; there will actually be contradictions between individuals and groups in society, even after all class differences have been completely erased. These will grow out of differences between individuals, who will continue to be good and bad, to think correctly or incorrectly, even under communism. Moreover, according to Mao's speech of 27 February 1957, which represents the next stage in the development of this strain in Chinese communist ideology, these continuing contradictions will also grow out of the very nature of any society in which there are differences of function and therefore contradictions between the leaders and the followers.

In the light of a text by Liu Shao-ch'i dating from 1941, it is interesting to speculate on the respective contributions of Mao and Liu to these theories. This is Part III of the book which used to be called in English *How To Be a Good Communist*, and of which the title is now translated more literally as *On the Self-cultivation of Communist Party Members*. Only the first two parts of this work, which was denounced in April 1967 as a 'big poisonous weed', were included in most editions available to the general public. These corresponded to lectures delivered in July 1939 at the Party School in Yenan. After his transfer to central China, where he was entrusted with the reorganization of the New Fourth Army following the incident of January 1941,[2] Liu delivered a third series of lectures, entitled 'On organizational and

1. See Text VI B 2.

2. On the New Fourth Army Incident, see Chalmers A. Johnson, *Peasant Nationalism and Communist Power*, Stanford University, Stanford, Calif., 1962, pp. 136–40.

disciplinary self-cultivation', which were normally available only for study within the Party.[1]

'What is the Party's organizational structure?' Liu begins. 'Like all other things, it is a contradictory structure, a contradictory entity, that is to say, the union of two opposing elements, which combine to form something new.' After discussing the unity of opposites as a general principle,[2] Liu goes on to talk in precise and most suggestive terms of the kind of opposites that make up the Communist Party, namely the leaders and the led:

Our Communist Party is also formed by the union of all sorts of different party members; its basic structure is the cell. For instance, three or more members of our Party can form a cell or small group, but the relationship which constitutes a cell does not consist merely in adding two party members to another party member. One party member plus two party members makes three party members; this is merely a relationship of addition, and does not constitute a Party structure (or organization). What, then, is the necessary condition for constituting an organization? Among the three members of the Party, there must be one secretary of the cell, and two members of the cell, or one head of

1. When I cited Liu's lectures in the first edition of this anthology, I had not yet identified them as part of his book on self-cultivation. For bibliographical details regarding the various editions of this work, see my article 'Mao Tse-tung as Marxist dialectician' cited above. I translate here from a complete text of the three parts of 'On self-cultivation', included in Liu Shao-ch'i's *Lun tang*, Ta-chung Shu-tien, Dairen, 1947, pp. 29–190. A French translation of this, with the indication of all the variants in the successive editions of Liu's book, an introduction by myself, and a facsimile of the text which I am using here, will be published late in 1969 by the Fondation Nationale des Sciences Politiques in Paris. See also my article 'The Party in Chinese communist ideology', to appear in *China Quarterly*, no. 38, 1969.

2. In the process, he gives the following singular example to illustrate the fact that combining similar things leads only to quantitative increase, but not to qualitative change: 'If one adds a cow to another cow, they are still just cows . . . but a bull plus a cow forms a new relationship, a man plus a woman gives rise to the relationship between man and wife. All things are contradictory entities' (ibid., p. 134). This has now led to his denunciation as a low individual whose 'self-cultivation' is 'vulgar bourgeois nonsense such as "a bull plus a cow" and "a man plus a woman".' See Yao Wen-yüan, 'Comments on Tao Chu's Two Books', *Peking Review*, no. 38, 1967, p. 12.

the group, and two members of the group. The union of the secretary and of the members of the cell, or of the head and the members of the group, is a union of contradictory elements, that is to say, the union of the leaders and the led. The union of the leaders and the led constitutes a unified organization, and only such a unified organization has strength. The unified organization is the Party – this is the Party's basic organizational structure.

The form taken by the union of the Party as a whole is that of the union of the leading organs at all levels and of all the Party members; that is to say, the union extending downward from the Central Committee, to all the Party branches, all the leading organs, and finally to all the cells; that is to say, the union of the Party leaders, of the Party cadres, and of the great mass of Party members; that is to say, the union of the upper-level and lower-level organizations of the Party. Thus, the structure of our Party is not that of a mixture. It is not simply the grouping together of several hundred thousand Party members, and it is not without a definite structure; on the contrary, it is the union of several hundred thousand Party members in accordance with a definite organizational form and definite rules. It is a union of contradictory elements, comprising the leaders and the led, the Party leaders and Party members, the upper-level and lower-level organizations of the Party. It is this type of organizational structure which gives to the Party its great fighting strength; otherwise, it would be nothing but an undisciplined mob.[74]

Quoting more briefly from this text of Liu Shao-ch'i in the first edition of this book, I suggested that Liu might well have been not simply Mao's spokesman in the domain of Party organization, but an independent thinker who had made his own contribution to Chinese communist ideology. The 'Cultural Revolution' has brought abundant confirmation that this is indeed the case. I shall have more to say about the differences in outlook and approach between the two men in discussing very recent developments. Here it is in order to point out that, while Liu went much farther in 1941 than Mao had done at that time in frankly recognizing the contradiction between the leaders and the led within the Party, he also showed the same concern with doing things in an orderly and disciplined way which we have noted in comparing his speech of June 1950 with that of Mao.

In any case, it is Mao who, in his speech of 27 February 1957, gave the idea of the inherently contradictory nature of all social relationships its sharpest and most celebrated expression. As far as the contradictions among the classes of Chinese society are concerned, Mao's 1957 speech can be regarded as a transposition into philosophical language of his concentric-circle theory of the people's democratic dictatorship. The ambiguous role of the national bourgeoisie is explained in terms of 'antagonistic' and 'nonantagonistic' contradictions (a distinction already made by Lenin[1]):

> The contradictions between ourselves and our enemies are antagonistic ones. Within the ranks of the people, contradictions among the working people are nonantagonistic, whereas those between the exploiters and the exploited classes have a nonantagonistic aspect as well as an antagonistic one. . . . Exploitation of the working class for profit is one aspect, while support of the Constitution and willingness to accept socialist transformation is the other. . . . The contradiction between exploiter and exploited that exists between the national bourgeoisie and the working class is in itself an antagonistic one. But, in the concrete conditions existing in China, such an antagonistic contradiction, if properly handled, can be transformed into a nonantagonistic one.[75]

In addition to reaffirming the attitude of conditional tolerance of the national bourgeoisie already enunciated in 1949, this text contains an interesting idea, which supports the interpretation of the theory of the people's democratic dictatorship as a modern equivalent of the theory of the General Will. The national bourgeoisie, says Mao, must *accept* the transformation it is undergoing – otherwise the contradiction between it and the workers will become antagonistic.[2]

There is an obvious link between these conceptions and the methods of indoctrination and thought reform that have played such a large part in Mao's thinking and the policy of the Chinese Communist Party since the 1930s. From the techniques of indoctrination of enemy soldiers practised in the Kiangsi days

1. See below the introduction to Chapter VI and Text VI B 1.
2. In a similar vein, Mao in 1937 made both the antagonistic and nonantagonistic character of the contradictions *within* the Communist Party dependent on the willingness of the 'comrades who have committed errors' to become conscious of this.

and in the anti-Japanese war, through the Cheng Feng movement of 1942–3, and the 'thought reform' practised during the Korean War [76] to the Hundred Flowers movement, there is a clear line of development.

This strain in Mao Tse-tung's thinking can be linked to the accent on conscious action manifested as early as the 1917 article on physical culture. Blind obedience is not enough; people must be made to understand and therefore to participate willingly and actively in the implementation of Party policy. 'Agitation' is, of course, also a characteristic feature of Soviet society; but it may fairly be claimed that the degree of Mao's preoccupation with this problem constitutes a case of the 'passage from quantitative to qualitative differences' that figures in Marxist dialectics.

The successful and peaceful resolution of the contradictions in Chinese society presupposes, according to Mao's 1957 speech, not merely a willingness to be transformed on the part of the national bourgeoisie, but also the 'correct' handling of these contradictions by the Party leadership. And the first prerequisite for this is that the Party cadres should recognize, as many of them it seems refused to do (despite the clear affirmations in the editorial of April 1956), that contradictions do in fact exist in Chinese society.

Not only do such contradictions exist between the various classes of society – they also exist between the government and society as a whole, between the leaders and the led.[1] This is the most revolutionary affirmation in Mao's speech of February 1957, and it is not surprising that it opened the door to developments that Mao was not prepared to accept.

For this speech in fact spans the transition between two epochs which appear totally divergent, but which nonetheless have a certain continuity. When Mao Tse-tung made this speech, the Hundred Flowers campaign was in full swing. Party members, and even simple citizens, were encouraged to indulge in unsparing criticism of the economic, administrative, and political authorities. The goal of this policy appears to have been a dual one; on the one hand, to avoid an explosion similar to that in Hungary,

1. See Text VI B 3.

which Mao blamed largely on the bureaucratism and repressive methods of the Hungarian leaders; and on the other hand, by allowing people to express themselves freely and thus to relieve their feelings, to call forth a wave of enthusiasm and good will to accelerate China's economic progress. Most probably Mao believed that if such latitude were granted to the citizens, they would use it to criticize particular abuses, but would not question the fundamental principles of the regime.

When a watered-down version of the speech was at last published in June 1957 (the original text has never been released), it was evident that this calculation had proved false. All over the country, students, peasants, and the intellectuals were openly criticizing the Party's domination over all spheres of society. That is, of course, a demand that no Leninist could ever accept. Mao therefore made a brusque turnabout and endeavoured to obtain by organization and discipline what he had not been able to obtain by the liberation of individual initiative, namely 'the acceleration of the economic and cultural development' of the country. In the domain of production, this meant the policy of the 'Great Leap Forward', and in the domain of social organization it meant the establishment of the people's communes; the whole of this radical policy found its ideological expression in the theory of the permanent revolution.[1]

This term was first rehabilitated by Liu Shao-ch'i in his speech of 5 May 1958, at the Party Congress, and most of the themes later developed under this heading were contained in his remarks. (I say 'rehabilitated' because the Chinese term is the same as that used earlier to designate Trotsky's theory, and Trotsky remains a villain and a heretic in China as in the Soviet Union.) Although the theory was invariably referred to at the time as 'Mao Tse-tung's theory of the permanent revolution', it was possible to have some doubts as to whether it was really his. Subsequent events, since the beginning of the 'Great Proletarian Cultural Revolution', appear to have settled the question; Liu Shao-ch'i, who claimed to be speaking for Mao, has been

1. For the reasons which lead me to translate 'permanent revolution' rather than 'uninterrupted revolution', see my *Documents sur la theorie de la 'révolution permanente' en Chine*, Mouton, Paris, 1963, pp. ix–x.

denounced, but the ideas he expounded in 1958 are still attributed to Mao.

The explicitly political content of the theory has varied considerably from time to time, depending upon the internal and external situation. Its core is a conception of the transition from socialism to communism based on an analogy with the Leninist conception of the transition from the democratic to the socialist revolution, as the latter was outlined by Mao Tse-tung in 'The Chinese revolution and the Chinese Communist Party'.[1]

This is the only aspect of the permanent revolution dealt with in an official pronouncement – the Wuchang resolution of the Central Committee of December 1958. This text appeared at a time when the Soviet leaders, deeply disturbed by the extravagant claims of an immediate passage from socialism to communism which had been voiced in Peking, had to be reassured. It stressed the importance of avoiding 'the utopian hope of bypassing the socialist stage' of the revolution. 'We are partisans of the Marxist-Leninist theory of the permanent revolution,' stated the resolution. 'We hold that there is not and cannot be a great wall between the democratic revolution and the socialist revolution, nor between socialism and communism. We are equally partisans of the Marxist-Leninist theory of stages in the development of the revolution, and we hold that the different stages of development reflect qualitative changes in reality and ... must not be confounded'.[77]

More interesting than this explicitly political aspect of the theory is its Promethean element. This was formulated as follows in one of the earliest articles devoted to the 'permanent revolution' following Liu Shao-ch'i's speech of May 1958:

> The more it is possible for men to carry out a conscious revolution in their own social relationships, the more they increase their power in the combat with nature, the more they can freely command as by magic the latent productive forces, making them appear everywhere and develop rapidly.[78]

The Promethean theme is an integral part of Marxist thought in general. At the same time, it may be asked whether the im-

1. See Text III K.

portance attached to this aspect of Marxism by the Chinese does not reflect the preoccupations of the peoples of the underdeveloped countries generally. Marx and Engels had an essentially Greek vision of nature, as an environment to be shaped by man, but at the same time a friendly environment. To their Chinese disciples, nature is an enemy against whom one 'declares war' in order to wrest from her the food necessary for survival and the resources necessary for economic and military power.

The two basic goals defined in the theory of the permanent revolution – the increasingly rapid transformation of society and of nature – are linked and reinforced by a philosophical theory drawn essentially from Engels and Lenin, as interpreted by Mao Tse-tung in his various writings on contradiction. From the idea of quantitative change leading over to qualitative change, the Chinese thinkers derive the conception of a universe in ceaseless and perpetual flux. In particular, even after all class conflict has been eliminated, contradictions will continue to arise between the productive forces and the relations of production because of the continuous development of the former, which in turn will engender contradictions between the members of society. These contradictions will be resolved by an endless series of 'qualitative changes', baptized 'revolutions', so that there will be an infinite number of revolutions, even after communism is fully established. For the moment, revolutions of the old type, engendered by the antagonistic contradictions between classes, and revolutions of the new type, caused by the nonantagonistic contradictions of socialist society, will continue to exist side by side; but ultimately the development of the productive forces and the efforts of men to adapt to them will replace the class struggle as the matrix of the endless revolutions to come.

This theory may be regarded as a distinctly original contribution to Leninism, growing out of the conditions of the underdeveloped countries. It reflects the characteristics of Chinese society mentioned earlier: the contrast between the old and the new, and the resulting instability and kaleidoscopic changes.

The theory of the permanent revolution, and indeed the whole of the ideology of the period of the Great Leap Forward, is in profound harmony with the most fundamental tendencies of

Mao's personality. It grows out of his Promethean urge to fashion nature, and out of his passionate desire to transform man, with its curious mixture of humanistic and totalitarian motives. It is infused with the combativeness that was so marked in him from the beginning and which was further accentuated by a quarter of a century of armed struggle. And it is characterized, too, by a certain impatience with reality, an implacable will to bend men, things, facts, and theories to his purposes, and to break them if they refuse to bend. 'In force and momentum, the attack is just like a tempest or hurricane; those who submit to it survive, and those who resist it perish,' wrote Mao in 1927 of the Hunanese peasants, echoing similar phrases in Chinese history and fiction. This sentence could very well serve as a description of his own approach to the transformation of Chinese society.

This heaven-storming approach finds graphic expression in Mao's contribution to the first issue of *Hung-ch'i* in 1958.[1] But this article not only expresses, like the theory of the permanent revolution, the will to advance very rapidly; it also formulates ideas regarding the sources of revolution which mark the beginning of a rupture with Leninism, and foreshadow the 'Cultural Revolution'.

The key formula in this respect, which to some extent symbolizes the most fundamental themes not only in Mao's thought but in China's revolutionary experience, is the celebrated thesis that the Chinese people draw strength and virtue from the fact that they are 'poor and blank'. The idea that poverty may lead to revolution bears some relationship to Marxism, though Marx singled out the proletariat as the saviour of society not merely because its members were poor but because of the decisive role they played in the productive process. The notion that 'blankness' qualifies the Chinese people for a revolutionary mission goes, on the contrary, entirely against the grain of Marxism. Marx himself, who had a profound admiration for the industrial revolution carried out by the European bourgeoisie in his own lifetime, saw the aim of the revolution in the re-shaping of the social and political order so as to permit the full development of this enterprise. The working class would be the bearer of this revolution

1. See Text VII C 3.

not merely because it incarnated the moral values of protest against injustice, but also by virtue of its skills.

Because the peasant societies of Asia did not possess this technical knowledge and economic drive, Marx proclaimed explicitly that the only solution for them lay in 'Europeanization'.[1] Lenin held similar views about 'semi-Asiatic' Russia. The clear implication of such a position is that, although the pre-capitalist societies of the non-European countries may give rise to revolutionary movements which will play a useful role in the world revolution as a whole, such movements must be guided by the communists of the advanced countries of Europe and North America, just as the peasants must be guided by the workers within each Western country. Soviet practice under both Lenin and Stalin distorted this emphasis on the role of an objectively-existing advanced class, possessing not merely fighting spirit but modern knowledge, in the direction of a voluntarist effort to bend objective reality to the aims of the revolutionaries, but the valorization of technical competence remained. And today, when the Soviet Union has become a great industrial nation which actually does possess the proletariat in the name of which the revolution was carried out in 1917, the leaders in Moscow are even more inclined to stress these orthodox principles.

For Mao Tse-tung, on the other hand, the implications regarding the inferiority of the Asian and African nations, and of their subordination to the leadership of the technically-advanced West, inherent in the logic of Marxism, are clearly intolerable. Hence his attempt to make of 'blankness' a virtue. The Chinese people may not have, for the moment, the same level of economic development and technical competence as the United States or the Soviet Union, but by the same token they are not afflicted with the maladies of crass materialism and selfish individualism that have perverted not only the West, but the land of 'modern revisionism'. This also provides an ideological justification for the decisive role of the countryside, both in the conquest of power, and in the socialist transformation of China. Mao's master, Li Ta-chao, taught him half a century ago that the cities were dens of

1. See *Marxism and Asia*, Text I 1, and the corresponding section of the introduction.

iniquity and that the veritable source of regeneration was to be found in the countryside. In 1958, when Mao exasperated the Soviets with the claim that China would establish full communism before they did, it was postulated that the evolution toward communism would begin in the villages, with the setting up of the people's communes, and only later be propagated toward the cities.[1]

Mao's praise of 'blankness' does not imply, of course, that he is uninterested in technical progress or that he is the enemy of modern knowledge. On the contrary, his aim has been and remains to build China into a 'modern socialist country, rich and strong'. But it does indicate an order of priorities. The choice in favour of the peasant rather than the worker, the army man rather than the Party cadre, the politically zealous Red Guard rather than the able student, in the end can be reduced to a single over-riding priority: to the man who wills rather than to the man who knows. Or, to put it somewhat more accurately, the preference goes to the man who is both resolute and malleable, who can be made to will and to do what Mao thinks he ought to will. These attitudes, as has often been pointed out, are a projection of the spirit of Yenan and of the Chingkangshan – of the guerrilla period when the ability to mobilize men was more important than technical knowledge, and when only unbending resolve enabled Mao's forces to hold out against a more numerous and far better equipped enemy. They have re-emerged in particularly extreme form today. Once more, Mao is confronted by an adversary infinitely superior in technical resources. Once more, he concludes that the revolutionary peoples will finally triumph because of the righteousness of their cause and their willingness to fight to the end.

In the preceding paragraph, the ideas and values of the 'Great Leap Forward' were juxtaposed with those of the 'Great Proletarian Cultural Revolution'. This telescoping of history is

1. The Soviets have not failed to seize on the parallel between these ideas and those of the Russian Populists, and have accused 'Mao and his partisans' of rediscovering 'an old S.-R. theory' and 'Narodnik-anarchist conceptions'. See P. N. Fedoseev, *Marksizm i voliuntarizm*, 'Znanie' Moscow, 1968, pp. 45–6.

justified not only because there is a close affinity between these two periods, but also because Mao had virtually nothing to say on China's internal problems from the end of 1958 until the eve of the Cultural Revolution. Even in 1958, some of Mao's comrades had denounced the attempt to produce steel by the mobilization of the masses as a 'guerrilla habit'.[1] When Mao's radical policies led to economic chaos, the Party bureaucracy took control and replaced these 'guerrilla methods' by an approach less drastically in conflict with the Soviet example, involving in particular a greater use of material incentives to stimulate production. The economic results were favourable, but Mao clearly viewed the proceedings with distaste. For the moment, he was obliged to accept the situation, and to find an outlet in writing or encouraging attacks on 'modern revisionism' abroad, and in issuing ringing denunciations of imperialism. As soon as circumstances permitted, however, he began his efforts to get China back on what he regarded as the true revolutionary path. In September 1962, at the Tenth Plenum of the Central Committee, he put forward the call 'never to forget the class struggle', and in the following May he warned against the danger that China might 'change its colour'.[2]

This last text can be regarded in a sense as the charter and fountain-head of the whole Cultural Revolution. It makes clear and explicit Mao's growing anxiety lest the 'right-wing deviations' in the Party which he had described as widespread in 1955 lead to the emergence of full-blown 'revisionist' tendencies such as he perceived in the Soviet Union, thereby ultimately jeopardizing the very survival of the revolutionary movement to which he had devoted himself for over forty years. A decisive factor in preventing such a process of degeneration would be the continuing fidelity of young people, who had not known the bitter sufferings of their elders at the hands of the Japanese and of the Kuomintang, to the revolutionary cause. In the spring of 1964, Mao therefore turned his attention to the problem of 'bringing up successors' to the veterans of the Long March.

This problem was first discussed on a large scale at the Ninth

1. See below Text VII C 4.
2. See the document dated 9 May 1963, Text VII E 8.

Congress of the Communist Youth League in June 1964. The fact now appears as singularly ironic, for a month earlier the General Political Department of the People's Liberation Army had published the first edition of *Quotations from Chairman Mao*, and this date can be taken as marking a decisive stage on the road to the replacement of the Party – and its emanation the Youth League – by the army as the dominant force in Chinese society and the arbiter of ideological orthodoxy. In July 1964, the ninth Chinese reply to the Soviet open letter of the previous July contained a passage, attributed to Mao, stressing once more the need to bring up 'millions of successors', and declaring that the final triumph of socialism over capitalism in China would require one or several centuries.

In January 1965, Mao for the first time designated 'people within the Party who are in authority and are taking the capitalist road' as the target of the 'socialist education movement' which he had been promoting since the plenum of September 1962, and which was now re-baptized 'the four clean-ups' (political, economic, organizational, and ideological).[1] Thus the battle lines were drawn, both from the standpoint of ideology and in terms of a power struggle among the principal leaders, for the 'Great Proletarian Cultural Revolution' of which the opening shots were to be fired in November 1965.

We cannot retrace here in detail the extremely complex events which ensued, and of which the end is not yet in sight.[2] In the context of the present volume, our concern is rather to spell out the ideological implications of the tactics adopted by Mao, or in any case carried out in his name. It would be difficult to exaggerate the importance of these. Although, as I have endeavoured to suggest in the foregoing pages, there is a clear line of continuity from the 'Socialist Upsurge' of 1955 and the 'Great Leap' of 1958 to the current 'Cultural Revolution', in many respects

1. See below Text VI C 10.

2. I have given my own account of this period in the conclusion to my Mao biography. This will be expanded and brought up to date in the new edition of the biography to be published in 1969. See also Jack Gray and Patrick Cavendish, *Chinese Communism in Crisis: Maoism and the Cultural Revolution*, Pall Mall Press, and Frederick A. Praeger, New York, 1968.

these tendencies have been carried so much farther that, to use Mao's vocabulary, quantitative change has given rise to a qualitative leap.

This is the case, first of all, as regards the role of the Party, and more generally the institutional framework of the revolution. We have seen that a decade ago, even as he denounced the right-wing opposition among his comrades, Mao still regarded the Party as the indispensable instrument for guiding the revolution. Although the Party's fortunes have varied considerably over the past two years, and at times the vicissitudes of the struggle have led Mao and his faction to seek a compromise with elements of the Party bureaucracy for tactical reasons, the mere fact that the Party's supremacy is no longer taken for granted indicates in itself a change without precedent in the history of the communist movement.

One reason for Mao's onslaught on the Party was, as already indicated, the fact that it was no longer an obedient instrument for carrying out his will. But while resentment at Liu Shao-ch'i, Teng Hsiao-p'ing and the other Party leaders who had thwarted him in the application of his radical policies undoubtedly influenced his attitude, his recent course corresponds too closely to tendencies long present in his thought and behaviour to be explained merely by pique and vanity. Stalin decimated the Party bureaucracy in order to maintain his own power, but he had nothing against bureaucracy as such; on the contrary, he could conceive of no other way of governing and of running the economy. Mao, on the other hand, although he exhibited very early a grasp of the importance of organization as a political weapon which I have called 'natural Leninism', has constantly sought to prevent all organizations, including the Party, from becoming ends in themselves. In the past, he combated the bureaucratization of the Party both from within, by the repeated rectification campaigns in which the cadres were obliged to participate, and from without, by constantly exposing the Party organization to popular scrutiny in accordance with the formula of the 'mass line'. This time, he chose to treat the Party cadres not, as in 1942 or 1957, as patients to be cured, but as enemies to be terrorized by the Red Guards and publicly humiliated.

The ideological justification offered for this policy was an idea put forward in passing by Mao three decades earlier, in a speech in Yenan on the occasion of Stalin's sixtieth birthday.[1] 'There are innumerable principles of Marxism,' he had then said, 'but in the last analysis they can all be summed up in one sentence: "To rebel is justified".' This maxim, according to Mao, was formulated by Marx, and further developed by Stalin. The attribution of such an anarchist notion to the late Soviet dictator is surely one of the greatest ironies of modern times.

The call to indiscriminate 'rebellion' against every form of authority could mark only a passing phase in Mao's strategic plan for the Cultural Revolution. The intervention of the Red Guards was necessary in order to paralyse the Party organization as previously constituted, and open the way to the creation of new political instruments more responsive to Mao's will. But, as already emphasized, Mao had displayed from the beginning an instinctive grasp of the importance of organization, and despite the references to the Paris Commune in the decisions of August 1966,[2] he cannot possibly have imagined at any time that the country could be run on a basis of completely spontaneous mass democracy. Once the power of the old Party apparatus loyal to Liu Shao-ch'i had been broken, something would therefore have to be put in its place.

The first stage in Mao's efforts to produce such a new political force adapted to his ends was that of the so-called 'seizure of power' which began early in 1967. This involved the establishment of 'Revolutionary Committees' in the various cities and provinces based on the 'three-in-one combination' of P.L.A. men, new revolutionary activists, and old Party and state cadres. The aim of this formula was to salvage a certain number of the old cadres, whose technical and administrative skills were necessary to the running of the country, without (at least for the moment) rehabilitating the Party as such. Sandwiched in between the army and the young Red Guard zealots, the Party bureaucrats could be utilized without any danger of their corrupting the

1. See Text X G.

2. See the decision of 8 August 1966, especially point 9, *Peking Review*, no. 33, 1966, pp. 9–10.

others with their revisionist and capitalist mentality. And in any case, effective control of the situation rested with the army.

These 'Revolutionary Committees' (of which the last were established only in the autumn of 1968) were supposed to take over all the powers of both the state and Party organizations in a given area. Moreover, the ideological justification for this process went so far as to speak of treating the apparatus of the Chinese Communist Party, hitherto supposed to be the vanguard of the proletariat, as Marx had said the Paris Commune showed the bourgeois state apparatus should be treated – i.e., by smashing it instead of trying to take it over. [79] Under the impact of such startling formulations, I ventured to speculate in March 1967 that perhaps there was no place at all for the Party in Mao's new scheme of things. This has now been proved false; there will indeed be a Communist Party in Mao Tse-tung's new, pure, 'proletarian' China, but a Party of a rather singular sort, explicitly deriving its authority exclusively from the leader.

The principle that the Party as a collective entity is the source of all authority and of all truth is the very keystone of the arch of Leninism. By openly setting himself above the Party as the incarnation of the will of the 'proletariat', Mao has perpetrated a heresy of which even Stalin was never guilty. Even as he established his own arbitrary dictatorship and purged the Party bureaucracy with the aid of the secret police, Stalin claimed to be merely the servant of the Party, exercising its collective authority in his capacity as Secretary General. Mao, in contrast, has allowed himself to be canonized – in his own lifetime, and not after death, as in Lenin's case – as the only fountain-head of both truth and authority.

This new conception of legitimacy receives striking expression in the Draft Party Constitution proposed by Mao in October 1968 (see Text VI C 13), not merely in the reference to a personal successor, but for example in the provision (in Article V) that Party members at any level can bypass their superiors and appeal directly to the Chairman himself. Even more astonishing, as a reflection of the mixture of the new and the old which prevails in China today, is the re-emergence of the concept of '*chung*' or loyalty to the ruler. This once designated a cardinal virtue of the faithful subject and minister; it now describes the highest attribute of a 'proletarian revolutionary' – absolute devotion to Chairman Mao.

These changes in the organizational framework within which power is exercised in China, and in their ideological expression, have been paralleled by a progressive modification in the aims of the Cultural Revolution. In early 1966 the Chinese press was filled with 'philosophical articles' by workers and peasants which described how the authors had assimilated what they called 'the dialectics of Mao Tse-tung', this being in fact simply a suitably revolutionary name for the experimental and Promethean mentality necessary to technical and economic progress. But we are now informed that during this period control of the Cultural Revolution had been captured by P'eng Chen, acting on behalf of Liu Shao-ch'i and Teng Hsiao-p'ing.[1] When Mao reasserted himself at the end of May 1966, the type of intellectual transformation involved took a different direction. The first phase, marked by the changing of the colours of traffic lights and the names of streets and shops, was, like the reign of the Red Guards in general, merely a transitory phenomenon. But this soon gave way to deeper and more significant tendencies.

In essence, Mao's Cultural Revolution aims to go beyond the humbling of the existing bureaucratic and technocratic élite, and to extirpate the very roots of any stratification which might emerge in the future, by destroying respect for the special status of the Party member or the special knowledge of the expert. The masses are henceforth to be, under Mao, the source of all political authority; they are also the repository of the wisdom and ingenuity which will enable China to forge ahead in her economic and technical development without reliance on 'reactionary bourgeois academic authorities' or specialists steeped in foreign knowledge and foreign theories.

In recent months, there has been tremendous emphasis on the need for working-class leadership in the Cultural Revolution. This obviously signifies above all an effort to re-establish order

1. See the directive of 16 May 1966, published on the first anniversary of its adoption, and the accompanying commentary, *Peking Review*, no. 21, 1967.

and put the Red Guards in their place. But as Mao's directives on education, included in Text VII E 10, make clear, 'workers' here means, not the bearers of knowledge and organizational skill, as in the Leninist tradition, but the common people, the 'poor and blank', whose majestic and all-conquering wisdom will put the intellectuals in their place.

The ultimate expression of these tendencies is to be found in the movement, which began in December 1968, to send students and other city-dwellers to the countryside. Mao launched this idea by a directive stating: 'It is very necessary for educated young people to go to the countryside to be re-educated by the poor and lower-middle peasants. Cadres and other people in the cities should be persuaded to send their sons and daughters who have finished junior or senior middle school, college or university to the countryside.' According to the commentaries which accompanied the publication of this teaching, the settling in the countryside of 'town-dwellers divorced from productive labour' and their participation in agricultural production was 'a long-term measure of fundamental importance in preventing and opposing revisionism and the correct path for gradually reducing the differences between town and countryside'. Moreover, the peasants did not merely teach these newcomers how to cultivate the land, but also gave them 'a profound class education'.[1]

This affirmation that the differences between town and countryside can best be eliminated by subjecting the town-dwellers to re-education in a rural environment, instead of penetrating the peasants with the technical knowledge and sense of discipline of the urban proletariat, and that class consciousness can best be acquired in the fields and not in the factories, is a spectacular manifestation of the populist strain in Mao's thinking, which has progressively re-asserted itself at the expense of his Leninist principles.

3. From the Chinese Revolution to the World Revolution

Mao Tse-tung's political thought consists essentially of generalizations based on his own revolutionary experience. We have

1. See *Peking Review*, no. 52, 1968, pp. 6–7.

now retraced that experience, and the conclusions Mao has drawn from it, through the two stages of the conquest of power and the effort since 1949 to transform Chinese society. Both these aspects of China's experience have been held up by Mao and his disciples as models for the rest of the world. Two decades ago, it was primarily Mao's road to power which was presented as of general relevance. Chinese statements on this theme (of which one of the most categorical was Liu Shao-ch'i's speech of November 1949 before a meeting of the World Federation of Trade Unions) were so bold as to arouse considerable dissatisfaction in Moscow.[1] But it is worth pointing out that as early as 1946, Liu Shao-ch'i, who had already praised Mao to the skies at the Seventh Party Congress in April 1945, hailed his thought as a guide to the future transformation of Asia:

> Mao Tse-tung's great accomplishment has been to change Marxism from a European to an Asiatic form. Marx and Lenin were Europeans; they wrote in European languages about European histories and problems, seldom discussing Asia or China. The basic principles of Marxism are undoubtedly adaptable to all countries, but to apply their general truth to concrete revolutionary practice in China is a difficult task. Mao Tse-tung is Chinese; he analyses Chinese problems and guides the Chinese people in their struggle to victory. He uses Marxist-Leninist principles to explain Chinese history and the practical problems of China. He is the first that has succeeded in doing so.... He has created a Chinese or Asiatic form of Marxism. China is a semi-feudal, semi-colonial country in which vast numbers of people live at the edge of starvation, tilling small bits of soil .... In attempting the transition to a more industrialized economy, China faces ... the pressures ... of advanced industrial lands.... There are similar conditions in other lands of south-east Asia. The courses chosen by China will influence them all.[80]

'A Chinese *or* Asiatic form of Marxism', that is the question. There is obviously no doubt that many of the problems – social, economic, and political – faced by other non-European countries are similar to those of China, and that the course chosen by China will therefore exert a certain influence. To the extent that Mao's

1. For extracts from the Chinese and Soviet contributions to these polemics, see *Marxism and Asia*, Chapter 9, which includes extensive passages from Liu Shao-ch'i's November 1949 speech.

thought and China's policies reflect the common interests and aspirations of all the underdeveloped countries, they may well have considerable appeal. But Mao is not only a revolutionary, but a Chinese revolutionary, and to the extent that his utterances reflect specifically Chinese interests and are clothed in language that is peculiarly Chinese, they may find little echo outside of China. The past thirty years have seen many changes in this respect, although despite the changes one can discern a certain continuity.

a. Sinification and universality. As noted previously, the slogan of the 'Sinification of Marxism' was first put forward by Mao Tse-tung himself in 1938, in his report to the Sixth Plenum of the Central Committee of the Chinese Communist Party. On that occasion, he said in part:

> Today's China is an outgrowth of historic China. We are Marxist historicists; we must not mutilate history. From Confucius to Sun Yat-sen we must sum it up critically, and we must constitute ourselves the heirs of all that is precious in this past. Conversely, the assimilation of this heritage itself turns out to be a kind of methodology that is of great help in the guidance of the revolutionary movement. A communist is a Marxist internationalist, but Marxism must take on a national form before it can be applied. There is no such thing as abstract Marxism, but only concrete Marxism. What we call concrete Marxism is Marxism that has taken on a national form, that is, Marxism applied to the concrete struggle in the concrete conditions prevailing in China, and not Marxism abstractly used. If a Chinese communist, who is a part of the great Chinese people, bound to his people by his very flesh and blood, talks of Marxism apart from Chinese peculiarities, this Marxism is merely an empty abstraction. Consequently, the Sinification of Marxism – that is to say, making certain that in all of its manifestations it is imbued with Chinese peculiarities, using it according to these peculiarities – becomes a problem that must be understood and solved by the whole Party without delay.... We must put an end to writing eight-legged essays on foreign models ... we must discard our dogmatism and replace it by a new and vital Chinese style and Chinese manner, pleasing to the eye and to the ear of the Chinese common people.[81]

It is clear from this passage how complex and ambiguous was

the meaning of 'the Sinification of Marxism', even in Mao's own mind. On the simplest level, it involved the use of a *language* accessible to the average Chinese, enlivened with popular proverbs and colourful turns of phrase, with an occasional classical quotation to give it added weight. Mao is an extremely skilful practitioner of this kind of Sinification, which undoubtedly has a favourable effect on Chinese readers,[82] and may make his writings appear more vivid and picturesque to foreigners as well. But this aspect of Sinification is unlikely to have much effect one way or another on whether an Indonesian or Cuban reader feels that Mao's brand of Marxism is peculiarly relevant to his own problems.

On a somewhat deeper level, Sinification clearly meant for Mao that those who professed to analyse China's current problems in Marxist terms should have a profound knowledge of their country's history and relate the present to the past. This type of Sinification is a two-edged sword as far as non-Chinese readers are concerned. To the extent that some of China's past has parallels in the past of other Asian countries, the efforts of Chinese Marxists to interpret their own past and salvage what is 'precious' in it may appear relevant. But on the other hand, what would the average foreign reader make of a passage such as this?

> In former times people used to say, 'He who reads Chu-ko's memorial on his military expedition and fails to shed tears is certainly not a faithful official; he who reads Li Mi's appeal to the Emperor and fails to shed tears is certainly not filial.' Today we ought to say, 'He who sees or hears how China's armies, forgetful of old enmities and mutually supporting one another, have intimately united, and is not moved, is certainly not a patriot.' [83]

This example goes slightly beyond the mere Sinification of *language*, for it is suggested that the Chinese of today should inherit, in modified form, the virtues of the men of the past. In the China of early 1939, when it appeared that effective collaboration between the communists and the Kuomintang to fight the Japanese had at last been established, this appeal was probably highly effective. But how many Indians or Algerians know – or care – that Chu-ko Liang was a minister of the Shu Han dynasty in the third century A.D., celebrated for his devotion to the throne, or that Li Mi was admired because he refused office in order to look after his ninety-six-year-old grandmother? Here the Sinification of Marxism merely makes it hermetic.

In fact, of course, we are dealing here with the Sinification of Marxists rather than the Sinification of Marxism. Indeed, it is a moot point whether there is not a good deal more of the former than of the latter in Mao himself. He is a very 'Chinese' Marxist, as his preoccupation with the glory of China amply demonstrates. But has he produced a Chinese variant of Marxism – that is, an ideology in which Marxism is not merely clothed in a Chinese dress, but in which the very concepts and methods by which reality is analysed have somehow become peculiarly Chinese?

If anywhere, one would expect to find such a contribution in Mao's analysis of Chinese history and society. In fact, if we look at the most detailed and lengthy piece of writing of this kind, the first part of 'The Chinese revolution and the Chinese Communist Party',[1] we find that Mao has changed his views since 1939, but neither the original nor the current version can be said to break new theoretical ground.

In the original version of this text, Mao affirms that traditional Chinese society has been completely stagnant for centuries and was only prodded into motion by the impact of the West. In the current version, he has inserted the thesis, more flattering to his countrymen, that changes were already at work that would have led to the birth of capitalism in China even without foreign intervention.[2] But far from advancing any original theoretical ideas to elucidate the unique traits of Chinese society, he endeavours, like any Soviet historian of the period, to force Chinese

1. Except for a few brief fragments (Texts I B, IV H, and VIII C), this first part of 'The Chinese revolution and the Chinese Communist Party' was judged to be of too specialized a character for inclusion in this introductory anthology. According to the note in the current edition of the *Selected Works*, it was not written by Mao, but revised by him. Nonetheless, since he has chosen to dignify it by inclusion in his works, it must be assumed that it corresponded rather closely to his ideas.

2. This theory regarding the existence of 'sprouts of capitalism' in China as early as the Ming dynasty was the subject of a vast debate among Chinese historians a decade ago.

society into the Procrustean bed of the schema 'primitive communism – slave-owning society – feudalism – capitalism – socialism', which Marx himself had clearly said was not necessarily valid for all societies.[1]

On the basis of this example, I concluded in the first edition of this book that, while Mao had indeed sinified the *form* of Marxism, his contributions to the *substance* of Leninist theory represented rather an adaptation of Marxism to Asian conditions. But the past five years have seen very singular developments, which require a new look at the whole problem.

In 1938, Mao Tse-tung declared that there was 'no such thing as abstract Marxism'. By 'abstract Marxism', he clearly meant a

1. Professor Wittfogel has dealt with the variants between the two versions of 'The Chinese revolution and the Chinese Communist Party', and in general with Mao's views regarding the 'feudal' character of Chinese society. (K. A. Wittfogel, 'The Marxist view of China (Part 2)', *China Quarterly*, no. 12, 1962, pp. 154–69.) He sees in the fact that Mao did not use the term 'feudal' in the original version of his 1926 article on the classes of Chinese society, but did adopt the term in his 1927 Hunan Peasant Report, evidence of an attempt to follow the wind in Moscow. While Mao always showed himself very skilful, throughout the period when his authority was not firmly established, in conforming outwardly to the line of the International, I would be inclined to explain his wavering on this point as the consequence of inadequate familiarity with Marxism rather than as a Machiavellian attempt to ingratiate himself with Stalin. As to the elimination of the statements made – or approved – by Mao in 1939 on the stagnant character of Chinese society before the impact of the West, and their replacement by the affirmation that China was already developing toward capitalism, Professor Wittfogel sees in this the liquidation of the last vestiges of Marx's theory of the 'Asiatic mode of production' and a new proof of Mao's subordination to Moscow. It is true that one of the imperatives governing the revisions of Mao's writings for the 1951 edition of the *Selected Works* was quite evidently the deletion of anything that might cause the least displeasure to Moscow. But the determination of Mao and other non-Western Leninists to fit themselves at all costs into Western patterns may also be explained by the prestige of the West even among those who are politically most hostile to it, and their rejection of certain ideas on the inherent inferiority of their own societies. In reality, there is no need to choose between a 'unilinear' theory of development, affirming that all societies everywhere must pass through identical phases, and a theory such as that of 'Oriental despotism', affirming that non-Western societies, if left to themselves, are incapable of change. The fact that Asian society was different does not in itself imply that it was either better or worse than

universally valid form of Marxism, and he did not even make an exception for the writings of Marx himself. The statement (removed in 1951) that Marxism is not only useless but non-existent apart from its concrete applications is an extreme one, but this exaggerated language serves to emphasize how strong was Mao's conviction thirty years ago that each nation must solve the problems of revolution in its own way. This attitude was, of course, natural enough when he was struggling for leadership of the Chinese revolution against men much better versed in 'abstract Marxism', and their supporters in Moscow. As we have seen, between 1942 and 1949 there was constant escalation in the claims made for Mao Tse-tung's achievements as a theoretician. Nevertheless, few people would have anticipated even five years ago (and I certainly did not) that Mao would one day go so far as to claim for his own thought the universality he denied to Marx. Yet this is precisely what he has done.

As late as August 1965, Mao Tse-tung's thought was regarded only as 'the application of the universal truths of Marxism-Leninism ... in the concrete practice of the Chinese revolution'. This is what Mao had advocated in 1938. But in the communiqué of the Eleventh Plenum of the Central Committee of the Chinese Communist Party, adopted on 12 August 1966, Mao's thought ceased to be merely one incarnation of Marxism-Leninism; henceforth, it *was* Marxism-Leninism.[1] Since then, the 'Cultural Revolution' has seen the constant repetition of the expression

---

Western society. The Chinese communists long failed to recognize this, or to advance a third interpretation of traditional society, different from either that of Stalin or that of Professor Wittfogel. In recent years, however, they have emphasized the 'peculiarities' of Chinese feudalism, although to the Western observer their list of 'peculiarities' appears to prove conclusively that Chinese society before the revolution was *not* feudal. For a discussion of recent Soviet views on Asian society, see the introduction to *Marxism and Asia*.

1. See the foreword of the General Political Department of the People's Liberation Army to *Quotations from Chairman Mao*, dated 1 August 1965, in the Corgi and Praeger editions of the *Quotations*. The communiqué of 12 August 1966 appears in *Peking Review*, no. 34. 1966, pp. 4–8. Lin Piao took over the new formulation in his preface of 16 December 1966 to the *Quotations*.

'Marxism-Leninism, Mao Tse-tung's thought', which places in effect a sign of equality between the two.

Thus, the substance of Mao's thought, and the claims made for it, have moved in opposite directions. When Mao was reputed to be Sinifying Marxism, he was in fact adapting it in ways relevant to many non-European countries. Now that his thought has been hailed as universal, it is in fact becoming in many ways increasingly Chinese – not the least in the underlying assumption that China is the centre of the world. But this growing Sinocentrism can, in turn, only be understood in the context of Mao's ideas regarding the evolution of the international situation as a whole, and in particular regarding events in the original homeland of revolution, the Soviet Union.

b. Mao Tse-tung versus the Soviet 'revisionist leading clique'. As I was making the final revisions of the first edition of this book, two editorials (dated 27 February and 4 March 1963) suddenly appeared in which the Chinese spelled out with striking clarity virtually all the basic points at issue between themselves and the Soviets. At the time, these texts seemed sufficiently novel and picturesque to justify analysing them in some detail. Since then, they have been left far behind by the even more vehement exchanges between Moscow and Peking. These recent polemics have been dissected in countless books and articles; I have given my own interpretation in *Marxism and Asia*. Rather than simply replacing the discussion of the 1963 editorials by an exegesis of the most recent texts in the Sino-Soviet controversy, it therefore seems appropriate here to focus on the influence these tensions have had on the development of Mao Tse-tung's own ideas and attitudes.

Although the roots of Sino-Soviet divergences and of Mao's own reaction to them go far deeper than considerations of individual or national pride, Chinese resentment at the high-handed manner in which the Soviets, even in recent years, have attempted to impose their will on the entire world communist movement is an aggravating factor which cannot be ignored. As early as 1936, Mao told Edgar Snow: 'We are certainly not fighting for an emancipated China in order to turn the country over to

Moscow!'[1] And in 1943, he referred to the cessation of 'meddling' by the Comintern in the affairs of the Chinese Communist Party in terms that suggested a certain bitterness.[2] This theme of dictation by Moscow to other parties featured prominently in the Chinese editorials of February and March 1963, which ridiculed Maurice Thorez for his '180 degree turnabouts' in response to a wave of Khrushchev's baton, and denounced the 'economic and political pressure' brought to bear on China in 1960 (involving in particular the tearing up of contracts for aid) as a manifestation of 'great-nation chauvinism'.[3]

Although the bitterness engendered by Soviet attempts to maintain 'abnormal, feudal-patriarchal relationships' with other parties lives on, accusations of this kind soon ceased to figure in the polemics because the Chinese no longer regarded the Soviet leaders as communists at all. The problem was therefore not to resist their attempts at domination, but to excommunicate them altogether. The Soviets, for their part, regard 'Mao Tse-tung and his group' as a band of petty-bourgeois fanatics who have betrayed socialism.[4] The unbridgeable gulf which has thus opened up between Moscow and Peking owes something to national sentiment, and something, too, to the difference in age between the Soviet and Chinese revolutions. But the Chinese conviction that Soviet society contains not an atom of genuine communism has not arisen simply because in Russia, half a century after 1917, revolutionary fervour has cooled; it grows out of a vision of revolution which rejects not only the capitalist system but the servitudes of technical rationality as such.

1. See Text X A.
2. See Text X C.
3. See 'Whence the Differences? A Reply to Thorez and Other Comrades', *Jen-min jih-pao*, editorial of 27 February 1963, *passim*. An English translation of this text was issued in pamphlet form by the Foreign Languages Press in Peking, and also included in numerous volumes of material on the Sino-Soviet polemics published in Peking and elsewhere.
4. For a recent and fairly complete statement of the Soviet case against Mao, see N. I. Kapchenko, *Pekin: Politika Chuzhdaya Sotsializmu* (*Peking: A Policy Alien to Socialism*), Izdatel'stvo 'Mezhdunarodnye Otnosheniia' Moscow, 1967.

As already suggested, the tendency toward the generalization of the spirit of Yenan which characterizes Mao's thinking since 1955 implies an emphasis on struggle rather than rationality, and on mass action rather than the technical and managerial élite, which in fact goes against the grain not only of 'Khruschevite revisionism' (with or without Khrushchev), but of Leninism itself. A parallel has been suggested, and does in fact exist, between certain aspects of Stalin's assault on the Party during the purges of the thirties, and Mao's assault on the Party today. But the similarities should not blind us to the profound differences between these two series of events, still less lead us to accept some theory of the identical wave of violence which grips all communist regimes two decades, more or less, after they are established. Stalin leaned on the government bureaucracy as a counterweight to the Party, Mao leans on the army, and this in itself is significant. Even more important, Stalin used mass hysteria backed by terror to exclusively political ends, to break resistance to his own rule. He did not regard mass mobilization as a useful instrument of economic progress. On the contrary, he stressed, like Lenin, both technological factors and organization as basic to the transformation of society. Worse still, for one praised today in Peking as a genuine revolutionary, he regarded not unselfish devotion to the common good, but material incentives, as the principal source of inspiration for 'building socialism'. Egalitarianism, he declared in 1934, was 'a reactionary petty-bourgeois absurdity worthy of some primitive sect of ascetics'.[84] And he ascribed the heroic exploits of the Stakhanovites essentially to the high standard of living they enjoyed.[85]

The accent on organization, rationality, and technical competence can, as already pointed out, be traced back to Marx himself, who saw in the European proletariat the class which would not only put an end to the injustice of capitalism, but at the same time inherit and carry on the Promethean mission of the bourgeoisie. Lenin made of the need for consciousness and organization the key to his whole revolutionary system, as it related to tactics both before and after the conquest of power. Mao, on the other hand, came to power not as a result of a skilfully-engineered coup by a minority, but after two decades of guerrilla warfare during which he had survived only by involving the whole of the Chinese people, or a large part of it, in the struggle to transform its own fate.

Out of this very different revolutionary experience have come the contrasting visions of revolution which we encounter today in China and in the Soviet Union. As suggested above in the second part of this introduction, there is room for doubt as to whether it was ever Mao's intention, in the course of the 'Cultural Revolution', to institute government by genuinely spontaneous mass action. But if this idealized stereotype must be rejected, it *is* a fact that Mao has involved the Chinese people more directly in their own fate than the Soviet people have ever been involved in theirs, except perhaps during the Second World War.

Once again, the writings of Stalin himself show how far removed was the spirit of the Soviet Union under his leadership from that which reigns in China today. Contradictions in socialist society, he declared in 1950, were resolved not by revolutions, but by gradual change, without qualitative leaps. Even such a profound transformation as agricultural collectivization in the Soviet Union had taken the form of a gradual transition, 'without ruptures', because it constituted a 'revolution from above'.[86]

In April 1960, when the Chinese seized the occasion of Lenin's ninetieth birthday to denounce the betrayers of his cause, they criticized 'certain theories' according to which 'it suffices to consolidate the socialist system, and there is no need to develop it; and even if it must still be developed, even if we must still advance toward communism, it is quite unneccessary to pass through a struggle or a qualitative leap'. In this way, they said, 'the process of permanent revolution of human society would continue to a certain point and then stop. On a philosophical level this corresponds to a metaphysical viewpoint and not to the viewpoint of dialectical materialism.'[87]

Although these attacks were directed explicitly against 'modern revisionism', the theories denounced were not those of Khrushchev, but those of Stalin. And in fact, the conception of 'revolution from above', by those who know best, was very much a part of Leninism. Mao, on the other hand, though he proposes to re-shape the 'poor and blank' Chinese people, attempts to do so from within, rather than from above.

The idea of 'revolution from above' not only inspires Soviet internal policy; it lies also at the root of Soviet thinking about the world revolution. Just as within the country revolution depends on organization and technology, so the world revolutionary movement must be led from Moscow, both because Russia is the oldest socialist country and therefore knows best, and because the Soviet Union has vast material and scientific resources at its command, whereas other revolutionaries have only words to offer. It would be hard to say whether the internal or the external applications of this spirit are more offensive to Mao. In any case, the two aspects are linked negatively in his mind, just as they are linked positively in the Russian view. Because the Soviet Union is not building socialism, but degenerating toward a technocratic order dominated by a 'new class', it is incapable of leading a genuine popular revolution on a world scale. Moreover, the vital forces of revolution are to be found not in the areas akin to the Soviet Union – the advanced industrial societies of Europe and North America – but in the peasant countries of Asia, Africa, and Latin America. China is the pathbreaker and model for revolution in these agrarian lands, and therefore the predestined leader of the world revolution today.

c. China and the non-European countries. China's foreign relations, like those of any revolutionary power animated by a universalist ideology, are a complex phenomenon made up of partially contradictory elements. At one extreme, we may encounter the pursuit of national interest and national grandeur in a virtually pure form. At the other, we observe an effort to promote or encourage social revolution within individual foreign countries, preferably in accordance with the example of the revolutionary power in question. Between the two lies a no-man's-land in which national and revolutionary motives are mingled, and it is often difficult to distinguish the one from the other. Thus, to encourage resistance to imperialist domination, especially on the part of non-European countries, can be regarded (and in fact has been regarded at various times and in varying degrees by both China and the Soviet Union) as in itself a contribution to world revolution because it contributes to weakening the strongholds of imperialism, especially the United States. But such a policy can also be pursued simply because it serves Chinese or Soviet national interests. And this may be the case even though an ideological rationalization is put forward tending to prove that such a policy of supporting non-revolutionary or even counter-revolutionary governments against imperialist pressures will in the long run encourage revolutionary tendencies within the countries of Asia, Africa, and Latin America.

Mao's own views on relations between China and the other non-European countries show a combination of all of these factors. Since 1936 at least, he has been persuaded that it is China's mission to show the other dependent and semi-dependent countries the way to liberation.[1] At the same time, it will be recalled that, as an adolescent, he was deeply affected by a pamphlet deploring the loss of Korea, Indochina, and Burma; and in 1939, he defined the territorial limits of China and its 'tributary states' in terms of the farthest extension of Peking's authority, including the Ryukyus, Korea, Bhutan, Nepal, and Burma.[2] It would, of course, be absurd to suggest that Mao intends to re-establish Chinese suzerainty over all these countries, but it is clear that he does intend to make them conscious of China's power.

In the course of the past few years, the contradiction between Mao's concern with revolution and his concern with China's power and prestige has progressively been resolved in his own mind – if not in reality – by the increasingly Sinocentric attitude already mentioned above. Just as, within China, a 'proletarian' is one who follows and reveres Chairman Mao, so on the world scene 'China' and 'revolution' are increasingly regarded as synonymous. Thus, editorials published in Peking constantly denounce the 'great anti-Chinese (*fan-Hua*) and counter-revolutionary (*fan-ko-ming*) chorus' inspired by the United States and the Soviet Union, as though opposition to China and opposition to revolution were merely two facets of a single form of wickedness. In this perspective, there can be no conflict between

1. See Text VIII A.
2. See Text VIII C.

the interests of China and the interests of the world revolution, since the two are by definition identical.

This trend is accompanied by the transposition to the world scene of the Chinese model of revolution by peasant-based guerrilla warfare. This transposition occurs on two levels. On the one hand, it is more and more categorically affirmed that only a revolution which takes the form of an armed struggle such as that led by Mao can bring about a real change in the society of a given Asian or African country. (Peking has shown a certain flexibility in applying these principles, frequently refraining from criticism of relatively conservative regimes so long as they did not adopt a hostile attitude toward China, but this is incidental in a discussion of the main thrust of Mao's theoretical ideas.) On the other hand, the global political struggle is viewed as analogous to Mao's road to power in China, in that the process as a whole involves the encirclement of the cities by the world's countryside.

This thesis was, of course, put forward in particularly detailed and striking terms by Lin Piao in his famous article of September 1965, 'Long live the victory of people's war!' The metaphor was not original with the Chinese, and had, in fact, been used in 1963 by D. N. Aidit, the leader of the Indonesian Communist Party.[1] But the Chinese could use it with far greater authority, for the victory of 1949 was the first and greatest example of the success of these tactics.

The idea of encircling the cities from the countryside was, in fact, in part a re-statement in terms of military imagery of a concept which had already been formulated in 1963 in meteorological language, when it was claimed that henceforth the storm-centre of world revolution had shifted to Asia, Africa, and Latin

1. For references and a discussion of Aidit's views, see Ruth T. McVey, 'Indonesian Communism and China', in Tang Tsou and Ping-ti Ho (editors), *China in Crisis, II: China's Policies in Asia and America's Alternatives*, University of Chicago, 1968. Not unnaturally, Aidit regarded South-east Asia rather than China as the centre of the world's countryside. P'eng Chen, who praised the Indonesian leader for the discovery of this idea during a visit to Djakarta in 1965, failed to mention this aspect of his conception. See *Peking Review*, no. 24, 1965, p. 11. The metaphor had in fact been put forward, with a very different meaning, in the Comintern programme of 1928. See *Marxism and Asia*, Text VII 1 B.

America.[1] And in advancing this view, which was hinted at already in his declarations of 1960 to delegations from various non-European countries,[2] Mao was placing himself in a direct line of descent from other Asian revolutionaries of the past, such as M. N. Roy, who argued at the Second Comintern Congress that the European workers were incapable of accomplishing anything until the masses of the colonies had shattered the power of imperialism,[3] or the Muslim Bolshevik Sultan Galiev,[4] who regarded Europe as a 'burnt-out revolutionary hearth'. In this respect, too, Mao has adapted Marxism to non-European conditions, in a way that is perhaps more significant and more effective than any other.

Such an adaptation of Marxism, which Mao began to propagate more or less explicitly a decade ago, clearly opens a gulf between himself and the leaders of the Soviet Union, though it should be viewed rather as a symptom and consequence of the split with Moscow than as a cause. In the first edition of this book, I wrote that such a position gave Mao an advantage in appealing to the underdeveloped countries that the Soviets could not hope to overcome. There is some truth in this, but the extent of this advantage has been greatly curtailed in recent years, as Mao's interpretation of revolutionary doctrine has become more and more overtly China-centred rather than Asia-centred. By early 1966, on the eve of the Cultural Revolution, this process had culminated in the categorical statement that China was henceforth the leader and the heart of the world revolution.[88] And by the following year, the point had been reached at which it was claimed: 'The radiant glory of the Great Proletarian Cultural

1. This was first stated in the eighth of the 'twenty-five points' of June 1963, *Peking Review*, no. 25, 1963, p. 9, and spelled out with still greater precision and vehemence in the fourth Chinese reply to the Soviet letter of 14 July 1963, entitled 'Apologists of neo-colonialism', *Peking Review*, no. 43, 1963, pp. 9–10. For extracts from this last text, see *Marxism and Asia*, Text XII 1.

2. See Text VIII G.

3. For extracts see *Marxism and Asia*, Text III 2.

4. At one time Stalin's assistant at the Commissariat for Nationalities. See A. Bennigsen and C. Lemercier–Quelquejay, *Islam in the Soviet Union*, Frederick A. Praeger, New York, 1967.

Revolution illuminates the future course of the world revolution and the future of humanity. In comparison, all other events in the world today, even the most important, pale into insignificance.'[89]

Mao's conceptions regarding the role of other Asian, African, and Latin American countries in the world revolution are obviously most intimately linked with his views on the Soviet Union on the one hand, and on the United States on the other. As already suggested, he has come to propagate the thesis that salvation will come only from the world's countryside because he no longer believes that the Soviet Union is in any way revolutionary, or that the Soviet leaders are prepared to risk their own tranquillity in order to aid the non-European peoples oppressed by imperialism. And the need and possibility of Afro-Asian solidarity rests on the existence of a common enemy in the shape of American imperialism.

d. Mao Tse-tung and the West. Whether or not one agrees with his criteria of judgement, there is no doubt that Mao Tse-tung knows a great deal about China, and something about the Soviet Union. About the capitalist West he knows nothing at all first hand. This means that he interprets it in terms of a combination of Marxist-Leninist stereotypes and the antiforeign prejudices of a Hunanese nationalist. And at the same time, his preference, both by temperament and experience, for military solutions, leads him to view problems instinctively in terms of struggle and firmness of will. These two factors are basic in considering his attitude toward the Occident.

Apart from the very natural resentment of a representative of a proud people against the contemptuous treatment inflicted on his countrymen by the West, another reason for the militancy of Mao's posture toward the outside world is his emphasis on the martial virtues. The language of war, strength, and courage runs like a red thread through all of Mao's works. This is not merely one of the *important* strains in Mao's personality and thought; it is almost the *central* strain.

To be sure, military metaphors are common enough in all communist writings. But the nature of these metaphors is significantly different in Mao's case. Lenin evokes above all the iron discipline required by any 'revolutionary army' if it is to achieve its objectives. Mao is by no means indifferent to discipline, but the source of his military metaphors is rather Chinese history and fiction, in which the individual hero plays the central role in deciding the issue of a battle. Whether it be the outlaw heroes of *Water Margin*, or the famous generals of the *Romance of the Three Kingdoms*, their very names, defiantly shouted or emblazoned on their banners, strike terror into the hearts of the enemy. Mao appears to think that the 'imperialists' tremble at the mention of his name in much the same way.

Whereas in relations with the Soviet Union nationalist and revolutionary motives may frequently come into conflict, in dealings with the West the visceral reaction of the Asian nationalist and the systematic anti-imperialism of the Leninist revolutionary are in full harmony. Despite the apparent simplicity of the problem, however, Mao's attitude toward the West in general and the United States in particular is one of the most curious and intriguing aspects of his thought. To be sure, the United States is the most powerful capitalist country and, therefore, in Mao's eyes the leader of the 'imperialist camp'.[1] Moreover, as early as 1923, Mao stigmatized America as 'the most murderous of hangmen'. Yet there was a time during World War II when the climate was quite different. It was, of course, quite different between the United States and the Soviet Union as well, and too much importance should not be attached to Mao's polite remarks about the American contribution to the war effort.[2] But it is curious to note that the Chinese communist press in these years not only referred to America as a democracy, but actually drew a parallel between America's war for independence in the eighteenth century and China's war for independence in the twentieth century. Washington was depicted as leading the struggle for democracy against the 'big landowners and big merchants', and it was emphasized that independence had not been attained easily, but had only been won after eight years of war. An editorial in *Chieh-fang jih-pao* of 4 July 1944 held that Roosevelt and Wallace were worthy heirs of Washington, Jeffer-

1. See Text IX J.
2. See Text IX G.

son and Lincoln. Mao Tse-tung did not sign this editorial, though he paid close attention to Yenan's press at this time and contributed a number of anonymous editorials. We do know, however, that during his adolescence he was deeply impressed by Washington's struggle for independence: 'Victory and independence only came to the United States after eight years of fighting under Washington,' he said to his friend Hsiao San, who had lent him a book on the subject, 'eight long, bitter years.'[90] And his writings and speeches of the war years contain many friendly references to America. The original version of his report to the Party Congress of April 1945 has the following passage, which has naturally been deleted from the current edition:

> The late American President Mr Roosevelt said: 'The world has become smaller.' The American people, whom the Chinese people used to regard as living in a faraway place, now seem next-door neighbours. The Chinese people will work together with the people of the great nations – America, Great Britain, the Soviet Union, and France – and also with the peoples of all nations to create a 'firm and lasting' world peace.[91]

The turnabout, which came a few weeks later, when American policy appeared to be veering toward support of Chiang Kai-shek against the communists, is vividly documented in Mao's editorials of 12 and 19 July 1945.[1] The tone suddenly becomes menacing and rather haughty. And yet, in the original version of the first editorial, Mao still expressed the conviction that a large part of American public opinion, as well as quite a few politicians and military men, were opposed to Washington's new policy.

Any such doubts about the utterly vicious nature of American policy, any attempts to discriminate between 'imperialist elements' and relatively progressive people within the American Government, have long since disappeared from Mao's statements. 'We should unite and drive U.S. imperialism from Asia, Africa, and Latin America back to where it came from,' he told delegates from Japan and Latin America in May 1960.[2] It is hardly necessary to add that Mao's militancy has not been diminished by recent events, including the war in Vietnam. For the

1. See Text IX F.
2. See Text VIII G.

moment, there appears to be little possibility of meaningful dialogue, let alone of agreement, between Mao Tse-tung and the United States. Yet in the long run, Sino-American relations may well prove to be the most important single factor in shaping the world of the future. Their evolution will depend in part on the balance between nationalist and revolutionary factors in the foreign policy of Mao or his successors. It will also depend on whether American policy combines the necessary firmness with an awareness of the complex nature of Mao's motives and a willingness to deal with people whose character and beliefs, deeply rooted in the tradition and situation of their own country, seem strangely alien to most Americans.

Wherever the responsibility may lie for Sino-American tensions and for Peking's situation on the margin of the world community – and there is no doubt that, however friendly American policy might have been, it could not have changed the basic facts of Mao's militancy and his hostility to 'imperialism', though it might possibly have attenuated their effects – the fact remains that the latent but permanent conflict with the United States has exacerbated the attitudes already engendered in the leaders of communist China by the twenty years of uninterrupted military conflict that brought them to power.

This experience of uninterrupted conflict, both before and after 1949, is one of the roots of the theory of the 'permanent' or 'uninterrupted' revolution. The parallel between 'uninterrupted revolution' (*pu-tuan ko-ming*) and uninterrupted warfare is apparent in Lu Ting-i's speech on the ninetieth anniversary of Lenin's birth, in which, after stressing that China had been the victim of continual attacks by the imperialists in general and American imperialism in particular, and that Mao Tse-tung had replied to these attacks by leading a 'permanent revolution', he continued:

> Lenin held that the proletariat of the socialist countries should, with the aid of the world proletariat and the toiling masses of the exploited people, defend the results already obtained through the victory of the proletarian revolution and at the same time support the unceasing (*pu tuan*) advance of the cause of the proletarian revolution, thus ceaselessly (*pu tuan*) weakening the forces of imperialism until capita-

lism has been annihilated and socialism has triumphed in the whole world.[92]

In earlier years, Mao himself frequently spoke of uninterrupted conflict. There is no doubt that, in this domain especially, the theory of the 'permanent revolution' bears Mao's stamp and reflects the temper of his mind.

Mao's views on the problem of war and peace have remained basically unchanged since he declared, at the 1957 Moscow meeting, that if half the world's population were wiped out, there would soon be '2,700 million people again and definitely more'.[1] Despite the growing destructive power of nuclear weapons, the Chinese ideologists hold to this position according to which an all-out war would mean not the end of civilization, but merely the end of imperialism, on the ruins of which 'the victorious people would very swiftly create a civilization thousands of times higher than the capitalist system and a truly beautiful future for themselves'. To justify this view, they cite Engels, according to whom 'the bourgeoisie broke up the feudal system and built upon its ruins the capitalist order of society', implying that ruins are ruins and that those to which Engels referred are no different from those of Hiroshima.[93] If Mao himself had a hand in writing this passage, which dates from 1963, it does not reflect very highly on his reasoning powers at that time.

Perhaps it would be fairer to refer to a deficiency in imagination rather than in intellect. Nearly all of Mao's experience of warfare has been with guerrilla operations, in which the individual combatant is indeed all-important, and in which superiority in *matériel* does not make up for the lack of popular support. In this context, it was logical to affirm, as he did in 1946, that the atomic bomb, like any new weapon, could not be a decisive factor in conflict.[2] And having coined the phrase 'the atomic bomb is only a paper tiger', he showed himself as reluctant to abandon it as he is to abandon any of his ideas and images once they have been launched. Stalin, who expressed similar opinions in 1946, modified his views somewhat once the Soviet Union had

1. See Text IX K.
2. See Text IX G.

tested its own nuclear weapons. Mao does not appear to have done so.

It should also be pointed out that Mao and his comrades, if they take an absurdly optimistic view of the consequences of atomic war, are not in favour of launching such a war or even of taking too great a risk of atomic war. On the contrary, they accuse the Soviets of having first committed the error of 'adventurism', and only then the error of 'capitulationism', in the Cuban crisis of October 1962.[94]

Their caution does not extend, however, to 'wars of liberation', which they support unreservedly. The cause of national liberation, they affirm, must not be subordinated to the attempt to reach an agreement with the imperialists on peace and disarmament. Here we are once more on ground that is not purely ideological but partly emotional and instinctive. In denouncing people who 'think that all is quiet in the world so long as there is no war in their own locality or neighbourhood', and 'only worry lest the "sparks" of resistance by the oppressed nations and peoples ... might lead to disaster and disturb their own tranquillity,'[95] the editorialist of *Red Flag* reveals one of the deepest roots of Sino-Soviet differences as an aspect of the differences between developed and underdeveloped countries in general. It is true that the rich, industrialized nations have a vested interest in preserving the accumulated benefits of civilization, and hence tend to place the avoidance of any situation that might conceivably degenerate into global warfare rather higher in their scale of values than those who have little to lose. And one can sympathize with the hostility of the inhabitants of some countries against a policy of maintaining the *status quo* at any price if this means the indefinite survival of certain oppressive regimes in Africa and elsewhere. But Mao's appeal on this point would probably carry more weight with the Soviet leaders if he did not accept quite so light-heartedly the consequences of an eventual error of calculation that might escalate into general conflict.

One of the most singular and contradictory aspects of Mao's thought concerns developments within the advanced industrial countries of Europe and North America. It is conceivable, though not certain, that Mao actually does believe that the United States Government is bitterly detested by 95 per cent of the American people, who are only kept down by sheer terror. His strange letter to Earl Browder in 1937,[1] implying that when the Chinese revolution was victorious Browder could hope to replace Roosevelt in the White House, would tend to support this image. Similarly, in his statement of 8 August 1963 denouncing racial discrimination in the United States, he declared: 'It is only the reactionary ruling clique among the whites which is oppressing the Negro people. They can in no way represent the workers, farmers, revolutionary intellectuals and other enlightened persons who comprise the overwhelming majority of the white people.'[2] In 1966 Mao proclaimed: 'The proletariat and working people of Europe, North America, and Oceania are in the midst of a new awakening.'[3] And by 1967 his spokesmen had reached the point of predicting a 'new October Revolution' in the Soviet Union.[96] But there are also indications that, despite his expressions of confidence in the 'peoples' of the 'imperialist' countries, Mao has come to regard Europe and America as a whole as hopelessly reactionary, and their inhabitants as all alike the beneficiaries of imperialism.[4] This is, as already suggested, the implication of the 'storm centre' hypothesis.

In any case, Mao's position regarding the tactics which ought to be followed by revolutionaries in Europe and America reflects an absolute refusal to accept as an accomplished fact the nature of modern industrial society. The bitter denunciations of Togliatti's 'revisionism' and 'opportunism' are rooted in a denial of the obvious truth that nowhere in Western Europe does there still exist a politically united working class whose members are interested in seizing power through violent revolution. Togliatti's efforts to develop a new strategy for the Italian Communist Party to fit these changed conditions were certainly not consistent with the letter of Leninism, and it was easy enough for the Chinese to point this out; but they themselves have not even recognized,

1. See Text X E.
2. See Text IX L.
3. See Text X M.
4. Text VIII G appears to suggest this.

in their theoretical formulations, that a problem exists. There is, however, a theoretical position implicit in the policy that China has adopted in supporting certain revolutionary groups in various European countries, namely that instead of accepting the altered mentality of the workers as the inevitable consequence of social and technological change, the revolutionary consciousness of the proletariat should be stirred up by the action of a vanguard until the proletarians once more begin to behave as they ought to do according to Marxist doctrine.

Conclusion

In attempting to evaluate Mao Tse-tung's place in the history of revolutionary thought and revolutionary activity, and his probable future impact on the world, I shall consider first his role as the leader of an Asian country, and then the general relevance of his contribution.

a. National revolution and social revolution in the non-European countries. At the beginning of this introduction, I defined three reactions to the impact of the West in the China in which Mao Tse-tung grew to manhood: tradition-oriented or conservative nationalism, radical Westernization, and revolutionary nationalism. Similar tendencies are manifest today throughout Asia and Africa. The first in its pure form obviously offers no real solution. No country today can escape the impact of modernization and industrialization; and once this process begins, the traditional élites will discover, as did the Chinese mandarins, that the acceptance of technological progress rapidly undermines both the social structure on which their rule is based and the ideas serving as its justification. Nor is the wholesale adoption of Western ideas and institutions a viable alternative. Quite apart from the questionable suitability of parliamentary democracy to the conditions in the non-European countries, it has become increasingly evident in recent years that the peoples of these areas regard as humiliating and unacceptable the idea that they are incapable of finding original solutions to their own problems, and must therefore model themselves on the West.

To be sure, revolutionary nationalism itself, despite its anti-Western political orientation, is in the broadest sense a vehicle for the Westernization of non-European societies. Though they may reject individualism and liberal democracy, its partisans wholeheartedly embrace other ideas such as the notions of progress and efficiency, and the goal of transforming nature. This last is typically a Western concept. It is totally alien to traditional Chinese thought, which preaches the adaptation of man to nature, and more alien still to the mystical philosophies of south-east Asia.

But if Asia and Africa are likely to be dominated for many years by 'revolutionary nationalism', must this necessarily be equated with Leninism? It is true that Leninism is an effective instrument for the Westernization of non-European societies in an anti-Western political context. A great deal of attention has been given recently to the problem of Marxism as the ideology of a phase in the development of agrarian societies, when change has proceeded far enough to produce rebelliousness among the victims of the economic dislocations resulting from industrialization, but not far enough to integrate the proletariat into the nation as sharers in the benefits of progress.[1] The reality of the world today shows that the appeal of Leninism in such a context is real enough, but Leninism is only one of several ideologies that may inspire and guide such an effort at the forced modernization of a backward country in an authoritarian context.

Indeed, the need for change, and for a strong government to hold the nation together during the period of continual social upheavals brought about by rapid economic development, together with the prevailing anti-Western and/or anti-imperialist sentiments, have created a climate in which virtually every Afro-Asian political leader, of whatever hue, endeavours to present himself as a revolutionary nationalist. Men as different as Mao Tse-tung, Nasser, and the Shah of Iran claim to be engaged in the radical transformation of society in order to further the double aim of social justice and national power. The political spectrum could thus be said to include, as the only alternatives to revolu-

1. The most stimulating and original work on this subject is Adam Ulam's *The Unfinished Revolution*, Random House, New York, 1960.

tionary nationalism, pseudo-revolutionary nationalism and semi-revolutionary nationalism.

Mao Tse-tung exhibits to the highest degree both strains in revolutionary nationalism – the anti-Western political animus, which is common to all nationalists in the underdeveloped countries, and the will to transform society and the Promethean attitude toward nature, which distinguish revolutionary nationalism from tradition-oriented nationalism. In his intellectual development, he leaped directly from tradition-oriented nationalism to revolutionary nationalism, without ever passing through the intermediate stage of radical Westernization. This is one of the traits that fitted him for the leadership of the Chinese revolution; conversely, men like Ch'en Tu-hsiu, insufficiently nationalist in outlook, had little chance of prevailing in the struggle for power.

If there can be no doubt that Mao is authentically nationalist, it is scarcely open to question that he is also authentically revolutionary. But what *kind* of a revolutionary is he? Does he, in fact, belong in the Leninist tradition at all?

b. Leninism and 'Maoism'. I have dealt with various aspects of Mao's contribution to the adaptation of Leninism to an underdeveloped, semi-dependent, non-European country in the mid-twentieth century. It is time to gather together all these scattered strands and summarize what Mao has taken over unchanged from Lenin, what he has added, and what he has transformed.

Mao's debt to Lenin is obvious. He owes him the conception that political consciousness does not manifest itself spontaneously among the proletariat but must be instilled by an élite or vanguard. He also is indebted to him for the theory and practice of organization in accordance with the principles of 'democratic centralism'. He owes him the theory of 'imperialism', which explains how normally hostile classes in dependent societies are united by a common interest in opposing foreign exploitation; he owes him also the idea of an alliance between the proletariat and certain other classes, particularly the peasantry, as the form of state power during the 'democratic' (i.e., pre-socialist) phase of the revolution. And to Lenin's disciple, Stalin, he owes the formula of the 'four-class bloc' (workers, peasants, petty bourgeoisie, and national bourgeoisie), which lies at the heart of his theory of 'people's democratic dictatorship'.

And yet, though much of this Leninist and Stalinist heritage is still apparent in Mao Tse-tung's thought, it has been transformed into something which is not only different but which has its own characteristic unity. If Lenin not only developed the general theory of imperialism, but went very far, especially at the Second Comintern Congress, in spelling out the detailed tactics of collaboration with 'bourgeois' nationalists to be applied by communists in colonial and semi-colonial areas, the fact remains that for him all such compromises with nationalism were dictated by necessity rather than by choice. Lenin was a European primarily interested in world revolution, who regarded the very existence of national differences as a misfortune, though as a realist he was quite prepared to compromise with nationalism if in this way he could harness the revolutionary energies of the colonial countries to his larger goal. Mao, on the other hand, is an Asian for whom nationalism is not a necessary evil but an authentic value in itself. Out of this grew his use of formulas such as that of the four-class bloc, which for Stalin was a mere passing phase in the development of the revolution, whereas in Mao's view – at least until the Cultural Revolution – it was possible to go all the way to communism under the joint dictatorship of the workers, peasants, petty bourgeoisie, and national bourgeoisie, even if some of these components were more equal than others.

Mao's contribution to the theory and practice of revolution is also characterized by an extreme voluntarism. To be sure, 'voluntarism', in the sense of an accent on conscious action, is by no means absent from Marx himself. But there is no doubt that it is carried much further in Lenin, and further still in Mao Tse-tung, and in the ideology of the Chinese Communist Party. This voluntarism attained a kind of apotheosis in the theory of the permanent revolution. Consider, for example, a passage such as this:

Men are not the slaves of objective reality. Provided only that men's consciousness be in conformity with the objective laws of the development of things, the subjective activity of the popular masses can manifest itself in full measure, overcome all difficulties, create the necessary conditions, and carry forward the revolution. In this sense, *the subjective creates the objective.*[1][97]

As emphasized previously, Lenin opened the door to this kind of development with his theory that in periods of revolution, politics takes precedence over economics. But there is no doubt that here the Chinese communists carry this trend a step further, a step that Lenin would have refused to take. One of the roots of this tendency in Chinese communist ideology is unquestionably the situation of China as an underdeveloped country, which has engendered a mood of impatience, a desire to transform the environment over night. But in Mao's case this situational factor has been tremendously reinforced by his love of struggle and drama.

How shall we evaluate the relative weight of the orthodox Leninist elements in Mao's thought and of his original contributions? Should he be called a Leninist, or even a Stalinist? Or does his thought deserve a name of its own – 'Maoism'?[2] In the first edition of this book, I concluded that everything considered, it was better *not* to use the term 'Maoism', because although Mao's thought contained original elements, he had never drawn these raw materials together in a system that deserved a name of its own. The intervening years have clearly shown that this judgement was erroneous.

The point at issue is not, of course, the term in itself. It matters little whether we speak of 'Maoism', of 'Mao Tse-tung's Thought', or of 'Mao Tse-tung-ism', as has occasionally been done by certain groups of Red Guards.[3] The important question is whether Mao's thought, whatever we call it, should be seen primarily as a variant of Leninism, or whether it is in fact of a quite different nature. The error which I committed in 1963 was,

1. Italics added.

2. This term is not, as some have suggested, the invention of certain Western scholars. It was used by Chang Ju-hsin, a Chinese communist writer, in an article that appeared in *Chieh-fang jih-pao*, 19 February 1942.

3. For example, among the signatories of the 'urgent notice' issued on 9 January 1967 by thirty-two 'revolutionary rebel' organizations in Shanghai, we find the 'North-east regional command of Mao Tse-tung-ism Red Guards', *Peking Review*, no. 4, 1967, p. 9.

no doubt, the result of viewing the matter too much in quantitative terms. There appeared to be more similarities than differences between Mao's thought and Leninism; therefore I chose to regard it in the first instance as an adaptation of Soviet theory and practice to Chinese conditions.

To be sure, the elements which entered into the sum five years ago were different. At that time, I set down the role of the Party as a key point which Mao had taken over from Lenin. Today, when the Party hierarchy has been subordinated to the army and victimized by the Red Guards, this item would weigh on the other side of the balance. But as already suggested, the fate of the Party is merely one manifestation of a general tendency, namely the downgrading of organization and technical knowledge in favour of (carefully controlled) spontaneity and revolutionary zeal. And this tendency was in fact clearly visible as much as a decade ago, in the 'poor and blank' thesis which was included in the first edition of this book.[1]

In Part 2 of this introduction, I developed at some length the contrast between Mao's revolution of the poor and blank, and the logic not only of Leninism but of Marxism itself. This contrast has become even more blatantly obvious with the emergence of the movement, mentioned above, for sending young people to the rural areas. There are good practical reasons for this policy in the lack of suitable employment in the cities at China's present stage of economic development, but the ideological justification offered is wildly unorthodox. Thus a 'veteran railway worker' is quoted as saying: 'We of the working class follow Chairman Mao's teachings faithfully . . . encouraging . . . our own children to settle in the countryside to be re-educated by the poor and lower-middle peasants so that they can temper themselves into reliable successors to the revolutionary cause of the proletariat.'[2] The suggestion that not merely the pampered children of the bourgeoisie, but the sons of the working class, can best learn from the peasant masses how to be proletarian revolutionaries, is the ultimate symbolic expression of Mao's reversion to the moral and intellectual universe of his childhood.

1. There Text VII C 4; now re-numbered Text VII C 3.
2. *Peking Review*, no. 1, 1969, p. 14.

Needless to say, the degree of Leninist orthodoxy attaching to Mao's theories is not the ultimate criterion of their relevance to the modern world. At first glance, however, his current policies would appear to be too deeply rooted in the situation and problems of China, and too strongly marked by the tendency to regard China as the centre of the world, to have much appeal in other countries. It is the more surprising that Mao Tse-tung's thought and example should today find perhaps an even greater echo in the advanced industrial societies of the West than in the agrarian lands of Asia, Africa, and Latin America.

c. Is Mao Tse-tung obsolete? When I put this rhetorical question in the first edition of this book, it was clearly implied that the answer was yes. I still believe that to a large extent Mao's ideas and methods *are* ill adapted to the problems of building a new society in the last third of the twentieth century, but despite the excesses of the Cultural Revolution there is a sense in which this is less clearly the case than five years ago.

Mao's personality is a complex and contradictory one; it includes an instinctive grasp of the importance of organization as a political weapon. But at the same time, he appears to see in organization a technique rather than an end in itself. One might sum up the difference between him and his Soviet counterparts by saying that whereas their utopia is one of rationality, his is one of struggle. Moreover, although his doctrine is collectivist, and although he has never shrunk back from the ruthless exercise of power, he is basically a romantic in search of adventure. The heart of political experience appears to be for him the outpouring (theoretically spontaneous) of the energies of the masses, with himself as the incarnation of the will of the masses. He is a combination of Lenin and Garibaldi – a strange blend of flamboyant leader and technician of power, just as twentieth-century China is a strange mixture of the renaissance and the age of automation. The era of individualist humanism, which spanned five centuries in the West, has run its course in China in one man's lifetime. Mao Tse-tung began his career as an iconoclast struggling against the restraints imposed on the individual by traditional society. He now finds himself grappling with the problems of organized and rationalized production in the era of automation.

Mao's tragedy is that of a man who has striven all his life to adapt to new and strange conditions and ideas, who has succeeded in doing this far better than most of his contemporaries, and who then discovers that the world with which he has sought to come to terms for half a century no longer exists, or in any case has been so profoundly modified that old formulas and old ideas are no longer applicable. Having begun life as a tradition-oriented Hunanese nationalist, he soon acquired the radically untraditional goal of breaking the grip of superstition, custom, and a hierarchical social structure on the lives of his compatriots, so that they might freely turn their energies to building a new China. In the course of a twenty-year apprenticeship, he learned how to combine to this end Leninist revolutionary techniques and the heritage of peasant revolt, and to mobilize the masses both in the name of class solidarity against the landlords and in the name of national solidarity against the Japanese. Thanks to a combination of talent, good luck, and blundering and corruption on the part of his adversaries, he succeeded, and in 1949 he found himself in more absolute and effective control of China than anyone had been since the heyday of the Manchu empire. But, as he stated himself at the time, 'to win country-wide victory is only the first step in a long march of ten thousand *li*'. And in this long march, the lessons he had learned in the struggle for power were of only limited relevance. 'We can learn what we do not know. We are not only good at destroying the old world, we are also good at building the new,' he added in 1949.[1] But in fact, the leap from guerrilla warfare in the countryside to the building of a modern industrial economy was a very great one indeed, an overwhelming challenge to Mao's flexibility.

To be sure, the tasks facing him are not precisely those that confront the leaders of the more advanced industrial nations. The Soviet Union on the one hand, and the United States and Western Europe on the other, are confronted by the problem of giving some meaning to human activity once a high level of material accomplishment has been achieved. For China, this particular

1. See Text VI C 7.

dilemma lies in the future; she is still at a stage where the 'war against nature' and the struggle for equality on the world scene in themselves constitute meaningful goals for social activity. But even at this early stage of economic development, China must face the problem of the immense and growing role of organization in society and in the economy. And in solving this problem, the myth of the Long March is as relevant – or as irrelevant – as the Marxian myth of the nineteenth-century proletariat to present Soviet conditions, or the myth of the lone frontiersman to the contemporary United States.

Mao himself clearly disagrees with this judgement; on the contrary, much of his effort in the past two years has been devoted precisely to demonstrating the relevance of the experience acquired on the Chingkangshan, during the Long March, and in Yenan days to the political and economic problems of China today. His attitude can clearly be explained in part by simple attachment to his own past, but it also grows out of the conviction that the spirit of adventure and sacrifice which characterized the past is the best antidote to the tendencies toward bureaucratization and routine which he regards as both tiresome and immoral.

There is a striking parallel between Mao's present attitude and that of his great Hunanese compatriot Tseng Kuo-fan a century ago. Just as Tseng regarded the values of the Chinese 'way' as superior to any economic or political gain, and preferred to sacrifice such strengthening of the country as could only be bought at the cost of inroads on what he regarded as its *raison d'être*, so Mao Tse-tung places the political criteria of doctrinal purity – which for him are also moral criteria – ahead of mere economic necessity. Like Tseng, he refuses to recognize that economics has its own logic, partly independent of any broader criteria; for him, as for Tseng, practical activity must be penetrated from beginning to end with moral values.

Having said this much in the first edition, I pointed out that no one had as yet discovered how to instil moral values – either communist or liberal – into the productive activity of advanced industrial society. This situation, I added, was certainly not ideal, but for the moment people had learned to live with it, both in the

United States and the Soviet Union; and I suggested that they were likely to go on living with it. Moreover, I assumed at that time that in the long run, the process of industrialization and modernization under way in China would lead to the emergence of the same tendencies which have been engendered by economic development in other countries: increasing functional differentiation and the birth of new forms of social stratification, the subordination of moral values to technical rationality, the primacy of economic incentives. This hypothesis seemed, at the time, so self-evident as not to require any further justification. After all, did not the United States and the Soviet Union, despite the vast differences between them, share to a large extent the traits just enumerated? In any case, five years ago similar assumptions were formulated by nearly everyone, including some who have since taken a different view. Thus Enrica Collotti-Pischel, who is today a wholehearted supporter of the Cultural Revolution, wrote in 1962:

> From the peasant Wu Sung, who strangles a tiger with his hands because he is unarmed and does not want to be eaten, chosen as a symbol of the invincibility of the Chinese revolution, to the 'East wind that now prevails over the West wind', Mao has elaborated a whole series of themes whose effectiveness with the Chinese masses can scarcely be appreciated by a European. This capacity for fertile and popular syntheses constitutes a fundamental instrument in the effort to call forth and direct the revolution in China, and also, within certain limits, for carrying over part of the momentum of the revolution to the period of peace and building of socialism. But it is of less and less weight as the technical and objective problems of building socialism come to take precedence over armed revolutionary struggle. In a more complex society, less easily influenced by mere human factors, above all by the action of voluntarist and moral factors, Mao's 'simplifications' lose part of their effectiveness and may all too easily become the source of mechanical and dogmatic repetition, and of escape from the concrete and specific problems posed by the modern world. [98]

Commenting on this in the first edition, I said that the Chinese were confronted with the undramatic character of the day-to-day organization of production in the modern world, as distinguished from the dramatic nature of the *results* of science. They had been obliged, in the aftermath of the Great Leap Forward, to adapt themselves to this reality, to rely less on 'redness' and more on 'expertness', less on the enthusiasm of the masses and more on the knowledge of the technician. But, I added, Mao would clearly have no part in formulating these concessions in ideological terms, for they went too much against the grain of his personality. *His* solution was to dramatize everything, including scientific research, in political terms.

The ensuing years have shown that this was indeed his solution, and that, far from being resigned to the triumph of 'economism', he was prepared to take even more radical measures than any which he had employed in the past in order to prevent China from 'changing colour' and following the Soviet Union down the path to the 'restoration of capitalism'. The charge that the homeland of the October Revolution has now become a capitalist country is in one sense so wildly absurd that the natural reaction is to dismiss it altogether. But it is important not to lose sight of what it means to Mao – and also to a goodly number of others, Maoist and non-Maoist, in the world today.

By 'capitalism', Mao obviously means a system in which economic privileges are enjoyed by those who exercise control – whether as bureaucrats or as entrepreneurs – over the means of production, and in which efficiency is more important than moral values. While we may regard it as an abuse of language to use the word in this way, it is hard to deny that the Soviet Union is effectively 'capitalist' in this sense. Indeed, the process has long been observed and noted – with pain by Djilas and other socialist critics of Soviet reality, and with some satisfaction by the theorists of '*embourgeoisement*' as the inevitable fate of all revolutions after a generation.

Mao has indignantly rejected the idea that this tendency is universal and inexorable, though the very zeal with which he has conducted his crusade against it would suggest that he feels only a miracle can preserve any people from succumbing. Indeed, he has recognized that even the Chinese, despite their remarkable revolutionary qualities, have not as yet succeeded in finally rooting out capitalist attitudes and sentiments in themselves, and will not do so for some time to come.

The egalitarian and anti-bureaucratic impulse inherent in the Cultural Revolution undoubtedly inspires sympathy in many quarters in Asia and Africa, despite the ambiguity of an appeal to the creativity of the masses which is in fact guided and controlled by the army. But there is clearly little evidence that these methods will contribute effectively, as Mao claims, to the development of the Chinese economy. The peoples of the non-European countries, who are intensely preoccupied with the problem of economic growth, which they regard as the only means for escaping from their situation of inferiority in the face of the West and of Japan, are therefore unlikely to be tempted to follow the Chinese example. But in the 'heartland of imperialism' itself, where increasing numbers of people, especially among the students, seek rather the wiser, juster and more humane use of the resources already available than the indefinite multiplication of the productive power of a system which appears as a heartless technocratic machine entirely beyond the control of the average man, Mao's refusal to accept progress at this price has had perhaps an even greater impact.

Mao is, of course, not the only one who has raised the standard of revolt against the consumer society, in its twin incarnations of 'goulash communism' and 'the American way of life', nor is the theory and practice of Chinese communism today in all respects well attuned to the aims of the protest movement in Paris, New York and Rome. The views of European and American students regarding relations between the sexes are certainly closer to those of the author of *Eros and Civilization* than to the puritanical ethos now dominant in Peking. And to many Che Guevara has more appeal, on both human and doctrinal grounds, than does Mao Tse-tung – not to mention the surprising resurgence of Trotskyite influence. The fact that such diverse currents, each of which is in strict logic totally incompatible with all the others, have on many recent occasions joined forces, is in itself an indication of how deep and real is the disenchantment with the fruits of modern civilization. Mao has, in my opinion, done very little to show the way to a free, spontaneous society not founded simply on the pursuit of individual self-interest. The moral pretensions of his Cultural Revolution are largely vitiated by the crudeness and mediocrity of the slogans, the narrow and primitive fanaticism which inspires the whole movement, and Mao's willingness to rely on naked military control in order to maintain his own power. In this sense, he is indeed obsolete, and the past two years have done nothing to enhance his ultimate historical stature. But the problems he has raised will be with us for a long time to come, not only in China but in the world at large. And as one of the first and most influential to reject the seemingly implacable logic of advanced industrial society, even though he was totally incapable of imagining a viable alternative, Mao may be remembered as a Janus-like figure looking forward to the future, despite the limitations resulting from his deep roots in the past.

Notes to the Introduction

1. Karl A. Wittfogel, *Oriental Despotism*, Yale University, New Haven, Conn., 1957.
2. Mary C. Wright, *The Last Stand of Chinese Conservatism: The T'ung Chih Restoration*, Stanford University, Stanford, Calif., 1957.
3. Joseph Levenson, *Confucian China and Its Modern Fate*, University of California, Berkeley, Calif., 1958–65; Routledge, 1958–65.
4. T'an Ssu-t'ung, *Jen hsüeh*, Part 2.
5. Chow Tse-tung, *The May Fourth Movement*, Harvard University, Cambridge, Mass., 1960.
6. For an account, perhaps somewhat exaggerated, of Mao's tribulations in this respect, see Siao-Yü (Hsiao Hsü-tung), *Mao Tse-tung and I Were Beggars*, Syracuse University, Syracuse, N.Y., 1959.
7. Edgar Snow, *Red Star over China*, Random House, New York, 1939, p. 118.
8. For extracts, see John K. Fairbank and Ssu-yu Teng, *China's Response to the West: A Documentary Survey, 1839–1923*, Harvard University, Cambridge, Mass., 1954, pp. 113–16.
9. Snow, op cit., pp. 116–21, 127, etc; Hsiao San (Emi Siao), *Mao Tse-tung, His Childhood and Youth*, People's Publishing House, Bombay, 1953, pp. 20–21. Li Jui, in *Mao Tse-tung t'ung-chih ti ch'u-ch'i ko-ming huo-tung*, Chung-kuo Ch'ing-nien Ch'u-pan She, Peking, 1957, p. 9, publishes facsimile pages from Mao's copies of Cheng Kuan-ying's book, and of the *Hsin-min ts'ung-pao*. (For further information regarding Li Jui's book, see the section on biographies in the bibliography at the end of this volume.)
10. Hsiao San, op. cit. (Chinese edition), p. 25.
11. Snow, op. cit., p. 129.
12. Li Jui, op. cit., p. 19.
13. ibid., pp. 40–44.
14. ibid.
15. ibid.
16. ibid.
17. ibid.
18. Snow, op. cit., p. 132.
19. Regarding the Hsin Min Hsüeh Hui, see Hsiao San, op. cit. (Chinese edition), pp. 42–3; Siao Yü, op. cit., pp. 56–63; Chou Shih-chao, 'My recollections of Chairman Mao Tse-tung in Changsha before and after the May 4th Movement', *Kung-jen jih-pao*, Peking, 20 April 1959;

translated in *Survey of the China Mainland Press* (S.C.M.P.), no. 2011; Snow, op. cit., pp. 130–32.

20. Li Jui, op. cit., p. 22.
21. Regarding the evolution of the two men, see Benjamin Schwartz, *Chinese Communism and the Rise of Mao* (third edition), Harvard University, Cambridge, Mass., 1958, pp. 12–27; and Maurice Meisner, *Li Ta-chao and the Origins of Chinese Marxism*, Harvard University, Cambridge, Mass., 1967. I have further elaborated my own interpretation with accompanying documents in *Marxism and Asia*.
22. Snow, op. cit., pp. 134–5, 137, 140.
23. *Hsin ch'ing-nien*, I, no. 2, 1915, p. 6. See my introduction to the French translation of an article written by Mao in 1917, *Une Étude de l'éducation physique*, Mouton, Paris, 1962, for an extract from this article.
24. All of the preceding paragraph is drawn from Meisner, op. cit.
25. Meisner, op. cit.; for the text of this article, see *Li Ta-chao hsüan-chi*, pp. 101–4.
26. *Hsin ch'ing-nien*, V, no. 5, 1918.
27. Snow, op. cit., p. 140.
28. Meisner, op. cit.; for the text of this article, see *Li Ta-chao hsüan-chi*, pp. 146–50.
29. See particularly his articles 'The victory of the masses', and 'A new era', published in October 1918 and January 1919, in *Li Ta-chao hsüan-chi*, pp. 109–11, 119–21.
30. *Mei-chou p'ing-lun*, no. 36, 1919, p. 4.
31. Li Jui, op. cit., p. 103.
32. Snow, op. cit., pp. 139–40.
33. Extracts cited by Li Jui, op. cit., p. 176.
34. 'Revolution in China and Europe', *New York Tribune*, 14 June 1853. Li Ta-chao translated this article in 1926, and used it to buttress his claims regarding the international significance of the Chinese revolution. For extracts see *Marxism and Asia*, Allen Lane, The Penguin Press, 1969, Texts I 2, and VI 13.
35. Regarding the importance of the peasantry, see in particular Marx's writings on France, *Die Klassenkämpfe in Frankreich 1848–1850*, and *Der 18. Brumaire des Louis Napoleon*. Regarding the progressive character of wars of national liberation and the role of various classes under such circumstances, see the writings of Marx and Engels regarding Eastern Europe, particularly Engels' writings on the Polish question. All of these issues are discussed in *Marxism and Asia*.
36. For an account of the evolution of Lenin's views on these two points – the relation between the stages of the revolution and the question of proletarian hegemony during the first stage – see Part 2 of my introduction to *Documents sur la théorie de la 'révolution permanente' en Chine*, Mouton, Paris, 1963.
37. There were precedents for this in Marx. See the introduction to *Marxism and Asia*.

38. Ch'en Kung-po, *The Communist Movement in China*, edited with an introduction by C. Martin Wilbur, East Asian Institute of Columbia University, New York, 1960, p. 109.
39. ibid., p. 84.
40. See the extracts from their correspondence in *Hunan li-shih tzu-liao*, no. 9, 1959, pp. 77–83.
41. Quoted in Meisner, op. cit.
42. Li Ta-chao, '*Jen-chung wen-t'i*' ('The racial question'), *Hsin Min-kuo*, no. 6, June 1924. Extracts in *Marxism and Asia*, Text VI 11.
43. Mao Tse-tung, *Selected Works I*, Foreign Languages Press, Peking, p. 20, note 6.
44. ibid., pp. 216–17 and 246–7.
45. ibid., p. 143.
46. Conrad Brandt, *Stalin's Failure in China, 1924–1927*, Harvard University, Cambridge, Mass., 1958, pp. 36–7.
47. Ch'en Kung-po, op. cit., p. 120.
48. *Cheng-chih chou-pao*, no. 1, 5 December 1925.
49. Stalin, *Works*, VIII, Foreign Languages Publishing House, Moscow, 1952–5, pp. 384–8.
50. Snow, op. cit., p. 144.
51. E. H. Carr, *Socialism in One Country*, III, Macmillan, 1964, pp. 769–72.
52. *Chung-kuo nung-min*, no. 5, 1926.
53. See Text IV E, pp. 179–88.
54. Lenin, op. cit., XXVI, 126.
55. See *Li Ta-chao hsüan-chi*, pp. 564–70.
56. *Strategiia i Taktika Kominterna v natsional'no-kolonial'noi Revoliutsii na primere Kitaia*, Moscow, 1934, p. 229. For other extracts from Comintern directives stressing this and related articles of orthodox doctrine, see *Marxism and Asia*, Text VII 3.
57. Text IV F, pp. 188–9.
58. Schwartz, op. cit., p. 191.
59. Boyd Compton (translator), *Mao's China: Party Reform Documents 1942–44*, University of Washington, Seattle, Wash., 1952, pp. xxi–xxii.
60. *Komintern v Dokumentakh*, p. 991.
61. *Su-wei-ai Chung-kuo*, pp. 71–4.
62. ibid., pp. 91–4.
63. *Mao Tse-tung*, pp. 158–61.
64. Snow, op. cit., pp. 84–92.
65. Chinese text in *Tou-cheng*, no. 110, 5 September 1936.
66. See C. B. McLane, *Soviet Policy and the Chinese Communists 1931–1946*, Columbia University, New York, 1958, pp. 79–91. Edgar Snow has stated that Mao wished to see Chiang brought to trial: *Random Notes on Red China*, Harvard University, Cambridge, Mass., 1957, pp. 1–11.
67. Stalin, *Works*, X, Foreign Languages Publishing House, Moscow, 1952–5, pp. 14–17.

68. University of California, 1962.
69. *Hsüan-chi*, (1947) Supplement, pp. 98–99.
70. J. Houska and K. Kara, *Otazky Lidove Demokracie*, Prague, 1955; Russian translation under the title *Kharakter Narodno-demokraticheskoi Revoliutsii*, Izdatel'stvo Inostrannoi Literatury, Moscow, 1958, pp. 464, 481–2. On this problem, see also the article of Benjamin Schwartz, 'Ideology and the Sino-Soviet Alliance', in Howard L. Boorman *et al.*, *Moscow-Peking Axis: Strengths and Strains*, Harper & Brothers, New York, 1957, pp. 112–41.
71. *Jen-min jih-pao*, 26 January 1956.
72. *Istoriia Vsesoiuznoi Kommunisticheskoi Partii* (*Bol'shevikov*). *Kratkii Kurs*, Gospolitizdat, Moscow, 1950, p. 118. For a survey of the evolution of Soviet writings on contradictions under socialism from 1927 to the present, see Part 3 of my introduction to *Documents sur la 'révolution permanente' en Chine*.
73. See, for example, M. Rozenthal's *Marksistskii Dialektichestii Metod*, Ogiz, Moscow, 1939, pp. 107–9.
74. Liu Shao-ch'i, *Lun Tang*, pp. 133–5.
75. Text VI B 3.
76. See the contrasting interpretations of Robert J. Lifton, *Thought Reform*, Gollancz, 1961; Penguin Books, 1967, and E. H. Schein, *Coercive Persuasion*, Norton, New York, 1961.
77. *Jen-min jih-pao*, 19 December 1958. For a longer extract from this resolution, see *Marxism and Asia*, Text X 8.
78. Wu Chiang, '*Pu-tuan ko-ming lun-che pi-hsü shih ch'e-ti pien-cheng wei-wu lun-che*', *Che-hsüeh yen-chiu*, no. 8, 1958, p. 25. For the complete text of this article see *Documents sur la 'révolution permanente' en Chine*.
79. *Peking Review*, no. 6, 1967, p. 13.
80. Anna Louise Strong, 'The thought of Mao Tse-tung', *Amerasia*, XI, no. 6, June 1947, p. 161.
81. See Text II A.
82. See John Fairbank, *The United States and China* (second edition), Harvard University, Cambridge, Mass.. 1958, p. 303.
83. This citation is from Mao's editorial for the first issue of the *Military Political Review* of the Eighth Route Army: *Pa-lu-chün chün-cheng tsa-chih*, no. 1, January 1939, p. 3.
84. Report to the Seventeenth Congress of the C.P.S.U., 26 January 1934, in *Voprosy Leninizma*, Moscow, 1952, p. 507.
85. See his speech of 17 November 1935 to the First All-Union Conference of Stakhanovites, ibid., pp. 532, 537 etc.
86. Stalin, *Marksizm i Voprosy Iazykoznaniia*, Gospolitizdat, Moscow, 1953, pp. 28–9.
87. Lu Ting-i, speech in *Jen-min jih-pao*, 23 April 1960.
88. *Yang-ch'eng wan-pao*, Canton, 2 February and 5 April 1966.
89. Feng Lei, article in *Jen-min jih-pao*, 13 March 1967.
90. Hsiao San, op. cit., pp. 20–21.

91. *Lun lien-ho cheng-fu*, p. 83; *On Coalition Government*, New China News Agency, Peking, 1945, p. 125. Strangely enough, this particular omission is indicated by asterisks in the current edition of the *Selected Works*, III, p. 308, though many other favourable references to the United States have been omitted and are not so marked.
92. *Jen-min jih-pao*, 23 April 1960.
93. See the editorial of 27 February 1963, *More on the Differences between Comrade Togliatti and Us*, Foreign Languages Press, Peking, 1963, p. 76.
94. ibid., p. 189.
95. ibid., p. 64.
96. See, for example, Lin Piao's speech on the occasion of the fiftieth anniversary of the October Revolution, in which he declared: 'The proletariat and the working people of the Soviet Union ... are sure to rise in revolution under the banner of Leninism, overthrow the rule of the reactionary revisionist clique and bring the Soviet Union back into the orbit of socialism' (*Peking Review* no. 46, 1967, p. 7).
97. Wu Chiang, op. cit., p. 28.
98. Enrica Collotti Pischel, *La Rivoluzione ininterrotta. Sviluppi interni e prospettive internazionali della rivoluzione cinese*, Einaudi, Turin, 1962, pp. 71–2.

A Note on the Texts

Anyone attempting to prepare a work based on selections from Mao Tse-tung's writings finds himself confronted with a staggering problem resulting from the nature of the source material. In the case of most political writers, there exist recognized, authentic texts, a literature that has been published, annotated, and translated. To be sure, the authenticity of one or another of these texts may occasionally be questioned, or (as in the case of Marx) unpublished writings may be discovered many years after the author's death. Nonetheless, there exists a nucleus of basic texts that, save for a few minor variants, may be considered definitive.

In contrast, the person dealing with Mao finds himself in the paradoxical situation of working with materials that have never been assembled, much less translated. The *Selected Works*, published in Peking in Chinese beginning in 1951, and then translated into various languages, include only about half of Mao's writings during the past half century.[1] Moreover, the texts included in the *Selected Works* have been subjected to such numerous and profound changes by the author that one cannot accept even a single sentence as being identical with what Mao had actually written without checking it against the original version.

In the face of such a situation, the logical solution would consist in first establishing the authentic Chinese text of Mao's complete works, to provide a solid basis for selecting extracts. Various people have thought of doing this. But the task is enormous, for it involves several thousand pages of Chinese texts, scattered throughout numerous books and periodicals, many of which are available in only one or two libraries outside of China. Moreover, the difficulties are compounded by the fact

1. For details, see the bibliographical appendix at the end of this volume.

that the 'Cultural Revolution' has seen the publication of a large number of texts attributed to Mao, dating from various periods. Although none of these passages can be taken as unquestionably authentic, they do set us the task of hunting down contemporary versions of items whose very existence has hitherto been unknown. It is therefore improbable that a complete edition of Mao's writings will be compiled in the foreseeable future. In view of the importance of Mao Tse-tung, both as a political figure and as an intellectual influence in the underdeveloped countries, there is perhaps a place for the present volume, despite the fact that it is premature and incomplete.

Since no authoritative edition of Mao's complete works exists, the orientation of this anthology is slightly different from that which might be expected in an introductory volume of this kind. Instead of presenting only the most typical and most fundamental extracts, many of which are already available in an English translation (even if this translation does not altogether correspond to the original Chinese text), I have interspersed a certain number of extracts that are perhaps not so central to Mao's thought, but that represent aspects of his personality and experience completely absent from the *Selected Works*. As for the basic texts already included in the *Selected Works* (of which a complete translation, published in Peking, is now available), I have extracted from them a number of particularly important passages. My translations frequently follow those already published, but they have been completely revised and corrected on the basis of the original Chinese texts.

Because of the nature of this volume, and also because of space limitations, I have not been able to indicate exhaustively all the discrepancies between Mao's original texts and the present official version. It did, however, seem useful and interesting to indicate the most important ones. Thus all italicized passages in the extracts have been either omitted or very extensively modified by the author in preparing the current edition of his *Selected Works*. Passages not to be found in the original texts and added by Mao for that edition are indicated by notes at the end of each extract.

Prologue: The Pre-Marxist Period in Mao Tse-tung's Development

I have attempted in the general introduction to place the article 'A study of physical culture', written by Mao in 1917 for the review *Hsin ch'ing-nien*, in its historical context, and to show how it throws light on Mao's further development.

Because this is the only complete and authentic text written before 1923 available in the West, and because the intellectual setting of this article is very different from that of Mao's writings after the May 4th Movement, it seems preferable to present the extracts I have selected from this article in a prologue, rather than attempt to insert them into the categories adopted for the writings of his Communist period.

In my monograph containing a complete French translation of this text, I have attempted to point out and to annotate all of the citations from the classics, and in general all the allusions that might cause difficulty for the Western reader. Here, for the sake of readability, I have merely annotated some allusions, in order to show the broad and rather eclectic nature of Mao's knowledge at the time. Those interested in further details can consult the complete French translation.

S.R.S.

A study of physical education[1]

Our nation is wanting in strength. The military spirit has not been encouraged. The physical condition of the population deteriorates

Editor's note: All the italicized passages are underscored in the original text and do not here represent discrepancies between two published versions. S.R.S.

1. Extracted from an essay published in April 1917 (in *Hsin ch'ing-nien*) under the pseudonym 'Twenty-eight-stroke Student' (Erh-shih-pa Hua

daily. This is an extremely disturbing phenomenon. The promoters of physical education have not grasped the essence of the problem, and therefore their efforts, though prolonged, have not been effective. If this state continues, our weakness will increase further. To attain our goals and to make our influence felt are external matters, results. The development of our physical strength is an internal matter, a cause. If our bodies are not strong we will be afraid as soon as we see enemy soldiers, and then how can we attain our goals and make ourselves respected? Strength depends on drill, and drill depends on self-awareness. The advocates of physical education have not failed to devise various methods. If their efforts have nevertheless remained fruitless, it is because external forces are insufficient to move the heart...

If we wish to make physical education effective, we must influence people's subjective attitudes and stimulate them to become conscious of physical education. If one becomes conscious of the problem, a programme for physical education will come easily, and we will attain our goals and make our influence felt as a matter of course...

1. An explanation of physical education. ... Physical education helps to maintain life. East and West differ in their interpretations of it. Chuang Tzu followed the example of the cook. Confucius drew on the lesson of the archer and the charioteer. In Germany, physical education has gained the greatest popularity. Fencing has spread all over the country. Japan has *bushidō*. Moreover, recently, following the traditions of our country, judo has developed there to an admirable degree. When we examine these examples, we see that they all begin with the study of physiology...

2. The place of physical education in our life. Physical education complements education in virtue and knowledge. Moreover, both virtue and knowledge reside in the body. Without the body there would be neither virtue nor knowledge. Those who understand this are rare. People stress either knowledge or morality. Know-

---

Sheng), the number of strokes required to write the three characters 'Mao', 'Tse', and 'Tung'.

Available translations: Mao Ze-dong, *Une étude de l'éducation physique*, Mouton, Paris, 1962. No English translation has been published.

ledge is certainly valuable, for it distinguishes man from animals. But wherein is knowledge contained? Morality, too, is valuable; it is the basis of the social order and of equality between ourselves and others. But where does virtue reside? *It is the body that contains knowledge and houses virtue*. It contains knowledge like a chariot and houses morality like a chamber. The body is the chariot that contains knowledge, the chamber that houses virtue. Children enter primary school when they reach the proper age. In primary school, particular attention should be paid to the development of the body; progress in knowledge and moral training are of secondary importance. Nourishment and care should be primary, teaching and discipline complementary. At present, most people do not know this, and the result is that children become ill, or even die young, because of studying. In middle and higher schools, stress should be placed equally on all three aspects of education. At present, most people over-emphasize knowledge. During the years of middle school, the development of the body is not yet completed. Since today the factors favouring physical development are few, and those deterring it numerous, won't physical development tend to cease? In the educational system of our country, required courses are as thick as the hairs on a cow. Even an adult with a tough, strong body could not stand it, let alone those who have not reached adulthood, or those who are weak. Speculating on the intentions of the educators, one is led to wonder whether they did not design such an unwieldy curriculum in order to exhaust the students, to trample on their bodies and ruin their lives. . . . How stupid! The only calamity that can befall a man is not to have a body. What else is there to worry about? If one seeks to improve one's body, other things will follow automatically. For the improvement of the body, nothing is more effective than physical education. *Physical education really occupies the first place in our lives. When the body is strong, then one can advance speedily in knowledge and morality, and reap far-reaching advantages*. It should be regarded as an important part of our study. Learning 'has its essential and its accessory parts, and affairs have their end and their beginning. To know what is first and what is last will bring one closer to the proper way.' [From *The Great*

Learning, one of the four Confucian classics, which Mao, like all Chinese of his generation, had studied since early childhood.] This is exactly what I intend to say.

3. Previous abuses of physical education and my method for remedying them. The three forms of education are equally important; students hitherto have paid much attention to moral and intellectual education but have neglected physical education. The unfortunate consequence has been that they bend their backs and bow their heads; they have 'white and slender hands' [from *Nineteen Old Poems*, a famous collection of poems of the Han dynasty]; when they climb a hill they are short of breath, and when they walk in the water they get cramps in their feet. That is why Yen Tzu had a short life, and Chia I died young. As for Wang Po and Lu Chao-lin, the one died young, and the other became a paralytic. All these were men of high attainments in morality and knowledge. But there comes a day when the body cannot be preserved, and then morality and wisdom are destroyed along with it. Only the men of the North are able 'to lie under arms and meet death without regret'. [From *The Doctrine of the Mean*, one of the Confucian classics.] In the regions of Yen and Chao there were many heroes, and martyrs and warriors often came from Liangchow. At the beginning of the Ch'ing dynasty, Yen Hsi-chai and Li Kang-chu practised both the literary and military arts. Yen Hsi-chai travelled over a thousand *li* to the north of the Great Wall to learn the art of fencing. He contended with brave soldiers and won. Hence he said: 'If one lacks either the literary or the military arts, is this the true way?' . . . As far as we students are concerned, *the installation of a school and the instruction given by its teachers are only the external and objective aspect. We also have the internal, the subjective aspect.* When one's decision is made in his heart, then all parts of the body obey its orders. Fortune and misfortune are of our own seeking. 'I wish to be virtuous, and lo, virtue is at hand.' [From the Confucian *Analects*.] How much more this is true of physical education! If we do not have the will to act, then even though the exterior and the objective are perfect, they still cannot benefit us. *Hence, when we speak of physical education, we should begin with individual initiative.*

4. The utility of physical education. Because man is an animal, movement is most important for him. And because he is a rational animal, his movements must have a reason. But why is movement deserving of esteem? Why is rational movement deserving of esteem? To say that movement helps in earning a living is trivial. To say that movement protects the nation is lofty. Yet neither is the basic reason. The object of movement is simply to preserve our life and gladden our hearts. Chu Hsi stresses respect, and Lu Chiu-yüan stresses tranquillity. Tranquillity is tranquil, and respect is not action; it is merely tranquil. Lao Tzu said that immobility was the ultimate goal; the Buddha sought quiet and methods of contemplation. The art of contemplation is esteemed by the disciples of Chu and Lu. Recently there have been those who, following these masters, have spoken of methods of contemplation, boasted about the effectiveness of their methods, and expressed contempt for those who exercise, thereby ruining their own bodies. This is perhaps one way, but I would not venture to imitate it. In my humble opinion, *there is only movement in heaven and on earth* . . .

One often hears it said that the mind and the body cannot both be perfect at the same time, that those who use their minds are deficient in physical health and those with a robust body are generally deficient in mental capacities. This kind of talk is also absurd and applies only to those who are weak in will and feeble in action, which is generally not the case of superior men. Confucius died at the age of seventy-two, and I have not heard that his body was not healthy. The Buddha travelled continually, preaching his doctrine, and he died at an old age. Jesus had the misfortune to die unjustly. As for Mohammed, he subjugated the world holding the Koran in his left hand and a sword in his right. All these men were called sages and are among the greatest thinkers . . .

Physical education not only strengthens the body but also enhances our knowledge. There is a saying: Civilize the mind and make savage the body. This is an apt saying. In order to civilize the mind one must first make savage the body. If the body is made savage, then the civilized mind will follow. *Knowledge consists in knowing the things in the world, and in discerning their laws. In this matter we must rely on our body, because direct observation depends on the ears and eyes, and reflection depends on the brain. The ears and eyes, as well as the brain, may be considered parts of the body. When the body is perfect, then knowledge is also perfect.* Hence one can say that knowledge is acquired indirectly through physical education. Physical strength is required to undertake the study of the numerous modern sciences, whether in school or through independent study. He who is equal to this is the man with a strong body; he who is not equal to it is the man with a weak body. The division between the strong and the weak determines the area of responsibilities each can assume.

Physical education not only enhances knowledge, it also harmonizes the sentiments. The power of the sentiments is extremely great. The ancients endeavoured to discipline them with reason. Hence they asked, 'Is the master [i.e., reason] always alert?' They also said: 'One should discipline the heart with reason.' But reason proceeds from the heart, and the heart resides in the body. We often observe that the weak are enslaved by their sentiments and are incapable of mastering them. Those whose senses are imperfect or whose limbs are defective are often enslaved by excessive passion, and reason is incapable of saving them. Hence it may be called an invariable law that when the body is perfect and healthy, the sentiments are also correct . . .

Physical education not only harmonizes the emotions, it also strengthens the will. The great utility of physical education lies precisely in this. The principal aim of physical education is military heroism. Such objects of military heroism as courage, dauntlessness, audacity, and perseverance are all matters of will. Let me explain this with an example. To wash our feet in ice water makes us acquire courage and dauntlessness, as well as audacity. In general, any form of exercise, if pursued continuously, will help to train us in perseverance. Long-distance running is particularly good training in perseverance. 'My strength uprooted mountains, my energy dominated the world' [from a poem attributed to Hsiang Yü] – this is courage. 'If I don't behead the Lou Lan, I swear I will not return' – this is dauntlessness. To replace the family with the nation – this is audacity. '[Yü] was away from his home for eight years, and though he thrice passed the door of it, he did not enter' [Like the preceding citation, this reference to Mencius attests to Mao's admiration for the warrior-heroes of the ancient past.] – this is perseverance. All these can be accomplished merely on the basis of daily physical education. *The will is the antecedent of a man's career.*

Those whose bodies are small and frail are flippant in their behaviour. Those whose skin is flabby are soft and dull in will. Thus does the body influence the mind. The purpose of physical education is to strengthen the muscles and the bones; as a result, knowledge is enhanced, the sentiments are harmonized, and the will is strengthened. The muscles and the bones belong to our body; knowledge, sentiments, and will belong to our heart. When both the body and the heart are at ease, one may speak of perfect harmony. Hence, physical education is nothing else but the nourishing of our lives and the gladdening of our hearts.

5. The reasons for disliking exercise. Exercise is the most important part of physical education. Nowadays students generally dislike exercise. There are four reasons for this: (1) They do not have self-awareness. If a thing is to be put into practice, one must first take pleasure in it. One must understand in detail the whys and the wherefores. To know in detail the whys and the wherefores is self-awareness. People generally do not know the interrelation between exercise and themselves – or they may know it in general terms but not intimately. . . . (2) They cannot change their long-established habits. Our country has always stressed literary accomplishment. People blush to wear short clothes. [The mode of dress of the swordsmen of King Wen of Chao, according to a chapter of the Taoist classic *Chuang Tzu*.] Hence there is the common saying, 'A good man does not become a soldier.' . . . (3) Exercise has not been propagated forcefully. . . . (4) Students feel that exercise is shameful. According to my humble observation, this is really their major reason for disliking exercise. Flowing garments, a slow gait, a grave, calm gaze – these constitute a fine deportment, respected by society. Why should one suddenly extend an arm or expose a leg, stretch and bend down? Is this not strange? Hence there are those who know well that their body needs exercise and, moreover, wish very much to do so, but they cannot. There are those who can exercise only with a group, not by themselves, and those who can exercise in privacy but not in public. In short, all this is due to feelings of shame. All four of these are reasons for disliking exercise. The first and the fourth are subjective, and changing them depends on ourselves; the second and third are objective, and changing them depends on others. 'What the superior man seeks is in himself' [*Analects*], that which depends on others is of lesser importance.

6. *The methods of exercise should be few.* Tseng Wen-cheng washed his feet before going to bed and walked a thousand steps after meals, benefiting greatly from this method. There was an eighty-year-old man who was still healthy. On being asked how he maintained his health, he replied, 'I don't eat hearty meals, that's all.' Nowadays the methods of exercise are very diverse, more than I can count. But although there may be several score or even several hundred, 'A branch in the forest is sufficient for the bird to lodge in, and if it drinks at the river it does not drink more than what its stomach can hold.' [From *Chuang Tzu*.] We have only this body and only these senses, bones, viscera, and veins. Even though there are several hundred methods of exercise, all of them *are aimed at improving the circulation of the blood.* If one method can accomplish this, the result of a hundred methods is the same as that of one. Therefore the other ninety-nine methods can be dispensed with. 'Our eyes can see only one thing at a time; our ears can hear only one sound at a time.' [From Hsün Tzu, a Confucian 'realist' considered a precursor of the Machiavellian school known as the Legalists.] To employ a hundred different methods to train the muscles and the bones only disturbs them . . .

7. *The points to which we must pay attention when we exercise.* We should have perseverance in all things. Exercise is no exception. Suppose there are two men who exercise. One practises and then stops, the other is unremitting in his practice. There will certainly be a difference in the results. First of all, perseverance in exercise creates interest. In general, that which is at rest cannot set itself in motion; there must be something to move it. And this something can only be interest . . .

Interest arises from unremitting daily exercise. The best way is to exercise twice a day – on getting up and before going to bed – in the nude; the next best way is to wear light clothes. Too much clothing impedes movement. If one does this daily, the idea of exercise is continually present and never interrupted. Today's exercise is a continuation of yesterday's exercise and thus leads to tomorrow's exercise. The individual exercise periods need not be long; thirty minutes are sufficient. In this way, a certain interest will naturally arise. *Secondly, perseverance in exercise can create pleasure. Exercise over a long time can produce great results and give rise to a feeling of personal value. As a result, we will be able to study with joy, and every day will see some progress in our virtue. Our heart is filled with boundless joy because we have persevered and obtained a result.* Pleasure and interest are distinct. Interest is the origin of exercise, and pleasure its consequence. Interest arises from the action, and pleasure from the result. The two are naturally different.

Perseverance without concentration of mind can hardly produce results. If we look at flowers from a galloping horse, even though we may look daily, it is like not having seen them at all. If one person's heart follows a swan in the sky, he cannot compete with the person who has meanwhile been studying carefully. Hence one should concentrate all one's effort on exercise. During exercise, the mind should be on the exercise. Idle and confused thoughts should all be put aside...

The superior man's deportment is cultivated and agreeable, but one cannot say this about exercise. Exercise should be savage and rude. To be able to leap on horseback and to shoot at the same time; to go from battle to battle; to shake the mountains by one's cries, and the colours of the sky by one's roars of anger; to have the strength to uproot mountains like Hsiang Yü and the audacity to pierce the mark like Yu Chi – all this is savage and rude and has nothing to do with delicacy. In order to progress in exercise, one must be savage. If one is savage, one will have great vigour and strong muscles and bones. The method of exercise should be rude; then one can apply oneself seriously and it will be easy to exercise. These two things are especially important for beginners.

There are three things to which we must pay attention in exercise: (*1*) *perseverance,* (2) *concentration of all our strength, and* (*3*) *that it be savage and rude.* There are many other things that require attention. Here I have merely indicated the most important ones...

I. To the Glory of the Hans

Although the first chapter of this anthology is the shortest this does not imply that it is the least important. In the introduction I have attempted to indicate the limitations imposed on Mao Tse-tung's nationalism by his being a Marxist-Leninist who thinks not only in national but also in class terms. But I also emphasized how deeply this nationalist impulse is rooted in his personality. If, from the standpoint of rational analysis, classes have a certain priority in his thinking, on the level of sentiment and instinctive reactions, it is probably his attachment to the nation that predominates, or has predominated until recently.

This nationalist reflex will be documented throughout this whole volume, whether it be with reference to the anti-Japanese war, to cultural policies, or to relations with Moscow and with the other underdeveloped countries. This chapter focuses on the admiration of Mao Tse-tung for his country and its inhabitants, and more particularly for the 'People of the Hans' (*Han-tsu*), who constitute the overwhelming majority of Chinese.

Whereas certain other ideas of Mao Tse-tung's have undergone considerable changes with the passing of the years, the theme treated in this chapter reveals an astonishing continuity of thought. Text I A, written in 1919, and Text I D, a speech delivered on the eve of the founding of the Chinese People's Republic, span a period of more than thirty years. And yet their essential ideas are almost identical: The Chinese people, a great people, is suffering under manifold oppression; only revolution can put an end to this oppression and sweep away internal and external reactionary forces, after which the people of the Hans will once more manifest all its genius. As pointed out in the introduction, the Great Proletarian Cultural Revolution has carried this glorification of the unique revolutionary capacities of the Chinese to new heights.

At the same time, Text I A shows Mao closer to a Westernizing attitude, blaming much of China's misfortunes on the backwardness of her own social system, than he has ever been before or since. It also reflects something of the fervour and exuberance that characterize the May 4th period as a whole, and of which Mao had more than his share.

To this hymn to the glory of the Hans, Text I B adds a few concrete details.

The two poems, which together constitute Text I C, illustrate the complexity of Mao Tse-tung's attitude toward his country's past. The first one, written in 1936,[1] displays the critical attitude of a revolutionary toward the grandeur of the past; the second, written after he came to power, puts greater emphasis on continuity with the past. One is struck in particular by the citation of two lines from a poem by Emperor Wu of Wei – the famous Ts'ao Ts'ao, whose name has become a synonym for cleverness and cruelty because of the highly unsympathetic manner in which he is presented in the *Romance of the Three Kingdoms* (although objective historians see in him a very able statesman set apart from his rivals by success rather than by a lack of morality). Hostile critics of Mao Tse-tung have made much of his admiration of Ts'ao Ts'ao, claiming that Mao identifies himself with a ruler whose vices he shares. However, the poem cited here transmits nothing more than a certain feeling of community with a man who, in ages past, contemplated the same sites, and who, like himself, knew the burdens of power.

S.R.S.

I · A Toward a new golden age[2]

... What is the greatest question in the world? The greatest question is that of getting food to eat. What is the greatest force? The greatest force is that of the union of the popular masses.

1. On the date of this poem, see *Mao Tse-tung*, p. 179, note.

2. Extracted from the manifesto written by Mao for the first issue of his magazine, *Hsiang-chiang p'ing-lun*, in July 1919, and from his article 'The great union of the popular masses', published in nos. 2–4 of the same periodical, July and August 1919. The original text of these materials is not available. This translation was prepared from extracts found in a number of

What should we not fear? We should not fear heaven. We should not fear ghosts. We should not fear the dead. We should not fear the bureaucrats. We should not fear the militarists. We should not fear the capitalists...

The time has come! The great tide in the world is rolling ever more impetuously! ... He who conforms to it shall survive, he who resists it shall perish...

As a result of the world war and the bitterness of their lives, the popular masses in many countries have suddenly undertaken all sorts of action. In Russia, they have overthrown the aristocrats and driven out the rich.... The army of the red flag swarms over the East and the West, sweeping away numerous enemies.... The whole world has been shaken by it.... Within the area enclosed by the Great Wall and the China Sea, the May 4th Movement has arisen. Its banner has advanced southward, across the Yellow River to the Yangtze. From Canton to Hankow, many real-life dramas have been performed; from Lake Tungt'ing to the Min River the tide is rising. Heaven and earth are aroused, the traitors and the wicked are put to flight. Ha! We know it! We are awakened! The world is ours, the nation is ours, society is ours. If we do not speak, who will speak? If we do not act, who will act? If we do not rise up and fight, who will rise up and fight?...

It is not that basically we have no strength; the source of our impotence lies in our lack of practice. For thousands of years the Chinese people of several hundred millions have all led a life of slaves. Only one person – the 'emperor' – was not a slave, or rather one could say that even he was the slave of 'heaven'. When the emperor was in control of everything, we were given no opportunity for practice...

We must act energetically to carry out the great union of the popular masses, which will not brook a moment's delay.... Our Chinese people possesses great intrinsic energy. The more profound the oppression, the greater its resistance; that which has accumulated for a long time will surely burst forth quickly. The

secondary sources recently published in Peking. For details, see the special note in the bibliography.

Available translations: none.

great union of the Chinese people must be achieved. Gentlemen! We must all exert ourselves, we must all advance with the utmost strength. Our golden age, our age of brilliance and splendour, lies ahead!

I · B The Chinese people[1]

Our China is one of the largest countries in the world, covering an area larger than the whole of Europe. In this vast territory there are large stretches of fertile land that provide us with food and clothing; there are mountain ranges, plateaux, and plains traversing the length and breadth of the country that provide us with extensive forests and rich mineral deposits; there are many rivers and lakes that provide us with facilities for water transport and irrigation; and there is a long coast line that facilitates communication with other nations beyond the seas. Since ancient times, our Chinese people have laboured, lived, and multiplied on this immense territory...

Developing along the same lines as the other *great* peoples of the world, the Chinese people (*chiefly the Hans*) first went through some tens of thousands of years of life in a classless, *equalitarian*, primitive, *communistic society*. Five thousand years have gone by since the collapse of primitive *communistic society* and the transition to class society – first a slave society, then that of feudalism. In the history of Chinese civilization (*chiefly that of the Hans*), agriculture and handicraft have always been highly developed; many great thinkers, scientists, inventors, statesmen, and strategists[2] have flourished, and there is a rich store of classical works. The compass was invented in China 3,000 years ago. The art of paper-making was discovered as early as 1,700 years ago. Block-printing was invented 1,200 years ago. Movable type was

1. Extracted from *The Chinese Revolution and the Chinese Communist Party*, *Chung-kuo ko-ming yü Chung-kuo Kung-ch'an-tang*, Chieh-fang She, n.d. (1940?), pp. 1–3.

Available translations: *Selected Works*, II, pp. 305–34. A translation of the original text is available in *Current Background*, no. 135, published by the U.S. Consulate General, Hong Kong.

2. In 1951, Mao added men of letters and artists to this listing.

invented 800 years ago. Gunpowder also was used in China much earlier than in Europe. China, with a recorded history of 5,000 years, is therefore one of the oldest civilized countries in the world.

The Chinese people is not only famous throughout the world for its endurance and industriousness; it is also a freedom-loving people with a rich revolutionary tradition. The history of the Hans, for instance, shows that the Chinese people would never submit to a rule of the dark forces and that in every case they succeeded in overthrowing or changing such a rule by revolutionary means. In thousands of years of Han history, there have been hundreds of peasant insurrections against the regime of darkness imposed by the landlords and nobility. As for the dynastic changes, *each and every one* has succeeded *only* by the force of the peasant uprisings. All the nationalities of China have always been unwilling to submit to the oppression of foreign peoples and have striven to shake it off by acts of resistance. They accept union only on the basis of equality, not on the basis of oppression of one people by another. In the thousands of years of Chinese history, many national heroes and revolutionary leaders have emerged. *China has also given birth to many revolutionary strategists, statesmen, men of letters, and thinkers.* So the Chinese people is also a people with a glorious revolutionary tradition and a splendid historical heritage.

I · C Old China, new China[1]

Snow

This is the scene in that northern land;
A hundred leagues are sealed with ice,
A thousand leagues of whirling snow.
On either side of the Great Wall

1. These and all succeeding poems cited in this volume are taken from the edition published in Peking under the title *Mao Chu-hsi shih tz'u san-shih-ch'i shou*. Some of the translations are adapted, with modifications, from Mao Tse-tung, *Nineteen Poems*, with notes by Chou Chen-fu and an appreciation by Tsang Keh-chia, Foreign Languages Press, Peking, 1958, and others are my own. (This is indicated in each case.) Here I follow the Peking translation, with substantial changes in the latter part of 'Snow'.

One vastness is all you see.
From end to end of the great river
The rushing torrent is frozen and lost.
The mountains dance like silver snakes,
The highlands roll like waxen elephants,
As if they sought to vie in height with the lord of heaven,
And on a sunny day
See how the white-robed beauty is adorned with rouge,
Enchantment beyond compare.

Lured by such great beauty in our landscape
Innumerable heroes have rivalled one another to bow in homage.
But alas, Ch'in Shih Huang and Han Wu Ti[1]
Were rather lacking in culture,
T'ang T'ai Tsung and Sung T'ai Tsu
Had little taste for poetry,
And Genghis Khan
The favourite son of heaven for a day
Knew only how to bend his bow to shoot great vultures.
Now they are all past and gone.
To find heroes in the grand manner
We must look rather in the present.

Peitaiho

A rainstorm falls on this northern land,
White breakers leap to the sky.
Of the fishing boats from Chinwangtao
There is not one to be seen on all the ocean.
Where have they gone?

More than a thousand years in the past
The Emperor Wu of Wei brandished his whip;
'Eastwards to Chiehshih', his poem, remains.
'The autumn wind is sighing' still today –
The world of men has changed!

1. It would seem that Mao's attitude toward the 'Martial Emperor' has undergone a change since his adolescence. (See the introduction, p. 22.)

I · D The Chinese people has stood up[1]

... Our conference is one of great nationwide popular unity.

Such great nationwide popular unity has been achieved because we have vanquished the Kuomintang reactionary government, which is aided by American imperialism. In the course of little more than three years, the heroic Chinese People's Liberation Army, an army such as the world has seldom seen, crushed the offensive of the several million troops of the American-supported Kuomintang reactionary government, thereby enabling us to swing over to the counter-offensive and the offensive...

We have a common feeling that our work will be recorded in the history of mankind, and that it will clearly demonstrate that the Chinese, who comprise one quarter of humanity, have begun to stand up. The Chinese have always been a great, courageous, and industrious people. It was only in modern times that they have fallen behind, and this was due solely to the oppression and exploitation of foreign imperialism and the domestic reactionary government.

For more than a century, our predecessors never paused in their indomitable struggles against the foreign and domestic oppressors. These struggles include the Revolution of 1911, led by Sun Yat-sen, the great pioneer of China's revolution. Our predecessors instructed us to carry their work to completion. We are doing this now. We have united ourselves and defeated both our foreign and domestic oppressors by means of the people's liberation war and the people's great revolution, and we proclaim the establishment of the People's Republic of China.

Henceforth, our nation will enter the large family of peace-loving and freedom-loving nations of the world. It will work bravely and industriously to create its own civilization and happiness, and will, at the same time, promote world peace and freedom. Our nation will never again be an insulted nation. We

1. Extracts from a speech delivered at the First Plenary Session of the Chinese People's Political Consultative Conference, 21 September 1949. (Source: *Hsin-hua yüeh-pao*, I, no. 1, 15 November 1949.)
Available translations: *Selected Works*, IV, pp. 411–24.

have stood up. Our revolution has gained the sympathy and acclamation of the broad masses throughout the world. We have friends the world over.

Our revolutionary work is not yet concluded. ... The imperialists and the domestic reactionaries will certainly not take their defeat lying down. ... Daily, hourly, they will try to restore their rule in China. ... We must not relax our vigilance ...

The people's democratic dictatorship and unity with international friends will enable us to obtain rapid success in our construction work. ... Our population of 475 million and our national territory of 9,597 million square kilometres are factors in our favour. It is true that there are difficulties ahead of us, a great many of them. But we firmly believe that all the difficulties will be surmounted by the heroic struggle of all the people of our country. The Chinese people has had ample experience in overcoming difficulties. If we and our predecessors could come through the long period of extreme difficulties and defeat the powerful domestic and foreign reactionaries, why can we not build up a prosperous and flourishing country after our victory? ...

An upsurge in cultural construction will inevitably follow in the wake of the upsurge of economic construction. The era in which the Chinese were regarded as uncivilized is now over. We will emerge in the world as a nation with a high culture.

Our national defence will be consolidated and no imperialist will be allowed to invade our territory again ...

Let the domestic and foreign reactionaries tremble before us. Let them say that we are no good at this and no good at that. Through the Chinese people's indomitable endeavours, we will steadily reach our goal.

II. Mao Tse-tung as a Marxist Theoretician

The word 'theory', applied to a strain of Marxism-Leninism, evokes a wide variety of subjects, extending from the most abstract questions to the systematic analysis of the tactics to be applied in a given country during a given period. This chapter deals with general problems: Mao's conception of the nature of Marxist theory and of the role of theory in the development of society and the universe; and Mao's method of setting forth the most general theses of Marxism on nature, history and society.

The inclusion of so long a chapter on questions of this type may seem highly paradoxical, for in the general introduction I emphasized that this aspect of Mao's thought is far from being the most interesting.

The relative mediocrity of Mao Tse-tung as a Marxist *philosopher*, that is to say as a systematic thinker dealing with problems on a high level of abstraction in terms of Marxist categories, can be explained no doubt in part by the difficulties in assimilating Western thought. But there is certainly more to be said on this. Mao Tse-tung unquestionably has a certain lack of interest in theoretical problems as such. He has a tendency to relate everything to the class struggle, and to certain other values: the affirmation by the Chinese people of its own personality, or the mastery of man over nature. These problems he envisages less in philosophical terms, than as aspects of the day-to-day struggle to carry out the revolution.

All of these themes will be dealt with in succeeding chapters, and we will see with what enthusiasm, with what wealth of imagination and imagery, he approaches these questions. When, on the other hand, he talks about dialectics – not about the dialectics of classes in China, nor about contradictions under socialism, but about dialectics in general – the result is much more lifeless.

The best example of this is the item called 'Dialectical materialism', which constitutes Text II C. The extracts from this work which appeared in the first edition of the present book were taken from Chapter 1, which was the only part available at that time. As explained above in the introduction, just as this revised edition was about to go to press, I obtained a portion of Chapter 2. I have therefore added a few brief passages from this newly-discovered part of the work, which is, if possible, even less inspired than Chapter 1 – no doubt because it deals at greater length with questions of the concepts and methods of philosophy. In the first edition of this book I said that 'Dialectical materialism', being Mao's only systematic exposition of certain basic questions, constituted a good introduction to his more specialized essays, 'On practice' and 'On contradiction' (Texts II D and II E). It is even more logical to regard it as an introduction to his other philosophical writings since we now know that it is actually the beginning of a series of lectures of which 'On practice' represents the last section.

Mao's lack of interest in pure theory is confirmed by the pedestrian character of the explicitly theoretical writings presented here; it is also confirmed by the vivacity of his exposition when he speaks of the link between theory and action. The first text, which I have entitled 'The Sinification of Marxism', constitutes a good transition from the theme of the first chapter to that of the present one. In it there are many echoes of the hymn to the glory of the Hans; there also is a strong stand in favour of the concrete application of Marxism, similar to that developed at much greater length in Text II B. This last text shows very well how audacious Mao can be in dealing with the fathers of Marxism-Leninism. It also contains some specimens of the down-to-earth humour that Mao Tse-tung employed to reach audiences untrained in Marxist dialectics.

In indicating the discrepancies between the original texts and the current edition of the *Selected Works*, I have confined myself to pointing out only the most important variants. Text II B in particular contains some excellent examples of the kind of language that Mao no longer allows himself to use today. And in Text II A, the key term, 'Sinification' (of Marxism), has now been deleted.

S.R.S.

II · A The Sinification of Marxism[1]

... Without revolutionary theory, without historical knowledge and an understanding of the concrete movement, it is impossible to lead a great revolutionary movement to victory.

The theories of Marx, Engels, Lenin, and Stalin can be applied to the whole universe. Their theories are not to be looked upon as dogma but as a guide for action. We must not study the letter of Marxism and Leninism, but the viewpoint and methodology of its creators, with which they observed and solved problems. It is only this guide to action, it is only this viewpoint and methodology, that constitute revolutionary science and provide us with the only correct orientation permitting us to take cognizance of the facts of the revolution and to lead the revolutionary movement. The Chinese Party has already made great progress in its Marxist-Leninist training as compared with the previous situation, but this training cannot yet be said to be universal and profound. *From this standpoint, we are more or less inferior to some of our fraternal parties in other countries.* And yet our task is to lead a great people of 450 million in an unprecedented historic struggle. Consequently, widespread and thorough study of theory is of decisive importance for us and can only be carried through by the utmost effort. Let us work hard at it. Following this Sixth Enlarged Plenum, let us begin a Party-wide competition in study.

1. Extracted from Chapter 7 of *On the New Stage* (*Lun hsin chieh-tuan*, Chieh-fang She, 1939), a report to the Sixth Plenum of the Sixth Central Committee, in October 1938. The original report comprises eight chapters.

Available translations: Mao Tse-tung, *On the New Stage*, New China Information Committee, Chungking (c/o Mr V. Robert, P.O. Box 1360, Hong Kong), pp. 73–5. (This translation is exceedingly mediocre and unfaithful, but it is the only translation from the original Chinese text. The translation in the *Selected Works* (II, pp. 195–211) is vastly superior, but includes only Chapter 7 of the report. The above extract is based partly on the New China Information Committee translation, with extensive revisions.)

Let us see who can really accomplish something in this respect, who can study more and better than the others. *Thus far our work has not been carried on too badly, but if we do not study theory more thoroughly, it will be impossible to improve on our best performance, and it is only such improvement that will make victory possible. The study of theory is consequently a precondition of victory.* From the viewpoint of the main task of leadership, if there are one or two hundred comrades who have learned to apply Marxism systematically rather than in petty detail, and to do so in concrete terms rather than indulging in empty talk, that will be equivalent to victory over the Japanese imperialists. Comrades, we must definitely study Marxism.

Another task of our study is to understand our historic inheritance and to evaluate it critically by the use of the Marxist method. The history of our great people over several millennia exhibits national peculiarities and many precious qualities. As regards all this, we are merely elementary-school students. Today's China is an outgrowth of historic China. We are Marxist historicists; we must not mutilate history. From Confucius to Sun Yat-sen we must sum it up critically, and we must constitute ourselves the heirs of all that is precious in this past. Conversely, the assimilation of this heritage itself turns out to be a kind of methodology that is of great help in the guidance of the revolutionary movement. A communist is a Marxist internationalist, but Marxism must take on a national form before it can be applied. *There is no such thing as abstract Marxism, but only concrete Marxism. What we call concrete Marxism is Marxism that has taken on a national form, that is, Marxism applied to the concrete struggle in the concrete conditions prevailing in China, and not Marxism abstractly used.* If a Chinese communist, who is a part of the great Chinese people, bound to his people by his very flesh and blood, talks of Marxism apart from Chinese peculiarities, this Marxism is merely an empty abstraction. Consequently, *the Sinification of Marxism – that is to say*, making certain that in all of its manifestations it is imbued with Chinese peculiarities, using it according to these peculiarities – becomes a problem that must be understood and solved by the whole Party without delay. ... We must put an end to writing eight-legged essays on foreign models; there must be less repeating of empty and abstract refrains; we must discard our dogmatism and replace it by a new and vital Chinese style and manner, pleasing to the eye and to the ear of the Chinese common people. To separate internationalist content from national form is the way of those who understand nothing of internationalism; we must link the two inseparably. As regards this question, serious shortcomings still persist in our ranks that must be resolutely eliminated.[1]

What are the peculiarities of our movement at the present time? What are its laws? How should we lead this movement? These are all extremely practical questions. To this day we have yet not acquired a full understanding either of Japanese imperialism or of China herself. As the movement develops, many new phenomena will arise unceasingly before our eyes. The great lesson to which we must apply ourselves constantly and with wide-open eyes is the study of all aspects of this movement and its development. If there is anyone who refuses this scrupulous and detailed study, *he is no better than a Don Quixote or Ah Q*, and can by no means be counted a Marxist. How shall we study? With the aid of our Marxist instrument, materialist dialectics. From whom shall we learn? Our teachers are numerous: the workers, the peasants, the petty bourgeoisie, the capitalists, the landlords, the Japanese imperialists, the whole world. All these are both the objects of our research and our teachers; we must learn something, great or small, from all of them.

The enemy of study is self-complacency. If we wish to study anything seriously, we must begin by not being complacent. As re-

1. In the New China Information Committee translation, the last three sentences of this paragraph have been replaced by the following text: 'There cannot be any separation of internationalist content from nationalist [*sic*] form. Such a separation leads to telling the backward masses what they like to hear, that is, a paean of praise about their own country. This is an actual promotion of chauvinism, not the work of internationalists. Communists must understand that internationalist content and nationalist form are indivisible. In our ranks there is still this kind of shortcoming, which should be overcome without delay.' It would be interesting to know who inserted this passage, which is in flagrant contradiction with the whole spirit of Mao's text, and why. As suggested in the introduction, Po Ku may have had something to do with it.

gards ourselves, we must 'learn without satiety', and as regards others, we must 'instruct them without being wearied'. [From the Confucian *Analects*.] Such must be our attitude.

II · B What is a Marxist theoretician?[1]

At the present time, confused concepts are prevalent on such questions as the nature of a theoretician, the nature of an intellectual, the relation between theory and practice, and so forth . . .

Can we claim that we possess theoreticians just because we have read a great many books on Marxism-Leninism? No, we cannot say this. Marxism-Leninism is the theory that Marx, Engels, Lenin, and Stalin created on the basis of actual fact, and it consists of general conclusions derived from historical and revolutionary experience. If we have only read this theory but have not used it as a basis for research in China's historical and revolutionary actuality, *have not created a theory in accordance with China's real necessities, a theory that is our own and of a specific nature*,[2] then it would be irresponsible to call ourselves Marxist theoreticians. If we who are communist Party members are so accustomed to looking at Chinese problems that we cannot see them, if we look *every day and see nothing, put on glasses and still see nothing, if we see only the complete works of Marx, Engels, Lenin, and Stalin on the shelf*, then our achievements on the theoretical front cannot but be poor. If we only know how to recite Marxist economics or philosophy, reciting from the first to the tenth chapters until they are thoroughly familiar

1. Extracted from 'Reform in learning, the Party, and literature', a speech delivered at the opening of the Party school in Yenan on 1 February 1942. Source: *Chieh-fang jih-pao*, 27 April 1942.

Available translations: *Mao's China*, pp. 9–22 *passim*.

2. In the current version, Mao speaks of applying the theories of Lenin and Stalin regarding the Chinese revolution, merely developing them a step further. (See *Selected Works*, IV, pp. 31, 37.) Here, in the original text, he demands that the Chinese communists, basing themselves on a Marxist-Leninist-Stalinist standpoint, create their *own* theories. This is something else again.

(laughter) but are completely unable to apply them, can we then be considered Marxist theoreticians? Hardly. *It would really be better if there were fewer such theoreticians.* If a man read ten thousand volumes by Marx, Engels, Lenin, and Stalin, and read each volume a thousand times so he could recite every sentence from memory, he still could not be considered a theoretician. What type of theoretician do we need? We need theoreticians who base their thinking on the standpoints, concepts, and methods of Marx, Engels, Lenin, and Stalin, who are able to *explain correctly the actual problems issuing from history and revolution, who are able to give a scientific interpretation and theoretical explanation of the various problems of Chinese economics, politics, military affairs, and culture.* This is the type of theoretician we need...

What about the problem of the so-called 'intelligentsia'? Because our China is a semi-colonial, semi-feudal country and its culture is undeveloped, the intelligentsia is of special value. According to a resolution of the Central Committee, we must strive to attract a broad stratum of the intelligentsia. It is very correct that an attitude of welcome be adopted toward them if they are revolutionary and willing to participate in the War of Resistance. *But as a result of this attitude, the intelligentsia has been glorified and the local bumpkins are handicapped.* We consider it entirely necessary to hold the intelligentsia in esteem, for without a revolutionary intelligentsia the revolution cannot succeed. However, we know that there are many intellectuals who consider themselves very learned and who make a great display of their knowledge, not realizing that this attitude is harmful and obstructs their progress. One truth that they should realize is that a great many so-called intellectuals are actually exceedingly unlearned and that the knowledge of the workers and peasants is sometimes greater than theirs. To this some may say, 'Aha! You're turning everything upside down. You're talking nonsense!' (Laughter.) But, Comrades, don't get excited. What I say is to a certain extent reasonable.

What is knowledge? From ancient times down to the present, there have only been two types of knowledge: knowledge of the struggle for production and knowledge of the class struggle.

(*Knowledge of the national struggle is also included in the latter category.*) What knowledge is there aside from this? There is none. Natural science and social science are nothing but the crystallization of these two types of knowledge. Philosophy is then a generalization and summary of natural science and social science. . . . Now let us consider those students who graduate and leave their schools where they have been completely isolated from the practical activities of society. In what position do they find themselves? A man studies from grade school to university, graduates, and is then considered learned. Yet, in the first place, he cannot till the land; second, he has no trade; third, he cannot fight; fourth, he cannot manage a job – in none of these fields is he experienced nor does he have the least practical knowledge. What he possesses is merely book knowledge. *Would it be possible to regard such a man as a complete intellectual? It would be very difficult; at the most I would consider him a half-intellectual, because his knowledge is still incomplete.* What is comparatively complete knowledge? All comparatively complete knowledge is formed in two stages: the first is that of knowledge through immediate perception; the second is knowledge through reason. Knowledge through reason is a higher stage of development of knowledge through immediate perception. Into which category does the book knowledge of students fall? Even if we suppose that their knowledge is correct, it is still theory drawn from the experience of their predecessors in the struggle of production and the class struggle, not knowledge drawn from their own personal experience. It is absolutely necessary that they obtain this [theoretical] knowledge, but they should realize that, for them, this knowledge is inverted, backward, one-sided; it has been proved by others, but not verified by the students themselves. They should know that it is not at all difficult to obtain this type of knowledge, that it is even extremely easy. *By comparison, the cook's task in preparing a meal is difficult. To create something edible, he must use a combination of wood, rice, oil, salt, sauce, vinegar, and other materials. This is certainly not easy, and to cook a good meal is all the more difficult. If we compare the tasks of the cook at the North-west Restaurant to those of the cooks in our homes, we find a great difference. If there is too much fire, the food will burn; too much vinegar, and it will be sour.* (Laughter.) *Cooking food and preparing dishes is truly one of the arts. But what about book knowledge? If you do nothing but read, you have only to recognize three to five thousand characters, learn to thumb through a dictionary, hold some book in your hand, and receive millet from the public. Then you nod your head contentedly and start to read. But books cannot walk, and you can open and close a book at will; this is the easiest thing in the world to do, a great deal easier than it is for the cook to prepare a meal, and much easier than it is for him to slaughter a pig. He has to catch the pig ... the pig can run ...* (laughter) *he slaughters it ... the pig squeals.* (Laughter.) *A book placed on a desk cannot run nor can it squeal.* (Laughter.) *You can dispose of it in any manner you wish. Is there anything easier to do? Therefore, I advise those of you who have only book knowledge and as yet no contact with reality, and those who have had little practical experience, to recognize their own shortcomings and become a bit more humble.*

How can half-intellectuals be transformed into people truly entitled to call themselves intellectuals? There is only one way: to see that those with only book knowledge become practical workers engaged in practical tasks, and those doing theoretical work turn to practical research. In this way we can reach our goal.

On hearing this, some people will lose their tempers, and say, 'According to your interpretation, Marx was also a half-intellectual. I would answer that it's quite true that, in the first place, Marx could not slaughter a pig, and second, he could not till a field. But he did participate in the revolutionary movement and also carried out research on commodity production. Millions see and use these commodities every day yet ignore them. Only Marx studied them in every aspect and scrutinized them from all angles, exhibiting none of the carelessness we show in reading the *History of the Communist Party of the Soviet Union.* He analysed the actual development of commodity production and derived a theory from observations on universally existent phenomena. He did personal research on nature, history, and proletarian revolution, and created the corresponding theories of dialectical materialism, historical materialism, and proletarian revolution. Thus Marx is to be regarded as a complete intellectual. The difference between him and the half-intellectual is that he participated in an actual revolutionary movement and carried on research and investigation by turning to a reality that was all-inclusive. This type of all-inclusive knowledge is called theory...

There is only one type of true theory: that which is derived from the observation of objective reality and proved by objective reality. Nothing else can measure up to the theory of which we speak. Stalin has argued that theory divorced from reality is empty. Empty theory is useless, incorrect, and must be rejected. We must single out those who delight in discussing such empty theories and put them to shame. Marxism-Leninism, derived from objective reality and tested by objective reality, is the most correct, scientific, and revolutionary truth. But many read Marxism-Leninism as dead dogma, thereby obstructing their own theoretical development and harming themselves and their comrades.

On the other hand, mistakes are also going to be made by those comrades engaged in practical work who make an incorrect application of their experience. It is quite true that such men have had a great deal of experience and should be valued highly. But there is great danger if they are satisfied with their experience. They should realize that the greater part of their knowledge is gained from immediate perception and is therefore limited, and that they fall short when it comes to reasoned, universal knowledge, that is to say, they fall short in theory. Thus their knowledge, too, is comparatively incomplete. Yet without comparatively complete knowledge it is impossible to finish the revolution...

In addition to the confusion prevailing about 'theoreticians' and 'intellectuals', there is a phrase we read every day – 'the union of theory and practice' – which still has a vague meaning for many of our comrades. Every day they speak of 'union' when what they actually mean is 'separation', for they take no steps toward 'union'. How can Marxist-Leninist theory and the reality of the Chinese revolution be united? Take the common saying, 'To shoot an arrow, have a target.' ... In shooting an arrow, you must aim at a target. The relation between Marxism-Leninism and the Chinese revolution is the same as between the arrow and the target. However, some comrades shoot arrows recklessly without a target. It is easy for them to harm the revolutionary cause. In addition, there are some comrades who merely take the arrow in hand, twist it back and forth, and say again and again in praise, 'Excellent arrow! Excellent arrow!' but are never willing to shoot it. This type of person is a connoisseur of antiques who has hardly any relationship with the revolution. The arrow of Marxism-Leninism must be used to hit the target of the Chinese revolution. If it were otherwise, why would we want to study Marxism-Leninism? . . .

Our comrades must understand that we do not study Marxism-Leninism because it is pleasing to the eye, or because it has some mystical value, like the doctrines of the Taoist priests who ascend Mao Shan to learn how to subdue devils and evil spirits. Marxism-Leninism has no beauty, nor has it any mystical value. It is only extremely useful. It seems that right up to the present quite a few have regarded Marxism-Leninism as a ready-made panacea: Once you have it, you can cure all your ills with little effort.[1] This is a type of childish blindness and we must start a movement to enlighten these people. Those who regard Marxism-Leninism as religious dogma show this type of blind ignorance. We must tell them openly, 'Your dogma is of no use,' *or, to use an impolite formulation, 'Your dogma is less useful than shit.' We see that dog shit can fertilize the fields and man's can feed the dog. And dogmas? They can't fertilize the fields, nor can they feed a dog. Of what use are they?* (Laughter.) *Comrades! You know that the object of such talk is to ridicule those who regard Marxism-Leninism as dogma, to frighten and awaken them, to foster a correct attitude toward Marxism-Leninism. Marx, Engels, Lenin, and Stalin have repeatedly said, 'Our doctrine is not dogma; it is a guide to action.' Of all things, these people forget this most important sentence. Theory and practice can be combined only if men of the Chinese Communist Party take the standpoints, concepts, and methods of Marxism-Leninism, apply them to China, and create a theory from*

1. In the current version, it is only 'isolated formulas, drawn from Marxist-Leninist literature' that are not to be regarded as panaceas (ibid., pp. 36–7); this new version places no limits on the magic value of Marxism-Leninism as a whole.

conscientious study of the realities of the Chinese revolution and Chinese history...

II · C Dialectical materialism[1]

CHAPTER 1: Idealism and Materialism

1. The struggle between two armies in philosophy. The whole history of philosophy is the history of the struggle and the development of two mutually opposed schools of philosophy, idealism and materialism. All philosophical currents and schools are manifestations of these two fundamental schools.

All philosophical theories have been created by men belonging to a definite social class. The ideas of these men have moreover been historically determined by a definite social existence. All philosophical doctrines express the needs of a definite social class and reflect the level of development of the productive forces of society and the historical stage in man's comprehension of nature...

The social origins of idealism and materialism lie in a social structure marked by class contradictions. The earliest appearance of idealism was the product of the ignorance and superstition of savage and primitive man. Then, with the development of the productive forces, and the ensuing development of scientific knowledge, it stands to reason that idealism should decline and be

1. The following text includes about two thirds of the first chapter, and about one fifth of the first six sections (all that is available to me) of the second chapter of Mao's '*Pien-cheng-fa wei-wu-lun* (*chiang-shou t'i-kang*)' ('Dialectical materialism – notes of lectures'), as published in *K'ang-chan ta-hsüeh*, nos. 6 to 8, April to June 1938. This magazine was issued in Canton by the T'ung-i Ch'u-pan-she. Chapter 1 appeared in no. 6, sections 1–4 of Chapter 2 in no. 7, and sections 5 and 6 of Chapter 2 in no. 8. As indicated in the introduction, this text of Chapter 1 is identical with that published in *Min-chu* (Shanghai) in 1940, from which I prepared the extracts in the first edition of this anthology.

Available translations: Chapter 1 has now been translated *in extenso* twice; for references see the introduction. There are no translations of Chapter 2, but I plan to publish the complete text of sections 1 to 6 in *China Quarterly* in the near future.

replaced by materialism. And yet, from ancient times to the present, idealism not only has not declined, but, on the contrary, has developed and carried on a struggle for supremacy with materialism from which neither has emerged the victor. The reason lies in the division of society into classes. On the one hand, in its own interest, the oppressing class must develop and reinforce its idealist doctrines. On the other hand, the oppressed classes, likewise in their own interests, must develop and reinforce their materialist doctrines. Both idealism and materialism are weapons in the class struggle, and the struggle between idealism and materialism cannot disappear so long as classes continue to exist. Idealism, in the process of its historical development, represents the ideology of the exploiting classes and serves reactionary purposes. Materialism, on the other hand, is the world view of the revolutionary class; in a class society, it grows and develops in the midst of an incessant struggle against the reactionary philosophy of idealism. Consequently, the history of the struggle between idealism and materialism in philosophy reflects the struggle of interests between the reactionary class and the revolutionary class. . . . A given philosophical tendency is in the last analysis a manifestation in a particular guise of the policy of the social class to which the philosophers belong.

The distinguishing characteristic of Marxist philosophy – i.e., dialectical materialism – is its effort to explain clearly the class nature of all social consciousness (including philosophy). It publicly declares a resolute struggle between its own proletarian nature and the idealist philosophy of the propertied class. Moreover, it subordinates its own special and independent tasks to such general tasks as overthrowing capitalism, organizing and building a proletarian dictatorship, and edifying a socialist society . . .

2. The difference between idealism and materialism. Wherein lies the basic difference between idealism and materialism? It lies in the opposite answers given by the two to the fundamental question in philosophy, that of the relationship between spirit and matter (that of the relationship between consciousness and existence). Idealism considers spirit (consciousness, concepts, the subject) as the source of all that exists on earth, and matter (nature and society, the object) as secondary and subordinate. Materialism recognizes the independent existence of matter as detached from spirit and considers spirit as secondary and subordinate ...

3. The source of the growth and the development of idealism. Idealism sees matter as the product of the spirit. This is turning the real world upside down. Where is the source of the growth and the development of such a philosophy?

As mentioned above, the earliest manifestation of idealism was brought about by the superstition and ignorance of primitive, savage man. But with the development of production, the separation between manual labour and intellectual labour was responsible for ranking idealism first among currents of philosophical thought. With the development of the productive forces of society, the division of labour made its appearance; the further development of the division of labour saw the emergence of persons devoting themselves entirely and exclusively to intellectual labour. But when the productive forces are still weak, the division between the two does not reach the stage of complete separation. Only after classes and private property appear and exploitation becomes the foundation of the existence of the ruling class do great changes occur. Intellectual labour then becomes the exclusive privilege of the ruling class, while manual labour becomes the fate of the oppressed classes. The ruling class begins to examine the relationship between themselves and the oppressed classes in an upside-down fashion: It is not the labourers who furnish them with means for existence, but rather they who supply the labourers with these means. Hence, they despise manual labour and develop idealist conceptions. To eliminate the distinction between manual labour and intellectual labour is one of the preconditions for eliminating idealist philosophy.

The social root that makes possible the development of idealist philosophy lies principally in the fact that this kind of philosophical consciousness is the manifestation of the interests of the exploiting class.[1] ... The final decline of idealism will come with the elimination of classes, after the establishment of a communist society.

1. I have corrected my previous reading of this sentence on the basis of C.S. Chao's translation, p. 272.

The source that enables idealism to develop and deepen and gives it the strength to struggle with materialism must be sought in the process of human knowing. ... When men think, they must use concepts. This can easily cause our knowledge to be split into two aspects: reality, which is of an individual and particular character; and concepts, which are of a general character. ... In the nature of things, the particular and the general are inseparably linked; once separated, they depart from objective truth. ... To separate the general from the particular, and to view the general as objective reality and the particular merely as the form in which the general exists – this is the method adopted by all idealists. All idealists put consciousness, spirit, or concepts in place of objective reality existing independently from human consciousness. ... They cannot point out the materialist truth according to which consciousness is limited by matter, but believe that only consciousness is active, whereas matter is only an inert composite entity. Urged on moreover by their own class nature, the idealists then use every method to exaggerate the activity of consciousness, developing this aspect unilaterally. ... Idealism in economics exaggerates beyond measure a non-essential aspect of exchange, raising the law of supply and demand to the status of the fundamental law of capitalism. ... Idealist historians regard heroes as the makers of history. Idealist politicians regard politics as omnipotent. Idealist military leaders practise the methods of desperate combat [*p'ing-ming-chu-i-ti tso-chan*]. Idealist revolutionaries advocate Blanquism. The die-hards say that the only way to revive our nation is to restore the old morality. All this results from exaggerating subjective factors beyond measure ...

Pre-Marxist materialism (mechanistic materialism) did not stress the thought process in the development of knowledge, but regarded thought merely as the object of action, as the mirror that reflects nature. ... Only dialectical materialism correctly shows the active role of thought, and at the same time points out the limitation imposed upon thought by matter. It points out that thought arises from social practice and at the same time actively shapes practice. Only this kind of dialectical theory of 'the unity of knowledge and action' can thoroughly vanquish idealism.

4. The origin of the inception and the development of materialism. The recognition that matter exists independently and apart from consciousness in the external world is the foundation of materialism. Man created this foundation through practice...

Obliged to submit to natural forces, and capable of using only simple tools, primitive man could not explain the surrounding phenomena and hence sought help from spirits. This is the origin of religion and idealism.

But in the long-range process of production, man came into contact with surrounding nature, acted upon nature, changed nature, and created things to eat, to live in, and to use, and adapted nature to the interests of man and caused man to believe that matter has an objective existence.

In the social existence of humanity, reciprocal relationships and influences arise between individuals. In a class society there is moreover a class struggle. The oppressed class considers the circumstances and estimates its strength, and then makes its plans. When they succeed in the struggle, the members of this class are convinced that their views are not the product of fantasy, but the reflection of the objectively existing material world. Because the oppressed class fails when it adopts the wrong plans and succeeds by correcting its plans it learns to understand that it can achieve its purposes only when its subjective plans rest upon the accurate understanding of the material nature of the objective world and the fact that the objective world is governed by laws.

The history of science furnishes man with proof of the material nature of the world and of the fact that it is governed by laws and helps man to see the futility of the illusions of religion and idealism and to arrive at materialist conclusions.

In sum, the history of man's practice comprises the history of his struggle with nature, the history of the class struggle, the history of science. Owing to the necessity to live and struggle, men have thought about the reality of matter and its laws, have proved the correctness of materialism, and have found the necessary intellectual tool for their struggle – materialist philosophy. The higher the level to which social production develops, the greater the development of the class struggle, and the more scientific knowledge reveals the 'secrets' of nature, the greater the development and consolidation of materialist philosophy. Thus man can be delivered gradually from the dual and crushing oppression of nature and society...

CHAPTER 2: Dialetical Materialism

1. Dialectical materialism is the revolutionary arm of the proletariat... The Chinese proletariat, having assumed at the present time the historical task of the bourgeois-democratic revolution, must make use of dialectical materialism as its mental arm ... The study of dialectical materialism is even more indispensable for the cadres who lead the revolutionary movement, because the two erroneous theories and methods of work of subjectivism and mechanism frequently subsist among the cadres, and as a result frequently cause the cadres to go against Marxism, and to lead the revolutionary movement on to the wrong path. If we wish to avoid or correct such deficiencies, the only solution lies in conscious study and understanding of dialectical materialism, in order to arm one's brain anew.

2. The relations between the old philosophical heritage and dialectical materialism ... After the May 4th Movement of 1919, as a consequence of the conscious appearance of the Chinese proletariat on the political stage, and the rise in the scientific level of the country, a Marxist philosophical movement arose and developed in China. In its first period, however, the level of understanding of materialist dialectics within the materialist current of thought was rather weak, and mechanistic materialism influenced by the bourgeoisie, as well as the subjectivism of Deborin, were its principal components. Following the defeat of the revolution in 1927 the level of understanding of Marxism and Leninism progressed, and the thinking of materialist dialectics gradually developed. Just recently, because of the severity of the national and social crisis, and also because of the influence of the movement for liquidating deviations in Soviet philosophy, a broad movement of materialist dialectics has developed in China's intellectual circles.

Because of the backwardness of China's social development, the dialectical materialist philosophical currents developing in China today do not result from taking over and reforming our own philosophical heritage, but from the study of Marxism-Leninism. However, if we wish to ensure that dialectical materialist thought shall penetrate profoundly in China, and continue to develop, and shall, moreover, give firm direction to the Chinese revolution and lead it to final victory in the future, then we must struggle with all the old and rotten philosophical theories existing in China on the ideological front throughout the whole country, raise the flag of criticism, and in this way liquidate the philosophical heritage of ancient China. Only thus we can attain our goal.

3. The unity of world view and methodology in dialectical materialism. Dialectical materialism is the world view of the proletariat. At the same time it is the method of the proletariat for taking cognizance of the surrounding world, and the method of revolutionary action of the proletariat. It is the unity of world view and methodology . . .

4. The question of the object of materialist dialectics – what do materialist dialectics serve to study? Marx, Engels and Lenin all explained materialist dialectics as the theory of development . . .

Under the heading of the object of philosophy we must still solve another problem, namely the problem of the unity of dialectics, logic and epistemology . . .

Materialist dialectics is the only scientific epistemology, and it is also the only scientific logic. Materialist dialectics studies the origin and development of our knowledge of the outside world. It studies the transition from not knowing to knowing, and from incomplete knowledge to more complete knowledge; it studies how the laws of the development of nature and society are daily reflected more profoundly and more extensively in the mind of humanity. This is precisely the unity of materialist dialectics with epistemology . . .

The essence of the concept of development consists in

regarding laws as the reflection in and transplanting to our minds (moreover further elaborated in our minds) of the manifestations of the movement of matter...

Only by using materialism to arrive at a solution of the problem of the relations between existence and thought, only by taking one's stand on the theory of the reflection, can one arrive at a thorough solution to the problems of dialectics, logic and epistemology...

5. *On matter*. The very first condition for belonging to the materialist camp consists in recognizing the independent existence of the material world, separate from human consciousness – the fact that it existed before the appearance of humanity, and continues to exist since the appearance of humanity, independently and outside of human consciousness. To recognize this point is a fundamental premise of all scientific research.

How shall we demonstrate this? The proofs are extremely numerous. Humanity is constantly in contact with the external world and must, moreover, struggle fiercely against the pressure and resistance of the outside world (nature and society). Moreover, we not only must, but can overcome this pressure and resistance. All of these real circumstances of the social practice of humanity, as manifested in the historical development of human society, are the best proof [of the existence of the material world]. China does not doubt the objective existence of Japanese imperialism which has invaded our country, nor of the Chinese people themselves. The students of the Anti-Japanese Military-Political University also do not doubt the objective existence of this university and of the students themselves...

If we consider this thing known as consciousness in the light of thoroughgoing materialism (that is to say in the light of materialist dialectics), then what we call consciousness is nothing else but a form of the movement of matter, a particular characteristic of the material brain of humanity; it is that particular characteristic of the material brain which causes the material processes outside consciousness to be reflected in consciousness. From this we see that when we distinguish matter from consciousness and when, moreover, we oppose them one to another, this is only conditional; that is to say, it has meaning only from the standpoint of epistemology...

In a word, matter is everything in the universe. 'All power belongs to Ssu-Ma I.' We say, 'All power belongs to matter.' This is the source of the unity of the world...

6. On movement (*on development*). The first fundamental principle of dialectical materialism lies in its view of matter ... This principle of the unity of the world has already been explained above in discussing matter.

The second fundamental principle of dialectical materialism lies in its theory of movement (or theory of development). This means the recognition that movement is the form of the existence of matter, an inherent attribute of matter, a manifestation of the multiplicity of matter. This is the principle of the development of the world. The combination of the principle of the development of the world with the principle of the unity of the world, set forth above, constitutes the whole of the world view of dialectical materialism. The world is nothing else but the material world in a process of unlimited development...

Dialectical materialism's theory of movement is in opposition first of all with philosophical idealism, and with the theological concepts of religion. The fundamental nature of all philosophical idealism and religious theology derives from their denial of the unity and material nature of the world, and in imagining that the movement and development of the world takes place apart from matter, or took place at least in the beginning apart from matter, and is the result of the action of spirit, God, or divine forces. The German idealist philosopher, Hegel, held that the present world results from the development of the so-called 'world idea'. In China the philosophy of the Book of Changes, and the metaphysics of the Sung and the Ming, all put forward idealist views of the development of the universe. Christianity says that God created the world, Buddhism and all of China's various fetishist religions attribute the movement and development of all the myriad phenomena (*wan wu*) of the universe to spiritual forces. All of these doctrines which think about movement apart from matter are fundamentally incompatible with dialectical materialism...

Dialectical materialism ... considers that rest or equilibrium are merely one element of movement, that they are merely one particular circumstance of movement. ... A sentence popular with the metaphysical thinkers of ancient China, 'Heaven does not change and the Way also does not change,' corresponds to ... a theory of the immobility of the universe. ... In their view, the basic nature of the universe and of society was eternally unchanging. The reason why they adopted this attitude is to be found primarily in their class limitations. If the feudal landlord class had recognized that the basic nature of the universe and of society is subject to movement and development, then most certainly they would have been pronouncing in theory a death sentence on their own class. The philosophies of all reactionary forces are theories of immobilism. Revolutionary classes and the popular masses have all perceived the principle of the development of the world, and consequently advocate transforming society and the world; their philosophy is dialectical materialism...

The cause of the transformation of matter is to be found not without, but within. It is not because of the impulsion of external mechanical forces, but because of the existence within the matter in question of two components different in their nature and mutually contradictory which struggle with one another, thus giving an impetus to the movement and development of the matter. As a result of the discovery of the laws of such movement and transformation, dialectical materialism is capable of enlarging the principle of the material unity of the world, extending it to the history of nature and society. Thus, not only is it possible to investigate the world considered as matter in perpetual movement, but the world can also be investigated as matter endlessly in movement from a lower form to a higher form. That is to say, it is possible to investigate the world as development and process...

Dialectical materialism investigates the development of the world as a progressive movement from the inorganic to the organic, and from thence to the highest form of the movement of matter (society)...

What we have just discussed is the theory of the movement of the world, or the principle of the development of the world, in accordance with dialectical materialism. This doctrine is the essence of Marxist philosophy. It is the world view and methodology of the proletariat. If the proletariat and all revolutionaries take up this consistently scientific arm, they will then be able to understand this world, and transform this world.

II · D On practice[1]

... A Marxist regards human productive activity as the most fundamental practice determining all other human activities ...

According to the Marxist, man's activity in social production develops step by step from a low stage to a high stage, and consequently man's knowledge, whether of nature or of society, also develops step by step from a low stage to a high stage, viz., from the elementary to the advanced, from the one-sided to the many-sided. For a very long period in human history, people were necessarily limited to a one-sided understanding of the history of society. This was due on the one hand to the constant distortion of it by the exploiting classes with their biased views, and on the other to the small scale of production that limited the scope of the people. Not until the modern proletariat appeared, along with the greatly increased productive forces of big industry, did man begin to have a comprehensive and historical understanding of the development of society and turn his knowledge of society into a science – the science of Marxism ...

Marxist philosophy, dialectical materialism, has two outstanding characteristics. One is its class nature: It openly declares itself to be in the service of the proletariat. The other is its practicality: It emphasizes the dependence of theory on practice, practice being the foundation of theory, which in turn serves practice ...

At first man sees practice only as the external aspect of things, their individual aspects, and their external relations to each other ...

1. Extracted from an article written in July 1937, and published in 1950 (*Hsüan-chi*, I, pp. 281–96).

Available translations: *Selected Works*, I, pp. 295–309.

With the continuation of man's social practice, the sensations and images of a thing are repeated innumerable times, and then a sudden change in the cognitive process takes place, resulting in the formation of concepts. Concepts as such no longer represent the external aspect of things, their individual aspects, or their external relations. Through concepts man comes to grasp a thing in its entirety, its essence, and its internal relations. Conception is not only quantitatively but also qualitatively different from perception. ... This is the second stage of knowledge. ... In the complete process of knowing a thing, this stage of conception, judgement, and inference is more important than the first stage. It is the stage of rational knowledge. The real task of cognition is to arrive at thought through perception, at a gradual understanding of the internal contradictions of objective things, their laws, the internal relations between this and that process, that is, a rational knowledge...

If anybody wants to know something, he cannot do otherwise than come into contact with that thing, that is to live (practise) in its setting. In a feudal society, one cannot know beforehand the laws of capitalist society, because, capitalist society not yet having appeared, there cannot be any practice appropriate to it. Marxism can only be the product of capitalist society. In the capitalist age of free competition, Marx could not know concretely beforehand some of the special laws of the age of imperialism, because this age, the last stage of capitalism, had not yet arrived and there was no practice appropriate to it. Only Lenin and Stalin could shoulder this task. Aside from their genius, the factor that enabled Marx, Engels, Lenin, and Stalin to formulate their theories was their personal participation in the practice of the class struggle and scientific experiments of their time. Without such participation, not even a genius can succeed in such a task...

All true knowledge originates from direct experience. But no one can directly experience everything. As a matter of fact, most of our knowledge is of things indirectly experienced. All our knowledge of ancient times and foreign lands belongs to this category, but for the ancients and foreigners it is knowledge of things directly experienced...

All knowledge originates in man's perception of the external world through his sensory organs. If one denies perception, direct experience, and personal participation in the practice of changing existing conditions, one is not a materialist . . .

The knowledge of capitalist society the proletariat had in the first period of its practice, the period of machine-smashing and spontaneous struggle, was only perceptual knowledge. It was knowledge merely of the individual aspects and the external relations of the various phenomena of capitalism. At that time, the proletariat was what is called a 'class in itself'. But when this class reached the second period of its practice, the period of conscious, organized economic and political struggle, there emerged the ideology of Marxism as a result of the practice of this class, its experience of constant and continuous struggle, and the scientific summary and integration of all these experiences by Marx and Engels. When this ideology was used to educate the proletariat and enabled it to understand the essence of capitalist society, the relation of exploitation between classes, and its own historic task, it transformed itself into a 'class for itself'.

The Chinese people came to know imperialism in the same way. The first stage was one of perceptual knowledge of the appearance of things. It was marked with the indiscriminately anti-foreign struggle of the T'aip'ing [1850–64] and the Boxer [1900] revolutionary movements. It was only in the second stage that the Chinese people arrived at rational knowledge. They saw the internal and external contradictions of imperialism. They also saw the essence of the exploitation of China's broad masses by imperialism in alliance with the comprador and the feudal classes. This kind of knowledge came to light only about the time of the May 4th Movement of 1919 . . .

If anyone thinks that knowledge can stop at the low stage of perception and that perceptual knowledge alone, not rational knowledge, is reliable, then one repeats the historical mistake of empiricism . . .

Rational knowledge depends upon perceptual knowledge and perceptual knowledge has to develop into rational knowledge. This is the epistemology of dialectical materialism. . .

But at this point the process of cognition is not yet concluded. If we stop the discussion of the dialectical-materialist process of cognition merely at rational knowledge, we have touched upon only half the problem. And from the point of view of Marxist philosophy, we have only touched upon the less important half. What Marxist philosophy considers most important is not understanding the laws of the external world and thereby explaining it, but actively changing the world by applying the knowledge of objective laws. Theory is important from the viewpoint of Marxism; its importance is shown in Lenin's statement: 'Without a revolutionary theory there can be no revolutionary movement.' [Lenin, *What Is To Be Done?*, p. 35.] But when Marxism emphasizes theory, it does so precisely and only because it can guide our actions. ... The active effect of cognition manifests itself not only in the active leap from perceptual knowledge to rational knowledge, but also, and more importantly, in the leap from rational knowledge to revolutionary practice. ... The problem whether theories correspond to objective realities is not entirely solved in the process of cognition from the perceptual to the rational as mentioned before; there it cannot be entirely solved. The only way to solve this problem completely is to redirect rational knowledge to social practice and apply theory to practice to see whether it can achieve preconceived results. ... The reason why Marxism-Leninism is regarded as truth lies in the fact that it was not only scientifically formulated by Marx, Engels, Lenin, and Stalin, but also subsequently verified in the revolutionary practice of class struggle and national struggle. ... Stalin rightly said: 'Theory becomes aimless if it is not connected with revolutionary practice, just as practice gropes in the dark if its path is not illumined by revolutionary theory.' [Stalin, *Foundations of Leninism*, p. 28.] ...

The development of the objective process is full of contradictions and conflicts, and so is the development of the process of man's cognition. All the dialectical movements of the external world can sooner or later find their reflection in man's knowledge. The process of coming into being, development, and elimination in social practice as well as in human knowledge is infinite. As the practice of changing objective existing conditions based upon certain ideas, theories, plans, or programmes moves forward step by step, man's knowledge of objective reality also deepens step by step. The movement or change of the world of objective realities is never finished, hence man's recognition of truth through practice is also never complete. Marxism-Leninism has in no way put an end to the discovery of truths, but continually [*pu-tuan-ti*] blazes the path toward the recognition of truths through practice. Our conclusion is that we stand for the concrete and historical unity of the subjective and the objective, of theory and practice, of knowledge and action . . .

The discovery of truths through practice, the verification and the development of them through practice, the active development of perceptual knowledge into rational knowledge and, by means of rational knowledge, the active direction of revolutionary practice and the reconstruction of the subjective and the external world – practice, knowledge, more practice, more knowledge, and the repetition *ad infinitum* of this cyclic pattern, and with each cycle, the elevation of the content of practice and knowledge to a higher level – such is the epistemology of dialectical materialism, such is its theory of the unity of knowledge and action.

II · E On contradiction[1]

The law of contradiction in things, that is, the law of the unity of opposites, is the most basic law in materialist dialectics. Lenin said: 'In its proper meaning, dialectics is the study of the contradiction within the very essence of things.' [Lenin, *Philosophical Notebooks*, Russian ed., p. 263.] . . .

1. The two world outlooks. In the history of human knowledge, there have always been two views concerning the laws of development of the world: the metaphysical and the dialectical, which form two mutually opposed world outlooks . . .

The so-called metaphysical world outlook or the world outlook of vulgar evolutionism consists in looking at the world from an isolated, static, one-sided viewpoint. It regards all things in the world, their forms and their species, as for ever isolated from one

1. Extracted from an article written in 1937 and published in 1952 (*Hsüan-chi* [first edition], II, pp. 765–805).

Available translations: *Selected Works*, I, pp. 311–47.

another and for ever changeless. Whatever change there is constitutes merely an increase or decrease in quantity or a transposition in space. Moreover, the cause of such an increase or decrease or transposition does not lie inside things but outside them, that is, propulsion by external forces . . .

Contrary to the metaphysical world outlook, the materialist-dialectical world outlook advocates the study of the development of things from the inside, from the relationship of one thing to other things, namely, that the development of things should be regarded as their internal and necessary self-movement, that a thing in its movement and the things surrounding it should be regarded as interconnected and interacting upon each other. The basic cause of development of things does not lie outside but inside them, in their internal contradictions. . . . Similarly, social development is chiefly due . . . to the development of the internal contradictions in society, namely, the contradiction between the productive forces and the relations of production, the contradiction between the classes, and the contradiction between the old and the new; it is the development of these contradictions that propels society and starts the process of the supersession of the old society by a new one . . .

The dialectical world outlook had already emerged in ancient times both in China and in Europe. But ancient dialectics was somewhat spontaneous and naïve; being based upon the social and historical conditions of those times, it was not formulated into an adequate theory, hence it could not fully explain the world and was later supplanted by metaphysics. The famous German philosopher Hegel, who lived from the late eighteenth century to the early nineteenth, made very important contributions to dialectics, but his is idealist dialectics. It was not until Marx and Engels, the great men of action of the proletarian movements, made a synthesis of the positive achievements in the history of human knowledge and, in particular, critically absorbed the rational elements of Hegelian dialectics and created the great theory of dialectical materialism and historical materialism that a great, unprecedented revolution took place in the history of human knowledge. Later, Lenin and Stalin further developed this great theory. Introduced into China, this theory immediately brought about tremendous changes in Chinese thought.

This dialectical world outlook chiefly teaches man how to observe and analyse skilfully the movement of contradictions in various things and, on the basis of such analysis, to point out the methods of solving the contradictions. Consequently, it is of paramount importance for us to understand concretely the law of contradiction in things.

2. The universality of contradiction. ... The universality or absoluteness of contradiction has a twofold meaning. One is that contradiction exists in the process of development of all things and the other is that in the process of development of each thing a movement in contradictions exists from beginning to end ...

There is nothing that does not contain contradiction; without contradiction there would be no world ...

Objective contradictions are reflected in subjective thought, constituting the contradictory movement of concepts, impelling the development of thought, and ceaselessly solving the problems that arise in man's thinking ...

3. The particularity of contradiction. ... The particular quality possessed by each form is determined by its own particular contradiction. ... Every form of society, every mode of thought has its particular contradiction and particular quality ...

Qualitatively different contradictions can only be solved by qualitatively different methods. For example, the contradiction between the proletariat and the bourgeoisie is solved by the method of socialist revolution; the contradiction between the great masses of the people and the feudal system is solved by the method of democratic revolution; the contradiction between colonies and imperialism is solved by the method of national revolutionary war; the contradiction between the working class and the peasantry in socialist society is solved by the method of collectivization and mechanization of agriculture; the contradiction within the Communist Party is solved by the method of criticism and self-criticism; the contradiction between society and nature is solved by the method of developing the productive forces. Processes change, old processes and old contradictions disappear, new processes and new contradictions emerge, and the methods of solving contradictions differ accordingly ...

In studying a problem, we must guard against . . . one-sidedness. . . . One-sidedness consists in not knowing how to look at a problem as a whole. For example: understanding only China but not Japan; understanding only the Communist Party but not the Kuomintang; understanding only the proletariat but not the bourgeoisie; understanding only the peasants but not the landlords; understanding only the favourable conditions but not the adverse; understanding only the past but not the future; understanding only the unit but not the totality; understanding only the defects but not the achievements; understanding only the plaintiff but not the defendant; understanding only clandestine revolutionary work but not overt revolutionary work; and so on. In short, not understanding the characteristics of each aspect of a contradiction. . . . In *Water Margin*, Sung Chiang launched three attacks on Chu village and was twice defeated because he had no clear knowledge of the conditions and applied the wrong methods. Later he changed his methods by first conducting an investigation into the situation. As a result he learned about the intertwining roads; succeeded in disrupting the alliance between the Li, Hu, and Chu villages; and won final victory in the third battle after secretly infiltrating his own soldiers in disguise into the enemy's camp, a stratagem similar to that of the Trojan Horse of foreign legend. There are numerous examples of materialist dialectics in *Water Margin*, and the episode of the three attacks on Chu village can be considered the best. . . .

The basic contradiction in the process of development of a thing, and the quality of the process determined by this basic contradiction, will not disappear until the process is completed; but the conditions of each stage in the long process of development of a thing often differ from those of another stage. This is because, although the nature of the basic contradiction in the development of a thing or in the quality of the process has not changed, the basic contradiction assumes an increasingly intensified form in the various stages of the long developmental process. Besides, some of the numerous big and small contradictions determined or influenced by the basic contradiction become intensified, some are temporarily or partially solved or mitigated, and some emerge anew; consequently, the process reveals itself as consisting of different stages. If people do not pay attention to the stages in the process of development of a thing, they cannot properly deal with its contradictions ...

When Marx and Engels applied the law of contradiction in things to the study of the process of social history, they saw the contradiction between the productive forces and the relations of production; they saw the contradiction between the exploiting class and the exploited class as well as the resultant contradiction between the economic foundation and its superstructures, such as politics and ideology; and they saw how these contradictions inevitably lead to different social revolutions in different class societies.

When Marx applied this law to the study of the economic structure of capitalist society, he saw that the basic contradiction of this society is the contradiction between the social character of production and the private character of ownership. It is manifested in the contradiction between the organized character of production in individual enterprises and the unorganized character of production in society as a whole. The class manifestation of this contradiction is the contradiction between the bourgeoisie and the proletariat ...

Stalin analysed the universality of the contradiction in imperialism, showing how Leninism is Marxism of the imperialist era and the proletarian revolution, and he also analysed the particularity of tsarist imperialism as compared to the contradictions of imperialism in general, showing how Russia became the birthplace of the theory and tactics of the proletarian revolution and how in such a particularity is contained the universality of contradiction. This kind of analysis made by Stalin serves as a model in understanding the particularity and the universality of contradiction and their interconnexion ...

4. The principal contradiction and the principal aspect of a contradiction. In the developmental process of a complex thing there are many contradictions; among these, one is necessarily the principal contradiction whose existence and development determine or influence the existence and development of other contradictions ...

But can we, in any contradiction, whether primary or secondary, treat the two contradictory aspects as being equal? No, we cannot. In any contradiction, the development of the contradictory aspects is uneven. ... Of the two contradictory aspects, one must be primary and the other secondary. ... The quality of a thing is determined mainly by the principal aspect of the contradiction that has taken the dominant position.

But this state is not a fixed one; the principal and the non-principal aspects of a contradiction transform themselves into each other and the quality of a thing changes accordingly...

In capitalist society, the position of capitalism has changed from a subordinate one in the old era of feudal society into the dominant one, and the nature of society has also changed from feudalism into capitalism. In the new era of capitalist society, feudal forces, originally dominant, have become subordinate, and then gradually approached extinction ...

Some people think that this is not true of certain contradictions. They claim, for example, that in the contradiction between the productive forces and the relations of production, the productive forces are the principal aspect; in the contradiction between theory and practice, practice is the principal aspect; in the contradiction between the economic foundation and its superstructure, the economic foundation is the principal aspect – and that there is no change in their respective positions. This is the view of mechanistic materialism, not of dialectical materialism. True, the productive forces, practice, and the economic foundation generally manifest themselves as the principal and decisive factors; whoever denies this is not a materialist. But under certain conditions, such aspects as the relations of production, theory, and the superstructure in turn manifest themselves as the principal and decisive factors; this must also be admitted. When the productive forces cannot be developed unless the relations of production are changed, the change in the relations of production plays the principal and decisive role. ... When the superstructure – politics, culture, and so on – hinders the development of the economic foundation, political and cultural reforms become the principal and decisive factors. In saying this, are we running counter to materialism? No. The reason is that although we recognize that in the development of history as a whole it is material things that determine spiritual things and social existence that determines social consciousness, we also do and must recognize the reaction of spiritual things and social consciousness upon social existence and the reaction of the superstructure upon the economic foundation. This does not run counter to materialism; this is the avoidance of mechanistic materialism and the firm upholding of dialectical materialism ...

5. The identity and struggle of the aspects of a contradiction. Identity, unity, coincidence, inter-permeation, inter-penetration, inter-dependence (or inter-dependence for existence), inter-connexion or cooperation – all these different terms mean the same thing and refer to the following two conditions: First, each of the two aspects of every contradiction in the developmental process of a thing finds the presupposition of its existence in the other aspect and both aspects coexist in an entity; second, each of the two contradictory aspects, according to given conditions, tends to transform itself into the other. This is what is meant by identity ...

A contradictory aspect cannot exist in isolation. Without the other aspect that is opposed to it, each aspect loses the condition of its existence. Just imagine, can any of the aspects of all the contradictory things or contradictory concepts in the human mind exist independently? Without life, there would be no death; without death, there would also be no life. Without 'above', there would be no 'below'; without 'below', there would also be no 'above'. Without misfortune, there would be no good fortune; without good fortune, there would also be no misfortune. Without facility, there would be no difficulty; without difficulty, there would also be no facility. Without landlords, there would be no tenant-peasants; without tenant-peasants, there would also be no landlords. Without the bourgeoisie, there would be no proletariat; without the proletariat, there would also be no bourgeoisie. Without imperialist oppression of nations, there would be no colonies and semi-colonies; without colonies and semi-colonies, there would also be no imperialist oppression of nations. All opposite elements are like this. Because of certain conditions, they are on the one hand opposed to each other and on the other hand they are inter-connected, inter-penetrated, inter-permeated, and inter-dependent; this character is called identity . . .

What is the relation between identity and struggle?

Lenin said: 'The unity (coincidence, identity, equivalence) of opposites is conditional, temporary, transitory, relative. The struggle of mutually exclusive opposites is absolute, just as development and motion are absolute.' ['On Dialectics', *Selected Works*, XI, 82.]

What does this passage from Lenin mean?

All processes have a beginning and an end; all processes transform themselves into their opposites. The stability of all processes is relative, but the mutability manifested in the transformation of one process into another is absolute . . .

Now we can make a few remarks to sum up. The law of the contradiction in things, that is, the law of the unity of opposites, is the basic law of nature and society and therefore also the basic law of thought. It is the opposite of the metaphysical world outlook. It means a great revolution in the history of human knowledge. According to the viewpoint of dialectical materialism, contradiction exists in all processes of objective things and subjective thought and runs through all processes from beginning to end – this is the universality and absoluteness of contradiction. Contradictory things and each of their aspects respectively have their specific features – this is the particularity and relativity of contradiction. Contradictory things, according to certain conditions, are characterized by identity and consequently can coexist in an entity and transform themselves into their opposite – this again is the particularity and relativity of contradiction. But the struggle within the contradiction is ceaseless; it exists both when the opposites coexist and when they are transforming themselves into each other, and the struggle is especially manifest in the latter case – this again manifests the universality and absoluteness of contradiction . . .

III. External and Internal Contradictions – The Bourgeoisie Between Imperialism and the Revolution

This and the following chapter contain selections bearing on the two fundamental problems in the tactics of a Communist Party in a pre-industrial country: relations with the bourgeoisie and relations with the peasantry. It seems more logical to begin with the bourgeoisie, for, on the one hand, according to Marxist conceptions this class is the only one capable of contending with the proletariat for hegemony over the revolution at the current stage; and, on the other hand, it is in analysing the behaviour of the bourgeoisie in a colonial country that Mao Tse-tung made the most extensive use of the concept of contradiction.

Although Mao Tse-tung may not have made any strikingly original contributions to theories on relations with the bourgeoisie, he may nevertheless be considered something of an innovator, for he has successfully navigated the shoals on which Soviet policy in the under-developed countries has so often foundered – an excessively sectarian attitude and subordination to the bourgeoisie. The early excerpts, although still very far from a theoretical solution to this problem, already reveal the basic impulse that permitted him, once he had acquired more experience and a more thorough knowledge of Marxism, to find a practical solution. This basic impulse combined a fierce revolutionary temperament and a strong feeling for national unity. In his articles of 1923,[1] only the 'militarists' are excluded from this unity and from participation in the 'national revolution' against the foreigners. In these articles, Mao appeals to his '400 million brothers'. In 1926, he adopted an attitude that would be labelled 'leftist' in Leninist terms;[2] his affirmation that

1. See Texts III A and III B.
2. See Text III C.

'the attitude of the various classes in China toward the national revolution is virtually identical with the attitude of the various classes in Europe toward the social revolution' goes even further than Roy did at the Second Congress of the International, and in any case has nothing to do with Leninism. But Mao Tse-tung succeeds in combining this rather sectarian position with an appeal to national union by an ingeniously simple expedient: He evaluates the strength of the different classes exclusively on the basis of their numbers, thus minimizing the influence of the bourgeoisie and landowners, and ends with the slogan 'Three hundred and ninety-five millions, unite!'

Two short extracts from 1928 writings[1] merely repeat the theses of the International at that time. The basic idea, that of a bourgeois-democratic revolution under the hegemony of the proletariat, was to be further developed by Mao Tse-tung and constitutes the essence of his thinking on relations with the bourgeoisie; here it has simply been taken over from the resolutions of the International. The same is true of the ideas set forth in the 1930 selection about the relation of internal and external contradictions.[2]

The 1931 text attests to his hatred of the Kuomintang,[3] the political representative of the bourgeoisie, but does not contain any theories on the nature of the bourgeoisie. (This text, like the two which follow it, is not signed by Mao alone, but the style seems to be his.) In it, he proposes the 'united front from below', which constituted the line of the International at the time, in its purest form. His declaration of 1933 reveals the first signs of originality on the subject. Although not yet suggesting the possibility of an understanding with the Kuomintang, still less with Chiang Kai-shek, for a common struggle against Japan, he no longer asks the soldiers to kill their officers and to join the soviets, as he did in 1931. The appeal is rather to the 'armed forces', that is, to the generals who command them. The position set forth by him in 1934[4] is essentially the same. As Hsiao Tso-

1. See Text III D.
2. See Text III E.
3. See Text III F.
4. See Text III G.

liang has pointed out, this document constitutes one of the first signs announcing the Long March.[1]

Mao's report of 27 December 1935[2] is one of the few selections that I have taken from the current Chinese edition of the *Selected Works* in the absence of a more reliable source. There are two reasons for this. First, this speech marks a turning point and cannot be ignored. Aligning himself with the decisions of the Seventh Congress of the International, Mao for the first time sets forth a position akin to his present position on this question. Secondly, although I have not been able to find a contemporary publication of this speech, I have a text of the resolution adopted a few days earlier by the Central Committee of the Chinese Communist Party confirming the position attributed to Mao by the text published in the *Selected Works*. There are, however, a few nuances: the insults of Chiang Kai-shek are somewhat more frequent and more violent, and the resolution also uses the phrase 'a government of national defence', which is not found in Mao's speech. More important, it contains this statement on the role of the workers which is not to be found in Mao's speech and which clearly reflects the line of the International rather than Mao's ideas: 'If we wish to defeat Japanese imperialism and its running dogs, the Chinese traitors, we must obtain the support of the majority of the working class.'

Even before the official conclusion of the alliance with the Kuomintang, Mao made it quite clear that he saw the relations between the two parties as a struggle for hegemony.[3] The brief fragment 'The Kuomintang has a brilliant future'[4] (this is the original title of one of the two paragraphs of Mao's report from which this was excerpted) shows how far Mao was prepared to go in his policy of collaboration with the Kuomintang. But it also shows the limits of this policy. While leaving official leadership of the anti-Japanese war to the Kuomintang, the communists affirmed that they were the only ones who were capable of effectively mobilizing the masses. By this, they

1. Hsiao Tso-liang, op. cit., pp. 293–4.
2. See Text III H.
3. See Text III I.
4. See Text III J.

already indicated clearly where real power would ultimately lie.

I have selected a large number of texts spanning the earlier years in order to illustrate Mao's groping search for a satisfactory position on his relation with the bourgeoisie. Now, at one stroke, he defined his position, which he never abandoned. He developed it at some length in January 1940, in a famous text the title of which has become one of the key phrases in Mao's thought: 'On new democracy'. Although this book contains new ideas on cultural problems, on the purely political level it largely restates ideas Mao had set forth much more concisely a month earlier in 'The Chinese revolution and the Chinese Communist Party'.[1] This latter text makes crystal clear his two essential theses with regard to the bourgeoisie: broad collaboration, but hegemony of the proletariat from beginning to end of the revolution.

If he chose this moment to express himself with such frankness, it is partly because the international communist movement had entered into a 'leftist' phase as a result of the Nazi-Soviet Pact, but above all because of the strengthening of his own position. In 1945, in contrast, in his report to the Seventh Party Congress (later given the title 'On coalition government'), Mao made many more verbal concessions to the Kuomintang – concessions that were carefully eliminated from the current edition of his works and replaced by affirmations of the hegemony of the proletariat. But this was merely an episode, important in the history of China, but secondary to the main lines of the development of Mao's thought.

With 'The Chinese revolution and the Chinese Communist Party', Mao's position toward the bourgeoisie was definitively established. Certain questions, however, were left unanswered, not only for tactical reasons (although Mao is extremely skilful in this respect) but because the problems involved had not yet arisen in concrete terms. This chapter therefore closes with an extract from 'On people's democratic dictatorship', which

1. See Text III K. As noted above in the introduction, 'On new democracy' does, however, differ from 'The Chinese Revolution and the Chinese Communist Party' by the presence of a few formal (and manifestly insincere) statements recognizing the leading role of the Kuomintang.

describes the fate of the bourgeoisie after the conquest of power by the Chinese Communist Party.[1]

S.R.S.

III · A The role of the merchants in the national revolution[2]

The present *coup d'état* has roused the merchants, who have persistently ignored politics, and has led them suddenly to look up and pay attention to politics. This is most welcome news! ... The Shanghai Chamber of Commerce ... has published a declaration to the whole nation. The declaration says: 'We venture to proclaim with sincerity to the Chinese and the foreigners that from the fourteenth day of this month our people do not recognize any action of Ts'ao K'un and Kao Ling-wei, following their usurpation of political power ... as qualified to represent the country ...'

At the same time, the Chamber of Commerce resolved not to recognize the national assembly, which 'cannot represent the people's will', and resolved, moreover, to organize a democratic committee as the organ for dealing positively with the affairs of the nation. This action ... may be regarded as the first gesture of the merchants to intervene in politics and as a manifestation of the fact that the merchants, who remained silent for three years, now speak in awesome tones.

The present political problem in China is none other than the problem of the national revolution [*kuo-min ko-ming*]. To use the strength of the people to overthrow the militarists and foreign imperialism, with which the former are in collusion to accomplish their treasonable acts, is the historic mission of the Chinese people. This revolution is the task of the people as a whole. The merchants, workers, peasants, students, and teachers should all come forward to take on the responsibility for a portion of the revolutionary work; but because of historical necessity and

1. See Text III L.

2. Extracted from the article 'The Peking *coup d'état* and the merchants', published in *Hsiang-tao*, nos. 31–2 (11 July 1923), pp. 233–4.

Available translations: none.

current tendencies, the work for which the merchants should be responsible in the national revolution is both more urgent and more important than the work that the rest of the people should take upon themselves. We know that the politics of semi-colonial China is characterized by the fact that the militarists and the foreign powers have banded together to impose a twofold oppression on the people of the whole country. The people of the whole country naturally suffer profoundly under this kind of twofold oppression. Nevertheless, the merchants are the ones who feel these sufferings most acutely and most urgently. Everybody knows that the *likin* and customs duties are matters of life and death for the merchants. The pressing demands of the merchants to 'abolish the *likin* and raise the tariffs' are the expression of their most immediate interests. But abolishing the *likin* and raising the tariffs is not something that can be easily done, because abolishing the *likin* hurts the interests of the militarists and raising the tariffs hurts the interests of foreign imperialism. If the *likin* were abolished completely, the militarists would grow thinner day by day, and the merchants fatter. In that case, the merchants would need only to shout in order to overthrow the militarists. But the clever militarists definitely will not do such a foolish thing as to lift a stone in this way and crush their own feet. And if one were to increase considerably the tariffs on foreign goods, or even go so far as to abolish the tariffs fixed by the treaties and replace them by protective tariffs freely set by the Chinese themselves, thus removing the fetters encumbering the Chinese merchants, the industry and commerce of the country would develop rapidly and foreign goods would no longer be able to gain a foothold in China. The cunning foreign imperialists are even less likely to do such a foolish thing. . . . The positions of the foreign powers and the militarists on the one hand and the merchants on the other are truly incompatible. . .

The merchants have hitherto 'loved peace' and have never imagined that political transformation necessitated a revolution which could not be accomplished by a few telegrams in favour of 'the reduction of the number of soldiers, the application of the constitution, and financial reforms'. Still less did they imagine that revolution necessitated their personal participation, and that only by calling for the organization of all the people and creating a mass movement could a revolutionary force be brought into existence. They even went so far as to think that political reform did not require a political party and to call the revolutionary efforts of the Kuomintang superfluous. It is impossible to compare these juvenile and timid attitudes with the present situation without being convulsed with laughter. ... Judging from the actions of the Shanghai merchants in response to the *coup d'état*, we know that they have already changed their attitudes, cast away their pacifism, adopted revolutionary methods, drummed up the courage to shoulder responsibility for the affairs of the nation, and progressed rapidly ...

The Shanghai merchants have arisen and begun to act. We hope that the merchants outside of Shanghai will all rise up and act together. The present situation is extremely pressing, as though the fire were already singeing our eyebrows, and does not permit us to fall idly asleep once more. At present, we must unite the whole nation in order to carry out the revolution. Factionalism among the merchants cannot be tolerated. They must know that foreign powers and the militarists are the common enemies of all the merchants, as well as of the whole nation. Moreover, the advantages obtained after a successful revolution will be common advantages. It is essential to unite and struggle so as to overthrow the common enemy and assure the common interest. ... The broader the organization of merchants, the greater will be their influence, the greater will be their ability to lead the people of the whole country, and the more rapid the success of the revolution!

In conclusion, we have the following warnings for the merchants of the whole country: (1) The great cause of revolution is no easy matter, even less so in China, a country under the twofold pressure of the foreign powers and the militarists. The only solution is to call upon the merchants, the workers, the peasants, the students, and the teachers of the whole country, as well as all the others who constitute our nation and who suffer under a common oppression, and to establish a closely knit united front. It is only then that this revolution will succeed. ... We must no longer neglect the lesson to be learned from previous experience, when the Association of Merchants and Teachers refused participation of the workers. (2) Now that the merchants have already courageously taken the first step in the revolution, they must take the second step ... endeavour to move forward, and never stop until they have attained their goal. Above all, they must never stop on meeting a slight obstruction, or set out on the false path of making an agreement with the foreign powers and the militarists. Everyone must believe that the only way to save both himself and the nation is through the national revolution. Many revolutionary causes throughout history may serve as our reference and our guide. Circumstances call upon us to perform a historic task. We can no longer be negligent! To open a new era through revolutionary methods, and to build a new nation – such is the historic mission of the Chinese people. We must never forget it!

III · B The Chinese Government and the foreigners[1]

We often say: 'The Chinese Government is the counting-house of our foreign masters.' Perhaps there are some who don't believe this. We also say: 'The false show of friendship by foreigners (especially Englishmen and Americans) is merely a pretence of "amity" in order that they may squeeze out more of the fat and blood of the Chinese people.' Perhaps there are some who don't believe this either. Ever since the prohibition against the export of cotton was repealed owing to the opposition of the foreigners, it has been impossible not to believe what we have just said to some extent. Now that the foreigners have put pressure on the government to abolish the cigarette tax in Chekiang and other provinces, it is impossible not to believe it a little more...

Of the cigarettes produced by English and American companies, a small portion is imported from England, America, and Japan, and a large portion is manufactured by English and

1. Extracted from the article 'The cigarette tax', published in *Hsiang-tao*, no. 38, 29 August 1923, p. 288.
Available translations: none.

American merchants using Chinese tobacco and Chinese labour in factories set up in Shanghai, Hankow, and elsewhere in China. When the manufactured cigarettes leave the factory, a small tax is paid, in accordance with the 'treaties'. They are then transported in bulk to the various provinces, and China is not allowed again to tax them 'freely'. In Chekiang Province alone, the sale of cigarettes amounts to 'over ten million yüan a year'. There is no accurate total figure for the annual sale of cigarettes in the whole nation; estimating on the basis of sales in Chekiang alone, it must be above 200 million yüan. This is really 'frightening to hear'! I ask my 400 million brethren to ponder awhile: What does the 'amity' of the foreigners really mean?

The 'Council of Ministers' of the Chinese Government is really both accommodating and agreeable. If one of our foreign masters farts, it is a lovely perfume. If our foreign masters want to export cotton, the Council of Ministers thereupon abolishes the prohibition of the export of cotton; if our foreign masters want to bring in cigarettes, the Council of Ministers thereupon 'instructs the several provinces by telegram to stop levying taxes on cigarettes'. Again, I ask my 400 million brethren to ponder a little: Isn't it true that the Chinese Government is the counting-house of our foreign masters?

III · C Analysis of all the classes in Chinese society[1]

Who is our enemy? Who is our friend? He who does not know how to distinguish his enemies from his friends cannot be a revolutionary, yet at the same time it is no easy task to distinguish them. If the Chinese revolution, although it has been going on for thirty years, has shown such meagre results, it is not the goal but the

1. Extracted from an article of the same title published in *Chung-kuo nung-min*, I, no. 2, February 1926, pp. 1–13.

Available translations: There are no translations of the original version. A translation of a revised version of 1951 appears in *Selected Works*, I, pp. 13–21, but the revised version bears little resemblance to the original, and only the middle third of the following extract appears in current editions. The passages eliminated or revised are so numerous that it did not seem worthwhile to indicate these departures by italics.

tactics that have been wrong. The tactical error committed is precisely the inability to rally one's true friends in order to strike at one's true enemies. ... The revolutionary party is the leader of the masses. No army has ever been known to achieve victory when its chiefs have led it in a false direction, and no revolutionary movement has ever been known to succeed when the revolutionary party has led it in a false direction. ... The Manifesto of the First National Congress of the Kuomintang fixed our tactics and traced the boundary between our enemies and our friends. But this programme is very concise. If we wish to understand these important tactics, if we wish to distinguish our true friends, we must analyse in general terms the economic position of the various classes of Chinese society, their class nature, their numerical strength, and their attitude toward the revolution.

In any country, wherever it be under the heavens, there are three categories of people: upper, middle, and lower. If we analyse things in more detail, there are five categories: big bourgeoisie [*ta tzu-ch'an chieh-chi*], middle bourgeoisie [*chung-ch'an chieh-chi*], petty bourgeoisie, semi-proletariat, and proletariat. As regards matters in the countryside ... the big landowners are the big bourgeoisie, the small landowners are the middle bourgeoisie, the peasant-landholders are the petty bourgeoisie, the peasants who own part of their land and rent the rest are the semi-proletariat, and the agricultural labourers are the proletariat. In the cities, the big bankers, the big merchants, and the big industrialists are the big bourgeoisie; the moneylenders, the merchants of middling importance, the owners of small factories are the middle bourgeoisie; the shop-keepers and master craftsmen are the petty bourgeoisie; the shop assistants, the street vendors, and the handicraft workers are the semi-proletariat; and the factory workers and the coolies are the proletariat. These five categories of people all have a different economic position and a different class nature. Consequently, they adopt different attitudes toward the revolution, i.e., complete opposition to the revolution, partial opposition to the revolution, neutrality toward the revolution, participation in the revolution, or being the principal force in the revolution.

The attitude of the various classes in China toward the national revolution is more or less identical with the attitude of the various classes of Western Europe toward the social revolution.[!] This may seem strange, but in reality it is not strange at all. For basically today's revolution is the same everywhere, its goals and its techniques are similar – to overthrow world capitalist imperialism and to unite the exploited peoples and classes to wage war. This is the unique feature that distinguishes today's revolution from all other revolutions in history.

What are the conditions of the various classes in Chinese society?

1. The big bourgeoisie. In economically backward and semi-colonial China, the big bourgeoisie is the vassal of the international bourgeoisie, depending upon imperialism for its existence and development. ... The goals of this class and those of the national revolution are absolutely incompatible. From beginning to end, they side with imperialism and form the extreme counter-revolutionary group ...

2. The middle bourgeoisie. ... This class aspires to attain the position of the big bourgeoisie, but it suffers from the blows of foreign capital and the oppression of the warlords and cannot develop. This class has a contradictory attitude toward the national revolution. When it suffers from the blows of foreign capital and the oppression of the warlords, it feels the need of a revolution and favours the revolutionary movement against imperialism and the warlords; but when the proletariat at home takes a militant part in the revolution and the international proletariat abroad gives its active support, it senses a threat to the realization of its desire to move up into the class of the big bourgeoisie and becomes sceptical about the revolution. This class is what is called the national bourgeoisie. Politically, it stands for nationalism [*Kuo-chia chu-i*] – that is to say, the establishment of a state dominated by a single class, the national bourgeoisie. A self-styled 'true disciple' of Tai Chi-t'ao wrote. ... 'Raise your left fist to knock down imperialism and your right fist to knock down the Communist Party.' This remark illustrates the contradictory character of this class. ... Its aim of establishing a state under its own rule is impracticable, because the present world situation is one in which the two big forces, revolution and counter-revolution are engaged in the final struggle. Two huge banners have been raised by these two massive forces: One is the red banner of revolution, held aloft by the Third International and rallying all the oppressed classes of the world; the other is the white banner of counter-revolution held aloft by the League of Nations and rallying all the counter-revolutionary elements of the world. The intermediate class . . . will beyond doubt disintegrate rapidly, some sections turning left and joining the ranks of the revolution and others turning right and joining the ranks of the counter-revolution; there is no room for any 'independence' on their part. . . . There is a group of which it is impossible to say whether or not its members belong to the comprador class. As for the merchants, there are certainly many who distinguish very clearly between foreign and domestic merchandise, but there are also shops that display both domestic and foreign merchandise. As for the class [*sic*] of the intellectuals, there are among them some sons and younger brothers of small landlords who have gone to study in the capitalist countries of Asia and who show very clearly that alongside their national characteristics they have also acquired foreign characteristics. . . . People of this kind do not have an unmixed national-bourgeois nature; one might call them the 'semi-national bourgeoisie'. They constitute the right wing of the middle bourgeoisie, and as soon as the revolutionary struggle becomes intense, these people will certainly rally to the ranks of imperialism and the warlords and make splendid partners of the comprador class. The left wing of the middle bourgeoisie is composed of those who absolutely refuse to follow imperialism. . . . But it is very difficult to get rid of their 'pacifist' attitudes, which are quite empty of meaning but to which they have been attached for a long time, and they are often seized with terror when faced with 'Red' tendencies. This is why their intermittent collaboration with the revolution cannot last. Hence the Chinese middle bourgeoisie, whether its right wing or its left wing, contains many dangerous elements, and one absolutely cannot expect it to strike out resolutely on the path of revolution . . .

Who is our enemy? Who is our friend? We can now answer these questions. All the warlords, bureaucrats, compradors, big landlords, and the reactionary section of the intelligentsia, who constitute what is called the Chinese big bourgeoisie and who are in league with imperialism, are our enemies, our true enemies. The whole of the petty bourgeoisie, the semi-proletariat, and the proletariat are our friends, our true friends. As to the vacillating middle bourgeoisie, its right wing must be considered our enemy; even if it is not already, it will soon become so. Its left wing may become our friend, but it is not a true friend and we must be constantly on our guard against it. We must not allow it to create confusion in our ranks. How many are our true friends? There are 395 million of them. How many are our true enemies? There are a million of them. How many are there of these people in the middle, who may be either our friends or our enemies? There are four million of them. Even if we consider these four million as enemies, this only adds up to a bloc of barely five million, and a sneeze from 395 million would certainly suffice to blow them down.

Three hundred and ninety-five millions, unite!

III · D The hegemony of the proletariat in the bourgeois-democratic revolution[1]

China is in urgent need of a bourgeois-democratic revolution, and this revolution can be completed only under the leadership of the proletariat. Because the proletariat was not firm in asserting its leadership in the revolution of 1926–7, which started from Kwangtung and spread toward the Yangtse River, the comprador class, the local bullies, and the bad gentry seized hold of it and *changed the nature of* the revolution. The bourgeois-democratic revolution thus met with a defeat of *historical*

1. The first paragraph of the following extract is from a resolution of 5 October 1928, written for the Second Party Congress of the Hunan-Kiangsi border area. The second paragraph is from a report of 25 November 1928 to the Central Committee. In the *Selected Works*, these two texts are called, respectively, 'Why is it that red political power can exist in China?' and 'The struggle in the Chingkang Mountains'. *Hsüan-chi*, 1947, Supplement, pp. 102, 81.

Available translations: *Selected Works*, I, pp. 64, 97.

significance. This defeat was on the whole similar to the defeat of the Russian revolution in 1905 . . .

We fully agree with the resolution of the Communist International concerning China. The present stage in China is indeed still the stage of the bourgeois-democratic revolution. The completion of a thorough democratic revolution in China implies, externally, the overthrow of imperialist privileges so as to achieve complete liberation and national unification, and, internally, the liquidation of the authority of the comprador class in the cities, the completion of the agrarian revolution, the elimination of feudal relations in the villages, and the overthrow of warlordism, *which is the political manifestation of the local bullies and bad gentry.* It is only through such a democratic revolution that the real basis *for a workers' government may be established, so as to go forward to the socialist revolution . . .*

III · E The relation between external and internal contradictions[1]

. . . If it is asked whether the revolutionary upsurge [*kao ch'ao* – a term employed at the time to translate the Russian word *pod"em*, generally rendered into English as 'upsurge'. To Mao, who knew no foreign languages, the words no doubt suggested an idea close to their literal meaning in Chinese – 'high tide'.] will arise soon in China, we can give a definite answer only after studying carefully whether the contradictions leading to the revolutionary upsurge are really developing. Since contradictions are developing internationally between the imperialist countries, between the imperialist countries and their colonies, and between imperialism and the proletariat in these countries, the imperialists feel all the more urgently the need to contend for China. As the imperialists' contention for China intensifies, both the contradiction between the imperialist powers and the whole

1. Extracted from the 'Letter to Comrade Lin Piao' of 5 January 1930, more commonly known under the title 'A single spark can start a prairie fire', *Hsüan-chi*, 1947, Supplement, pp. 92–3.

Available translations: *Selected Works*, I, pp. 120–21.

Chinese nation, and the contradictions among the imperialists themselves, develop simultaneously in China. A daily expanding and intensifying mêlée thus ensues within the ruling class[1] in China, and the contradictions within the ruling class also develop daily. From these contradictions within the ruling class[2] – the mêlée among the warlords – ensues a pitiless increase of taxation and, as a consequence, the growing contradiction between the broad masses of taxpayers and the rulers is accentuated with every passing day. As a result of the contradictions between imperialism and Chinese capitalism[3] the latter fails to obtain concessions from the former; this leads to the aggravation of the contradiction between the Chinese bourgeoisie and the Chinese working class, the Chinese bourgeoisie having no other issue but to increase its exploitation of the working class.[4] The dumping of commodities by imperialism, the corrosion by Chinese mercantile capital, and the increase of taxation by the government bring about the sharpening of the contradiction between the landlords and the peasants, and the exploitation through rent and usury becomes heavier. Because of the pressure of foreign goods, the exhaustion of the purchasing power of the broad masses of the workers and peasants, and the increase of taxation by the government, dealers in domestic products and independent producers are forced daily further on the road to bankruptcy. . . . Once we understand all these contradictions, we shall see in how desperately precarious a situation and how anarchic[5] a state China finds herself. We shall see also how, inevitably, the revolutionary upsurge against the imperialists, the warlords, and the landlords will arise, and very speedily at that. All of China is littered with dry firewood, which will soon be kindled into a conflagration. The proverb 'A single spark can start a prairie fire' appropriately describes how the current situation will develop. We need only look at the development of the many workers' strikes, peasant

1. In 1951, Mao adopted a less neutral term, i.e., 'the various cliques of the reactionary rulers'.

2. Ibid.

3. In 1951, this was replaced by 'China's national industry'.

4. Here Mao inserted 'The Chinese workers put up resistance', in the 1951 edition.

5. In 1951, the un-Marxist term 'anarchic' was replaced by 'chaotic'.

uprisings, soldiers' mutinies, and merchants' and students' strikes to see that it will undoubtedly not take long for these 'sparks' to become 'a prairie fire'...

III · F A letter from the Chinese workers' and peasants' Red Army to our brothers the soldiers of the White Army on the subject of the forced occupation of Manchuria by Japanese imperialism[1]

Soldiers, Our Brothers!

Do not the Kuomintang militarists frequently tell you that it is your responsibility to 'defend the country and protect the people'? But look, at present Japanese imperialist troops have already occupied all the most important cities of Manchuria; they have massacred the toiling masses of workers and peasants in Manchuria and our soldiers with guns, cannons, and bombs, and already regard Manchuria as their colony. May I ask: How are the Kuomintang militarists carrying out their responsibility to 'defend the country and protect the people'? What do they tell you now?

Confronted by such violent behaviour on the part of Japanese imperialism, the Kuomintang militarists tell you 'we must not resist'; they tell you 'reasonable people should submit to violence'; they ask you to stretch out your neck and let the Japanese imperialist robbers butcher you; they ask you to submit peacefully and to become 'men without a country', slaves of Japanese imperialism. From this you can see that the Kuomintang militarists can only toady and capitulate to imperialism, can only act as the running dogs of imperialism. They cannot 'defend the country' nor can they 'protect the people'.

And yet, for the sake of enlarging their own spheres of influence, and of exploiting and butchering the Chinese people on a still larger scale, the Kuomintang militarists have, year after year, carried on a confused military struggle among themselves.

1. The following is the full text of a proclamation disseminated in 1931 under this title. Source: *Su-wei-ai Chung-kuo*, pp. 60–64.
Available translations: none.

And in the name of these wars among militarists, they bravely urge you to go to the battlefield to kill your own brothers, to destroy the lives and property of the people; they levy vexing and irregular taxes, impress men into coolie service and requisition horses; they suck the last drop of blood of the toiling masses; they butcher the revolutionary workers and peasants; they force people to grow opium to poison the masses; they have created calamities (floods, drought, and famine) without precedent throughout China; in exploiting and butchering the masses, they have shown great resolution and courage!

Especially when the masses of workers and peasants of our soviet area arose on their own initiative and drove out all the imperialists, overthrew the rule of the Kuomintang, confiscated all the land of the landlord class, enforced the eight-hour day, created the Workers and Peasants' Red Army and established the Soviet Government of the workers, peasants, and soldiers, all the militarists of the Kuomintang were mortally offended and manifested their resolution and courage. Once, twice, three times, they attacked us with the aid of the imperialists; they used airplanes, bombs, poison gas, cannons, and machine guns to butcher the people of the soviet area. If we do not destroy them root and branch, they will definitely not leave us alone, although their attacks have all been defeated through strenuous effort by us and by the masses. They are also extraordinarily brave in attacking the people's soviet political power and the People's Red Army!

Soldiers, our brothers! You have had enough of the deception and oppression of such militarists. Think for a moment. Why do you risk your lives on behalf of these militarists? Can you say you do so in order to live and feed your families? In reality, you yourselves often do not receive a copper of pay. You yourselves have neither enough to eat nor warm clothing. How can you feed a family? Your superior officers treat you like cattle, like cannon fodder; they want you to risk your lives to massacre your own worker and peasant brothers so that they can rise in rank and enrich themselves.

Soldiers, our brothers! You must think of another way out. There is a way out for you – revolution! You now have guns and cannons in your hands. First kill your reactionary superior officers; then unite with the workers, peasants, and all the toiling masses of your area to overthrow the fucking Kuomintang Government [*Kuomintang ti tiao cheng-fu*]; confiscate the land of the landlord class and distribute it among the poor peasants; confiscate the food and the houses of the wealthy and distribute them among the poor; let the workers do only eight hours of work a day; then, organize yourselves to run your own affairs. In this way, you will have created a government of the workers, peasants, and soldiers, that is, a Soviet Government. You will have become the armed force of the workers and peasants – the Workers' and Peasants' Red Army. If there is a Soviet Government and a Red Army near your garrison area, then when you have either taken prisoner or killed your reactionary superior officers present yourself there to join the Red Army. Only the Soviet Government and only the Red Army can protect the interests of the workers, peasants, and soldiers, overthrow the Kuomintang, overthrow imperialism, and really defend the people.

Soldiers, our brothers! Turn your guns in the opposite direction and fight to overthrow imperialism and the Kuomintang, which exploit, oppress, and butcher the Chinese labouring masses; fight to establish the Soviet Government and the Red Army of the workers, peasants, and soldiers! We your brothers, the hundreds of thousands of soldiers of the Red Army, truly welcome you to our ranks.

Down with imperialism and the Kuomintang!

Establish the Workers', Peasants', and Soldiers' Soviet Government!

Long live the Chinese Workers' and Peasants' Red Army!

Long live the victory of the Chinese Soviet Revolution!

Commander in Chief of the Chinese Workers' and Peasants' Red Army and Commander of the First Army: CHU TE

Chief of the Central Political Department of the Chinese Workers' and Peasants' Red Army: MAO TSE-TUNG

Commander of the Second Army of the Chinese Workers' and Peasants' Red Army: HO LUNG

Commander of the Third Army of the Chinese Workers' and Peasants' Red Army:

P'ENG TE-HUAI

General of the Third Army of the Chinese Workers' and Peasants' Red Army:

HUANG KUNG-LÜEH

25 September 1931

III · G Proclamation on the northward march of the Chinese workers' and peasants' Red Army to fight Japan[1]

The hateful Japanese imperialism ... intends to transform China into its colony and turn the people of all China into slaves without a country doomed to suffer eternally the massacre, rape, exploitation, and trampling of the Japanese bandits.

In their reaction toward the invasion of Japanese imperialism, the Kuomintang militarists – Chiang Kai-shek, Chang Hsüeh-liang, and all the others – have all capitulated and sold out. ... Under the slogan 'No strength to fight Japan', they have instituted ceaseless 'campaigns of encirclement' of the Soviet Government, which is the only anti-Japanese and anti-imperialist government in all China, and the Workers' and Peasants' Red Army. All this proves that the Kuomintang is the most faithful running dog of Japanese imperialism and that the Kuomintang militarists are the greatest traitors in all Chinese history. In the face of the ceaseless aggressions of Japanese imperialism, the Chinese Soviet Government has repeatedly called upon the Chinese masses to arm themselves for a national revolutionary war ... and it is preparing for a direct combat with Japanese imperialism. Under ... three conditions [for the three conditions, see the Introduction, p. 65] the Soviet Government is willing to conclude an agreement regarding military operations with any armed force anywhere in China. ... The Kuomintang attacks make it impossible for our Soviet Government to unite directly with the masses of all China and to wage a revolutionary war

1. Extracted from a proclamation published in 1934 under the same title. Source: *Min-tsu chan-hsien hsün-pao*, no. 2, 10 August 1935.
Available translations: none.

against Japanese imperialism together with the anti-Japanese volunteers in the North-east, in order to drive the Japanese imperialist bandits out of China . . .

Therefore, if the Soviet Government and the Workers' and Peasants' Red Army is to mobilize all its forces to fight Japanese imperialism, it can do nothing else but fight a bloody war with the millions of Kuomintang bandit troops that are attacking us. Only thus can it protect and maintain the free Soviet area that has already been saved from imperialist bondage, so that it will not again be trodden underfoot and sold out by the imperialist running dogs, the Kuomintang bandits. We will definitely not abandon the revolutionary anti-imperialist bases that have been created as a result of countless bloody fights with Kuomintang bandit troops. But the Soviet Government definitely cannot sit by and watch the ruin of the Chinese people at the hands of Japanese imperialism. . . . The Soviet Government and the Workers' and Peasants' Red Army, fearing no difficulties and with the greatest resolution, are sending an advance guard detachment northward to fight the Japanese. If this detachment should encounter any armed force that will accept the three conditions we have put forth, the main units of our Workers' and Peasants' Red Army will follow the advance guard to unite with all armed forces in China for a common struggle against Japan. . . . More concretely, the Soviet Government proposes:

1. To oppose resolutely the selling out . . . of the whole of China by the Kuomintang Government . . .

2. To proclaim the immediate breaking off of diplomatic relations with Japan . . .

3. To call upon the masses of all China to arm themselves with the weapons that can be found in the Kuomintang arsenals and factories as well as with all the imported weapons and to organize popular anti-Japanese volunteer units and guerrillas . . .

4. To confiscate all the enterprises and property of the Japanese imperialists and the Chinese traitors . . .

5. To organize everywhere anti-Japanese groups of the masses. . . . Let the running dogs of imperialism, the Kuomintang, let the Kuomintang traitors who are selling out their country, shout 'no strength to fight Japan'. By mobilizing the masses of all China

against Japan, by arming the masses of all China against Japan, by uniting the masses of all China against Japan, we shall gain the strength to overthrow Japanese imperialism and the band of traitors of the Kuomintang!

Chairman of the Provisional Central Government of the Chinese Soviets: MAO TSE-TUNG

Chairman of the Military Committee of the Chinese Workers' and Peasants' Red Army: CHU TE

15 July 1934

III · H On the tactics of fighting Japanese imperialism[1]

Comrades! A very great change has now taken place in the political situation. Our Party has defined its tasks on the basis of this change . . .

The main characteristic of the present situation is that . . . the Japanese imperialists . . . want to change the whole of China from a semi-colony shared among several imperialist powers into a colony monopolized by Japan. . . . In such circumstances, all classes and all political groups in China are faced with the following question: What is to be done? Resist? Surrender? Or vacillate between these two alternatives?

Now, let us see how the various classes in China answer this question.

Both the workers and peasants of China demand resistance . . .

The Chinese petty bourgeoisie also demands resistance. Have not the young students and the urban petty bourgeoisie already started a broad anti-Japanese movement? . .

But what of the national bourgeoisie, the comprador and landlord classes, what of the Kuomintang, when they are confronted with the question?

The big local bullies, the big bad gentry, the big warlords, the

1. Extracted from a report of 27 December, 1935, to a conference of Party activists, *Hsüan-chi*, I, pp. 139–56.

Available translations: *Selected Works*, I, pp. 153–78.

big bureaucrats, and the big compradors have long made up their minds. They have said and are still saying that revolution (of whatever kind) is after all worse than imperialism. They have formed a camp of traitors: for them such a question as whether or not they are to become slaves of a foreign nation does not exist, because they have already obliterated national demarcations and their interests are inseparable from those of imperialism; and their chief of chiefs is none other than Chiang Kai-shek...

The national bourgeoisie presents a complicated problem. This class took part in the revolution of 1924–7, but, badly frightened by the flames of that revolution, it subsequently went over to the side of the people's enemies, i.e., the Chiang Kai-shek bloc. The question is whether, under the present circumstances, the national bourgeoisie can change. We believe it can. ... The national bourgeoisie does not have the same feudal character as the landlord class; nor does it have the same comprador character as the comprador class. Within the national bourgeoisie there is a section of people who have more affiliations with foreign capital and Chinese landed interests, people who constitute its right wing, and we shall not for the time being speculate whether they can or cannot change. The problem lies with the sections that have no or comparatively little affiliation of this kind. We believe that in the new situation, when China is in threat of being reduced to a colony, the attitude of these sections of the national bourgeoisie can change. And the change is marked by their vacillation. They dislike imperialism on the one hand and fear the thoroughness of the revolution on the other, and thus vacillate between the two. ... But at certain stages of our struggle, one section of [the national bourgeoisie] can take part in the struggle. And the other section can pass from vacillation to neutrality ...

In making a general analysis of the attitude of the Chinese landlord class and bourgeoisie in this great upheaval, another aspect should be pointed out, namely, that even within the camp of the landlords and compradors there is no complete unity. This results from the circumstances of a semi-colony, i.e., circumstances in which many imperialist powers are contending for China. When our struggle is directed against Japanese imperialism, the running dogs of the United States or even Britain, obeying the varying tones of their masters' command, may engage in a veiled strife or even an open conflict with the Japanese imperialists and their running dogs . . .

Summing up the problem of class relations, we may say that, along with the basic change in the situation caused by the Japanese invasion of China proper, the relationship of the various classes in China has changed, with an increase in the strength of the camp of the national revolution and a decrease in the strength of the camp of the national counter-revolution . . .

What is the basic tactical task of the Party? It is none other than to form a broad national revolutionary united front . . .

If we say that our government has hitherto been one based on the alliance of the workers, peasants, and the urban petty bourgeoisie, then from now on it must be so transformed as also to represent the members of all other classes who are willing to take part in the national revolution.

For the present, this government's basic task is to oppose the attempt of Japanese imperialism to annex China. This government will broaden its scope of representation: Not only the representatives of those who are interested only in national revolution but not in the agrarian revolution may join the government; the representatives of those who will not oppose European and American imperialism because of their affiliations, but will oppose Japanese imperialism and its running dogs, may also join the government if they want to . . .

The Communist Party and the Red Army are not only acting at present as the initiators of the Anti-Japanese National United Front, but will inevitably become the powerful mainstay of the anti-Japanese government and anti-Japanese army, preventing the Japanese imperialists and Chiang Kai-shek from attaining their ultimate end in their policy of disrupting the national united front . . .

So long as the Communist Party and the Red Army live and grow, the Anti-Japanese National United Front, too, will live and grow. Such is the hegemony of the Communist Party and the Red Army in the national united front . . .

Why should we change the workers' and peasants' republic into a people's republic?

Our government represents not only the workers and peasants but the whole nation . . .

Beyond doubt, the people's republic does not represent the interests of the enemy classes. On the contrary, the people's republic stands in direct opposition to the jackals of imperialism, the landed gentry and the comprador class, and does not include them among the 'people'.[1] . . . The sum total of the interests of the workers, peasants, and other sections of the people constitutes the interests of the Chinese nation. Though the comprador and the landlord classes also live on Chinese soil, they do not care about the interests of the nation; their interests clash with those of the majority of the people. As we part company only with this small number of landlords and compradors and clash only with them, we have the right to call ourselves the representatives of the whole nation.

There is also a clash of interest between the working class and the national bourgeoisie. . . . But if the national bourgeoisie joins the united front against imperialism, then the working class and the national bourgeoisie will have interests in common. The people's republic will not, in the era of the bourgeois-democratic revolution, abolish non-imperialist and non-feudal private property, but will encourage the development of industrial and commercial enterprises of the national bourgeoisie rather than confiscate them. We shall protect any national bourgeois so long as he does not support the imperialists and traitors. In the stage of democratic revolution, a limit is set to the struggle between labour and capital . . .

In giving the urban petty bourgeoisie, the intellectuals, and other elements who support the anti-imperialist and anti-feudal programme the right to voice their opinion and to work in the government of the people's republic, the right to elect and to be elected, we are not jeopardizing the interests of the basic section of the masses – the workers and peasants. The essential part of our programme must be the protection of the interests of the basic section of the masses – the workers and peasants. The

1. This reference to the categories that compose the 'people', which echoes Mao's later ideas (cf. Text III L), may well have been added after the fact.

majority formed in this government by the representatives of the basic section of the masses, the workers and peasants, and the leadership and activities of the Communist Party in it, all ensure that the participation of the representatives of those people involves no danger. It is perfectly obvious that the Chinese revolution at the present stage is still a bourgeois-democratic revolution, not a proletarian-socialist one. Only the counter-revolutionary Trotskyites will talk such nonsense as that China has already completed her bourgeois-democratic revolution and that any further revolution can only be a socialist one. The revolution of 1924–7 was a bourgeois-democratic revolution that was not completed and failed. The agrarian revolution led by us from 1927 to the present is also a bourgeois-democratic revolution, because its task is to oppose imperialism and feudalism, not capitalism. The revolution will remain such for quite a long time to come.

The motive forces of the revolution are still, in the main, the workers, the peasants, and the urban petty bourgeoisie, but now the national bourgeoisie may be added. ... It is much more difficult and requires a good deal more time and effort for China than for Russia to complete her democratic revolution politically and economically.

III · I The stages in the development of the revolution[1]

In the case of a two-part essay, the second part can be written only after the first part has been completed. Resolute leadership of the democratic revolution is the condition for achieving the victory of socialism. We are fighting for socialism and thus are different from any revolutionary followers of the Three People's Principles. Our effort of today is directed towards the great objective of tomorrow; he who loses sight of this great objective

1. Extracted from a speech given on 7 May 1937, before a conference of Party delegates in Yenan, which appeared under the title 'Let us strive to draw the broad masses into the Anti-Japanese National United Front', *Chieh-fang*, 1 (2), May 1937, p. 19.

Available translations: *Selected Works*, I, pp. 290–91.

is no longer a communist. But he who relaxes his efforts today is not a communist either.

We advocate the theory of the transition [*chuan-pien*, which was the term used to translate the Russian term *pererastanie*, or 'growing over'. Lenin opposed this conception to Trotsky's 'permanent revolution', as did Mao in 1937. It is questionable, however whether this meant 'growing over' to Mao, or simply 'transition', in accordance with the literal meaning of the Chinese characters.] of the revolution, of the transition from a democratic revolution to a socialist orientation. The democratic revolution will undergo several stages of development, all under the slogan of a democratic republic, not that of a soviet regime. It is a long struggle from the hegemony of the bourgeoisie to the hegemony of the proletariat, a process of striving for leadership, which depends on the condition that the Communist Party raise the level of awareness and organization of the proletariat, the level of awareness and organization of the peasantry as well as the petty bourgeoisie.

The peasantry is the staunch ally of the proletariat; after it comes the petty bourgeoisie. It is the bourgeoisie that will contend with us for hegemony.

We depend on the strength of the masses and on our correct policies to overcome the vacillation and the lack of thoroughness of the bourgeoisie; otherwise the bourgeoisie will turn round and overcome the proletariat.

A sound and healthy transition (without bloodshed) is what we hope for and what we must fight strenuously for; the result will be decided by the strength of the masses.

We advocate the theory of the transition of the revolution, not the Trotskyite theory of permanent revolution [*pu-tuan ko-ming lun*] *nor semi-Trotskyite* '*Li Li-sanism*'. We stand for going through all the necessary stages of a democratic republic in order to arrive at socialism. We are opposed to tailism [translation of the Russian word *khvostizm*, invented by Lenin to stigmatize those Social Democrats who believed that the party should follow the workers rather than take them in hand and instil class consciousness.] but also to adventurism and precipitation.

We cannot agree with the Trotskyite approach, which rejects

the bourgeoisie and stigmatizes the alliance in the semi-colonial countries with the *revolutionaries* among the bourgeoisie as capitulationism simply because of the transitory nature of the bourgeoisie's participation in the revolution.[1] Such an alliance today with the revolutionary[2] group among the bourgeoisie is a bridge that has to be crossed on our way to socialism.

III · J The Kuomintang has a brilliant future[3]

... The Kuomintang and the Communist Party are the foundation of the Anti-Japanese United Front, but of these two it is the Kuomintang that occupies first place. Without the Kuomintang, it would be inconceivable to undertake and pursue the War of Resistance. In the course of its glorious history, the Kuomintang has been responsible for the overthrow of the Ch'ing, the establishment of the Republic, opposition to Yüan Shih-k'ai, establishment of the Three Policies of uniting with Russia, with the Communist Party, and with the workers and peasants, and the great revolution of 1926–7. Today it is once more leading the great anti-Japanese war. It enjoys the historic heritage of the Three People's Principles; it has had two great leaders in succession – Mr Sun Yat-sen and Mr Chiang Kai-shek; it has a great number of faithful and patriotic active members. All this should not be underestimated by our compatriots and constitutes the result of China's historical development.

In carrying out the anti-Japanese war, and in organizing the

1. The original text says simply 'provisional character of the bourgeoisie', which could be interpreted to mean that the bourgeoisie as a class is condemned to disappear. But it seems more likely in this context that Mao was thinking rather of the provisional character of the alliance between the proletariat and the bourgeoisie, and it is in this sense that he modified the text in 1951. We follow the latter version here.

2. The 1951 text speaks of the 'anti-Japanese' rather than the 'revolutionary' sector of the bourgeoisie.

3. Extracted from a report to the Sixth Plenum of the Central Committee of the Chinese Communist Party, in October 1938. The first half of this text comes from the portion of Mao's report omitted completely in the current edition of the *Selected Works*.

Available translations: See note to Text II A.

Anti-Japanese United Front, the Kuomintang occupies the position of leader and framework. ... Under the single great condition that it support to the end the war of resistance and the United Front, one can foresee a brilliant future for the Kuomintang ...

Comrades! There is a further point, pertaining to the proper position of the Chinese Communist Party in the national war. This is the question of the way in which the communists should become conscious of their own role and strengthen themselves, *in order to be in a position to assume their great responsibilities in the national war* ...[1]

The communists must display great activity in the national war, and this activity should manifest itself concretely in every domain. In other words, the communists should exercise the role of vanguard and model in every domain. ... In a war of long duration and amidst difficult conditions, only the communists, with[2] the other friendly parties and armies, and all the advanced elements of our people, can, by carrying out fully their role of vanguard and model, mobilize all the vital forces of the nation, *raise the level of the stragglers*, conquer all difficulties, and struggle to vanquish the enemy and to build a new China ...

III · K The Chinese revolution and the Chinese Communist Party[3]

What, after all, is the character of the Chinese revolution at the present stage? Is it a bourgeois-democratic or a proletarian-socialist revolution? Obviously, it is the former, not the latter.

Chinese society is still a colonial, semi-colonial, and semi-

1. The current version replaces the italicized words as follows: 'organize themselves in order to be in a position to lead this war and to achieve victory and not defeat'.

2. In the current version 'with' is replaced by 'in agreement with', a change which emphasizes the role of the communists.

3. Extracted from the last three sections of the final chapter of *The Chinese Revolution and the Chinese Communist Party*. Unlike the passages included in Chapter I of this anthology, this extract was written exclusively by Mao.

Available translations: See note to Text I B.

feudal society; the principal enemies of the Chinese revolution are still imperialism and the semi-feudal forces; the task of the Chinese revolution consists in a national revolution and a democratic revolution for overthrowing these two principal enemies; furthermore, the motive forces of this revolution include at times the *national bourgeoisie and even a part of the big bourgeoisie*, and, even if the big bourgeoisie betrays the revolution and becomes its enemy, the spearhead of the revolution will still be directed at imperialism and feudalism rather than at capitalism and capitalist private property in general. That being so, the character of the Chinese revolution at the present stage is not proletarian-socialist but bourgeois-democratic.

However, the bourgeois-democratic revolution in present-day China is no longer of the general, old type, which is now obsolete, but of the special, new type. This kind of revolution is developing in China as well as in all other colonial and semi-colonial countries, and we call it the new-democratic revolution. This new-democratic revolution is part of the world proletarian-socialist revolution; it resolutely opposes imperialism, i.e., international capitalism. Politically, it means the joint *revolutionary-democratic* dictatorship of several revolutionary classes over the imperialists and reactionary traitors, and opposition to the transformation of Chinese society into a society under bourgeois dictatorship. Economically, it means nationalization of all big capital and big enterprises of the imperialists and reactionary traitors, distribution of large landed property among the peasants, and at the same time assistance to private middle and small enterprises[1] without the elimination of the rich-peasant economy. Hence, while clearing the way for capitalism, this democratic revolution of a new type creates the precondition for socialism. The present stage of the Chinese revolution is a transitional stage between putting an end to the colonial, semi-colonial, and semi-feudal society and establishing a socialist society – a new revolutionary process, that of the new-democratic revolution. This process began only after World War I and the Russian October Revolution; it started in China with the May 4th Movement of 1919. A

1. Here the 1951 edition has the words 'general preservation of private capitalist enterprises'.

new-democratic revolution is a revolution of the broad masses of the people led by the proletariat and directed against imperialism and feudalism; *it is a revolution of the united front of several revolutionary classes.* China must go through this revolution before she can go forward to a socialist revolution;[1] otherwise, it is impossible.

This kind of new-democratic revolution differs greatly from the democratic revolutions in the history of European and American countries in that it results in the dictatorship of the united front of all revolutionary classes,[2] not in the dictatorship of the bourgeoisie. During the Anti-Japanese War, the anti-Japanese democratic regime that ought to be established[3] is a regime of the Anti-Japanese National United Front, which is neither a 'one-class dictatorship' of the bourgeoisie nor a 'one-class dictatorship' of the proletariat, but a 'joint dictatorship of several parties' belonging to the Anti-Japanese National United Front.[4] All those who stand for resistance to Japan and for democracy are qualified to share this political power, regardless of their party affiliations.

This kind of new-democratic revolution differs also from a socialist revolution in that it aims only at overthrowing the rule of the imperialists and reactionary traitors, but not at overthrowing any capitalist elements still able to take part in the anti-imperialist, anti-feudal struggles.

This kind of new-democratic revolution is in line with the revolution of the Three People's Principles as advocated by Sun Yat-sen in 1924 [in the Manifesto of the First National Congress of the Kuomintang]...

Since China's bourgeois-democratic revolution at the present stage is not a bourgeois-democratic revolution of the general, old type, but a democratic revolution of a special, new type – a new-

1. In 1951, Mao looked farther ahead, replacing 'socialist revolution' by 'socialist society'.

2. In 1951, Mao added 'under the leadership of the proletariat'.

3. In 1951, this was changed to read 'the political power built up in the anti-Japanese base areas under the leadership of the Chinese Communist Party'.

4. In 1951, Mao eliminated the term 'one-class dictatorship' and changed his definition of new democracy to 'a joint dictatorship of several revolutionary classes under the leadership of the proletariat'.

democratic revolution – and since the Chinese revolution is now taking place in the new international setting of the 1940s and 1950s, characterized by the rise of socialism and the decline of capitalism, on the eve of the Second Great Imperialist War and of the second great global revolution [this was standard communist terminology for World War II between the Nazi-Soviet Pact and the German invasion of the Soviet Union. For Mao's views on this theme, see Text IX E, pp. 394–400.], there can be no doubt whatever that the ultimate perspective of the Chinese revolution is not capitalism but socialism . . .[1]

It is an inevitable result of the victory of the democratic revolution in economically backward China that capitalism will develop to a certain degree. Of course, it is undeniable that this will be merely one aspect of the result of the Chinese revolution, not its whole outcome. The whole outcome of the Chinese revolution will be the development of the capitalist factors on the one hand and of the socialist factors on the other. What are the socialist factors? They are the growing political weight of the proletariat and the Communist Party in the whole country and the actual or possible recognition of the leadership of the proletariat and the Communist Party by the peasantry, the intelligentsia, and the petty bourgeoisie.[2] All these are the socialist factors. Together with the favourable international situation, they are bound to make it highly possible that the Chinese bourgeois-democratic revolution will finally steer clear of a capitalist future and head toward the realization of socialism . . .

The Chinese revolution as a whole involves a twofold task. That is to say, it embraces a revolution that is bourgeois-democratic in character (a new-democratic revolution) and a revolution that is proletarian-socialist in character. It embraces the twofold task of the revolution at both the present and the future stages. The leadership in this twofold revolutionary task rests on the shoulders of the party of the Chinese proletariat, the Chinese Communist Party, for without its leadership no revolution can succeed.

1. In 1951, Mao added 'and communism'.
2. Here Mao added 'the state enterprises of the people's republic and the cooperatives of the labouring people' in 1951.

The completion of China's bourgeois-democratic revolution (the new-democratic revolution) and its transformation into a socialist revolution once all the necessary conditions are present, that is the sum total of the great and glorious revolutionary task of the Chinese Communist Party. All members of the Party should strive for its accomplishment and should never stop half-way. Some immature communists think that the present task – the democratic revolution – is our only task, and that we do not have to face that of the socialist revolution at the future stage; or they think that the present revolution or the agrarian revolution is in fact the socialist revolution. It must be emphatically pointed out that both views are erroneous. Every communist must know that the Chinese Communist movement[1] as a whole is a complete revolutionary movement embracing the two revolutionary stages, democratic and socialist, which are two revolutionary processes differing in character, and that the socialist stage can be reached only after the democratic stage is completed. The democratic revolution is the necessary preparation for the socialist revolution, and the socialist revolution is the inevitable trend of the democratic revolution. And the ultimate aim of all communists is to strive for the final building of socialist society and communist society. We can give correct leadership to the Chinese revolution only on the basis of a clear understanding of both the differences between the democratic and socialist revolutions and their interconnexions.

Except for the Communist Party, none of the political parties, bourgeois or petty-bourgeois, is equal to the task of leading China's two great revolutions, democratic and socialist, to their complete realization. And the Chinese Communist Party, from the very day of its birth, has placed this twofold task upon its own shoulders and has strenuously fought for it for eighteen years.

A task like this is at once most glorious and most arduous. It cannot be accomplished without a Bolshevized Chinese Communist Party of nationwide scope and broad mass character, fully consolidated ideologically, politically, and organizationally. It is

1. This was replaced by 'revolutionary movement led by the Chinese Communist Party'.

therefore the duty of every communist to take an active part in building up such a Communist Party . . .

III · L The bourgeoisie and the people[1]

. . . 'You are autocrats.' My dear sirs, you are right, that is just what we are. All the experience the Chinese people have accumulated through several decades teaches us to enforce the people's democratic dictatorship – which one could also call people's democratic autocracy, the two terms mean the same thing – that is, to deprive the reactionaries of the right to speak and let the people alone have that right.

Who are the people? At the present stage in China, they are the working class, the peasantry, the urban petty bourgeoisie, and the national bourgeoisie. These classes, led by the working class and the Communist Party, unite to form their own state and elect their own government; they enforce their dictatorship over the running dogs of imperialism – the landlord class and bureaucrat-bourgeoisie, as well as the representatives of those classes, the Kuomintang reactionaries and their accomplices – suppress them, allow them only to behave themselves and not to be unruly in word or deed. . . . Democracy is practised within the ranks of the people, who enjoy the rights of freedom of speech, assembly, association, and so on. The right to vote belongs only to the people, not to the reactionaries. The combination of these two aspects, democracy for the people and dictatorship over the reactionaries, is the people's democratic dictatorship . . .

The people's democratic dictatorship is based on the alliance of the working class, the peasantry, and the urban petty bourgeoisie, and mainly on the alliance of the workers and the peasants, because these two classes comprise eighty to ninety per cent of China's population. These two classes are the main force in overthrowing imperialism and the Kuomintang reactionaries.

1. Extracted from 'On the people's democratic dictatorship', 1949. *Hsüan-chi*, IV, pp. 1480, 1483–4.

Available translations: *Selected Works*, IV, pp. 417–18, 421–2.

The transition from new democracy to socialism also depends mainly upon their alliance.

The people's democratic dictatorship needs the leadership of the working class. For it is the working class that is most far-sighted, most selfless, and most thoroughly revolutionary. The entire history of revolution proves that without the leadership of the working class revolution fails and that with the leadership of the working class revolution triumphs. In the epoch of imperialism, no other class anywhere can lead a genuine revolution to victory. This is clearly proved by the fact that the many revolutions led by China's petty bourgeoisie and national bourgeoisie all failed.

The national bourgeoisie at the present stage is of great importance. Imperialism, a most ferocious enemy, is still with us. China's modern industry still forms a very small proportion of the national economy. . . . If China is to counter imperialist oppression and raise her backward economy to a higher level, she must utilize all the factors of urban and rural capitalism that are beneficial to the national economy and the people's livelihood; and we must unite with the national bourgeoisie in common struggle. Our present policy is to regulate capitalism, not to destroy it. But the national bourgeoisie cannot be the leader of the revolution, nor should it have the chief role in state power. The reason it cannot be the leader of the revolution and should not have the chief role in state power is that the social and economic position of the national bourgeoisie determines its weakness; it lacks foresight and sufficient courage and many of its members are afraid of the masses.

Sun Yat-sen advocated 'arousing the masses of the people' or 'giving assistance to the peasants and workers'. But who is to 'arouse' them or 'give assistance' to them? Sun Yat-sen had the petty bourgeoisie and the national bourgeoisie in mind. As a matter of fact, they cannot do so. Why did forty years of revolution under Sun Yat-sen end in failure? Because in the epoch of imperialism, the petty bourgeoisie and the national bourgeoisie cannot lead any genuine revolution to victory . . .

IV. The Peasantry and Working-Class Leadership

The problem of the respective roles of the workers and the peasants, like that of the relations between the revolutionary forces and the national bourgeoisie, is one of the basic problems of the Leninist strategy of the revolution in the underdeveloped countries. It constitutes a crucial point around which revolve the controversies over the orthodoxy of Mao's peasant strategy.

The first text in this chapter belongs to a period when Mao Tse-tung had begun the study of Marxism but did not yet consider himself a Marxist. Li Jui gives a summary of this article, including some textual citations, which attributes to Mao the idea that the workers and peasants should constitute the basis of the 'great union of the popular masses'. He also affirms that Mao said this method of struggle was invented by 'a German, Marx'. Unfortunately, a comparison of Li Jui's presentation of this text with certain other sources, and in particular with a facsimile of part of the article, shows that he does not hesitate to modify the wording of the original when it does not serve his purposes.[1] I am therefore inclined to doubt that Mao's ideas in 1919 were as precise as this. The article 'The great union of the popular masses' belongs rather to Mao's 'populist' phase, when he wished to unite the whole of the Chinese people against the tiny minority of 'aristocrats' and 'capitalists', but had not yet clearly distinguished the role of each social category in the 'great union' which he advocated.

The later texts contained in this chapter do deal specifically with the question of the respective roles of these two classes and with the leading role of the workers. It will be noted that this leading role is not explicitly recognized in the original version of

1. For an example, see the note on the sources of this text at the end of the bibliography.

Text IV C, the 'Analysis of all the classes in Chinese society' of February, 1926, and that the formula was inserted only in 1951. Similarly, as I have already pointed out, all the references to the leading role of the working class or the Communist Party were added later to the 'Report of an investigation into the peasant movement in Hunan'. At the same time, Mao Tse-tung has deleted many of the passages that give the poor peasants exclusive credit for the revolution. Several of these references occur in the part of the Hunan Report included in Text IV E, particularly the reference to 'the leadership of the poor peasants'. In 1929, on the other hand, conforming to the ruling orthodoxy, Mao Tse-tung voiced the principle of working-class direction, although he affirmed at the same time that there would be no disadvantage if the *strength* of the peasants surpassed that of the workers. His interpretation of this doctrine in practice reduced 'working-class leadership' to a fiction.[1] Text III D, in the preceding chapter, recognized the hegemony of the proletariat over the revolution, and such affirmations were common during the whole Kiangsi period, when the Soviet Government presided over by Mao Tse-tung was officially characterized by Lenin's formula of a 'dictatorship of the workers and peasants'. But this constituted the repetition of formulas learned by rote rather than the manifestation of Mao's own thinking. Only in 1935 did he really begin to use the categories of Marxist thought in an original manner.

The previous chapter illustrates the evolution of his ideas on the role of the proletariat, i.e., the Communist Party, and its relation to the bourgeoisie during the years 1935–49. The present chapter contains only one text dealing explicitly with the relations between the peasants and the workers, taken from 'The Chinese revolution and the Chinese Communist Party', which fixes once and for all the basic outlines of Mao's thought on the strategy of the Chinese revolution down to the conquest of power.[2] In a sense the two texts of 1926,[3] as well as the extracts from the 'Report of an Investigation into the Peasant Movement in Hunan',[4] are

1. See Text IV F.
2. See Text IV H.
3. See Texts IV B and IV D.
4. See Text IV E.

more revealing than this explicit analysis. On the one hand, they show Mao Tse-tung's preoccupation with the revolutionary strength of the peasants, to whom he attributed the capacity to act autonomously in their own sphere. This is particularly clear in the Hunan Report. But at the same time, these three texts give us a picture of a Mao instinctively drawn toward a Leninist attitude on the means and techniques of revolutionary action even before he had really understood Lenin's theses on the role of the various classes in the revolution, let alone assimilated them. One finds here an emphasis on the importance of *organization*, not only in the Hunan Report, but also in the 1926 article on the peasantry of Kiangsu and Chekiang. There is also an insistence on the priority of politics over economics, which is also one of the cornerstones of Lenin's system.

Side by side with this implicit Leninism, this natural tendency to adopt a Leninist attitude on the role of organization and of force in the revolution, there is also a striking manifestation of the Chinese and tradition-bound side of Mao's personality. One might point out particularly the passages praising the *éléments déclassés* – bandits, robbers, and even prostitutes – as a revolutionary force. There is certainly something of the admiration for the outlaw, for the men who find themselves excluded from an unjust society and in conflict with society, which Mao absorbed from the famous novel *All Men Are Brothers* and which manifests itself also in the appeal to the *Ko Lao Hui*,[1] with its reference to popular heroes. Incidentally, it is interesting to note that the passage in Text IV B on the *éléments déclassés* has been deprived of its picturesque quality in the *Selected Works*.[2]

1. See Text IV G.
2. In 1926, Mao Tse-tung had published two articles in *Chung-kuo nung-min*, the first one dealing with the 'classes' among the peasantry, and the second with the classes of Chinese society in general. The text of the two is similar but not identical. In the case of the *éléments déclassés*, the passage of the second article, the one included in the *Selected Works*, is shorter than the corresponding one in the first, the one cited here. Nevertheless, it does contain the enumeration of the five categories constituting the *éléments déclassés;* this enumeration was expunged in 1951.

S.R.S.

IV · A The great union of the popular masses[1]

The decadence of the state, the sufferings of humanity, and the darkness of society have all reached an extreme. To be sure, among the methods of improvement and reform, education, industrialization, strenuous efforts, creation, destruction [of that which is bad and outmoded], and construction are all right, but there is a method more fundamental than these, which is that of the great union of the popular masses.

If we study history, we find that all the movements that have occurred in the course of history, of whatever type they may be, have all without exception resulted from the union of a certain number of people. A greater movement naturally requires a greater union, and the greatest movement requires the greatest union. All such unions are more likely to appear in a time of reform and resistance . . .

That which decides between victory and defeat is the solidity or weakness of the union and whether the ideology that serves as its basis is new or old, true or false . . .

[The aristocrats and capitalists and other powerful people in society have carried their oppression to an extreme] . . . and consequently the decadence of the state, the sufferings of humanity, and the darkness of society have also reached an extreme. It is then that reform and resistance arise, and that the great union of the popular masses is achieved.

When the great union of the popular masses of France opposed the great union of the adherents of the monarchy and the victory of 'political reform' had been attained, many countries followed the French example and undertook all sorts of 'political reforms'. After last year's struggle in Russia, which pitted the great union of the popular masses against the great union of the aristocracy and the great union of the capitalists and led to the victory of 'social reform', many countries – Hungary, Austria, Czechoslovakia,

1. Extracted from an article in Mao's review *Hsiang-chiang p'ing-lun*, nos. 2, 3, and 4, July and August 1919. For the sources of this extract, see the bibliography.

Available translations: none.

Germany – have followed Russia's example and have undertaken all sorts of social reforms. Although this victory is not complete ... it may certainly become so, and one can also imagine that it will spread throughout the whole world.

Why is the great union of the popular masses so terribly effective? Because the popular masses in any country are much more numerous than the aristocracy, the capitalists, and the other holders of power in society ...

We should know that our brothers of other lands have often employed this method in pursuing their interests. We must arise and imitate them, we must carry out our great union. ... As soon as we arise and let out a shout, the traitors will get up and tremble and flee for their lives ...

If we wish to achieve a great union, in order to resist the powerful people whom we face who harm their fellow men, and in order to pursue our own interests, we must necessarily have many small unions to serve as its foundation. ... Because our circumstances and professions are different, there are also certain differences, large or small, in the sphere of our common interests. ... Hence, the method (union) for seeking our common interests also displays certain differences, large or small ...

We are peasants, and so we want to unite with others who cultivate the land like we do, in order to pursue our various interests. The interests of us who cultivate the land can only be protected by ourselves! ... How do the landlords treat us? Are the rents and taxes heavy or light? Are our houses satisfactory or not? Are our bellies full or not? Is there enough land? Are there those in the village who have no land to cultivate? We must constantly seek answers to all these questions. ... We are workers, we wish to unite with others who work like ourselves in order to pursue the various interests of us workers. ... We cannot fail to seek a solution to such questions concerning us workers as the level of our wages, the length of the working day, and the equal or unequal sharing of dividends ...

We are students, we are already living in the twentieth century, and yet they still compel us to observe the old ceremonies and the old methods. The country is about to perish, and yet they still paste up posters forbidding us to love our country. ... We want our own union. . . . We are women, we are sunk even deeper in a sea of bitterness, we want to carry out our union . . .

IV · B An analysis of the various classes of the Chinese peasantry and their attitudes toward revolution[1]

No matter where you go in the villages, if you are a careful observer, you will see the following eight different types of people: big landlords; small landlords; peasant landholders; semi-landholders; sharecroppers; poor peasants; farm labourers and rural artisans; *éléments déclassés.* These eight types of people form eight separate classes. Their economic status and standard of living differs, this in turn influences their psychology, so that their attitudes toward revolution also differ.

A large portion of China's big landlords are descendents of the Ch'ing officials and nobles; some are present-day officials and militarists. There is also a small group of rich urban merchants who have bought land. There are very few who raised themselves to the status of big landlords by their industrious cultivation of the land. Their interests are built on the exploitation of the five types of peasants: the peasant landholders, the semi-landholders, the sharecroppers, the poor peasants, and the agrarian workers. . . . Hence China's big landlords are the deadly enemies of the Chinese peasantry, the real rulers in the villages, and the solid supporters of the imperialists and the militarists, the only solid bulwark of a clannish feudal society, the final cause of the emergence of all anti-revolutionary forces. If we consider those who manage 500 mou or more as big landlords, they constitute about 0.1 per cent of the peasantry (including their families). Of the 320 million Chinese peasants (eighty per cent of the total population), about 320,000 belong to this category.

The small landlords are more numerous than the big landlords,

1. Extracted from an article of the same title published in *Chung-kuo nung-min*, I, no. 1, January 1926, pp. 13–20.

Available translations: none. Long passages of this article are identical with sections of 'Analysis of all the classes in Chinese society', published in the following issue of the same magazine, and available in English translation (see note to Text III C).

numbering at least two million. Most of them are peasant proprietors who have raised themselves to this status by hard work, but a small fraction of them are urban merchants who have bought land; another fraction are descendants of officials who have seen better days, or present-day small officials.[1] ... They oppose the Kuomintang's policy of alliance with Russia, and its admission of communist elements. These people constitute the right wing of the Chinese middle bourgeoisie and are inclined to oppose the revolution. But within the middle bourgeoisie there is a left wing, which, under certain conditions, can be led toward the path of revolution. For instance, when the enthusiasm for the peasants' association movement rises, the left wing among the small landlords can be led to help in the work of the peasants' associations. But they tend toward compromise, and because of ties of blood in the last analysis they feel closer to the right wing of the small landlords and to the big landlords than to the peasants' associations. We definitely cannot expect them to set out courageously on the path of revolution ...

The peasant landholders belong to the petty bourgeoisie. They are also of three types. The first type of peasant landholder consists of those who have some surplus money and food. That is to say, after they have satisfied their needs, the product of their annual labour leaves them a surplus that can be employed for so-called primitive accumulation of capital. Such people are very much preoccupied with 'enriching themselves'. Although they do not indulge in the vain hope of enriching themselves greatly, nonetheless they wish to attain the position of small landlords. ... These people are very timid; they are afraid of the officials and also a little afraid of revolution. ... This group of people with surplus money and food constitutes the right wing of the petty bourgeoisie. ... But they form only a minority of the peasant landholders, perhaps not more than ten per cent. The number of peasant landholders in China ... is roughly between 100 million and 120 million. The wealthy portion of the peasant landholders forms about ten per cent of the total number, or twelve million. The second type of peasant landholder is just able to meet his

1. Here follows a passage identical with one on the middle bourgeoisie in general that occurs in the second paragraph of Text III C.

needs. ... This type of landholder differs greatly from the first type. He, too, wishes to enrich himself, but Marshal Chao will not permit him to do so. As a result of his recent oppression and exploitation by the imperialists, the militarists, and the landlord class, he feels that the world is not what it used to be. He realizes that if he now works only as hard as before, he will not be able to maintain himself. He must work longer hours, rise earlier, work longer, and devote more attention to his job, simply in order to maintain his standard of living. He begins to become somewhat abusive, calling the foreigners 'devils', the militarists 'money-grabbing commanders', and the local bullies and bad gentry 'the heartless rich'. As for the anti-imperialist, anti-militarist movement, he suspects that it may not succeed (the reason being that the foreigners and warlords have so much power behind them); consequently he refuses to join it recklessly and remains neutral. But he will absolutely not oppose the revolution. This group of people is very large, accounting for roughly half the peasant landholders, approximately sixty million.

The third type of peasant landholder has an annual deficit.... Many of this group formerly belonged to so-called well-to-do families, but gradually they fell first to a bare subsistence level, then to a situation where they have a deficit.... Spiritually, these suffer more than the others, because they see the contrast between the past and the present. This type of people is very important in the revolutionary movement and can contribute great strength to the advancement of the revolution. They number roughly forty per cent of the peasant landholders, i.e., forty-eight million – a not inconsiderable number, which constitutes the left wing of the petty bourgeoisie. In normal times, the above three types of peasant landholders differ in their attitude toward the Chinese revolution. But as soon as war breaks out, i.e., when the tide of revolution is rising and the dawn of victory is in sight, not only will the third type of left-wing peasant landholder immediately join the revolution, but the second type of middle-of-the-road peasant landholder may also join. And even the first type of right-wing peasant landholder, carried along by the high tide of revolution created by the sharecroppers and the left-wing peasant landholders, will also have no alternative but to go along with the revolution . . .

The semi-landholders, sharecroppers, and poor peasants number roughly between 150 million and 170 million. The semi-landholders number about fifty million, and the sharecroppers and poor peasants about sixty million each. This is an extremely large mass. The so-called 'peasant problem' is in large part their problem. Although all three of these types of peasants belong to the semi-proletariat, they differ greatly in their economic conditions. The life of the semi-landholders is harder than that of the peasant landholders, because the former are short of half of their food each year. They must rent land from others, or find employment as workers, or engage in petty trading to make up the shortage. Between spring and summer, when the new crops are not yet ripe and last year's yellow grain is exhausted, they borrow at high rates of interest and buy grain at high prices from others. Naturally, their lot is much harder than that of peasant landholders, who do not depend on others. Yet they are better off than the sharecroppers, because the latter have no land and receive only half of what they grow each year. Although semi-landholders receive only half or even less than half the crop from the land they rent, still they receive the entire crop from their own land. Hence the revolutionary spirit of the semi-landholders is better than that of the peasant landholders, but not equal to that of the sharecroppers.

The sharecroppers and the poor peasants are both tenant peasants subject to the landlord's exploitation, but there is a certain difference in their economic status. The sharecroppers have no land, but they have relatively adequate farm implements and a reasonably adequate amount of circulating capital. These peasants receive half of the product of their annual labour. They make up the deficit by growing side crops, catching fish and crayfish, and raising poultry and pigs. In this way they eke out a living. Surrounded by difficulties and privations, they are continually preoccupied with how they will make out each year. Hence their life is harder than that of the semi-landholders, but better than that of the poor peasants. Their revolutionary spirit thus is better than that of the semi-landholders, but does not match that of the poor peasants.

The poor peasants do not have sufficient farm implements nor do they have any circulating capital. They are short of fertilizers and reap only a meagre harvest from the fields. After paying the rent, very little is left for them. During years of famine or difficult months, they beg from relatives and friends, appealing for a few measures of grain to tide them over for four or five days. Their debts pile up like the burden on the backs of draught oxen. They are the most miserable among the peasants and are most receptive to revolutionary propaganda.

The farm labourers, or agricultural proletariat, include those hired by the year, the month, or the day. These farm labourers possess neither land nor tools, nor do they have any circulating capital. Hence they can subsist only by their labour. With their long hours of work, their low salaries, the treatment they receive, and the insecurity of their employment, they are worse off than the other workers. This group of people is the most distressed in the rural areas and should be given the greatest attention by those who are organizing peasant movements. The position of the rural handicraftsmen is higher than that of the hired agrarian workers, because they possess their own tools and belong to a kind of liberal profession. But because of their heavy family burdens and the disparity between their earnings and the cost of living, the constant burden of poverty and the fear of losing their jobs, their situation is not much different from that of the farm labourers.

The *éléments déclassés* consist of peasants who have lost their land, handicraftsmen who have lost all opportunity of employment as a result of oppression and exploitation by the imperialists, the militarists, and the landlords, or as a result of floods and droughts. They can be divided into soldiers, bandits, robbers, beggars, and prostitutes. These five categories of people have different names, and they enjoy a somewhat different status in society. But they are all human beings, and they all have five senses and four limbs, and are therefore one. They each have a different way of making a living: the soldier fights, the bandit robs, the thief steals, the beggar begs, and the prostitute seduces.

But to the extent that they must all earn their livelihood and cook rice to eat, they are one. They lead the most precarious existence of any human being. They have secret organizations in various places: for instance, the Triad Society in Fukien and Kwangtung; the Ko Lao Hui [Society of Brothers] in the provinces of Hunan, Hupei, Kweichow, and Szechwan; the Big Sword Society in the provinces of Anhwei, Honan, and Shantung; the Society of Morality in Chihli and the three north-eastern provinces; the Blue Band in Shanghai and elsewhere. These serve as their mutual-aid societies in the political and economic struggle. To find a place for this group of people is the greatest and the most difficult problem faced by China. China has two problems: poverty and unemployment. Hence, if the problem of unemployment can be solved, half of China's problems will be solved. The number of *éléments déclassés* in China is fearfully large; it is roughly more than twenty million. These people are capable of fighting very bravely, and, if properly led, can become a revolutionary force.[1]

Our work of organizing the peasantry involves gathering the five kinds of peasants into a single organization: the peasant land-holders, semi-landholders, sharecroppers, poor peasants, and farm labourers and handicraftsmen. In principle, the peasants should adopt the method of struggle in their relations with the landlord class, demanding from them economic and political concessions. In special circumstances, when one encounters particularly reactionary and bad gentry and local bullies who exploit the people savagely, as in Haifeng or Huangning, the peasants should overthrow them altogether. As for the *éléments déclassés*, one should exhort them to side with the peasants' associations and to join the big revolutionary movement to help solve the problem of unemployment; one should never force them to go over to the side of the enemy and become a force in the service of the counter-revolutionaries.

1. In 1951, Mao added (in his 'Analysis of all the classes'), 'but they are inclined to be destructive'.

IV · C The Chinese proletariat[1]

Since China is economically backward, the number of her industrial workers (industrial proletariat) is not large. Of the two million industrial workers, the majority are engaged in five industries, i.e., railways, mining, maritime transport, textiles, and shipbuilding; most of them work in enterprises owned by foreign capital. Consequently, the industrial proletariat, though small in number, has become the major force[2] of the national revolutionary movement. If we examine the strength shown in the strike movements of the last four years, such as the seamen's strike, the railway strike, the strikes in the Kailan and Tsiaotso coal mines, and the big strikes in Shanghai and Hong Kong after the 30 May incident, we become aware of the importance of the industrial proletariat in the national revolution. The primary reason why the industrial workers can act in this way is their concentration. No other group has such 'organized concentration'. The second reason is their low economic status. Having been deprived of the means of production and left with nothing but their two hands, they are especially well suited for struggle, because they have despaired of ever becoming rich and are subjected to the most ruthless treatment by the imperialists, the warlords, and the comprador class. The strength of the coolies in the cities is also worthy of attention. This group includes mostly stevedores and rickshawmen, but also garbage men and street cleaners. Having nothing but their hands, their economic status is similar to that of the industrial workers, but they are inferior to them in organized concentration, and also as regards their importance among the productive forces . . .

1. Extracted from 'Analysis of all the classes in Chinese society', published in *Chung-kuo nung-min*, I, no. 2, February 1926.

Available translations: *Selected Works*, I, p. 18.

2. In 1951, Mao replaced 'major force' by 'leading force'. He also added two phrases justifying this leading role of the industrial proletariat, saying that it 'incarnates the new productive forces' and 'constitutes the most progressive class in modern China'.

IV · D The bitter sufferings of the peasants in Kiangsu and Chekiang, and their movements of resistance[1]

If one takes the boat from Wuhsi, the first place at which one arrives is the market town of Kushan. It is situated between the three *hsien* of Chiangyin, Shangshu, and Wuhsi. In these three *hsien* there are many big landlords who oppress the farmers very severely. Last autumn, a certain Kushan student who had studied in Japan, by the name of Chou Shui-p'ing, returned to this village. (Chou had first graduated from Wuhsi Provincial Teachers' College.) He could not bear the sight [of such oppression], and encouraged the tenant farmers to organize into a body called the 'Tenant Farmers' Cooperative Self-help Society'. Chou moved from village to village, speaking with tears in his eyes of the sufferings of the peasants. A large number of Kushan peasants followed him, and those in the neighbouring areas of Chiangyin, Shangshu, and Wuhsi *hsien* were all inflamed. They rose like clouds and opposed the rich but heartless big landlords, and with one voice demanded the reduction of rent. But before the peasants had completely united themselves, the bad landlords had already united themselves and the gentry and landlords of the three *hsien*, Chiangyin, Shangshu, and Wuhsi acted simultaneously. Letters and telegrams fell like snowflakes on Sun Ch'uan-fang; Sun Ch'uan-fang of course obeyed the orders of the landlords. Last November, he dissolved the 'Tenant Farmers' Cooperative Self-help Society' and arrested Chou Shui-p'ing, who was executed in January of this year. It seemed that the movement for rent reduction had been suppressed for a time. But when Chou Shui-p'ing's coffin was returned to Kushan to be exhibited in his house, the farmers went up to the coffin daily in crowds and kowtowed before it, saying, 'Mr Chou died for us, we will avenge his death.' This year there was a big drought, and the harvest was poor; the farmers again thought of rising up to demand rent reduction. This shows that they are not in the least

1. Extracted from an article of the same title (signed by Mao's *tzu*, Jun-chih) published in *Hsiang-tao*, no. 179, 25 November 1926, pp. 1869–71. Available translations: none.

afraid to die. They know that a united struggle to reduce the exploitation of the avaricious and cruel landlords is their only way out . . .

Tz'u Hsi is located in Chekiang, east of Ningpo. In recent months there occurred a great insurrection in the Shanpei area of this *hsien.* The peasants of this Shanpei area are violent by nature, and frequently indulge in armed combat. On top of this, in recent years the officials and police have been unreasonably oppressive and the bad landlords have stepped up their exploitation. So the accumulated exasperation of the peasants was already deep. By chance the climate this year was unstable, and as a result the rice and cotton crops failed, but the landlords refused to make any reduction whatever in their harsh rents. The peasants' insurrection against famine thereupon exploded. Once the farmers' insurrection broke out, all the *éléments déclassés* joined them very courageously. In the morning of 13 September, there assembled more than 2,000 people, who went to the police station to report the famine, and clashed with the police. They burned down the police station, and distributed the arms of the police among themselves. They then turned to go to the homes of the village gentry landlords to 'eat up powerful families'. After eating them up, and out of anger at the evils of the village gentry landlords, they destroyed the landlords' screens, paintings, and sculptured ancient doors and windows. They did this every day; they did not listen much to others' exhortation, but let off their steam in this manner. The day after [each such outburst], the landlord in question ran to the city to report, and soldiers and police came down to the village and turned everything upside down, but the leaders of the peasants had already mostly escaped. There was widespread propaganda about 'Violation of the law' and 'Crimes', the farmers became fearful, and thus the movement was suppressed. The reason for the failure of this movement is that the masses did not fully organize themselves, and did not have leadership, so that the movement barely got started and then failed.

IV · E Report of an investigation into the peasant movement in Hunan[1]

Agrarian revolution. ... In a very short time, several hundred million peasants in China's central, southern, and northern provinces will rise like a tornado or tempest – a force so extraordinarily swift and violent that no power, however great, will be able to suppress it. They will break through all the trammels that now bind them and push forward along the road to liberation. They will send all imperialists, warlords, corrupt officials, local bullies, and evil gentry to their graves. All revolutionary parties and all revolutionary comrades will stand before them to be tested, to be accepted or rejected by them. To march at their head and lead them? To follow in the rear, gesticulating at them and criticizing them? To face them as opponents? Every Chinese is free to choose among the three, but circumstances demand that a quick choice be made...

The peasant movement in Hunan, so far as it concerns the *hsien* in the central and southern sections of the province, where the movement is already developed, can be roughly divided into two periods. The first period was that of organization, extending from January to September of last year. ... The second was the period of revolution, extending from last October to this January...

After the peasants had organized themselves, action ensued. The main targets of the peasants are the local bullies, the evil gentry, and the lawless landlords; they also hit out against various patriarchal ideologies and institutions, corrupt officials in the cities, and evil customs in the rural areas. In force and momentum, the attack is just like a tempest or hurricane; those who submit to it survive, those who resist perish. As a result, the privileges the feudal landlords have enjoyed for thousands of

1. Extracted from a report written in February 1927, *Hsüan-chi*, 1947, Supplement, pp. 1–22.

Available translations: The current version is translated in *Selected Works*, I, pp. 23–59. The first half of the original version (including sections 1 and 2 of Text IV E) can be found in *Documentary History*, pp. 80–89.

years are shattered to pieces. The dignity and prestige of the landlords are dashed to the ground. With the fall of the authority of the landlords, the peasant association becomes the sole organ of authority, and the slogan 'All Power to the Peasant Association' has become a reality. Even trifling matters, such as quarrels between man and wife, have to be settled by the peasant association. Nothing can be settled in the absence of association representatives. *Whatever nonsense the people from the association talk in the meetings is considered sacred.* The associations actually dictate in all matters in the countryside, and it is literally true that 'whatever they say, goes'. The public can only praise the association, not condemn it. . . . Fear of the peasant association has caused the top local bullies and evil gentry to flee to Shanghai, the second-ranking ones to Hankow, the third-ranking ones to Changsha, and the fourth-ranking ones to the *hsien* towns. The fifth-ranking ones and still lesser fry are forced to remain in the countryside and bow to the peasant association.

'I'll donate ten dollars, please admit me to the peasant association,' one of the lower-ranking evil gentry would say.

'Pshaw! Who wants your filthy money!' the peasants would reply.

Many middle and small landlords, rich peasants, and even middle peasants, formerly opposed to the peasant association, now seek in vain to be admitted. While visiting various places, I have often come across such people who solicited my help; 'I beg the committeeman from the provincial capital to be my guarantor!' they would say . . .

In short, what was generally sneered at four months ago as the 'peasants' gang' has now become something most honourable. Those who prostrated themselves before the power of the gentry now prostrate themselves before the power of the peasants. Everyone admits that the world has changed since last October . . .

When I first arrived in Changsha, I met people from various circles and picked up a good deal of gossip. From the middle strata upward to the right-wingers of the Kuomintang, there was not a single person who did not summarize the whole thing in one phrase: 'An awful mess!' Even people with revolutionary inclinations, carried away by the opinion of the 'awful-mess' school that hovered like a storm over the whole city, became downhearted when they tried to picture the conditions in the countryside and felt unable to deny the 'mess'. The very progressive people could only remark, 'Indeed a mess, but inevitable in the course of the revolution.' In a word, nobody could categorically deny the 'mess'. But the fact is ... that the broad peasant masses have risen to fulfil their historical mission, that the democratic forces in the rural areas have risen to overthrow the rural feudal power. The overthrow of this feudal power is the real objective of the national revolution. What Mr Sun Yat-sen wanted to but failed to accomplish in the forty years he devoted to the national revolution, the peasants have accomplished in a few months. The patriarchal-feudalistic class of local bullies, evil gentry, and lawless landlords has formed the basis of autocratic government for thousands of years, the firm support of imperialism, warlordism, and corrupt officialdom. [To overthrow them] is a marvellous feat, one which had not been achieved in the last forty vears – or even in thousands of years. It is 'very good indeed'. It is not a 'mess' at all. It is anything but an 'awful mess'. *To give credit where due, if we allot ten points to the accomplishments of the democratic revolution, then the achievements of the urban dwellers and the military rate only three points, while the remaining seven points should go to the peasants in their rural revolution.* ... Every revolutionary comrade should know that the national revolution requires a profound change in the countryside. The revolution of 1911 did not bring about this change, hence its failure. Now the change is taking place, and this is an important factor necessary for completing the revolution. Every revolutionary comrade must support this change, else he will be taking a counter-revolutionary stand ...

There is another section of people who say, 'Although the peasant association is necessary, it has gone rather too far in its actions.' ... True, the peasants do in some ways 'act unreasonably' in the countryside. ... Turning everything upside down, they have even created a kind of terrorism. This is what some people call 'going too far'. ... A revolution is not the same as inviting people to dinner or writing an essay or painting a picture or embroidering a flower; it cannot be anything so refined, so calm and gentle, or so 'mild, kind, courteous, restrained, and magnanimous'. [The virtues of Confucius, as described by one of his disciples.] A revolution is an uprising, an act of violence whereby one class overthrows the authority of another. A rural revolution is a revolution in which the peasantry overthrows the authority of the feudal landlord class. If the peasants do not use the maximum of their strength, they can never overthrow the deeply rooted, age-old authority of the landlords. The rural areas must experience a great, fervent revolutionary upsurge, which alone can arouse hundreds and thousands of the people to form a great force. All the actions mentioned above, labelled as 'going too far', are caused by the power of the peasants, generated by a great, fervent revolutionary upsurge in the countryside. Such actions were quite necessary in the second period of the peasant movement [the period of revolution]. In this period, it was necessary to establish the absolute authority of the peasants. It was necessary to prevent criticisms against the peasant association. It was necessary to overthrow all the authority of the gentry, to knock them down, even stamp them underfoot. All actions labelled as 'going too far' had a revolutionary significance in the second period. To put it bluntly, it was necessary to bring about a brief reign of terror in every rural area, else one could never suppress the activities of the counter-revolutionaries in the countryside or overthrow the authority of the gentry. To right a wrong it is necessary to exceed the proper limit; the wrong cannot be righted without doing so . . .

The vanguard of revolution. The right wing of the Kuomintang says, 'The peasant movement is a movement of the riffraff, a movement of the lazy peasants.' This feeling has gained much currency in Changsha. I went to the countryside and heard the gentry say, 'It is all right to set up the peasant association, but the people now running it are incompetent; better put others on the job!' This opinion and the dictum of the right wing amount to the same thing; both admit that the peasant movement may continue (since the peasant movement is already a fact, no one dare say that it should not), but they regard the people leading the movement as incompetent. Their hatred is directed against the lower-level administrators, particularly of the associations, labelling them 'riffraff'. *These people, who used to go around in worn-out leather shoes, carry broken umbrellas, wear blue gowns and gamble*, in short, all those who were formerly despised or kicked into the gutter by the gentry, who had no social standing, and who were denied the right to speak, have now dared to raise their heads. Not only have they raised their heads, they have also taken power into their hands. They are now running the *hsiang* peasant association [peasant association at the lowest level] and have turned it into a formidable force. They raise their rough, blackened hands and lay them on the heads of the gentry. They tie the evil gentry with ropes, put tall paper hats on them, and lead them in a parade through the villages. ... Every day the coarse, harsh sounds of their denunciations pierce the ears of the gentry. They are giving orders and directions in all matters. They rank above everybody else, they who used to rank below everyone else – that is what people mean by 'upside down'...

The peasants have accomplished a revolutionary task for many years left unaccomplished, and done the most important work[1] in the national revolution. But have all the peasants taken part in accomplishing such a great revolutionary task and doing this most important work? No. The peasantry consists of three sections – the rich peasants, the middle peasants, and the poor peasants...

The *only group* in the countryside that has always put up the bitterest fight is the poor peasants. Throughout the period of underground organization and that of open organization, *it was they who fought, who organized, and who did the revolutionary work. They alone* are the deadliest enemies of the local bullies and evil gentry and attack their strongholds without the slightest hesitation; *they alone are able to carry out the work of destruction.* ...[2] This enormous mass of poor peasants is the backbone of the peasant association, the vanguard in overthrowing the

1. In 1951, the phrase 'the most important work' was changed to 'important work'.

2. All the italicized passages giving the poor peasants sole credit for the revolution were expunged from the 1951 edition. Instead, Mao inserted the following sentence: 'They accept the leadership of the Communist Party most willingly.'

feudal forces, and the foremost heroes who have accomplished the great revolutionary undertaking left unaccomplished for many years. Without the poor peasants (the 'riffraff', as the gentry calls them), it would never have been possible to bring about the present state of revolution in the countryside, to overthrow the local bullies and evil gentry, or to complete the democratic revolution. Being the most revolutionary, the poor peasants (*particularly the poorest ones*) have won the leadership in the peasant association. In both the first and second periods, almost all the posts of chairmen and committee members in the peasant associations at the lowest level (i.e., the *hsiang* associations) were held by poor peasants. ... This leadership of the poor peasants is extremely necessary. Without the poor peasants there can be no revolution. To reject them is to reject the revolurion. To attack them is to attack the revolution. From beginning to end, the general direction they have given the revolution has never been wrong. They have hurt the dignity of the local bullies and evil gentry. They have knocked down the big and small local bullies and evil gentry and trampled them underfoot. Many of their deeds in the period of revolution, described as 'going too far', were in fact dictated by the very needs of the revolution. ... We must oppose such counter-revolutionary calumnies as 'riffraff movement' and 'movement of the lazy peasants' and must be especially careful not to commit the error of helping – even unintentionally – the local bullies and evil gentry in their attacks on *the leadership* of the poor peasants ...

Dealing political blows to the landlords. After the peasants are organized, the first thing they do is to smash the political prestige of the landlord class, especially of the local bullies and evil gentry, i.e., curtail the social power of the landlords in the countryside and build up the power of the peasants. This is a most serious and vital matter. It is the main struggle during the second period, the period of revolution. If this struggle is not won, there can be no victory in any economic fight, such as the struggle for rent and interest reduction or for securing capital and land. ... The peasants are able to deal political blows to the landlords in the following ways:

1. Auditing of accounts. Most of the local bullies and evil gentry are guilty of embezzling public funds entrusted to them, and the accounts are not in order. Now the peasants have used the auditing of accounts as a lever to overthrow a great many local bullies and evil gentry. In many places auditing committees are set up for the specific purpose of settling accounts with the local bullies and evil gentry, who shudder at the mere sight of such committee offices. Auditing campaigns like these have been carried out extensively in all counties where the peasant movement has risen, and their significance lies not so much in recovering the funds as in exposing the crimes of the local bullies and evil gentry and knocking them down from their political as well as social position . . .

2. *Contributions.* Raising funds among the rich and brutal landlords for the relief of the poor, for the organization of co-operatives and rural credit agencies, or for other purposes . . .

3. Major demonstrations. A big crowd is rallied to demonstrate at the house of a local bully or one of the evil gentry who is hostile to the association. The demonstrators take their meals at his house, slaughtering his pigs and consuming his grain; quite a few such cases have occurred . . .

4. Parades through the villages in tall paper hats. Such things have been staged many times in various places. The local bullies and evil gentry are crowned with tall paper hats bearing slogans such as 'Local bully so and so' or 'So and so, one of the evil gentry'. They are walked on a lead and escorted by big crowds both in front of and behind them. Sometimes gongs are beaten and flags waved to attract attention. This form of punishment, more than any other, makes the local bullies and evil gentry shudder with fear. He who has once been crowned with the tall paper hat loses face forever and can never hold up his head again . . .

5. Imprisonment in the hsien *jail.* This is a greater punishment than donning the tall paper hat. The local bullies and evil gentry are arrested and locked up in the *hsien* jail, and the *hsien* magistrate is asked to sentence them. The people sent to prison now are different from those in the past: Formerly it was the gentry who sent the peasants to jail; now it is the other way round . . .

6. *Shooting*. This punishment was invariably meted out to the biggest of the local bullies and evil gentry by request of the peasants and the people as a whole. ... The execution of one such big local bully or one member of the evil gentry has its repercussions throughout the whole *hsien* and is very effective in eradicating any remnant of feudalism. Scores or at least a few such big local bullies and evil gentry are to be found in every *hsien*, and the only effective way of suppressing the reactionaries is to execute at least one or two guilty of the most serious crimes and wrongdoing in every *hsien*. When the local bullies and evil gentry were at the height of their power, they killed peasants without batting an eyelid. ... In view of these atrocities of the local bullies and evil gentry as well as the White terror let loose by them in the rural areas, how can one say that the peasants should not now rise and shoot *one or two*[1] of them and bring about a small-scale reign of terror in suppressing the counter-revolutionaries?

Overthrowing the clan authority of the elders and ancestral temples, the religious authority of the city gods and local deities, and the masculine authority of husbands. A man in China is usually subjected to the domination of three systems of authority: (1) the system of the state (political authority), ranging from the national, provincial, and *hsien* government to the *hsiang* government; (2) the system of the clan (clan authority), ranging from the central and branch ancestral temples to the head of the household; and (3) the system of gods and spirits (religious authority), including the system of the nether world ranging from the King of Hell to the city gods and local deities, and that of supernatural beings ranging from the Emperor of Heaven to all kinds of gods and spirits. As to women, apart from being dominated by these three systems, they are further dominated by men (the authority of the husband). These four types of authority – political authority, clan authority, religious authority, and the authority of the husband – represent the ideology and institution of feudalism and patriarchy; they are the four bonds that have bound the Chinese people, particularly the peasants. We have already seen how the peasants overthrow the political authority of the landlords in the

1. In the current edition this reads 'a few'.

countryside. The political authority of the landlords is the backbone of all other systems of authority. Once this has been overthrown, so clan authority, religious authority, and the authority of the husband all begin to totter. Where the peasant association is powerful, the clan elders and administrators of temple funds no longer dare oppress the younger members of the clan or embezzle the funds. The evil clan elders and administrators have been overthrown, along with the local bullies and evil gentry . . .

Religious authority begins to totter everywhere as the peasant movement develops. In many places the peasant associations have taken over the temples of gods as their offices. Everywhere they advocate the appropriation of temple properties to maintain peasant schools and to defray association expenses, calling it 'public revenue from superstition'. Forbidding superstition and smashing idols has become quite the vogue in Liling. . . . In the Lungfeng Nunnery in the North Third District, the peasants and school teachers chopped up the wooden idols to cook meat. . . . *Everywhere, by the nature of things*, only the older peasants and women still believe in gods, while the young and middle-aged peasants no longer do so. Since it is the young and middle-aged peasants who are in control of the peasant association, the movement to overthrow religious authority and eradicate superstition is gathering momentum everywhere. As to the authority of the husband, it has always been comparatively weak among the poor peasants, because the poor peasant women, for financial reasons compelled to engage more in manual work than women of the wealthier classes, have obtained greater rights to speak and more power to make decisions in family affairs. *They also enjoy considerable sexual freedom. Among the poor peasantry, triangular and multilateral relationships are almost universal.* In recent years, the rural economy has become even more bankrupt, and the basic condition for men's domination over women has already been undermined. Lately, with the rise of the peasant movement, women have begun to organize rural women's associations in many places; they have been given the opportunity to lift up their heads, and the authority of the husband is tottering more and more with every passing day. In short, all feudal and patriarchal ideologies and institutions are tottering with the rise of the power of the peasants. ... At present, however, such attacks have just 'begun', and there can be no complete overthrow of the three until the economic struggle of the peasants is completely victorious. Hence, our task at present is to guide the peasants to wage political struggles with their utmost strength so that the authority of the landlords will be thoroughly uprooted. An economic struggle should also be started immediately, so that the economic problems[1] of the poor peasants can be completely solved. The abolition of the clan system, of superstitions, and of one-sided notions of chastity[2] will follow as a natural consequence of victory in the political and economic struggles. If we crudely and arbitrarily devote excessive efforts to the abolition of such things, we shall give the local bullies and evil gentry a pretext for undermining the peasant movement by raising such slogans as 'The peasant association does not show piety toward ancestors'; 'The peasant association abuses the gods and destroys religion'; and 'The peasant association advocates the sharing of women'. ... The idols should be removed by the peasants themselves, and the temples for martyred virgins and the arches for chaste and filial widowed daughters-in-law should likewise be demolished by the peasants themselves ...

IV · F The force of the peasantry and the leadership of the workers[3]

Proletarian leadership is the sole key to the victory of the revolution. The laying of the Party's proletarian basis and the establishment of the Party cells in industrial enterprises in key centres are

1. This was changed to 'the problem of land and other economic problems' in 1951. Although this reference is an afterthought, there was at least one reference to the land problem in the original version of the Hunan report (see this extract, p. 255).

2. Chastity of women, of course, not of men. In the current version, Mao has changed this to read 'abolition ... of inequality between men and women'.

3. Extracted from a report of the Front Committee to the Central Committee of the Party, dated 5 April 1929, cited in Mao's letter to Lin Piao, of 5 January 1930, *Hsüan-chi* 1947, Supplement, p. 94.

Available translations: *Selected Works*, I, pp. 122–3.

the greatest organizational tasks[1] of the Party at present. At the same time, the development of the struggle in the countryside, the establishment of soviets in small areas, and the creation and expansion of the Red Army, are conditions[2] for helping the struggle in the cities and accelerating the revolutionary upsurge. It is therefore a very great mistake to abandon the struggle in the cities and *to sink into peasant guerrilla-ism.*[3] But in our opinion it is also a mistake – if any of our Party members hold such views – to fear the development of the power of the peasants lest it overwhelm the leadership[4] of the workers and hence become detrimental to the revolution. For the revolution in semi-colonial China will fail only if the peasant struggle is deprived of the leadership of the workers; it will never suffer just because the peasant struggle develops in such a way that the peasants become more powerful than the workers.

IV · G Appeal to the Ko Lao Hui[5]

Brothers of the Ko Lao Hui!

... Formerly, following its principles – 'Restore the Han and exterminate the Ch'ing', 'Strike at the rich and aid the poor' – the Ko Lao Hui participated actively in the anti-Manchu revolutionary movement of 1911. The revolution in northern Shensi has also benefited from the considerable aid, support, and active participation of comrades from the Ko Lao Hui. Comrades such as Hsieh

1. In the 1951 text, the 'greatest organizational tasks' became simply 'important tasks'.

2. In the 1951 text, the 'conditions' became 'the essential conditions'.

3. This phrase was eliminated in 1951. It is clear that the effect of the three changes just noted is to attenuate slightly the manner in which Mao, who in 1929 found himself in a dependent and precarious position, minimized his own role and paid verbal homage to the 'working-class' strategy of Li Li-san in addressing himself to the Central Committee.

4. In 1951, 'leadership' was replaced by 'force'; this change makes the paragraph read somewhat more logically.

5. Extracted from the appeal published in *Tou-cheng*, no. 105, 12 July 1936, 3(b)–5(a).

Available translations: For the full text see the appendix to my article 'Mao Tse-tung and Secret Societies', *China Quarterly*, no. 27, 1966, pp. 11–13.

Tzu-ch'ang or Liu Chih-tan are not only leaders of the Red Army; they are also exemplary members of the Ko Lao Hui. This revolutionary spirit, these glorious feats, must be manifested even more widely in today's heroic struggle to save the country and save ourselves . . .

In the past, you supported the restoration of the Han and the extermination of the Manchus; today, we support resistance to Japan and the saving of the country. You support striking at the rich and helping the poor; we support striking at the local bullies and dividing up the land. You despise wealth and defend justice, and you gather together all the heroes and brave fellows [*hao han*] in the world; we do not spare ourselves to save China and the world; we unite the exploited and oppressed peoples and groups of the whole world. Our views and our positions are therefore quite close; there is even more complete correspondence as regards our enemies and the road toward salvation. Consequently, we once more make a special and very sincere appeal to all our brothers of the Ko Lao Hui throughout the whole country. Regardless of our past subjects of discord or mutual grievances, we must now forget them in order to unite under the slogan of resisting Japan and saving the country, and constitute a close and intimate alliance of brothers! . . .

Show the revolutionary spirit that characterized the Ko Lao Hui in the past!

Let the Ko Lao Hui and the whole of the Chinese people unite to strike at Japan and to restore China!

Long live the liberation of the Chinese people!

Chairman of the Central Government of the Chinese People's Soviet Republic:

MAO TSE-TUNG

15 July 1936

IV · H The particular characteristics of the Chinese peasantry and the Chinese proletariat[1]

Under this age-old feudal system of economic exploitation and political oppression, the poverty-stricken, suffering Chinese peasants led a slavelike life. Under the yoke of feudalism they had no freedom of person. The landlords had the right to beat and insult them, even to put them to death at will, while the peasants had no political rights whatever. The extreme poverty and backwardness of the peasants that resulted from such ruthless exploitation and oppression by the landlord class is the reason for China's backward and stagnant economy and social life.

In feudal society, the main contradiction is between the peasantry and the landlord class.

Yet in this society, the peasants and the handicraftsmen were the principal creators of wealth and culture.

The ruthless economic exploitation and political oppression of the peasantry by the landlord class could not fail to force the peasants to rise repeatedly in revolt against its rule. From Ch'en Sheng, Wu Kuang, Hsiang Yü, and Liu Pang of the Ch'in dynasty ... down to the T'aip'ing Heavenly Kingdom in the Ch'ing dynasty, there have been several hundred uprisings, all of them peasant movements of resistance, that is, peasant revolutionary wars. The gigantic scale of such peasant uprisings and peasant wars in Chinese history is without parallel[2] in world history. These[3] peasant uprisings and peasant wars alone formed the real motive force of China's historical evolution.[4] For each peasant uprising and peasant war dealt a blow to the existing

1. Extracted from 'The Chinese revolution and the Chinese Communist Party', *Chung-Kuo ko-ming yü Chung-kuo Kung-ch'an-tang*. Chieh-fang She, n.d. (1940), pp. 5–6, 27–9.

Available translations: See note to Text I B, p. 164.

2. In 1951, Mao Tse-tung, slightly modifying his Sinocentrism, changed this to read 'there are few examples in the history of the world'. But curiously enough, the Peking translation of this passage still reads 'is without parallel in the world'.

3. In 1951, Mao inserted: 'This class struggle of the peasantry'.

4. In 1951, the scope of this sentence was slightly reduced; Mao rewrote it so that the peasant movements are presented as the sole motive force of Chinese *feudal* society, and not of Chinese history as a whole.

feudal regime; *thus to some extent it changed the productive relations of society* and to some extent furthered the development of the productive forces of society. However, since neither new productive forces nor new modes of production nor a new class force nor an advanced political party existed in those days, and the peasant uprisings and wars consequently lacked the *leadership of an advanced class and an advanced political party, such as the* correct leadership given by the proletariat and the Communist Party today, the peasant revolutions invariably failed, and the peasants were utilized during or after each revolution by the landlords and the nobility as a tool for bringing about dynastic changes. Thus, although some social progress was made after each peasant revolutionary struggle, the feudal economic relations and feudal political system remained basically unchanged.

Only in the last hundred years did fresh changes take place ...

The Chinese proletariat has many particularly outstanding qualities, which *permit it to become the leading force in the Chinese revolution.*[1]

What are the particularly outstanding qualities of the Chinese proletariat?

First, the Chinese proletariat is subjected to threefold oppression (by imperialism, by the bourgeoisie, and by the feudal forces) with a severity and ruthlessness seldom found in other nations of the world, and consequently it is more resolute and more thorough-going in the revolutionary struggle than any other class. Moreover, there is no economic basis in colonial and semi-colonial China for social reformism like that of *Western* [In deleting the word, 'Western', Mao now applies the stigma of reformism to all of Europe, East as well as West.] Europe. (*But one must be careful; at times Chinese national reformism* [*Chung-kuo min-tsu kai-liang chu-i*] *may easily exercise some influence on a part of the workers.*) Hence, the proletariat as a whole, with the exception of a few scabs, is most revolutionary.

1. For once, the 1951 text eliminated rather than added a reference to the leading role of the workers. At the same time, Mao added a few sentences to indicate that the Chinese proletariat also possesses the outstanding qualities of all proletariats, not only its own unique qualities.

Secondly, ever since its appearance on the revolutionary scene, the Chinese proletariat has been under the leadership of its own revolutionary political party – the Chinese Communist Party – and has become the most politically conscious class in Chinese society.

Thirdly, because the Chinese proletariat is largely made up of bankrupt peasants, it has natural ties with the vast peasantry, which facilitate a close *revolutionary* alliance between the two.

Therefore, in spite of certain unavoidable weaknesses – for example, its small size (as compared with the peasantry), its youth (as compared with the proletariat in capitalist countries), and its low cultural level (as compared with the bourgeoisie), the Chinese proletariat has nonetheless become the basic motive force of the Chinese revolution. The Chinese revolution certainly will not succeed without the *participation and* leadership of the proletariat . . .

V. The Military Principles of Mao Tse-tung

The term 'military principles', as applied to Mao Tse-tung, immediately evokes the strategic and tactical principles of guerrilla warfare that have aroused so much interest in recent years in the most diverse contexts – from China to Cuba and from Algeria to Vietnam. This chapter includes texts setting forth his basic ideas regarding the conduct of revolutionary war, but the accent has been placed rather on the organic link between Mao's military thought and his mind and personality as a whole.

Mao's admiration for the martial spirit, courage, and violence have already been discussed. These characteristics are once more expressed in striking fashion in the poems that constitute Texts V C and V G. The poem 'Chingkang Mountain' appears in a particular light when one reads it in the context of the selections that precede and follow it and that provide graphic details about the real situation of Mao's army at that period. The high praise bestowed on the fighting qualities of the *éléments déclassés* in Text V B, and the admission that these elements constitute the *majority* of the Red Army in Text V D, emphasize the parallel between Mao Tse-tung's situation in 1928 or 1929 and that of the heroes of the novel *All Men are Brothers*. (Needless to say, these two points were eliminated from the texts in question in the current edition of Mao's writings.) But at the same time, Texts V B and V D show clearly that Mao is a Leninist revolutionary concerned not only with political goals, but also with the organizational means necessary for their attainment. Here, as when he identifies himself with the emperors of bygone days, Mao affirms his link with China's past even as he repudiates certain aspects of that past and affirms his will to transform his country in order to restore its ancient greatness.

The theme of China's grandeur and uniqueness, to which this anthology devotes a special chapter, is indeed present here, as it is present in everything that Mao Tse-tung has said or written. In this respect one is particularly struck by the affirmations in Text V E of the importance of the Chinese experience of revolutionary war, which is declared to be even more important than the Soviet experience. These statements were replaced in the current edition of the *Selected Works* by passages saying the exact opposite.

Two other basic themes are treated here: the primacy of politics and of the human factor. The first one is developed particularly in Texts V D and V J; the second especially in Texts V H and V I. But both of them underlie all of Mao's military writings. Moreover, they are linked and constitute two aspects of the voluntarism that Mao Tse-tung inherited from Lenin and has carried one step further, in a context in which reliance on the economic determinism of orthodox Marxism for the accomplishment of the hoped-for revolution was even less possible than in the Russia of 1917.

Mao's military principles in the narrow sense are illustrated by texts V F and V M. Although the first analyses the problem in terms of conditions in the mid-thirties, when the Red Army was relatively weak, while the second dates from late 1947, when the Chinese communists were already fighting the Kuomintang virtually on a basis of equality, the central idea is the same: to concentrate a force overwhelmingly superior to that of the enemy in each engagement, although the enemy may be vastly superior in the overall balance of forces. As emphasized in both these texts, Mao is persuaded that these tactical principles can be applied only by the revolutionaries and not by their opponents, because only the revolutionaries can obtain the support of the population so that their armed forces can move among the peasant masses like a fish in water. (See the last paragraph of Text V J.)

Text V K, written in 1938, contains one of Mao's earliest and sharpest formulations of the idea – recently made famous by Lin Piao – of encircling the cities from the countryside. And Text V L, which declares that 'the army is the chief component of the political power of a state', foreshadows recent theoretical pronouncements, during the Great Proletarian Cultural Revolution, regarding the place of the army in the dictatorship of the proletariat.

S.R.S.

V · A Why can China's Red political power exist?[1]

The prolonged existence within a country of one or several small areas under Red political power amid the encirclement of White political power is a phenomenon that has never been found elsewhere in the world. There are peculiar reasons for this unusual phenomenon. . . . First, it cannot occur in any imperialist country or in any colony under direct imperialist rule, but only in economically backward, semi-colonial China, which is under indirect imperialist rule. For this unusual phenomenon can occur only in conjunction with another unusual condition, namely, the warfare within the White regime. The most striking characteristic[2] of semi-colonial China is that, since the first year of the Republic, the various cliques of old and new warlords, supported by the comprador class and the landed gentry, have waged incessant, internecine warfare. Such a phenomenon is found neither in any of the imperialist countries of the world nor in any colony under direct imperialist rule, but only in China, which is under indirect imperialist rule. Two things account for its occurrence, namely, China's localized agricultural economy (instead of a unified capitalist economy) and the imperialist policy of division and exploitation by marking off spheres of influence. The prolonged splits and wars within the White regime provide the conditions under which one or several small Red areas[3] can emerge amid the encirclement of the White political power.

1. Extracted from a resolution of 5 October 1928, *Hsüan-chi*, 1947 Supplement, p. 103.

Available translations: *Selected Works*, I, pp. 64–5.

2. In 1951, this became 'One of the characteristics'.

3. The phrase 'under the direction of the Communist Party' was added in 1951.

V · B The composition and training of the Red Army in earliest days[1]

1. *Origin of the Red Army soldiers.* They may be divided *into the following six groups:* (1) troops formerly under Yeh [T'ing] and Ho [Lung] in Chaochow and Swatow; (2) the former Guards Regiment of Wuchang; (3) peasant *militiamen* from Liuyang and P'ingkiang; (4) peasant *militiamen* from southern Hunan and workers from Shuikoushan; (5) men captured from the forces under Hsü K'e-hsiang, T'ang Sheng-chih, Pai Ch'ung-hsi, Chu P'ei-te, Wu Shang, and Hsiung Shih-hui; and (6) *workers* and peasants from the various *hsien* in the border area. *The first four groups form the backbone of the Army*, but after more than a year of *endless* battles, the troops formerly under Yeh and Ho, the Guards Regiment, and the peasant *militiamen* from Liuyang and P'ingkiang ... have been reduced to only one-third of their original strength. The *Red Army* from southern Hunan, *after eight months of struggle in the border area*, has also suffered heavy losses in killed and wounded. Therefore, although the first four groups, *owing to their superior quality*, have remained the basic force of the Fourth Red Army, ... they are far outnumbered by the last two. In the last two groups, the prisoners are more numerous; without reinforcements from this group, manpower would have become a serious problem for the Fourth Army. However, *even with these reinforcements*, *of which the quality is inferior to the former groups* (*though quite a few among them are good soldiers*), enlistment still cannot keep up with the increase in rifles; the rifles, once increased in number, are seldom lost, but soldiers may be lost at any time when they are wounded or killed, fall ill or desert (*a few soldiers desert every time we are defeated*). *Few of the peasants in the border areas are willing to serve as soldiers. Since the land has been divided up, they have all gone to till it. Now the soldiers of peasant or working-class origin in the Fourth Army in the border area constitute an extreme minority.*

1. Extracted from a report of 25 November 1928, to the Central Committee of the Chinese Communist Party, *Hsüan-chi*, 1947, Supplement, pp. 62–7.

Available translations: *Selected Works*, I, pp. 80–83.

Thus the problem is still serious. The Hunan Provincial Party Committee has promised to send workers here from Anyüan, and we hope this will be done at once.

2. *Composition.* One part consists of workers, the other of *éléments déclassés.* (*So it is not true to say, as the Hunan Provincial Committee did, that all the soldiers are* éléments déclassés.) The *contingent of* éléments déclassés *should be replaced by peasants and workers, but these are not available now.* On the one hand, when fighting is going on every day, the *éléments déclassés are after all especially good fighters.* Moreover, casualties are mounting high. *Consequently, not only can we not diminish the* éléments déclassés *now in our ranks*, but it is even difficult to find more for reinforcements. In these circumstances, the only method is to intensify political training, *so as to effect a qualitative change in these elements.*

3. *Nature.* The majority of the Red Army soldiers come from mercenary armies; but once they join the Red Army, the mercenary system is abolished.[1] The Red Army has never instituted the system of regular pay, but issues only food and pocket money...

4. *Political training.* The Red Army soldiers have *generally* become class conscious and acquired elementary political knowledge about land distribution, establishment of soviets, arming the workers and peasants, etc. They already know that they are fighting for themselves and for the workers and peasants. Consequently they can endure even this miserable life and bitter struggle without complaint.... The system of Party commissars has developed from experience, and in our opinion it cannot *yet* be abolished. The Party commissars at the army and division levels may be abolished.... But the commissars at the regiment, battalion, and company levels, particularly at the company level, must not be abolished *now.* Since the Party cell is organized on a company basis, the Party commissar of the company has to supervise the soldiers' committee of the whole company in carrying out political

1. In 1951, Mao added that the soldiers were conscious of fighting for the people.

training and directing the work of the mass movement and within the Party act as cell secretary. It has been proved that companies that have a better than average Party commissar are *somewhat* sounder than the others. Because the casualties among the lower cadres are heavy, soldiers captured from the enemy one day have often been made platoon or even company commanders the next, and some of those captured only last February or March are now battalion commanders. It is absurd to believe that the Party commissars can be abolished simply because our army is now called the Red Army . . .

5. *Military training.* The soldiers of other armies need six months' or a year's training before they can fight, but our soldiers, recruited only yesterday, have to fight today with practically no training to speak of. Consequently, part of the middle and higher cadres and many soldiers have only an extremely poor mastery of military techniques. Courage is their only strength. *This is very dangerous . . .*

6. *Problems of supply.* The Hunan Provincial Committee has asked us to pay attention to the material life of the soldiers and to make it at least a little better than that of the average worker or peasant. At present, the very reverse is the case in the army; *perhaps no one's life is so miserable as that of the Red Army soldiers. Owing to the shortage of funds*, each man gets only five cents a day for *food* (though rice is supplied *by local sources*); often even this rate is hard to maintain. *The common saying of the soldiers, 'Overthrow the capitalists, and eat pumpkin every day' expresses their misery . . .*

7. *Democracy in the Army.* Apart from the role played by the Party, the reason the Red Army can sustain itself without being exhausted, in spite of such miserable material conditions and such incessant engagements, is the thoroughness of its democratic[1] practice. The officers do not beat the soldiers; officers and

1. Here and throughout this selection, Mao in 1928 employed the term *min-ch'üan* (the second of Sun Yat-sen's 'Three People's Principles') to convey the idea of democracy. In 1951, he substituted the term *min-chu*, the more usual word for democracy.

soldiers have the same food and clothing and receive equal treatment; soldiers enjoy freedom of assembly and speech; cumbersome formalities and ceremonies are abolished; the financial administration is absolutely open to [the inspection of] all; and the *soldiers' representatives inspect the final accounts.* ... All these measures give great satisfaction to the soldiers; the newly captured soldiers in particular feel that the camp of today and the camp of yesterday are worlds apart. They feel that, although they are materially worse off in the Red Army than in the White, spiritually they are liberated; therefore, they are reasonably content. The fact that the same soldier fights more bravely in the Red Army today than he did for the enemy yesterday testifies to the effectiveness of these democratic practices. The Red Army is like a furnace in which all captured soldiers are melted down and transformed the moment they come over. In China not only the masses of workers and peasants[1] need democracy, but the army needs it even more urgently. The thoroughness of democratic practices in the army will be an important policy for destroying the feudal mercenary army in China ...

V · C Chingkang Mountain[2]

Below the hill were our flags and banners,
To the hilltop sounded our bugles and drums.
The foe surrounded us thousands strong,
But we were steadfast and never moved.

Our defence was strong as a wall already,
Now did our wills unite like a fortress.
From Huangyangchieh came the thunder of guns,
And the enemy army had fled in the night!

1. In 1951, the 'masses of workers and peasants' was replaced by 'people'.

2. See note to Text I C. Here I follow the Peking translation.

V · D Erroneous conceptions and their social origins[1]

On the purely military viewpoint. The purely military viewpoint is unusually widespread among a number of comrades in the Red Army. It manifests itself as follows:

1. To regard military work and political work as opposed to each other; to fail to recognize military work as only one of the means for accomplishing political tasks. Even to declare, 'When military work is well done, political work will naturally be well done; when military work is not well done, political work cannot be well done either.' This is to go a step further and to regard military work as leading political work.

2. To regard the task of the Red Army as similar to that of the White army – merely fighting. Not to understand that the significance of the tasks of the Chinese Red Army lies in the fact that it is an armed group for carrying out political tasks of a class nature. In order to carry out this task, particularly in present-day China, the Red Army must not merely fight; besides fighting, it should also shoulder such important tasks as agitating among the masses, organizing them, arming them, and helping them to set up political power.[2] When the Red Army fights, it fights not merely for the sake of fighting but *exclusively* to agitate among the masses, to organize them, to arm them, and to help them establish political power; apart from such objectives, fighting loses its meaning, and the Red Army the reason for its existence . . .

1. Extracted from a resolution written in December 1929, for the Ninth Conference of the Communist Party Organization of the Fourth Army of the Red Army. Only the first part of this resolution – from which the present extracts have been taken – is reproduced in the 1951 edition of *Hsüan-chi*, where it is presented as constituting the complete text. The present translation was made from Mao's *Chung-kuo Kung-ch'an-tang Hung-chün ti-ssu-chün ti-i-tz'u tai-piao ta-hui chüeh-i-an*, Hsin-min Ch'u-pan She, Hong Kong, 1949, pp. 4, 10–11, 14–15.

Available translations: *Selected Works*, I, pp. 105–14. This translation includes only the part printed in the *Hsüan-chi.*

2. Here the phrase 'and even establishing organizations of the Communist Party' was added in 1951.

On absolute equalitarianism. At one point, absolute equalitarianism in the Red Army developed to a very serious extent. *It is true that after numerous struggles it has been greatly reduced, but traces of it still exist.* For example ... denying the necessity for officers to ride horses in the performance of their duties and to regard horseback riding as a sign of inequality. To demand absolutely equal distribution of supplies and to object to larger allotments in special cases ...

Like extreme democratization in political matters, the source of absolute equalitarianism can be traced to an economy of handicrafts and small peasant farming ...

Not only is absolute equalitarianism merely an illusion of the peasants and small proprietors in an era in which capitalism has not yet been abolished, but even in the era of socialism material things will be distributed according to the requirements and work of each person, and there is definitely no such thing as absolute equalization. The distribution of material things among the personnel of the Red Army must be as equal as possible. ... But absolute, unreasonable equalitarianism must be opposed, because it is not needed in our struggle; on the contrary, it hinders the struggle.

On the mentality of roving insurgents.[1] The mentality of roving insurgents in the Red Army arises for the following reasons: (1) the *éléments déclassés* form the majority[2] of the Red Army soldiers – this is the immediate cause; and (2) there are great masses of *éléments déclassés* in the country, especially in the southern provinces – this is the indirect cause. As a result, a political mentality of roving insurgents and a point of view favourable to continual movement have arisen in the Fourth Army. But the type of large-scale actions by roving insurgents carried out by Huang Ch'ao, Li Ch'uang, and *Hung Hsiu-ch'üan*[3] are no longer valid in imperialist-ruled China, particularly

1. There are such great differences between the original and the 1951 versions of the text of this paragraph that no attempt has been made to indicate all the variants systematically.

2. In the 1951 edition, Mao admits to the presence of only 'a very large proportion' of *éléments déclassés*.

3. In 1951, the name of Hung Hsiu-ch'üan, the leader of the Taipings, was

in present-day China, into which advanced weapons (hand grenades, cannons, and machine guns), advanced methods of communication (military telephone and radio), and advanced methods of transportation (motorcar, steamship, and railroad) have already been imported. Consequently, the mentality of roving insurgents naturally cannot predominate in the Red Army. However, its influence is still great, manifesting itself as follows:

1. By an unwillingness to expand our political influence by strenuously helping the masses to establish political power, but instead attempting to expand it by applying only mobile guerrilla methods.

2. An unwillingness to expand the Red Army by first expanding the local detachments of the Red guards, then the local units of the Red Army, and finally the main forces of the Red Army, but instead attempting to do so by 'hiring men and buying horses' and 'recruiting deserters and taking in mutineers' [phrases used to describe the activities of ringleaders of rebellions or of outlaws].

3. Impatience in carrying on hard struggles together with the masses, and instead looking forward to go to the big cities and indulge in eating and drinking.

These manifestations of the mentality of the roving insurgents seriously hamper the Red Army in accomplishing the great tasks imposed upon it by the revolution; thus the elimination of this mentality is indeed one of the important aims of the ideological struggle in the Party organization of the Red Army.

The following methods of rectification should be applied:

1. Intensified education to change the incorrect ideas *that have their basis in the éléments déclassés* and eliminate the mentality of roving insurgents.

2. Intensified education to change the vagabond outlook among the basic sections of the Red Army and the newly captured soldiers.

3. Attracting active workers and peasants experienced in

deleted, evidently because Peking now considers the Taipings a great revolutionary movement and precursor of the Chinese Communist Party. Therefore it would not be proper to call Hung Hsiu-ch'üan merely the head of a band of roving insurgents, like the other peasant leaders mentioned in the same sentence.

struggle into the ranks of the Red Army in order to change the composition of the Red Army.

4. Creating new Red Army units composed of the masses of workers and peasants who are in the midst of struggle . . .

V · E The particularities of China's revolutionary War[1]

The laws of war must be studied and understood by anyone directing a war.

The laws of a revolutionary war must be studied and understood by anyone directing a revolutionary war.

The laws of China's revolutionary war must be studied and understood by anyone directing China's revolutionary war.

We are now engaged in a war; our war is a revolutionary war; and our revolutionary war is being waged in this semi-feudal, semi-colonial country of China. Thus we must not only study the laws of war in general, but also the laws of a particular revolutionary war and, moreover, the laws of the even more particular revolutionary war in China . . .

There is one group that holds an incorrect view, which we refuted long ago. These people maintain that it is enough merely to study the laws of war in general or, specifically, that it is enough to follow the rules published by the Chinese Government or the military academies. They do not see that these rules represent only the laws of war in general and, moreover, are copied entirely from abroad; if we copy them and apply them mechanically, without the slightest change in form or content, it will be like whittling down our feet to fit the shoes and we shall be defeated. Their argument is: Such things were learned at the cost of blood in the past, why are they of no use? They do not see that although we must value the experience acquired in the past at the cost of blood, we must

1. Extracted from *Strategic Problems of China's Revolutionary War*, written in 1936 and first published in 1941 (*Hsüan-chi*, 1947, Supplement, pp. 109–12, 128–30).

Available translations: *La Stratégie de la guerre révolutionnaire en Chine*, Éditions sociales, Paris, 1950. *Selected Works*, I, pp. 179–81, 196–9. This French translation is of the original text; only the revised text has been translated into English.

also value experience acquired at the cost of our own blood.

Another group holds a second incorrect view, which we also refuted long ago. These people declare that it is enough to study Russia's experience of the revolutionary war or, specifically, that it is enough to follow the laws that guided the Civil War in the Soviet Union and the military directives published there. They do not see that these laws and directives in the Soviet Union embody the special characteristics of the Civil War and the Red Army of the Soviet Union; if we copy them and apply them mechanically, allowing no change whatsoever, it will also be like whittling down our feet to fit the shoes and we shall be defeated. Their argument is: Ours, like the war in the Soviet Union, is a revolutionary war; since the Soviet Union has won victory, how can there be any alternative but to follow its example? They do not see that *although we must value Soviet experience, and even value it somewhat more than experiences in other countries throughout history, because it is the most recent experience of revolutionary war, we must value even more the experience of China's revolutionary war*,[1] because there are a great number of conditions special to the Chinese revolution and the Chinese Red Army . . .

What then are the characteristics of China's revolutionary war? I think there are four principal characteristics:

The first is that China is a semi-colonial country with a vast territory and rich resources, unevenly developed both politically and economically, and it has gone through the great revolution of 1924–7.

This characteristic indicates that it is possible for China's revolutionary war to develop and attain victory . . .

Let us now analyse this problem.

The unevenness of political and economic development in China is manifested in the coexistence of a few semi-modern industrial and commercial cities and the boundless expanses of

1. In the current edition, Mao has changed the italicized passages into their precise opposite. He now affirms that Soviet experience must be valued 'particularly' (not merely 'somewhat more'), adding that this experience was acquired under the leadership of Lenin and Stalin. As for Chinese experience, instead of being the most important, it becomes merely something that should also be valued.

rural districts *still stuck in the middle ages;* the coexistence of several millions of industrial workers on the one hand and, on the other, hundreds of millions of peasants under the old regime; the coexistence of big warlords controlling the central government and small warlords controlling the provinces; the coexistence of the regular army and a variety of heterogeneous armed forces; and the coexistence of a few railway and steamship lines and motor roads on the one hand and, on the other, the vast number of wheelbarrow paths and trails for pedestrians only, many of which are difficult to negotiate even for them.

China is a semi-colonial country. The disunity among the imperialist countries has caused the disunity among the various ruling blocs in China. A semi-colonial state controlled by several countries is different from a colony controlled by a single country.

China is a vast country – 'When the east is still dark, the west is lit up; when night falls in the south, the day breaks in the north'; hence one need not worry about whether there is room enough to move around.

China has gone through a great revolution, which has provided us with the seeds of the Red Army, the Chinese Communist Party, which leads the Red Army, and the masses who have participated in the revolution.

We have said, therefore, that the first characteristic of China's revolutionary war is that China is a semi-colonial country with a vast territory and rich resources that has gone through a revolution and is unevenly developed politically and economically. This characteristic determines not only our political strategy and tactics but our military strategy and tactics as well.

The second characteristic is the great strength of the enemy.

What is the situation of the Kuomintang, the enemy of the Red Army? It is a party that has seized political power and has stabilized it somewhat. It has gained the support of the principal counter-revolutionary countries in the world. It has remodelled its army, which has thus become different from any other army in Chinese history and, on the whole, similar to the armies of the modern states in the world; its army is supplied much more abundantly with arms and other equipment than the Red Army, and it is greater in numerical strength than the army in any other period of Chinese history, greater even than the standing army of any country in the world. There is a world of difference between the Kuomintang army and the Red Army . . .

The fact that the Chinese Red Army is confronted with such a powerful enemy constitutes the second characteristic of China's revolutionary war. This characteristic inevitably makes the war waged by the Red Army different in many ways from wars in general, from the Civil War in the Soviet Union, and from the Northern Expedition.

The third characteristic is that the Red Army is weak and small . . .

The *soviet* regimes are dispersed and isolated in mountainous or remote regions and deprived of any outside help. In economic and cultural conditions, the *soviet* areas are more backward than the Kuomintang areas. These bases were extremely small in the beginning and have not grown much larger. Moreover, they are often shifted about, and the Red Army possesses no really consolidated bases.

The Red Army is small in number, its arms are poor, and its access to food, bedding, clothing and other supplies is extremely difficult . . .

The fourth characteristic is the Communist Party's leadership and the agrarian revolution.

This characteristic is the inevitable result of the first one. It gives rise to the following two features: On the one hand, China's revolutionary war, though taking place in a period of reaction in China and throughout the world, can yet be victorious because it is led by the Communist Party and supported by the peasantry. Because we have secured the support of the peasantry, our soviet areas, though small, possess great political power and stand firmly opposed to the huge Kuomintang regime; in a military sense, this creates colossal difficulties for the attacking Kuomintang. The Red Army, though small, has great fighting capacity, because its men[1] have sprung from the agrarian revolution and are fighting for their own interests, and because officers and men are politically united.

1. Here, too, Mao inserted the phrase 'under the direction of the Communist Party' in the 1951 edition.

On the other hand, our situation contrasts sharply with that of the Kuomintang. Opposed to the agrarian revolution, the Kuomintang is deprived of the support of the peasantry. Despite the great size of its army, it cannot arouse the bulk of the soldiers or many of the lower-rank cadres, who come from the group of small producers, to risk their lives consciously for its sake. Officers and men are politically disunited and this reduces their fighting capacity.

A vast semi-colonial country that is unevenly developed politically and economically and that has gone through a great revolution; a powerful enemy; a weak and small Red Army, and the agrarian revolution – these are the four principal characteristics of China's revolutionary war . . .

V · F One against ten and ten against one: the essence of guerrilla tactics[1]

An army operating on strategically interior lines suffers from many disadvantages, and this is especially so in the case of the *Chinese* Red Army, confronted as it is with 'encirclement and suppression'. But in campaigns and battles we can and absolutely must change this situation. We can turn a big 'encirclement and suppression' campaign waged by the enemy against us into a number of small, separate campaigns of encirclement and suppression waged by us against the enemy. We can change the converging attack directed by the enemy against us on the plane of strategy into converging attacks directed by us against the enemy on the plane of campaigns and battles. We can change the enemy's strategic superiority over us into our superiority over him in campaigns and battles. We can put the enemy who is in a strong position strategically into a weak position in campaigns and battles. At the same time we can change our own strategically weak position into a strong position in campaigns and battles. This is what we call exterior-line operations within interior-line

1. For the source and available translations, see the note to Text V E. This passage occurs on pp. 168–73 of the Supplement to the 1947 edition of the *Hsüan-chi*, and on pp. 235–9 of the *Selected Works*, I.

operations, encirclement and suppression within 'encirclement and suppression', blockade within blockade, the offensive within the defensive, superiority within inferiority, strength within weakness, advantage within disadvantage, and initiative within passivity. The winning of victory in the strategic defensive depends basically on this measure – concentration of troops.

In the war annals of the [Chinese] *soviets*,[1] this has often been an important controversial issue. ... In 1933 the exponents of military equalitarianism put forward the theory of 'striking with two fists' and splitting the main force of the Red Army in two, to seek victories simultaneously in two strategic directions. As a result, one fist remained idle while the other was tired out with fighting, and we failed to win the greatest victory possible at the time. In my opinion, *whether we have ten thousand, a million,*[2] *or ten million troops*, we should employ our army in only one main direction, not two. I am not objecting to operations in two or more directions, but at any given time there ought to be only one main direction. *During the European War, the powerful German Army had only one main direction of operations at a time from beginning to end. Among the military critics, there are those who consider that it was an error to withdraw part of the troops from the western theatre of operations in August and September 1914 in order to reinforce the eastern front, because of the danger to East Prussia. If we assume that these withdrawals are the principal cause, or one of the causes, of the lack of success in the western theatre of operations, then these criticisms are justified.* The Chinese Red Army, which entered the arena of the civil war as a small and weak force, has since repeatedly defeated its powerful antagonist and won victories that have astonished the world, and it has done so by relying largely on the employment of concentrated strength. Any one of its great victories can prove this point. When we say, 'Pit one against ten, pit ten against a hundred', we are speaking of strategy, of the whole war and the

1. Here and elsewhere in this text (and in many other texts), Mao has today found various substitutes for the term 'soviet' in referring to the period 1931–4, in order to avoid this reminder of too-slavish imitation of Russian terms and methods.

2. The slogan of the Central Committee in 1933–4 was 'a Red Army a million strong'.

overall balance of forces, and in this sense that is just what we have been doing. However, we are not speaking of campaigns and tactics, in which we must never do so. Whether in counter-offensives or offensives, we should always concentrate a big force to strike at one part of the enemy forces. ... Our strategy is 'pit one against ten', and our tactics are 'pit ten against one' – these contrary and yet complementary propositions constitute one of our principles for gaining mastery over the enemy ...

To abandon *arming the people and* small-scale guerrilla warfare and 'concentrate every single rifle in the Red Army', as advocated by Li Li-san-*ism*,[1] has long since been proved wrong. Considering the wars of *the* [*Chinese*] *soviets*, the operations of the *armed* people *and of small-scale* guerrilla units, and those of the main forces of the Red Army complement each other like a man's two arms, and if we had only the main forces of the Red Army without the *armed* people *and the small-scale* guerrilla units, we would be *nothing but* a warrior with only one arm. ... The kind of concentration of forces we advocate does not mean the abandonment of arming the people and of small-scale guerrilla warfare.[2]

... The kind of concentration we advocate is based on the principle of guaranteeing absolute or relative superiority on the battlefield. To cope with a strong enemy or to fight on a battlefield of vital importance, we must have an absolutely superior force; for instance, a force of forty thousand was concentrated to fight the nine thousand men under Chang Hui-tsan on 30 December 1930. To cope with a weaker enemy or to fight on a battlefield of no great importance, a relatively superior force is sufficient; for instance, only some ten thousand Red Army men were employed to fight Liu Ho-ting's seven thousand men in Chienning on 29 May 1931, in the last battle of the second campaign of encirclement and suppression.

That is not to say that we must have numerical superiority on every occasion. In certain circumstances, we may go into battle with a relatively or absolutely inferior force. The case of going

1. In the current edition, Li Li-san's ideas are no longer dignified by calling them an 'ism'; the term has been replaced by 'Li Li-san line'.

2. In the current edition, this sentence has been moved from the end to the beginning of this paragraph.

into battle with a relatively inferior force may occur, for example, when we have only a rather small Red Army force in a certain area (not when we have more troops and have not concentrated them). Then, in order to *withstand* the attack of the stronger enemy in conditions where popular support, terrain and weather are greatly in our favour, it is of course necessary to concentrate the main part of our Red Army force for a surprise attack on a segment of one flank of the enemy while containing his centre and his other flank with guerrillas or small detachments, and in this way victory can be won. In our surprise attack on this segment of the enemy flank, the principle of using a superior force against an inferior force, of using the many to defeat the few, still applies. The same principle also applies when we go into battle with an absolutely inferior force, for example, when a guerrilla force makes a surprise attack on a large White Army force, but is attacking only a small part of it.

As for the argument that the concentration of a large force for action in a single battle area is subject to the limitations of terrain, roads, supplies and billeting facilities, it should be evaluated according to the circumstances. There is a difference in the degree to which these limitations affect the Red Army and the White Army, as the Red Army can stand greater hardships than the White Army.

We use the few to defeat the many – this we say to the rulers of China as a whole. We use the many to defeat the few – this we say to the enemy on the battlefield. That is no longer a secret, and in general the enemy is by now well acquainted with our ways. However, he can neither prevent our victories nor avoid his own losses, because he does not know when and where we shall *attack him*. This we keep secret. The Red Army generally operates by surprise attacks.

V · G Poems on the Long March[1]

The Long March

The Red Army fears not the trials of a distant march;
To them a thousand mountains, ten thousand rivers are nothing;
Before their eyes the Five Ridges ripple like little waves,
And the mountain peaks of Wumeng are like mud balls beneath
  their feet.
Warm are the cloud-topped cliffs washed by the River of Golden
  Sand,
Cold are the iron chains that span the Tatu River.
The myriad snows of Minshan only make them happier,
And when the three Armies have crossed, each face is smiling.

Loushan Pass

Keen is the west wind;
In the endless void the wild geese cry at the frosty morning moon.
  The frosty morning moon.
The clatter of horses' hoofs rings sharp,
And the bugle's note is muted.

They say that the strong pass is iron hard
And yet this very day with a mighty step we shall cross its summit,
  We shall cross its summit!
The hills are blue like the sea,
And the dying sun like blood.

Mount Liupan

The sky is high, the clouds are pale,
We watch the wild geese flying south till they vanish;
If we reach not the Great Wall, we are no true men!
Already we have come ten thousand *li*.

High on the crest of Liupan Mountain
Our banners idly wave in the west wind.
Today we hold the long cord in our hands;
When shall we bind fast the Grey Dragon?[2]

1. See note to Text I C. Here I follow the Peking translation with some modifications.

2. Name of an Eastern constellation. Here it refers to the Japanese invaders from the East.

V · H Conscious activity in war[1]

... When we say we are opposed to the subjective approach to a problem, we mean that we must oppose ideas of individuals not based upon or not corresponding with objective facts, because, being fancies and falsehoods, they will lead to failure if we act on them. But everything must be done by man; the protracted war and final victory will not take place without human action. And action presupposes ideas, arguments, opinions, plans, directives, policies, strategies, and tactics; only thus can one act, and act successfully. Ideas, etc., are subjective, while endeavours or actions are manifestations of the subjective component of the objective, but both are part of an activity peculiar to human beings. We term such activity 'conscious activity', a characteristic distinguishing men from objects. All ideas based upon and corresponding to objective facts are correct ideas, and all endeavours or actions based upon correct ideas are correct actions. We must develop such ideas and actions, such conscious activity. The Anti-Japanese War is waged to drive out an imperialist power and to transform the old China into a new China. The people throughout China must be mobilized and their conscious activity in resisting Japan developed before this objective can be achieved ...

Conscious activity is a distinctive characteristic of man, *especially of man at war*. This characteristic is manifested *in all of man's acts*, but *nowhere more strongly* than in war. Victory or defeat in a war is decided on the one hand by the military, political, economic, and geographical conditions, by the character of the war, and by international support on both sides. But it is not decided by these alone; these alone constitute only the possibility of victory or defeat; they do not in themselves decide the issue. To decide the issue, subjective efforts must be added, efforts in directing and waging the war, i.e., conscious activity in war.

People who direct a war cannot strive for victories beyond the

1. Extracted from 'On protracted war', published in *Chieh-fang*, no. 43, 1 July 1938, p. 22.

Available translations: *Selected Works*, II, pp. 151–2.

limit allowed by the objective conditions, but within that limit they can and must strive actively for victory. The stage of action for these commanders in a war must be built upon objective conditions, but on this stage, they can direct the performance of many living dramas, full of sound and colour, of power and grandeur ..

V · I We must not fear the enemy[1]

... We must not, because we are undergoing the suffering of a war more cruel than any seen in the past, immediately capitulate; nor must we, under the influence of a long war, suddenly lose our endurance and give way to lassitude. We must inspire ourselves with the most resolute spirit of unyielding struggle, with the most burning patriotic sentiments, and with the will to endurance, and carry out a protracted struggle against the enemy. We must know that, although the circumstances and the duration of the war are cruel and protracted, this is nothing compared to what would happen if the war were lost; if our country were destroyed and the whole of our people reduced to a position of irretrievable ruin, the suffering would be even more cruel and would never come to an end. Therefore, however cruel the war may be, we must absolutely and firmly endure until the last five minutes of struggle. This is especially the case with our present enemy, who finds his advantage in a rapid decision in the war, whereas our advantage is to be found in the strategy of a protracted war.

When we see the enemy, simply because he has a weapon in his hands, we must not be frightened to death like a rat who sees a cat. We must not be afraid of approaching him or of infiltrating into his midst in order to carry out sabotage. We are men; our enemies are also men; we are all men, so what should we fear? The fact that he has weapons? We can find a way to seize his

1. Extracted from *Chi-ch'u chan-shu*, Tzu-ch'iang Ch'u-pan-she, Hankow, 1938 (Transcript of lectures by Mao).

Available translations: Mao Tse-tung, *Basic Tactics*, translated with an introduction by Stuart R. Schram. Foreword by Brigadier General Samuel B. Griffith, II, Frederick A. Praeger, New York, 1966, pp. 52–3.

weapons. All we are afraid of is getting killed by the enemy. But when we undergo the oppression of the enemy to such a point as this, how can anyone still fear death? And if we do not fear death, then what is there to fear about the enemy? So when we see the enemy, whether he is many or few, we must act as though he is bread that can satisfy our hunger, and immediately swallow him.

V · J War and politics[1]

... 'War is the continuation of politics'; in this sense war is politics and war itself is a political action; there has not been a single war since ancient times that did not bear a political character. The Anti-Japanese War is a revolutionary war waged by the whole Chinese nation. Victory in this war is inseparable from the over-all policy of persistently carrying on our war of resistance and maintaining the united front. It is inseparable from the mobilization of all the people in the nation, from political principles such as unity of officers and men, unity of the army and the people, and the disintegration of the enemy forces, from the implementation of the united-front policy; from cultural mobilization, and from efforts to win the support of international forces and of the people of the enemy's country. In short, war cannot be separated from politics. Any tendency among the anti-Japanese soldiers to belittle politics, to isolate war from it, and to make war an absolute, is erroneous and must be corrected.

But war has its special characteristics and in this sense it is not identical with politics. 'War is a special political technique for the realization of certain political objectives.'[2] When politics has developed to a certain stage beyond which it cannot proceed by the usual means, war is made to sweep away the obstacles in the

1. The first three paragraphs of this text are taken from 'On protracted war' (see note to Text V G); tle fourth is from *All the Problems of the anti-Japanese Guerrilla War* (see below the bibliography), p. 55 of the Chinese text.

Available translations: For the first three paragraphs, see note to Text V H; regarding translations of the fourth paragraph see the note in the bibliography.

2. In the current edition, this sentence has been replaced by Clausewitz's well-known dictum about war, which had been used by Lenin as well.

way of politics. For instance, the semi-independent status of China has been an obstacle to the political development of Japanese imperialism, and so Japan started her war of aggression to sweep away that impediment. . . . It can therefore be said that politics is bloodless war, while war is the politics of bloodshed . . .

Such a gigantic national revolutionary war as ours cannot succeed without universal and thoroughgoing political mobilization. China was greatly remiss in failing to undertake anti-Japanese political mobilization before the war of resistance. By this, she lost a move to the enemy. Even after the war of resistance began, political mobilization had been far from universal, let alone thoroughgoing. News about the war reached the great majority of the people through the enemy's shelling and air bombing. That also constituted a kind of mobilization, but it was done by the enemy, not by ourselves. People in remote regions who cannot hear the guns lead a tranquil life even now. This situation must be changed, otherwise there can be no victory for our life-and-death struggle. We must not again fail to make the move against our enemy; on the contrary, we must fully exploit this move to vanquish him. Such a move is of the highest significance, in fact a matter of paramount importance, whereas our inferiority in things like weapons is but secondary. With the common people of the whole country mobilized, we shall create a vast sea of humanity in which the enemy will be swallowed up, obtain relief for our shortage in arms and other things, and secure the prerequisites to overcome every difficulty in the war. In order to achieve victory, we must persistently carry on the war of resistance, maintain the united front, and keep up the protracted war. But none of these can be separated from the mobilization of the common people. To aim at attaining victory while neglecting political mobilization means 'trying to drive one's chariot southward by heading northward', a step that would inevitably forfeit victory . . .

There are those who feel that it is hardly conceivable for a guerrilla unit to exist for a long period behind the enemy lines. This is a viewpoint based on ignorance of the relations between the army and the people. The popular masses are like water, and the army is like a fish. How then can it be said that when there is water, a fish will have difficulty in preserving its existence? An army which fails to maintain good discipline gets into opposition with the popular masses, and thus by its own actions dries up the water. In this case, it naturally cannot continue to exist. All guerrilla units must thoroughly understand this principle.

V · K Encircling the cities from the countryside[1]

The question is as follows: the enemy has occupied China's principal cities and lines of communication, and bases himself on the cities to oppose us; we base ourselves on the countryside to oppose the enemy. Can the countryside defeat the cities? The answer is that it is difficult, but it can be done. . . . The question of China's cities and countryside today is qualitatively different from that of the cities and the countryside in capitalist countries abroad. In capitalist countries, the cities rule the countryside in reality as well as in outward form, and when the head constituted by the cities is cut off, the four limbs of the countryside cannot continue to exist. It is impossible to conceive of a protracted guerrilla war carried on by the peasants in the countryside against the cities in a country such as England, America, France, Germany, Japan, etc. Such a thing is also impossible in a small semi-colonial country. . . . In a big semi-colonial country such as China, this possibility has now emerged, but very obviously three inter-related conditions are required. The first is that it should be a semi-colonial country. In a semi-colonial country, although the cities have a leadership function, they cannot altogether rule the countryside. For the cities are too small, and the countryside is too enormous, and the vast human and material resources are to be found in the countryside rather than in the cities. The second condition is that it should be a big country. If you lose part of it, there is still another part remaining. The enemy is controlling a big country with few troops, and if you add to this our resolute resistance, the enemy is forced into a situation where he experiences the difficulties of having an insufficient military force,

1. Extracted from Chapter 3, paragraph 14 of *On the New Stage*, 1938. For source and available translations, see note to Text II A.

and of having this force split up. Thus, not only do we have a main base area from which to wage a war of resistance ... but we also have a broad area behind the enemy lines in which we can carry on guerrilla warfare.... The third condition is given by present circumstances. If, a few decades ago, China had been conquered militarily by a great imperialist country, as England conquered India, then we could hardly have avoided losing our state (*wang kuo*).[1] But today things are different. Today, in particular, China has progressed: there are new political parties, new armies, and a new type of people, and this is the basic force for defeating the enemy. Less important is a decline in Japan's own position ... and still less important is the change in the international situation.... I have already explained these points in detail in *On Protracted War*. To sum up, in today's big semi-colonial countries such as China, there exist many favourable conditions. If we rely fundamentally on organizing a resolute, prolonged and widespread war of resistance against the enemy who has occupied our cities, if we wage war on many interlocking fronts, encircle the cities and isolate them, meanwhile gradually increasing our own strength over a long period, and so transform the relations between the enemy and ourselves; and if we co-ordinate these tactics with changes in the international situation – in this case, we will be able to drive out the enemy progressively and to regain control of the cities. There is not the slightest doubt that it is difficult, even in China today, for the countryside to oppose the cities. For the cities as a whole are concentrated, whereas the countryside is scattered.... Nevertheless we must state that the countryside can defeat the cities.... In the conditions prevailing during the civil war, a very small portion of the countryside carried on a protracted war against the cities, even at a time when all of the imperialist countries together were opposing communism. Who would venture to say that under the conditions of the national war, and moreover at a time when the imperialist camp is divided, the greater part of the Chinese

1. On the concept of 'losing one's state' and becoming 'slaves without a country', regarded in late nineteenth and early twentieth century China as the worst of all misfortunes, see *Marxism and Asia*, Text VI 2, and the related passage in the introduction.

countryside cannot carry on a protracted war against the enemy in the cities? There is not the slightest doubt that we can. Moreover, there is a great difference between what we call the countryside today, and the countryside at the time of the civil war. Not only is the area much greater, and not only do we possess in addition, in the broad rear made up of such provinces as Yünnan, Kweichow and Szechuan, a number of cities and of industrial enterprises, but we have established relations with foreign countries, or are in a position to establish them.... As Chairman [of the Military Council] Chiang pointed out in his message to the citizens last December: 'The heart of China's protracted war of resistance, the source of her ultimate victory, is to be found neither in Nanking nor in any other great city, but lies in reality in the villages of the whole country, and in the firmness of heart of the people.' This is altogether correct; although the war is difficult, a victorious future awaits us.

V · L Political power grows out of the barrel of a gun[1]

Every communist must understand this truth: Political power grows out of the barrel of a gun. Our principle is that the Party commands the gun; the gun shall never be allowed to command the Party. But it is also true that with the gun at our disposal we can really build up the Party organizations; the Eighth Route Army has built up a powerful Party organization in North China. We can also rear cadres and create schools, culture and mass movements. Everything in Yenan has been built up by means of the gun. Anything can grow out of the barrel of the gun. Viewed from the Marxist theory of the state, the army is the chief component of the political power of a state. Whoever wants to seize and hold on to political power must have a strong army. Some people have ridiculed us as advocates of the 'theory of the omnipotence of war'; yes, we are, we are advocates of the theory of the omnipotence of revolutionary war. This is not a bad thing;

1. Extracted from Mao's concluding remarks at the Sixth Plenum of the Central Committee, in November 1938, *Hsüan-chi*, II, p. 511.
Available translations: *Selected Works*, II, pp. 224–5.

it is good and it is Marxist. With the help of guns, the Russian communists brought about socialism. We want to bring about a democratic republic. Experience in the class struggle of the era of imperialism teaches us that the working class and the toiling masses cannot defeat the armed bourgeois and landlord except by the power of the gun; in this sense we can even say that the whole world can be remoulded only with the gun. As advocates of the abolition of war, we do not desire war; but war can only be abolished through war – in order to get rid of the gun, we must first grasp it in hand.

V · M The military principles for defeating Chiang Kai-shek[1]

. . . Our principles of operation are:

1. To attack dispersed, isolated enemy forces first; to attack concentrated, strong enemy forces later.

2. To take small and medium cities and extensive rural areas first; to take big cities later.

3. To make the wiping out of the enemy's effective strength our main objective, rather than the holding or seizure of a city or place. Holding or seizing a city or place is the outcome of wiping out the enemy's effective strength, and often a city or place can be held only after it has changed hands a number of times.

4. In every battle, to concentrate an absolutely superior force (two, three, four, and sometimes even five or six times the enemy's strength), to encircle the enemy forces completely, to strive to wipe them out thoroughly and not let any escape from the net. In special circumstances, to deal crushing blows to the enemy, that is, to concentrate all our strength on a frontal attack and also to attack one or both of his flanks, with the aim of wiping out one part and routing another, so that our army can swiftly move its troops to smash other enemy forces. To avoid battles of attrition

1. Extracted from a report of 25 December 1947, entitled 'The present situation and our tasks', *Mu-ch'ien hsing-shih ho wo-men ti jen-wu*, Chieh-fang She, 1948.

Available translations: *Selected Works*, IV, pp. 161–2.

in which we lose more than we gain or only break even. In this way, although we are inferior as a whole (in terms of numbers), we are absolutely superior in every part and every specific campaign, and this ensures victory in the campaign. As time goes on, we shall become superior as a whole and eventually wipe out the enemy.

5. To fight no battle unprepared, to fight no battle if we are not sure of victory; to try to be well prepared for each battle, to make every effort to ensure victory in the prevailing conditions.

6. To give full play to our style of fighting – courage in battle, no fear of sacrifice or fatigue, and continuous fighting (that is, fighting successive battles in a short time without rest).

7. To wipe out the enemy through mobile warfare, at the same time paying attention to the tactics of positional attack and capturing fortified enemy points and cities.

8. With regard to attacking cities, resolutely to seize all weakly defended fortified enemy points and cities. To seize at opportune moments all moderately defended fortified enemy points and cities if circumstances permit. As for strongly defended fortified enemy points and cities, to wait until conditions are ripe and then take them.

9. To replenish our strength with all the arms and most of the personnel captured from the enemy. Our army's main sources of manpower and *matériel* are at the front.

10. To make good use of the intervals between campaigns to rest, train, and consolidate our troops. In general, periods of rest, training, and consolidation should not be very long, and the enemy should so far as possible be permitted no breathing space.

These are the main methods employed by the People's Liberation Army in defeating Chiang Kai-shek. They are the result of the tempering of the People's Liberation Army in long years of fighting against domestic and foreign enemies and are completely suited to our present situation. The Chiang Kai-shek bandit gang and the U.S. imperialist military personnel in China are very well acquainted with our military methods. Seeking ways to counter them, Chiang Kai-shek has often assembled his generals and field officers for training and made them study our military literature and captured documents. The U.S. military has recommended to

Chiang Kai-shek one strategy and tactics after another for destroying the People's Liberation Army; it has trained Chiang Kai-shek's troops and supplied them with military equipment. But none of these efforts can save the Chiang Kai-shek bandit gang from defeat, because our strategy and tactics are based on a people's war; no army opposed to the people can use our strategy and tactics...

VI. Dictatorship, Contradictions and the Mass Line

As explained in the preface to the revised edition, it is this chapter and the next one that have been most extensively recast. They still deal with internal policies in China since 1949, and the antecedents of these policies in Mao's previous thinking, but the material has been redistributed according to different criteria. In a word, the present chapter now deals with the forms of political power, and the next one with the way in which power is used to reshape society.

The first of the three sub-divisions of Chapter VI is devoted to general statements regarding the form of government appropriate to a socialist state. Text A 1 contains Mao's refutation of Bertrand Russell's arguments for communism without dictatorship. (Russell expounded these ideas in a lecture in Changsha in the autumn of 1920 which Mao attended.) Text A3, which is the continuation of the extract from 'On People's Democratic Dictatorship' in Chapter III, shows clearly that for Mao the reign of freedom – which he defines in Marxist terms as a classless society and in traditional Chinese terms as the 'great harmony' – is to be reached only after society has been transformed by strict discipline. This text, written in 1949, offers an interesting contrast with Text A 2, which dates from 1945 and which rejects dictatorship in favour of a broad coalition of democratic forces.

Part B of this chapter is devoted to Mao's overall vision of Chinese society in terms of the central idea of contradictions. Text B 1 is a brief extract from the 1937 article 'On contradiction', containing a citation of Lenin's famous phrase, published in the *Leninskii Sbornik* in 1929, which constitutes the *locus classicus* of the idea of non-antagonistic contradictions under socialism. The brief but striking passage constituting Text B 2 is taken from an editorial of the *Jen-min jih-pao* of April 1956, which although not signed by Mao, has been attributed to him. (According to the note accompanying its publication the editorial was written after a meeting of the newspaper's editors with the Central Committee of the Chinese Communist Party.) There is no doubt, in any case, that it reflects Mao's viewpoint. Text B 3 consists of substantial extracts from Mao's speech of 27 February 1957 on solving contradictions among the people. This speech was discussed in the general introduction, and is too well known to require lengthy commentary here. It straddles, as it were, the subject matter of this chapter and the next one, since it deals at some length with the function of dictatorship in society, and also with the problems of cultural transformation.

Part C of this chapter, which contains a number of new texts not included in the first edition, deals with the role of the Chinese Communist Party and its working style. Text C 1 contains Mao's statement of the well-known Leninist principle of democratic centralism. Texts C 2 and C 4 express his desire to proceed by persuasion rather than constraint in changing the mentality of his fellow citizens, and Text C 3 is the classic statement of the 'mass line'. Text C 6 very clearly shows the limits of Mao's tolerance of 'erroneous' ideas, and of his desire to arouse the masses to genuinely spontaneous action. Text C 5 strongly emphasizes both the key role of the Communist Party in the revolutionary process, and the Chinese debt to the Russian example in building such a political instrument. Text C 7, which dates from 1949, displays the emphasis on 'plain living and hard struggle' which is such an important theme of the current Great Proletarian Cultural Revolution. Text C 8, which dates from the first great wave of radicalism in China in 1955, shows Mao still insisting heavily on the role of the Party cadres, but Text C 9, which comes from the same volume (*Socialist Upsurge in China's Countryside*), indicates that already at that time he was becoming suspicious of the 'right opportunism' which he found 'prevalent almost to the point of becoming universal' in the Party. Text C 10 consists of extracts from the twenty-three-point directive of January 1965 regarding the 'socialist education' movement in the countryside. It is in this document, today attributed to Mao, that 'people within the Party who are in authority and are taking the capitalist road' were first singled out as the principal object of attack. The last three texts, from the period of the cultural revolution (Texts C 11 to C 13) show Mao struggling with the basic contradiction of this whole movement: to make use of the old cadres, and at the same time to break their monopoly of administrative and political power and shake them up by contact with the masses.

S.R.S.

VI · A 1 Communism and dictatorship[1]

In his lecture at Changsha, Russell ... took a position in favour of communism but against the dictatorship of the workers and peasants. He said that one should employ the method of education to change the consciousness of the propertied classes, and that in this way it would not be necessary to limit freedom or to have recourse to war and bloody revolution.... My objections to Russell's viewpoint can be stated in a few words: 'This is all very well as a theory, but it is unfeasible in practice.' ... Education requires (1) money, (2) people, and (3) instruments. In today's world, money is entirely in the hands of the capitalists. Those who have charge of education are all either capitalists or slaves of capitalists. In today's world, the schools and the press, the two most important instruments of education, are entirely under capitalist control. In short, education in today's world is capitalist education. If we teach capitalism to children, these children, when they grow up, will in turn teach capitalism to a second generation of children. Education thus remains in the hands of the capitalists. Then the capitalists have 'parliaments' to pass laws protecting the capitalists and handicapping the proletariat; they have 'governments' to apply these laws and to enforce the advantages and the prohibitions that they contain; they have 'armies' and 'police' to defend the well-being of the capitalists and to repress the demands of the proletariat; they have 'banks' to serve as repositories in the circulation of their wealth; they have 'factories', which are the instruments by which they monopolize the production of goods.

1. Extracted from two letters to Ts'ai Ho-sen, in November 1920 and January 1921, published in *Hunan li-shih tzu-liao*, no. 9, 1959, pp. 83–4. Available translations: none.

Thus, if the communists do not seize political power, they will not be able to find any refuge in this world; how, under such circumstances, could they take charge of education? Thus, the capitalists will continue to control education and to praise their capitalism to the skies, so that the number of converts to the proletariat's communist propaganda will diminish from day to day. Consequently, I believe that the method of education is unfeasible. ... What I have just said constitutes the first argument. The second argument is that, based on the principle of mental habits and on my observation of human history, I am of the opinion that one absolutely cannot expect the capitalists to become converted to communism. ... If one wishes to use the power of education to transform them, then since one cannot obtain control of the whole or even an important part of the two instruments of education – schools and the press – even if one has a mouth and a tongue and one or two schools and newspapers as means of propaganda ... this is really not enough to change the mentality of the adherents of capitalism even slightly; how then can one hope that the latter will repent and turn toward the good? So much from a psychological standpoint. From a historical standpoint ... one observes that no despot, imperialist, and militarist throughout history has ever been known to leave the stage of history of his own free will without being overthrown by the people. Napoleon I proclaimed himself emperor, and failed; then there was Napoleon III. Yüan Shih-k'ai failed; then, alas, there was Tuan Ch'i-jui. ... From what I have just said, based on both a psychological and a historical standpoint, it can be seen that capitalism cannot be overthrown by the force of a few feeble efforts in the domain of education. This is the second argument. There is yet a third argument, most assuredly a very important argument, even more important in reality. If we use peaceful means to attain the goal of communism, when will we finally achieve it? Let us assume that a century will be required, a century marked by the unceasing groans of the proletariat. What position shall we adopt in the face of this situation? The proletariat is many times more numerous than the bourgeoisie; if we assume that the proletariat constitutes two-thirds of humanity, then one billion of the earth's one billion five hundred million inhabitants are proletarians (I fear that the figure is even higher), who during this century will be cruelly exploited by the remaining third of capitalists. How can we bear this? Furthermore, since the proletariat has already become conscious of the fact that it, too, should possess wealth, and of the fact that its sufferings are unnecessary, the proletarians are discontented, and a demand for communism has arisen and has already become a fact. This fact confronts us, we cannot make it disappear; when we become conscious of it we wish to act. This is why, in my opinion, the Russian revolution, as well as the radical communists in every country, will daily grow more powerful and numerous and more tightly organized. This is the natural result. This is the third argument...

There is a further point pertaining to my doubts about anarchism. My argument pertains not merely to the impossibility of a society without power or organization. I should like to mention only the difficulties in the way of the establishment of such a form of society and of its final attainment.... For all the reasons just stated, my present viewpoint on absolute liberalism, anarchism, and even democracy is that these things are fine in theory, but not feasible in practice...

VI · A 2 Chinese forms and Soviet forms[1]

... Only through democracy can one arrive at socialism. This is an axiom of Marxism. In China, the period of struggling for democracy will be a long one. Without a unified state based on a new-democratic coalition; without the development of a new-democratic state economy; without the development of a *vast* private capitalist economy and cooperative economy; without the development of a national, scientific, and mass culture, that is, a new-democratic culture; without the liberation and development of the individual initiative of hundreds of millions of people; in short without a thorough bourgeois-democratic

1. Extracted from *On Coalition Government*, Mao's report to the Seventh Party Congress, 1945. (*Lun lien-ho cheng-fu*, Chieh-fang She, 1945, pp. 42, 46.)

Available translations: *Selected Works*, III, pp. 283–4.

revolution of a new type,[1] the establishment of socialism on the debris of a colonial, semi-colonial, and semi-feudal China is an empty dream...

Some people suspect that after the communists come to power they will perhaps, following the example of Russia, establish a proletarian dictatorship and a one-party system. Our answer is that a new-democratic state based on the union of several democratic classes is different in principle from a socialist state based on a proletarian dictatorship.[2] China, during the entire period of the new-democratic system, cannot and therefore should not be a system of one-class dictatorship and a one-party monopoly of government. If any party, any social group, any individual outside the Communist Party adopts a cooperative, friendly attitude toward the Communist Party, we can have no reason for not cooperating with them. Russian history has created the Russian system. There they have eliminated the social system of exploitation of man by man and have realized the newest type of democracy, namely the socialist political, economic, and cultural system. All anti-socialist political parties have been thrown out by the people. They support only the Bolsheviks. In this way they have created the Russian state, which is entirely necessary and reasonable for them. ... Chinese history[3] will create the Chinese system. For a long period there will exist a special type of system that is entirely necessary and reasonable for us, but different from that of Russia – a new-democratic type of state and government with a union of several democratic classes.

1. Here the current edition has added: 'led by the Communist Party'.

2. In the 1951 edition, Mao has added: 'To be sure, the new-democratic system we defend is created under the leadership of the proletariat, under the leadership of the Communist Party.'

3. In the current edition, this reads: 'The *contemporary* history of China'.

VI · A 3 The function of dictatorship in the transformation of society[1]

... 'Don't you want to abolish state power?' Yes, we do, but not right now; we cannot do it yet. Why? Because imperialism still exists, because domestic reaction still exists, because classes still exist in our country. Our present task is to strengthen the people's state apparatus – mainly the people's army, the people's police, and the people's courts – in order to consolidate national defence and protect the people's interests. Given this condition, China can develop steadily, under the leadership of the working class and the Communist Party, from an agricultural into an industrial country and from a new-democratic into a socialist and communist society, abolish classes, and realize the Great Harmony [*ta-t'ung*]. The state apparatus, including the army, the police, and the courts, is the instrument by which one class oppresses another. It is an instrument for the oppression of antagonistic classes; it is violence and not 'benevolence'. 'You are not benevolent!' Quite so. We definitely do not apply a policy of benevolence to the reactionaries and the reactionary activities of the reactionary classes. Our policy of benevolence is applied only within the ranks of the people, not to the reactionaries or to the reactionary activities of reactionary classes, for these are outside the people.

The people's state protects the people. Only when the people have such a state can they educate and remould themselves on a countrywide scale by democratic methods and, with everyone taking part, shake off the influence of domestic and foreign reactionaries (which is still very strong, will survive for a long time, and cannot be quickly destroyed), rid themselves of the bad habits and ideas acquired in the old society, not allow themselves to be led astray by the reactionaries, and continue to advance – to advance toward a socialist and communist society.

Here, the method we employ is democratic – the method of

1. Extracted from 'On the people's democratic dictatorship', 1949 *Hsüan-chi*, IV, pp. 1480–82.

Available translations: *Selected Works*, IV, pp. 418–19.

persuasion, not of compulsion. When anyone among the people breaks the law, he too should be punished, imprisoned, or even sentenced to death; but this is a matter of a few individual cases and differs in principle from the dictatorship exercised over the reactionaries as a class.

As for the members of the reactionary classes and individual reactionaries, so long as they do not rebel, sabotage, or create trouble after their political power has been overthrown, land and work will be given to them as well to allow them to live and remould themselves through work. If they are not willing to work, the people's state will compel them. Propaganda and educational work will be done among them too and, moreover, will be done with as much care and thoroughness as among the captured army officers in the past. This, too, may be called a 'policy of benevolence' if you like, but it is imposed by us on the members of the enemy classes and cannot be mentioned in the same breath with the work of self-education that we carry on within the ranks of the revolutionary people.

Such remoulding of members of the reactionary classes can be accomplished only by a state of the people's democratic dictatorship under the leadership of the Communist Party. When it is well done, China's major exploiting classes, the landlord class and the bureaucrat-bourgeoisie (the monopoly-capitalist class), will be eliminated for good. There remain the national bourgeoisie; at the present stage, we can already do a good deal of suitable educational work with many of them. When the time comes to realize socialism, that is, to nationalize private enterprise, we shall carry the work of educating and remoulding them a step further. The people have a powerful state apparatus in their hands. There is no need to fear rebellion by the national bourgeoisie.

The serious problem is the education of the peasantry...

VI · B 1 Nonantagonistic contradictions[1]

... Within the Party, opposition and struggle between different ideas occur constantly; they reflect the class contradictions and

1. Extracted from *On Contradiction*, 1937. (See note to Text II E.)

the contradictions between the old and the new things in society. If there were neither contradictions nor ideological conflicts through which the contradictions are resolved, the Party's life would come to an end . . .

Even under the social conditions of the Soviet Union, a difference exists between the workers and the peasants; this difference is a contradiction, though, unlike that between labour and capital, it will not become intensified into antagonism or assume the form of class struggle. In the course of socialist construction, the workers and the peasants have formed a firm alliance and will gradually solve this contradiction in the process of development from socialism to communism. This is a question of distinction in the character of contradictions, not a matter of the presence or absence of them. Contradiction is universal, absolute, existing in all processes of the development of things and running through all processes from beginning to end . . .

As we have pointed out above, the contradiction between correct ideology and erroneous ideologies within the Communist Party reflects the class contradictions when the classes exist. In the beginning, or with regard to certain matters, such a contradiction need not immediately manifest itself as antagonistic. But with the development of the class struggle, it can also grow and become antagonistic. The history of the Communist Party of the Soviet Union shows us that the contradiction between the correct ideology of Lenin and Stalin and the erroneous ideologies of Trotsky, Bukharin, and others initially was not manifested in an antagonistic form, but subsequently developed into antagonism. A similar case occurred in the history of the Chinese Communist Party. The contradiction between the correct ideology of many of our comrades in the Party and the erroneous ideologies of Chen Tu-hsiu, Chang Kuo-t'ao, and others was also not manifested in an antagonistic form initially, but subsequently developed into antagonism. At present the contradiction between the correct ideology and the erroneous ideologies in our Party is not manifested in an antagonistic form and, if comrades who have committed mistakes can correct them, it will not develop into antagonism. Therefore, the Party on the one hand must carry on a serious struggle against erroneous ideologies, and on the other must give the comrades who have committed mistakes sufficient opportunity to become aware of them. Under such conditions, conflicts pushed to excess are obviously not appropriate. But if those people who have committed mistakes persist in thcm and increase the gravity of their mistakes, then it is possible that such contradictions will develop into antagonisms.

Economically, in capitalist society (where the town under bourgeois rule ruthlessly exploits the countryside) and in the Kuomintang-controlled areas in China (where the town under the rule of foreign imperialism and the native big comprador bourgeoisie savagely exploits the countryside), the contradiction between the town and the countryside is one of extreme antagonism. But in a socialist country and in our revolutionary bases, such an antagonistic contradiction becomes a nonantagonistic contradiction; and it will disappear when a communist society is realized.

Lenin said: 'Antagonism and contradiction are utterly different. Under socialism, antagonism disappears, but contradiction subsists.' That is to say, antagonism is only one form of struggle between contradictions, but not its universal form; we cannot apply this formula everywhere.

VI · B 2 Contradictions under socialism[1]

Some naïve ideas seem to suggest that contradictions no longer exist in a socialist society. To deny the existence of contradictions is to deny dialectics. The contradictions in various societies differ in character, as do the forms of their solution, but society at all times develops through continual contradictions. Socialist society also develops through contradictions between the productive forces and the conditions of production. In a socialist or communist society, technical innovations and improvement in the social system inevitably continue to take place; otherwise the development of society would come to a standstill and society

1. Extracted from an editorial in the *Jen-min jih-pao* of 5 April 1956, entitled 'On the historical experience of the dictatorship of the proletariat'.

Available translations: *On the Historical Experience of the Dictatorship of the Proletariat*, Foreign Languages Press, Peking, 1956.

could no longer advance. Humanity is still in its youth. The road it has yet to traverse will be no one knows how many times longer than the road it has already travelled. Contradictions between progress and conservatism, between the advanced and the backward, between the positive and the negative, will constantly occur under varying conditions and different circumstances. Things will keep on like this: One contradiction will lead to another, and when old contradictions are solved new ones will arise. It is obviously incorrect to maintain, as some people do, that the contradiction between idealism and materialism can be eliminated in a socialist or communist society. As long as contradictions exist between the subjective and the objective, between the advanced and the backward, and between the productive forces and the conditions of production, the contradiction between materialism and idealism will continue in a socialist or communist society and will manifest itself in various forms. Since man lives in society, he reflects, in different circumstances and to varying degrees, the contradictions existing in each form of society. Therefore, not everybody will be perfect, even when a communist society is established. By then there will still be contradictions among the people, and there will still be good people and bad, people whose thinking is relatively correct and others whose thinking is relatively incorrect. Hence there will still be struggle between people, though its nature and form will be different from those in class societies. Viewed in this light, the existence of contradictions between the individual and the collective in a socialist society is nothing strange . . .

VI · B 3 On the correct handling of contradictions among the people[1]

Never has our country been so united as it is today. The victories

1. Extracted from a speech of 27 February 1957, published (in revised form) on 10 June 1957 under the same title. My source was *Kuan-yü cheng-ch'üeh ch'u-li jen-min nei-pu mao-tun ti wen-t'i*, Jen-min Ch'u-pan-she, Peking, 1960, pp. 1–6, 10, 25–8, 30–33.

Available translations: Mao Tse-tung, *On the Correct Handling of Contradictions Among the People*, Foreign Languages Press, Peking, 1957.

of the bourgeois-democratic revolution and the socialist revolution, coupled with our achievements in socialist construction, have rapidly changed the face of old China. Now we see before us an even brighter future. The days of national disunity and turmoil, which the people detested, have gone forever. Led by the working class and the Communist Party, and united as one, our 600 million people are engaged in the great work of building socialism. ... However, this does not mean that there are no longer any contradictions in our society. It would be naïve to imagine that there are no more contradictions. To do so would be to fly in the face of objective reality. We are confronted by two types of social contradictions – contradictions between ourselves and the enemy and contradictions among the people. These two types of contradictions are totally different in nature...

The term 'the people' has different meanings in different countries and in different historical periods in each country.... At this stage of building socialism, all classes, strata, and social groups that approve, support, and work for the cause of socialist construction belong to the category of the people, while those social forces and groups that resist the socialist revolution and are hostile to and try to wreck socialist construction are enemies of the people.

The contradictions between ourselves and our enemies are antagonistic ones. Within the ranks of the people, contradictions among the working people are nonantagonistic, whereas those between the exploiters and exploited classes have a non-antagonistic aspect as well as an antagonistic one.... In the conditions existing in China today what we call contradictions among the people include the following: contradictions within the working class, contradictions within the peasantry, contradictions within the intelligentsia, contradictions between the working class and the peasantry, contradictions between the working class and other sections of the working people on the one hand and the national bourgeoisie on the other, contradictions within the national bourgeoisie, and so forth. Our people's government is a government that truly represents the interests of the people and serves the people, yet certain contradictions do exist between the government and the masses. These include contradictions between the interests of the state, collective interests, and individual interests; between democracy and centralism; between those in positions of leadership and the led; and contradictions arising from the bureaucratic practices of certain state functionaries in their relations with the masses. All these are contradictions among the people. Generally speaking, underlying the contradictions among the people is the basic identity of the interests of the people.

In our country, the contradiction between the working class and the national bourgeoisie is a contradiction among the people. . . . This is because of the dual character of the national bourgeoisie in our country. . . . Exploitation of the working class for profit is one aspect, while support of the Constitution and willingness to accept socialist transformation is the other. . . . The contradiction between exploiter and exploited that exists between the national bourgeoisie and the working class is in itself an antagonistic one. But, in the concrete conditions existing in China, such an antagonistic contradiction, if properly handled, can be transformed into a nonantagonistic one and resolved in a peaceful way. But if it is not properly handled, if, say, we do not follow a policy of uniting with, criticizing, and educating the national bourgeoisie, or if the national bourgeoisie does not accept this policy, then the contradiction between the working class and the national bourgeoisie can turn into an antagonistic contradiction as between ourselves and the enemy . . .

Our state is a state of the people's democratic dictatorship, led by the working class and based on the worker-peasant alliance. What is this dictatorship for? Its first function is to suppress the reactionary classes and elements and those exploiters in the country who range themselves against the socialist revolution, to suppress all those who try to wreck our socialist construction, that is to say, to solve the contradictions between ourselves and the enemy within the country . . .

The second function of this dictatorship is to protect our country from subversive activities and possible aggression by the external enemy . . .

Our constitution states that citizens of the People's Republic of China enjoy freedom of speech, of the press, of assembly, of association, of procession, of religious practices, and so on.... Our socialist democracy is democracy in the widest sense, such as is not to be found in any capitalist country...

But this freedom is freedom with leadership and this democracy is democracy under centralized guidance, not anarchy. Anarchy does not conform to the interests or wishes of the people.

Certain people in our country were delighted when the Hungarian events took place. They hoped that something similar would happen in China, that thousands upon thousands of people would demonstrate in the streets against the People's Government. Such hopes ran counter to the interests of the masses and therefore could not possibly get their support. In Hungary, a section of the people, deceived by domestic and foreign counter-revolutionaries, made the mistake of resorting to acts of violence against the people's government, with the result that both the state and the people suffered for it...

Democracy sometimes seems to be an end, but it is in fact only a means. Marxism teaches us that democracy is part of the superstructure and belongs to the realm of politics. That is to say, in the last analysis, it serves the economic base. The same is true of freedom. Both democracy and freedom are relative, not absolute, and they come into being and develop under specific historical circumstances. Within the ranks of our people, democracy stands in relation to centralism, and freedom to discipline. They are two conflicting aspects of a single entity, contradictory as well as united, and we should not one-sidedly emphasize one to the detriment of the other. Within the ranks of the people, we cannot do without freedom, nor can we do without discipline; we cannot do without democracy, nor can we do without centralism.... Under democratic centralism, the people enjoy a wide measure of democracy and freedom, but at the same time they have to keep themselves within the bounds of socialist discipline. All this is well understood by the masses of the people.

While we stand for freedom with leadership and democracy under centralized guidance, in no sense do we mean that coercive measures should be taken to settle ideological matters and questions involving the distinction between right and wrong among the people. Any attempt to deal with ideological matters or questions involving right and wrong by administrative orders or coercive measures will be not only ineffective but harmful.... Administrative orders issued for the maintenance of social order must be accompanied by persuasion and education, for in many cases administrative orders alone will not work...

Contradictions in a socialist society are fundamentally different from contradictions in old societies, such as capitalist society. Contradictions in capitalist society find expression in acute antagonisms and conflicts, in sharp class struggle, which cannot be resolved by the capitalist system itself, but only by socialist revolution. But contradictions in socialist society are not antagonistic and can be resolved one after the other by the socialist system itself.

The basic contradictions in socialist society are still those between the relations of production and the productive forces, and between the superstructure and the economic base...

'Let a hundred flowers bloom,' and 'let a hundred schools contend,' 'long-term coexistence and mutual supervision' – how did these slogans come to be?

They were put forward in the light of the specific conditions in China, on the basis of the recognition that various kinds of contradictions still exist in a socialist society, and in response to the country's urgent need to speed up its economic and cultural development.

The policy of letting a hundred flowers bloom and a hundred schools contend is designed to promote the flourishing of the arts and the progress of science; it is designed to enable socialist culture to thrive in our land...

Questions of right and wrong in the arts and sciences should be settled through free discussion in artistic and scientific circles and in the course of practical work in the arts and sciences. They should not be settled in summary fashion. A trial period is often needed to determine whether something is right or wrong. In the past, new and correct things often failed at the outset to win recognition from the majority of people and had to develop by twists and turns in struggle. ... Copernicus' theory of the solar system and Darwin's theory of evolution were once dismissed as erroneous and had to win over bitter opposition. Chinese history offers many similar examples. In a socialist society, conditions for the growth of new things are radically different from and far superior to those in the old society. Nevertheless, it still often happens that new, rising forces are held back and reasonable suggestions smothered...

Marxism has also developed through struggle. At the beginning, Marxism was subjected to all kinds of attack and regarded as a poisonous weed. It is still being attacked and regarded as a poisonous weed in many parts of the world. But in the socialist countries it enjoys a different position. Yet even in these countries there are non-Marxist as well as anti-Marxist ideologies. ... In China ... remnants of the overthrown landlord and comprador classes still exist, the bourgeoisie still exists, and the petty bourgeoisie has only just begun to remould itself. The class struggle is not yet finished. The class struggle between the proletariat and the bourgeoisie, the class struggle between various political forces, and the class struggle in the ideological field between the proletariat and the bourgeoisie will still be long and arduous and at times may even become very acute. The proletariat seeks to transform the world according to its own world outlook. So does the bourgeoisie. In this respect, the question whether socialism or capitalism will win is still not really settled. Marxists are still a minority of the entire population as well as of the intellectuals. Marxism therefore must still develop through struggle. ... That which is correct always develops in the course of struggling against that which is wrong. ... As mankind in general rejects an untruth and accepts a truth, a new truth will begin struggling with new erroneous ideas. Such struggles will never end. This is the law of development of Marxism...

Ideological struggle is not like other forms of struggle. Crude, coercive methods should not be used in this struggle, only the method of painstaking reasoning. Today, socialism enjoys favourable conditions in the ideological struggle. The main power of the state is in the hands of the working people led by the proletariat. The Communist Party is strong and its prestige stands high. Although there are defects and mistakes in our work, every fair-minded person can see that we are loyal to the people, that we are both determined and able to build up our country together with the people, and that we have achieved great successes and will achieve still greater ones. The vast majority of the bourgeoisie and intellectuals who come from the old society are patriotic; they are willing to serve their flourishing socialist motherland, and they know that if they turn away from the socialist cause and the working people led by the Communist Party, they will have no one to rely on and no bright future to look forward to.

People may ask: Since Marxism is accepted by the majority of the people in our country as the guiding ideology, can it be criticized? Certainly it can. Marxism, being a scientific truth, fears no criticism. ... Quite the contrary. Marxists need to steel and improve themselves and win new positions in the teeth of criticism and the storm and stress of struggle. Fighting against wrong ideas is like being vaccinated – a man develops greater immunity from disease after the vaccine takes effect. Plants raised in hothouses are not likely to be robust. Carrying out the policy of letting a hundred flowers bloom and a hundred schools contend will strengthen, not weaken the leading position of Marxism in the ideological field.

What should our policy be toward non-Marxist ideas? As far as unregenerate counter-revolutionaries and wreckers of the socialist cause are concerned, the matter is easy: We simply deprive them of their freedom of speech. But it is quite a different matter when we are faced with incorrect ideas among the people. ... It is not only futile but very harmful to use crude and summary methods to deal with ideological questions among the people, with questions relating to the spiritual life of man. You may ban the expression of wrong ideas, but the ideas will still be there. On the other hand, correct ideas, if pampered in hothouses without exposure to the elements or immunization against disease, will not win out against wrong ones ...

What, from the point of view of the broad masses of the people, should be the criteria today for distinguishing between fragrant flowers and poisonous weeds? ...

Basing ourselves on the principles of our Constitution, the will of the overwhelming majority of our people and the political programmes jointly proclaimed on various occasions by our political parties and groups, we believe that, broadly speaking, words and actions can be judged right if they:

1. help to unite the people of our various nationalities rather than divide them;

2. are beneficial, not harmful, to socialist transformation and socialist construction;

3. help to consolidate, not undermine or weaken, the people's democratic dictatorship;

4. help to consolidate, not undermine or weaken, democratic centralism;

5. tend to strengthen, not to cast off or weaken, the leadership of the Communist Party;

6. are beneficial, not harmful, to international socialist solidarity and the solidarity of the peace-loving peoples of the world.

Of these six criteria, the most important are the socialist path and the leadership of the Party.... These are political criteria. Naturally, in judging the truthfulness of scientific theories or assessing the aesthetic value of works of art, other pertinent criteria are needed, but these six political criteria are also applicable to all activities in the arts or sciences. In a socialist country like ours, can there possibly be any useful scientific or artistic activity that runs counter to these political criteria?...

In 1956, small numbers of workers and students in certain places went on strike. The immediate cause of these disturbances was the failure to satisfy certain of their demands for material benefits, of which some should and could be met, while others were out of place or excessive, and therefore could not be met for the time being. But a more important cause was the bureaucratism of those in positions of leadership. In some cases, responsibility for such bureaucratic mistakes should be placed on the higher authorities, and those at lower levels should not be made to bear all the blame. Another cause for these disturbances was the inadequacy of the ideological and political educational work done among the workers and students. In the same year, members of a small number of agricultural cooperatives also created disturbances, and the main causes were also bureaucratism on the part of the leadership and lack of educational work among the masses...

We do not approve of disturbances, because contradictions among the people can be resolved in accordance with the formula 'unity – criticism – unity', while disturbances inevitably cause losses and are detrimental to the advance of socialism. ... With regard to this question, we should pay attention to the following:

1. In order to get rid of the root cause of disturbances, we must stamp out bureaucratism, greatly improve ideological and political education, and deal with all contradictions in a proper way. If this is done, there usually will not be any disturbances.

2. If disturbances should occur as a result of bad work on our part, then we should guide those involved in such disturbances toward the correct path, make use of these disturbances as a special means of improving our work and educating the cadres and the masses, and work out solutions to questions neglected in the past.... The guiding spirits of disturbances should not be removed from their jobs or expelled without good reason, except for those who have committed criminal offences or active counter-revolutionaries who should be dealt with according to law. In a big country like ours, it is nothing to get alarmed about if small numbers of people create disturbances; rather we should turn such things to advantage to help us get rid of bureaucratism.

In our society, there is ... a small number of people who, unmindful of public interests, refuse to listen to reason, commit crimes, and break the law. They may take advantage of our policies and distort them, deliberately put forward unreasonable demands in order to stir up the masses, or deliberately spread rumours to create trouble and disrupt social order. We do not propose to let these people have their way. On the contrary, proper legal action must be taken against them. The masses demand that these persons be punished. Not to do so would run counter to popular will...

VI · C 1 On democratic centralism[1]

... Some comrades see only the interests of the part and not the whole; they always put undue stress on that part of the work for which they themselves are responsible and always wish to subordinate the interests of the whole to the interests of their own part. They do not understand the Party's system of democratic centralism; they do not know that the Communist Party not only needs democracy, but needs centralization even more. They forget the system of democratic centralism, in which the minority is subordinate to the majority, the lower level to the higher level, the part to the whole, and the entire membership to the Central Committee...

... We must definitely build a centralized, unified Party and make a clean sweep of all unprincipled factional struggles. We must combat individualism and sectarianism so as to enable our whole Party to march in step and fight for one common goal.

VI · C 2 Against the intimidation of comrades[2]

The second charge against Party formalism is that of 'Making a False Show of Authority to Instil Terror'. Some types of Party formalism are expressed not only as the mouthing of empty phrases and words without substance, but also as a false show of authority to instil terror, an attitude that contains a deadly poison. The mouthing of empty phrases and words without substance may be considered merely childish, but making a false show of authority to instil terror is not only childish but knavish.

1. Extracted from Mao's speech of 1 February 1942 (see note to Text II B).

Available translations: The original version has been translated by Boyd Compton in the volume cited in the note to Text II B. Since the above passage has been left virtually untouched in the current edition of the Chinese text, we here follow *Selected Works*, III, pp. 43–5.

2. Extracted from a speech of 8 February 1942, entitled 'Against party formalism', published in *Chieh-fang jih-pao*, 18 June 1942.

Available translations: *Mao's China*, pp. 39–41.

... That which is scientific never fears public criticism. Because science is the truth, it does not fear refutation. On the other hand, subjectivism and sectarianism, as displayed in formalistic Party essays and speeches, are deeply afraid of refutation and show extreme cowardice when they rely on a false show of authority to instil terror. Faced with this terror, people shut their mouths. Subjectivism and factionalism can then 'return to court, having achieved the victory'. This false show of authority cannot reflect the truth; on the contrary, it is detrimental to it.... Hitherto, two phrases have recurred in our essays and speeches: One is, 'struggle savagely'; the other is, 'attack mercilessly'. It is necessary to use such means in dealing with the enemy and with opposition thought, but it is a mistake to use them in dealing with our own comrades. Quite often, as is stated in the fourth section of the conclusion of the *History of the Communist Party of the Soviet Union*, enemies and opposition thought sneak into the Party. Without a doubt savage struggle and merciless attack must be used as means against these persons and types of thought, for scoundrels take advantage of these means in dealing with the Party. If we persist in being lenient with them, we fall into their trap. But we cannot use the same means in dealing with comrades who unwittingly commit errors. With such comrades we must make use of criticism and self-criticism. This is the method referred to in the fifth section of the conclusion of the *History of the Communist Party of the Soviet Union.* No matter with whom you are dealing, a false show of authority to instil terror is always uncalled for. This strategy of terror is not of the slightest use against the enemy; against our comrades it only does harm.... The Chinese Communist Party does not rely on terror for nourishment: it relies on the truth, on arriving at the truth by a verification of facts, and on science.... All organs that make decisions and issue directives, and all comrades who write essays or deliver speeches, must always rely on truth[1] and utility. Only when they do this can victory in the revolution be attained.

1. In the current version, the reference is not merely to 'truth' but to 'Marxist-Leninist truth'. There are a number of other variations, but they are of minor importance not worth noting here.

VI · C 3 On the mass line[1]

1. There are two methods which must be employed in whatever work we do. One is to combine the general with the particular; the other is to combine the leadership with the masses.

2. In any task, if no general and widespread call is issued, the broad masses cannot be mobilized for action. But if persons in leading positions confine themselves to a general call – if they do not personally, in some of the units, participate deeply and concretely in the application of *this call*, make a break-through at some single point, gain experience, and afterwards use this experience for guiding other units – then they will have no way of testing the correctness or of enriching the content of their general call, and there is the danger that nothing may come of it. . . . This is the method by which the leaders combine leading and learning. No one in a leading position is competent to give general guidance to all the units unless he has *studied concrete* individuals and events in *concrete* subordinate units. This method must be promoted everywhere so that leading cadres at all levels learn to apply it.

3. . . . However active the leading group may be, its activity will be transformed into fruitless effort by a handful of people unless combined with the activity of the broad masses. On the other hand, if the broad masses alone are active without a strong leading group to organize their activity properly, such activity cannot be sustained for long, or carried forward in the right direction, or raised to a high level. The masses in any given place are generally composed of three parts, the relatively active, the intermediate and the relatively backward. *If we compare these three groups of people, then in general the two extremes are small, while the middle group is large.* The leaders must therefore be skilled in uniting the small number of active elements to form a

1. Extracts from a directive of the Central Committee of the Chinese Communist Party dated 1 June 1943, and originally published anonymously (*Chieh-fang jih-pao*, 4 June 1943). This text is attributed to Mao in the current edition of the *Selected Works*.

Available translations: *Selected Works*, III, pp. 117–22.

leading group, and must rely on this leading group to raise the level of the intermediate elements and to win over the backward elements. A leading group that is genuinely united and linked with the masses can be formed only gradually in the process of mass struggle, *such as in rectification or study campaigns*, and not in isolation from it. In the process of *any* great struggle, the composition of the leading group should not and cannot remain entirely unchanged throughout the initial, middle and final stages; the activists (*heroes*) who come forward in the course of the struggle must constantly be promoted to replace those original members of the leading group who are inferior by comparison or who have degenerated. One fundamental reason why the work in many places and many organizations cannot be pushed ahead is the lack of a leading group which is united, linked with the masses and kept constantly healthy.... In every organization, school, or army unit, whether large or small, we should give effect to the ninth of Stalin's conditions for the bolshevization of the Party, namely, that regarding the establishment of a nucleus of leadership.[1] The criteria for such a leading group should be the four which Dimitrov enumerated in his discussion of cadre policy – absolute devotion to the cause, contact with the masses, capacity for independent work, and observance of discipline...

4. In all the practical work of our Party, all correct leadership is necessarily from the masses, to the masses. This means: take the ideas of the masses (scattered and unsystematic ideas) and concentrate them (through study turn them into concentrated and systematic ideas), then go to the masses and propagate and explain these ideas until the masses embrace them as their own, hold fast to them and translate them into action, and test the correctness of these ideas in such action. Then once again concentrate ideas

1. In an interview of February 1925, on the German Communist Party, Stalin put forward twelve conditions for achieving the bolshevization of the Communist Parties in other countries, of which the ninth reads as follows: 'The Party must be able to recruit for its main leading group the best elements of the advanced fighters who are sufficiently devoted to the cause to be genuine spokesmen of the aspirations of the revolutionary proletariat, and who are sufficiently experienced to become real leaders of the proletarian revolution, capable of applying the tactics and strategy of Leninism.' (Stalin, *Works*, Vol. 7, p. 39.)

from the masses and once again take them to the masses so that the ideas are persevered in and carried through. And so on, over and over again in an endless spiral, with the ideas becoming more correct, more vital and richer each time. Such is the Marxist-*Leninist* theory of knowledge, *or methodology* ...

5. ... Many comrades do not see the importance of, or are not good at, drawing together the activists to form a nucleus of leadership, and they do not see the importance of, or are not good at, linking this nucleus of leadership closely with the broad masses, and so their leadership becomes bureaucratic and divorced from the masses. Many comrades do not see the importance of, or are not good at, summing up the experience of mass struggles, but fancying themselves clever, are fond of voicing their subjectivist ideas, and so their ideas become empty and impractical. Many comrades rest content with making a general call with regard to a task and do not see the importance of, or are not good at, following it up immediately with particular and concrete guidance, and so their call remains on their lips, or on paper or in the conference room, and their leadership becomes bureaucratic...

...

9. ... The harder the struggle, the greater the need for communists to link their leadership closely with the demands of the broad masses, and to combine general calls closely with particular guidance, so as to smash completely subjectivist and bureaucratic methods of leadership. All leading comrades of our Party must at all times counterpose scientific[1] methods of leadership to subjectivist, bureaucratic methods of leadership and use the former to overcome the latter. Subjectivists and bureaucrats do not understand the principles of combining the leadership with the masses and the general with the particular; they greatly impede the development of the work of the Party. Hence, to combat subjectivist and bureaucratic methods of leadership, we must promote scientific methods of leadership both extensively and intensively.

1. In the present official version, Mao has changed this to read: 'scientific, Marxist methods'. Similar variants, in which he originally referred to science in general and now limits this to Marxist science, are scattered through his works.

VI · C 4 Let us transform the consciousness of the masses[1]

... *All intellectuals must absolutely get rid of the bad habit of isolating themselves from the masses. They must give themselves to the people in a spirit of abnegation, unite closely with the workers, peasants, and soldiers. For their part, the worker and peasant cadres must respect these revolutionary intellectuals and have confidence in them.*

In working for the masses we must start from their needs, not from our wishes, however good, *nor from historical dogmas. Everything must be adapted to the time and place....* It sometimes happens that the masses objectively need some reform but are not yet subjectively awakened to it and willing or determined to bring it into effect. In that case, we should wait patiently and introduce the reform only when, through our work, the great majority of the masses have become awakened to the need and are willing and determined to start it. *We absolutely must not proceed by orders or constraints.* Unless the masses are awakened and willing, all work that needs their participation will turn out to be an empty formality and end in failure. The saying 'haste brings no success' [from the Confucian *Analects*] does not mean that we should not make haste, but that we should not take reckless action that will inevitably lead to failure...

VI · C 5 Without a party, there can be no revolution[2]

If there is to be a revolution, there must be a revolutionary party. Without a revolutionary party, without a party built on the

1. Extracted from a speech of 30 October 1944 at a mass meeting of cultural workers of the border regions; published in *Ch'ün-chung*, X, no. 2 10 February 1945, p. 49.

Available translations: *Selected Works*, III, pp. 236–7.

2. Extracted from an article written by Mao in November 1948 for the Cominform journal *For a Lasting Peace, for a People's Democracy*. (Source: *Ch'ün-chung* II, no. 44, 11 November 1948, pp. 2–3.)

Available translations: *Selected Works*, IV, p. 284.

revolutionary theory and style *of Marx*, *Lenin and Stalin*, it is impossible to lead the working class and the broad masses of the people to defeat imperialism and its running dogs. In the more than one hundred years since the birth of Marxism, it was only through the example of the Russian Bolsheviks in leading the October Revolution, in leading socialist construction and in defeating fascist aggression that revolutionary parties of a new type were formed and developed in the world. With the birth of revolutionary parties of this type, the face of the world revolution has changed. The change has been so great that transformations utterly inconceivable to people of the older generation have come into being amid fire and thunder. The Communist Party of China is a party built and developed on the model of the Communist Party of the Soviet Union. With the birth of the Communist Party of China, the face of the Chinese revolution took on an altogether new aspect. Is this fact not clear enough?

VI · C 6 Learning from one's subordinates[1]

... Ask your subordinates about matters you don't understand or don't know, and do not lightly express your approval or disapproval. Some documents, after having been drafted, are withheld from circulation for a time because certain questions in them need to be clarified and it is necessary to consult the lower levels first. We should never pretend to know what we don't know, we should 'not feel ashamed to ask and learn from people below' [from the Confucian *Analects*], and we should listen carefully to the views of the cadres at the lower levels. Be a pupil before you become a teacher; learn from the cadres at the lower levels before you issue orders. In handling problems, this should be the practice of all bureaus of the Central Committee and Party committees of the fronts, except in military emergencies or when the facts of the matter are already clear. To do this will not lower one's prestige; it can only raise it. Since our decisions incorporate the

1. Extracted from a speech of 13 March 1949, at the Second Plenum of the Seventh Central Committee (*Hsüan-chi*, IV, pp. 1442–3).
Available translations: *Selected Works*, IV, pp. 378–9.

correct views of the cadres at the lower levels, the latter will naturally support them. What the cadres at the lower levels say may or may not be correct; we must analyse it. We must heed the correct views and act upon them. The reason why the leadership of the Central Committee is correct is chiefly that it synthesizes the material, reports, and correct views coming from different localities. . . . Listen also to the mistaken views from below; it is wrong not to listen to them at all. Such views, however, are not to be acted upon but to be criticized . . .

VI · C 7 Victory is only the first step[1]

. . . To win country-wide victory is only the first step in a long march of ten thousand *li*. Even if this step is worthy of pride, it is a comparatively minor one; what will be more worthy of pride is yet to come. After several decades, the victory of the Chinese people's democratic revolution, viewed in retrospect, will seem like only a brief prologue to a long drama. A drama begins with a prologue, but the prologue is not the climax. The Chinese revolution is great, but the road after the revolution will be longer, the work greater and more arduous. This must be made clear now in the Party. The comrades must be taught to remain modest, prudent, and free from arrogance and rashness in their style of work. The comrades must be taught to preserve the style of plain living and hard struggle. . . . We can learn what we did not know. We are not only good at destroying the old world, we are also good at building the new. Not only can the Chinese people live without begging alms from the imperialists, they will live a better life than that of the imperialist countries.

1. Extracted from a report to the Second Plenum of the Seventh Central Committee, 5 March 1949, *Hsüan-chi*, IV, pp. 1439–40.
Available translations: *Selected Works*, IV, p. 374.

VI · C 8 Everything depends on the Party secretaries[1]

The line followed in this locality is correct. This township (*hsiang*) already has five agricultural producers' cooperatives, seven combined mutual-aid teams, three year-round mutual-aid teams, and fourteen seasonal mutual-aid teams. Their total membership amounts to 98.4 per cent of those peasant households which ought to be organized. Prior to December 1954, the Party branch in this township had still not placed the main emphasis, in its work of leadership, on the mutual aid and cooperative movement; Party members feared the difficulties in leading the mutual-aid teams. The Party branch relied not on the method of 'The Party secretary takes the lead and all the Party members help run the cooperatives',[2] but on the work team (sent there apparently from a higher level). At the present time, rural Party branches in quite a number of places throughout the country show this weak and impotent attitude toward the question of agricultural cooperation. And it is not only the branches – there may well be some higher-level Party committees that do the same. This is the crux of the problem. Whether or not the socialist transformation of our agriculture can keep pace with the rate of advance of industrialization in our country, whether or not the cooperative movement can develop in a healthy fashion with very few flaws and guarantee an increase in production, depends on whether or not the local party committees at all levels can quickly and correctly shift the emphasis to this task. Work teams must be sent, but it must be stated very clearly that they are sent to help local Party organizations, and not to replace them – not to incite them to make no use of their own hands and brains, and rely exclusively on the work teams. This township in Kweichow showed very great achievements in the period of only a little over five months after

1. Extracted from Mao's editorial notes to *Chung-kuo nung-ts'un ti she-hui-chu-i kao-ch'ao*, Jen-min Ch'u-pan-she, Peking, 1956, pp. 1125–6.

Available translations: *Socialist Upsurge in China's Countryside*, Foreign Languages Press, Peking, 1957, pp. 206–7. This translation is made from the one-volume abridgement of the three-volume Chinese edition cited above.

2. This was the slogan put forward in the very first article of the collection. See pp. 11–26 of the English edition.

it changed its attitude in December 1954. They didn't rely on the work team, but pitched in themselves, and the Party members no longer feared difficulties. A change of this kind depends first and foremost on the secretaries of the Party committees at various levels . . . and on the Party branch secretaries. They must assume responsibility for the whole process of forming agricultural cooperatives. If they are afraid of trouble, of difficulties, if they do not throw themselves personally into this great task confronting them but merely pass it on to the rural work departments [of the Party] or to the work teams, not only will they be unable to carry out the task, but they may also cause a great deal of disorder.

VI · C 9 The danger of right opportunism within the Party[1]

In many localities there is a practice prevalent almost to the point of being universal: right opportunists within the Party, working hand in glove with the forces of capitalism in society, are preventing the broad masses of poor and lower middle peasants from taking the road to the formation of cooperatives [literally, *ho-tso-hua*, 'cooperativization']. . . . Some people, although they call themselves communists, manifest little interest in the cause of socialism we are now endeavouring to advance. Not only do they fail to support the enthusiastic masses, but on the contrary they throw cold water on the masses' heads. In China, 1955 was the year of decision in the struggle between socialism and capitalism. This decisive struggle was reflected first and foremost in the course of the three conferences called by the Central Committee of the Chinese Communist Party in May, July and October. The first half of 1955 was murky and obscured by dark clouds. But in the second half, the atmosphere changed completely. Tens of millions of peasant households swung into action. In response to the call of the Central Committee, they carried out the formation of cooperatives [*ho-tso-hua*]. As the editor [i.e., Mao] writes these

1. Extracted from *Socialist Upsurge* . . . (see note to Text VI C 8), pp. 729–30 of the Chinese edition.

Available translations: pp. 159–60 of the English edition.

few lines, more than sixty million peasant households throughout the country have already joined cooperatives. It is as if a raging tidal wave has swept away all the demons and ghosts. Now we can look at every member of society and see exactly who is who. It is the same in the Party. By the end of this year, the victory of socialism will be assured to a very large extent. Of course, many more battles still lie ahead. We must continue to fight hard.

VI · C 10 The socialist education movement in the countryside [1]

Since the Tenth Plenum of the Eighth Central Committee of the Party in September 1962, as a result of the socialist education movement which has developed in the cities and in the countryside, as a result of the application of a series of Central Committee policies by the whole Party, as a result of the active efforts of the popular masses, numerous party members and cadres, an excellent situation has come into being on the political, economic, ideological and cultural, and military fronts in our country. In the course of the past few months, more than a million cadres throughout the country have gone deep down into units at the grass-roots level in the villages, and a new high tide has emerged in the movement for socialist revolution.

The many great successes which our country has obtained so rapidly in the course of the past year, demonstrate that our Party's general line for building socialism is correct. At the same time, this has demonstrated even further that our Chinese Communist Party, headed by Comrade Mao Tse-tung, is a great, glorious and correct Party . . .

Serious and sharp class struggles persist both in our cities and

1. Extracts from the directive of 14 January 1965 on the socialist education movement in the countryside, known as the twenty-three-point directive. *Nung-ts'un she-hui-chu-i chiao-yü yün-tung chung mu-ch'ien t'i-ch'u ti i-hsien wen-t'i*, 14 January 1965, paragraphs 1, 2, 3, 4 and 5.

Available translations: R. Baum and F. C. Teiwes, *Ssu-ch'ing: the Socialist Education Movement of 1962–66*, University of California, Berkeley, Calif., 1968, pp. 118–26. I have revised my own translation in the light of this version, which became available only when this book was in proof.

in the countryside. Once the socialist transformation of the system of property has been basically carried out, the class enemies who oppose socialism endeavour to use the method of 'peaceful evolution' in order to re-establish capitalism. This situation of class struggle is necessarily reflected within the Party. The leadership of some communes, brigades, enterprises, and other units has been corrupted, or usurped. ... Experience has shown that if only the whole Party ... thoroughly applies the various directives of the Party Central Committee regarding the Socialist Education Movement, grasps the essential principle of class struggle, relies on the working class, the poor and lower middle peasants, the revolutionary cadres, the revolutionary intellectuals, and other revolutionary elements, and takes care to unite over ninety-five per cent of the masses, and over ninety-five per cent of the cadres – provided we do this, the numerous questions still persisting in the cities and in the countryside will not be hard to locate and to solve...

The important point in this campaign is rectifying those people within the Party who are in authority and are taking the capitalist road...

Some of those people in authority taking the capitalist road do so openly, others act behind the scenes.

Some of those who support them are at lower levels, some are at higher levels.

At the lower levels, there are landlords, rich peasants, counter-revolutionaries, and other bad elements who have already been identified, and also similar elements who have not been detected.

At the higher levels, there are those who oppose building socialism in the communes, the *ch'ü*, the *hsien*, the special districts, and even in the work of provincial and Central Committee departments. Among them are those who were originally class-alien elements; there are those who have shed their skins and changed their nature; and there are those who have taken bribes and traitorously banded together to break the law and cause disorder...

The overwhelming majority of our cadres want to take the socialist road, but there are a few people among them who do not have a clear understanding of the socialist revolution, do not employ people properly, do not investigate the work energetically, and commit bureaucratic errors...

The socialist education movement in the cities and the countryside will henceforth be called simply the four clean-ups movement, i.e. political, economic, organizational and ideological clean-up. In the cities, the socialist education movement was known in the past as the 'five-antis' movement.[1] Henceforth, it will also be known as the four clean-ups, and the term five-antis will be abolished...

In June 1964, at a meeting of the Standing Committee of the Politburo of the Central Committee, attended by the first secretaries of all the regional bureaus of the Central Commttiee, Comrade Mao Tse-tung said:

What are the criteria for carrying out the socialist education movement well?

1. One must see whether the poor and lower middle peasants are really stirred into action or not.
2. Has the problem of the 'four uncleans' among the cadres been solved or not?
3. Have the cadres taken part in manual labour or not?
4. Has a good leadership core been established or not?
5. When landlords, rich peasants, counter-revolutionaries and bad elements are discovered who indulge in disruptive activities, is this contradiction simply handed over to higher authorities, or are the masses mobilized to watch them seriously and reform them on the spot?
6. One must see whether the result is to increase or to decrease production.

... Throughout the whole movement, we must make use of contradictions, win over the majority, oppose and smash the minority; those who resolutely take the capitalist road are always an extreme minority. There are some people who have committed errors who can still correct them. As for those people who are the target of the four clean-ups, we must be good at dissociating them, at treating them in a discriminating fashion, and at isolating the worst offenders to the greatest extent possible...

1. On the 'five antis', see *Mao Tse-tung* pp. 252–3.

VI · C 11 Old cadres must not rest on their laurels[1]

Veteran cadres performed meritorious services in the past, but they must not rest on their past achievements; they should temper and remould themselves very well in the Great Proletarian Cultural Revolution, win new merit, and make new contributions.

VI · C 12 Getting rid of the stale and taking in the fresh[2]

A human being has arteries and veins through which the heart makes the blood circulate, and he breathes with his lungs, exhaling carbon dioxide and inhaling fresh oxygen, that is, getting rid of the stale and taking in the fresh. A proletarian party must also get rid of the stale and take in the fresh, for only thus can it be full of vitality. Without eliminating waste matter and absorbing fresh blood the Party has no vigour.

VI · C 13 The Party is the leading nucleus[3]

The Chinese Communist Party is the political party of the proletariat.

The basic programme of the Chinese Communist Party is completely to overthrow the bourgeoisie, to replace the dictatorship of the bourgeoisie by the dictatorship of the proletariat, and

1. Quoted in an editorial regarding the formation of a Revolutionary Committee in Chinghai, *Jen-min jih-pao*, 13 August 1967, p. 1.
Available translations: *Peking Review*, no. 34, 1967, p. 25.

2. Quoted in the editorial 'Absorb fresh blood from the proletariat', *Hung-ch'i*, no. 4, 1968, p. 7.
Available translation: *Peking Review*, no. 43, 25 October 1968, p. 5.

3. Extracts from the draft constitution of the Chinese Communist Party elaborated on the basis of suggestions by Mao Tse-tung and submitted at his request to the Twelfth Plenum of the Central Committee in October 1968. Text as given in the Hong Kong newspaper *Hsing-tao jih-pao* on 9 January 1969.
Available translation: *China Quarterly*, no. 37, 1969.

to use socialism to defeat capitalism. The ultimate aim of the Party is to realize communism.

The Chinese Communist Party 'is composed of advanced elements of the proletariat; it is a vigorous and vital vanguard organization which leads the proletariat and the revolutionary masses in the struggle against the class enemy.'[1]

The Chinese Communist Party takes Marxism, Leninism and Mao Tse-tung's thought as the theoretical basis guiding its thinking. Mao Tse-tung's thought is the Marxism-Leninism of the era when imperialism is heading for total collapse and socialism is advancing towards world-wide victory.

During the past half century Comrade Mao Tse-tung, in leading China in the great struggle for the completion of the new democratic revolution, in leading China's great struggle for socialist revolution and socialist construction, and in the great struggle of the international communist movement in the present era to oppose imperialism, oppose modern revisionism and oppose the reactionaries of all countries, has combined the universal truth of Marxism-Leninism with concrete revolutionary practice, and has inherited, defended, and developed Marxism-Leninism, raising it to a completely new stage.

Comrade Lin Piao has consistently held high the great red banner of Mao Tse-tung's thought, and has most loyally and resolutely implemented and defended the proletarian revolutionary line of Comrade Mao Tse-tung. Comrade Lin Piao is the close comrade-in-arms and successor of Comrade Mao Tse-tung.

Socialist society is a relatively long historical stage. Classes, class contradictions, and class struggle will exist from beginning to end of this historical stage as will the struggle between the two roads of socialism and capitalism, the danger of a capitalist restoration, and the threat of subversion and aggression from imperialism and modern revisionism. These contradictions can only be resolved by relying on the theory and practice of Marxist permanent revolution. The great proletarian cultural revolution in our country is precisely a great political revolution under con-

1. The words in quotation marks are substantially identical with Mao's directive quoted in the New Year's Day editorial of 1 January 1968, except for the replacement of 'should be' by 'is'.

ditions of socialism, in which the proletariat opposes the bourgeoisie and all exploiting classes.

In order to consolidate and strengthen the dictatorship of the proletariat, the whole Party must hold high the great red banner of Marxism, Leninism, and Mao Tse-tung's thought, and lead the 700 million people of the whole country in building socialism independently, through hard struggle, going all out, aiming high, and achieving greater, faster, better and more economical results.

The Chinese Communist Party firmly upholds proletarian internationalism, resolutely unites together with the genuinely Marxist-Leninist political parties of the whole world, unites with the oppressed peoples and the oppressed nations of the whole world, giving mutual support and learning from each other, and struggles to overthrow imperialism headed by the United States, modern revisionism headed by the Soviet revisionist renegade clique and the reactionaries of all countries, to establish a new world where there will be no imperialism, no capitalism, and no system of exploitation.

The Chinese Communist Party was consolidated and developed in the great storms of class struggle, and in the struggle against right and 'left' opportunist lines. In the course of the class struggle, and the struggle between opposing lines, the Party must unceasingly 'get rid of the stale and take in the fresh',[1] in order to guarantee that hegemony in the Party and the state will be firmly grasped in the hands of the Marxists for ever.

The Chinese Communist Party with Comrade Mao Tse-tung as its leader is a great, glorious and correct Party and is the leading nucleus of the Chinese people.

A Chinese Communist Party member who swears to fight to the death for communism must firmly resolve not to fear sacrifices, to overcome all difficulties, and go on to seize victory!

Article I. Any Chinese worker, poor peasant, lower middle peasant, revolutionary soldier or other revolutionary element of eighteen years or over, who accepts the Party Constitution, participates in a Party organization and works within it, carries out

1. Slogan attributed to Mao in October 1968; see Text VI C 12.

the Party's decisions and pays the Party subscription, may become a member of the Chinese Communist Party.

Article II. A person who applies to join the Party must individually complete the formalities for entering the Party, must be introduced by two Party members, and must fill in a certificate of desire to enter the Party; he must be examined by the Party branch, the views of the broad masses within[1] the Party must be heard, the application must be passed by a full meeting of the Party branch, and it must be approved by the Party Committee one level higher.

Article III. A member of the Chinese Communist Party must:

(i) creatively study and apply Marxism, Leninism and Mao Tse-tung's thought;

(ii) seek to promote the interests of the majority of the people of China and of the world;

(iii) be able to unite with the majority, including those who have wrongly opposed him but have sincerely corrected their errors. However, he must be particularly vigilant against careerists, plotters, and two-faced people, and must prevent this kind of bad person from usurping the leadership of the Party and the state at any level;

(iv) discuss with the masses any matter which arises;

(v) boldly practise criticism and self-criticism ...

Article V. The principle of the Party's organization is democratic centralism.

The leading organs of the Party at every level are produced by democratic consultation and election.

The whole Party must obey a uniform discipline; the individual must obey the organization, the minority must obey the majority, lower ranks must obey higher ranks, and the whole Party must obey the Centre.

Leading organs of the Party at every level must report on their work at regular intervals to the Party Congress or to a general assembly of Party members, and must constantly listen to the

1. Certain texts read 'within and without'.

opinions of the masses both inside and outside the Party and be subject to their supervision. A Party member has the right to raise criticism and to make proposals to the Party organization and to the leaders at every level. If he does not agree with the decisions and directives of the Party organization, a Party member may reserve his opinion; moreover he has the right to by-pass his immediate superiors and report directly to the Central Committee and the Chairman of the Central Committee. We must create a lively political situation characterized by both centralism and democracy, both discipline and freedom, both unity of will and a happy mood on the part of each individual.

The organs of proletarian dictatorship, the Communist Youth League, and all the people's organizations must accept the leadership of the Party . . .

Article XII. Basic-level Party organizations must raise high the great red banner of Marxism, Leninism, and Mao Tse-tung's thought, put proletarian politics to the fore, resolutely support the 'four firsts' and extensively promote the 'three-eight' working style. Their main tasks are:

(i) to lead Party members and the revolutionary masses in the creative study and application of Mao Tse-tung's thought;

(ii) constantly to carry out education of Party members and the revolutionary masses in class struggle and the struggle between the two lines, and to lead them in resolute struggle against the class enemy;

(iii) to propagate Party policies, thoroughly carry out Party resolutions, and fully accomplish every task given them by the Party and the state;

(iv) to establish close links with the masses, constantly listen to the opinions and demands of the masses, develop active ideological struggle within the Party and make the life of the Party vigorous and vital;

(v) to develop Party members, carry out Party discipline, constantly rectify the Party organization, and resolutely maintain the purity of the Party ranks.

VII · Transforming Man, Nature, and Society

This chapter deals with Mao's efforts, culminating in the Great Proletarian Cultural Revolution, to change the face of China both by reshaping the country's society and economy so as to turn it into a powerful modern nation, and by transforming the patterns of thought and behaviour of the Chinese people. The first sub-division is devoted to a subject which has always been close to Mao's heart: the family system and relations between the sexes. Texts A 1 and A 2, dating respectively from the May 4th period and from the years of the Kiangsi Soviet Republic, illustrate the liberal side of Mao's thinking in this domain: 'freedom to love' for the individual rather than the servitude of arranged marriages, and equal rights for women. Text A 3 reveals one of the utilitarian aims of this policy: making women available for productive labour. (Another and equally important goal, not touched on by the texts in this chapter, is of course to weaken the family as an obstacle to social mobilization for political ends.) I have substituted Text A 4 (in praise of the women's militia) for Mao's poem in memory of his first wife, because it seems more characteristic of his state of mind today.

Part B of this chapter deals with agrarian policy, and spans the successive stages from land reform to the establishment of the communes. The first three texts, B 1, B 2, and B 3, illustrate Mao's position before taking power on the first stage in the agrarian transformation of China. On the one hand, Mao is constantly preoccupied with the problem of the link between changes in this field and the social bases of the communists' power; and on the other hand, there is his clear affirmation that the collectivization of agriculture was the ultimate goal – even if he did not say explicitly then, as he did in today's revised edition, that the Chinese form of collectivization would necessarily be identical with the Soviet form. Once solidly established in power, he expounded, as shown by Text B 4, the very ideas about preserving a rich-peasant economy in order to restore production for which Liu Shao-ch'i is today branded a traitor to the revolution. Text B 5 contains extracts from Mao's speech of July 1955 on forming cooperatives by which he turned his back on moderation and launched China on a new and radical path. Text B 6 shows Mao once more concerned with the priority which should be accorded to the political objective of maintaining the control of the poor peasants in the villages, rather than to the economic objective of increasing production. Text B 7, published in December 1955, calls for a transition from 'semi-socialist' to 'socialist' co-operatives within three years, but in less time than that, Mao was calling, as illustrated by Text B 8, for the creation of people's communes.

The texts in part C illustrate the mood which suffused both the 'Socialist Upsurge' of 1955 and the 'Great Leap Forward' of 1958, and which has erupted even more spectacularly in the current Great Proletarian Cultural Revolution – the belief that 'revolution can change everything', coupled with the will to take advantage of China's 'poverty' and 'blankness' in order to paint 'the most beautiful pictures' on this blank sheet of paper and ultimately live 'better than the imperialist countries'. This last concern with collective well-being has receded today in favour of a puritanical doctrine of abstention from the pleasures of this life, and an evident anxiety about the corrupting effects of wealth and ease. But the link between Mao's impatience in the face of natural and human obstacles, and his warlike temperament and guerrilla experience, illustrated by Text C 4, remains as strong as ever.

Part D of this chapter, dealing with youth, once more illustrates the antinomy we have so often emphasized in our analysis of Mao's thought: a simultaneous insistence on spontaneity and discipline. On the one hand, Mao shows an appreciation of the role of youthful enthusiasm in revolution, independently of class origins, which he has attenuated in the current edition of the *Selected Works*. Thus, in Text D 2, the following sentence has now been eliminated: 'The whole of the Chinese revolutionary movement found its origin in the action of young students and intellectuals.' But at the same time, Mao strongly emphasized in 1939 (Texts D 1 and D 2) that young people must listen to their elders, who have the experience they lack, and look to them for guidance. But, as shown by Text D 3, he had already, by 1955, arrived at the view, put into practice on a vast scale in 1966 in the role attributed to the Red Guards, that young people must lead the way and force their more conservative elders to follow.

The ten texts constituting part E of this chapter illustrate various aspects and stages in the development and application of Mao's ideas about 'cultural revolution', both in the narrow sense of the reform of art and literature and in the broad sense of reshaping the ideas and habits of an entire nation. Text E 1, a brief extract from 'On new democracy', contains Mao's views regarding the selective assimilation of elements from China's traditional culture. These principles are theoretically still in force today, though in the course of the Great Proletarian Cultural Revolution they have been more honoured in the breach than in the observance. Text E 2, dating from 1942, stresses the difficulty of mastering the use of language in a way hardly compatible with today's doctrine of 'do-it-yourself' writing by workers and peasants. Text E 3 contains extracts from Mao's principal utterance on art and literature, his interventions at the forum held in Yenan in May 1942. On this occasion, Mao expressed views corresponding essentially to the tenets of 'socialist realism' as practised in the Soviet Union: namely, that the people are the source of all art and that all art must serve the people and be comprehensible to the people. Text E 4 is an extract from an anonymous editorial written by Mao in 1951 and now refurbished as one of the 'five militant documents' on art and literature. In it, Mao stressed the political criterion of popular culture versus the 'feudal' culture of the ruling classes in the evaluation of China's heritage. In Text E 5, written in 1955, Mao complained bitterly that the 'party formalism' he had denounced in 1942 still flourished in the writings of the average cadre. Text E 6 reveals the fundamental anxiety which is, in a sense, the starting-point of the whole 'Cultural Revolution': that inspired by the 'selfish, capitalistic spontaneous tendencies' which are prone to emerge in man and society. Text E 7 is a brief quotation from

Mao's remarks at the Tenth Plenum of the Central Committee of the Chinese Communist Party in September 1962, denouncing the use of literature for 'anti-party activities', i.e. for the propagation of ideas different from his. Text E 8, written in 1963 and published in 1964, first put forward the clarion call to prevent China from 'changing colour' by constantly mobilizing the masses for 'class struggle'. Text E 9, a directive written in December 1963, denounces the lag of the superstructure, and in particular of the arts, as compared to the economic base of Chinese society. In Text E 10, I have gathered together eighteen of the brief quotations attributed to Mao in the course of the Great Proletarian Cultural Revolution, arranging them roughly in chronological order. Although these 'supreme directives' continue to stress mobilizing the masses, one can see the evolution from attacks on the cadres to a reconciliation with important elements in the Party in order to save China from chaos.

S.R.S.

VII · A 1 Miss Chao's suicide[1]

A person's suicide is entirely determined by circumstances. Was Miss Chao's original idea to seek death? On the contrary, it was to seek life. If Miss Chao ended up by seeking death instead, it is because circumstances drove her to this. The circumstances in which Miss Chao found herself were the following: (1) Chinese society; (2) the Chao family of Nanyang Street in Changsha; (3) the Wu family of Kantzuyüan Street in Changsha, the family of the husband she did not want. These three factors constituted three iron nets, composing a kind of triangular cage. Once caught

1. Extracted from several articles published in the Changsha *Ta-kung-pao*, beginning on 16 November 1919. Our translation is made from the text appearing in *Hunan li-shih tzu-liao*, no. 8, 1959, pp. 28–31, supplemented by the extracts given by Chou Shih-chao in the *Kung-jen jih-pao* of 20 April 1959.

Available translations: Since the appearance of the first edition of this book, Roxane Witke has translated extensive passages from Mao's articles in her study 'Mao Tse-tung, women, and suicide in the May Fourth era', *China Quarterly*, no. 31, 1967, pp. 128–47. The Chou Shih-chao extracts appear in translation in S.C.M.P., no. 2011, 12 May 1959.

in these three nets, it was in vain that she sought life in every way possible. There was no way for her to go on living; the contrary of life is death, and Miss Chao thus felt compelled to die. . . . If, among these three factors, there had been one that was not an iron net, or if one of these nets had opened, Miss Chao would certainly not have died. (1) If Miss Chao's parents had not had recourse to compulsion but had yielded before Miss Chao's free will, Miss Chao would certainly not have died; (2) if Miss Chao's parents had not resorted to compulsion but had permitted Miss Chao to explain her point of view to the family of her future husband, and to explain the reasons for her refusal, and if in the end the family of her future husband had accepted her point of view, and respected her individual freedom, Miss Chao would certainly not have died; (3) even if her parents and the family of her future husband had refused to accept her free will, if in society there had been a powerful group of public opinion to support her, if there were an entirely new world where the fact of running away from one's parents' home and finding refuge elsewhere were considered honourable and not dishonourable, in this case, too, Miss Chao would certainly not have died. If Miss Chao is dead today, it is because she was solidly enclosed by the three iron nets (society, her own family, the family of her future husband); she sought life in vain and finally was led to seek death . . .

Yesterday's incident was important. It happened because of the shameful system of arranged marriages, because of the darkness of the social system, the negation of the individual will, and the absence of the freedom to choose one's own mate. It is to be hoped that interested persons will comment on all aspects of this affair, and that they will defend the honour of a girl who died a martyr's death for the cause of the freedom to choose her own love . . .

The family of the parents and the family of the future husband are both bound up with society; they are both parts of society. We must understand that the family of the parents and the family of the future husband have committed a crime, but the source of this crime lies in society. It is true that the two families themselves carried out this crime; but a great part of the culpability was transmitted to them by society. Moreover, if society were good, even if the families had wanted to carry out this crime, they would not have had the opportunity to do so . . .

Since there are factors in our society that have brought about the death of Miss Chao, this society is an extremely dangerous thing. It was capable of causing the death of Miss Chao; it could also cause the death of Miss Ch'ieh, Miss Sun, or Miss Li. It is capable of killing men as well as women. All of us, the potential victims, must be on our guard before this dangerous thing that could inflict a fatal blow on us. We should protest loudly, warn the other human beings who are not yet dead, and condemn the countless evils of our society . . .

If we conduct a campaign in favour of marriage reform, it is first of all the superstitions about marriage that must be demolished, above all the belief that marriages are predestined by fate. Once these beliefs are demolished, the pretext behind which the arrangement of marriages by parents hides itself will disappear at the same time, and then the concept of 'incompatibility of husband and wife' will immediately appear in society. And with the appearance of the concept of incompatibility of husband and wife, the army of the family revolution will arise in countless numbers, and the great wave of the freedom of marriage and of the freedom to love will sweep over China . . .

My attitude toward suicide is to reject it. . . . First of all, man's goal is to seek life, and he should not go against the grain of his natural tendency and seek death. . . . Secondly, although suicide results from the fact that society deprives people of all hope . . . we should struggle against society in order to regain the hope that we have lost. . . . We should die fighting. . . . Thirdly, if people show respect for those who have courageously put an end to their own lives, that does not at all mean that they respect suicide as such, but rather that they respect the courageous spirit of 'resistance to brute force', which inspires the person who commits suicide . . .

It is so much better to be killed in fighting than to take one's own life! The goal of struggle is not 'to be killed by others' but 'to aspire toward the emergence of a true personality'. If a person does not attain this despite all his efforts, if he fights to the death and sacrifices himself, then he will be the most courageous of all on earth, and his tragedy will make a great impression on men's minds! . . .

VII · A 2 Decree regarding marriage[1]

Under feudal domination, marriage is a barbaric and inhuman institution. The oppression and suffering borne by woman is far greater than that of man. Only the victory of the workers' and peasants' revolution, followed by the first step toward the economic emancipation of men and women, brings with it a change in the marriage relationship and makes it free. In the soviet districts, marriages now are contracted on a free basis. Free choice must be the basic principle of every marriage. The whole feudal system of marriage, including the power of parents to arrange marriages for their children, to exercise compulsion, and all purchase and sale in marriage contracts shall henceforth be abolished.

Although women have obtained freedom from the feudal yoke, they are still labouring under tremendous physical handicaps (for example, the binding of the feet) and have not obtained complete economic independence. Therefore on questions concerning divorce, it becomes necessary to protect the interests of women and place the greater part of the obligations and responsibilities entailed by divorce upon men.

Children are the masters of the new society. Under the old system little attention was paid to children. Consequently special regulations have been established concerning the protection of children.

These present regulations are hereby made public and shall enter into force as of 1 December 1931.

MAO TSE-TUNG

Chairman of the Central Executive Committee

1. This is the full text of a decree of the First Session of the Central Executive Committee of the Chinese Soviet Republic entitled 'Provisional Marriage Regulations', (*Su-wei-ai Chung-kuo*, pp. 207–8).

Available translations: *Fundamental Laws of the Chinese Soviet Republic*, with an introduction by Bela Kun, International Publishers, New York, 1934, pp. 83–4.

HSIANG YING
CHANG KUO-T'AO
Vice-Chairmen

28 January 1931

VII · A 3 China's women are a vast reserve of labour power[1]

Prior to the formation of cooperatives (*ho-tso-hua*), many localities throughout the country had a problem of surplus labour. Since cooperatives have been formed, many cooperatives are finding themselves short of labour. It has become necessary to get the broad masses of the women, who in the past did not work in the fields, to take their place on the labour front. This is an important development, quite unexpected for many people. In the past, people commonly said that after the formation of cooperatives, there would certainly be a labour surplus. 'We have too big a labour force already,' they used to say; 'what shall we do if there is a further surplus?' In a great many places, when the formation of cooperatives was carried out, this anxiety was dissipated.... In a great many localities, when the scale of production is expanded, the number of types of activity increased, the sphere of the exploitation of nature extended and deepened, and work done more skilfully, a lack of labour power will be felt. This condition is only beginning to make its appearance, and in the future it will develop from year to year. The same thing will happen after the mechanization of agriculture. In the future there will be all sorts of enterprises that people have never dreamed of, raising our agricultural output to several times, ten times, or even several tens of times its present level. The development of industry, transportation, and exchange will go even farther beyond the bounds of our ancestors' imagination. Science, culture, education and hygiene will do the same. China's women are a vast reserve of labour power. This reserve should be tapped

1. Extracted from *Socialist Upsurge* ... (see note to Text VI C 8), pp. 674–5 of the Chinese edition.
Available translations: pp. 285–6 of the English edition.

and used in the struggle to build a mighty socialist country. To encourage women to join in productive labour, we must put into effect the principle of equal pay for equal work, men and women alike...

VII · A 4 Lines written on a picture of the Women's Militia[1]

Proud and alert, they carry five-foot guns,
The first rays of the morning sun illuminate the drill-field.
The daughters of China are filled with high resolve,
To red garments they prefer the uniform.

VII · B 1 Let's get organized![2]

For thousands of years a system of individual production has prevailed among the peasant masses under which a family or a household forms a productive unit. This scattered, individual form of production was the economic foundation of feudal rule and has plunged the peasants into perpetual poverty. The only way to change this state of affairs is gradual collectivization, and, according to Lenin, the only way to bring about collectivization is through cooperatives. Here in the border region, many peasants' cooperatives have been set up, but they are still not the soviet-type cooperatives known as collective farms.[3] Our economy is new-democratic, and our cooperatives are at present still organizations of collective labour founded on the basis of individual ownership (i.e., the basis of private property). Such cooperatives,

1. The above poem was written in February 1961. Regarding the source see note to Text I C. The translation is my own.

2. Extracted from a speech given at a reception in honour of labour heroes, 29 November 1943. My source was *Ching-chi wen-t'i yü ts'ai-cheng wen-t'i* (revised edition, Chieh-fang She, Yenan, January 1944), pp. 228–9.

Available translations: Mao Tse-tung, *Selected Works*, IV, pp. 151–2.

3. In the current edition, Mao has amplified this point somewhat and speaks of 'several stages of development' that the Chinese cooperatives must undergo before turning into soviet-type cooperatives.

again, fall into several types.... No matter what names they have; no matter whether they are each composed of a few, or dozens or hundreds of people ... no matter whether their mutual aid is rendered in terms of manpower, animal power, or implements, or whether their members may or may not live and board together during the busy season; and no matter whether they are of a temporary or permanent nature – all are good so long as they are collective mutual-aid organizations in which the masses take part of their own free will (no compulsion whatever is allowed). This method of collective mutual aid was discovered by the masses themselves ...

VII · B 2 On the enlightened gentry[1]

... The enlightened gentry are individual landlords and rich peasants with democratic leanings. Such people have conflicts with bureaucrat-capitalism and imperialism and to a certain extent also with the feudal landlords and rich peasants. We unite with them not because they are a political force to be reckoned with or because they are of any economic importance (their feudal landholdings should be handed over with their consent to the peasants for distribution), but because they gave us considerable help politically during the War of Resistance and during the struggle against the United States and Chiang Kai-shek. During the period of land reform, it will help the land reform throughout the country if some of the enlightened gentry favour it. In particular, it will help win over the intellectuals (most of whom come from the landlord or rich peasant families), the national bourgeoisie (most of whom have ties with the land), and the enlightened gentry throughout the country (who number several hundred thousand), and it will help isolate the chief enemy of the Chinese revolution, the Chiang Kai-shek reactionaries.... At the present stage, what we require of them is that they favour the struggle against the United States and Chiang Kai-shek, favour

1. Extracted from an inner-Party directive dated 1 March 1948, drafted by Mao. *Hsüan-chi*, IV, pp. 1287–8.
Available translations: *Selected Works*, IV, pp. 209–10.

democracy (not be anti-communist), and favour the land reform. If they can meet these requirements, we should unite with them without exception and while uniting with them educate them.

VII · B 3 The general line of land reform: unite ninety per cent of the population[1]

... Feudalism is the ally of imperialism and bureaucrat-capitalism and the foundation of their rule. Therefore, the reform of the land system is the main content of China's new-democratic revolution. The general line in the land reform is to rely on the poor peasants, unite with the middle peasants, abolish the system of feudal exploitation step by step and in a discriminating way, and develop agricultural production. Only the poor peasants can and must be the basic force to be relied upon in the land reform. Together with the farm labourers, they make up about seventy per cent of China's rural population. The main and immediate task of the land reform is to satisfy the demands of the masses of poor peasants and farm labourers. In the land-reform programme it is necessary to unite with the middle peasants; the poor peasants and the farm labourers must form a solid united front with the middle peasants, who account for about twenty per cent of the rural population. Otherwise, the poor peasants and farm labourers will find themselves isolated and the land reform will fail.... A section of the middle peasants must be allowed to keep some land over and above the average obtained by the poor peasants. We support the peasants' demand for equal distribution of land in order to help arouse the broad masses of peasants speedily to abolish the system of landownership by the feudal landlord class, but we do not advocate absolute equalitarianism.... There is a kind of thinking now current in the countryside that undermines industry and commerce and advocates absolute

1. Extracted from a speech delivered at a conference of Party cadres, in April 1948, and published in *Ch'ün-chung*, II, no. 18, 30 May 1948, pp. 5–6.

Available translations: With the exception of the few words italicized in this extract, the text appearing in the *Selected Works*, IV, pp. 235–6, is identical with that of 1948. A translation based on the original text appears in *China Digest*, 1 June 1948.

equalitarianism in land distribution. Such thinking *corresponds to a kind of agrarian socialism;* it is reactionary, backward, and retrogressive in nature. We must criticize it. The sole target of the land reform is and must be the system of feudal exploitation by the landlord class and by the old-type rich peasants, and there should be no encroachment either upon the liberal bourgeoisie[1] or upon the industrial and commercial enterprises run by the landlords and rich peasants. . . . The aim of the land reform is to abolish the system of feudal exploitation, that is, to eliminate the feudal landlords as a class, not as individuals. Therefore a landlord must receive the same allotment of land and property as does a peasant and must be made to learn productive labour and participate in the nation's economic life. Except for the most heinous counter-revolutionaries and local tyrants who have incurred the bitter hatred of the broad masses, who have been proved guilty and who therefore may and ought to be punished, a policy of leniency must be applied to all, and any beating or killing without discrimination must be forbidden. The system of feudal exploitation should be abolished step by step, that is, in a tactical way. In launching the struggle, we must determine our tactics according to the circumstances and the degree to which the peasant masses are awakened and organized. We must not attempt to wipe out overnight the whole system of feudal exploitation . . .

VII · B 4 We must preserve a rich peasant economy[2]

The work of agrarian reform should be carried forward by stages

1. In the current edition, 'liberal bourgeoisie' has been replaced by the more usual term 'national bourgeoisie'.

2. Extracted from Mao's speech of 6 June 1950 at the Third Plenum of the Seventh Central Committee of the Chinese Communist Party, entitled 'Fight for a fundamental turn for the better in the financial and economic situation in China', as given in *Hsin-hua yüeh-pao*, no. 7, 1950, p. 488.

Available translations: *New China's Economic Achievements, 1949–1952*, China Committee for the Promotion of International Trade, Peking, 1952, pp. 6–7.

and in an orderly manner. Since the war has virtually ended on the mainland, the situation is completely different from that during the 1946–8 period when the People's Liberation Army was locked in a life-and-death struggle with the Kuomintang reactionaries and the issue had not yet been decided. The state can now, by means of loans to poor peasants, help them solve their difficulties, and make up for the fact that they received less land [than under the policy in force from 1946 to 1948]. Therefore, there should be a change in our policy toward the rich peasants, a change from the policy of requisitioning the surplus land and property of the rich peasants to one of preserving a rich peasant economy, in order to further the early restoration of production in the rural areas. This change of policy will also serve to isolate the landlords, while protecting the middle peasants and those who rent out small plots of land.

... Blindness and anarchy in the economic field should be gradually eliminated in line with the principle of unified planning and of considering the interests of all sections. Existing industry and commerce should be properly readjusted, while practical and appropriate steps should be taken to improve relations between public and private enterprises and between labour and capital. Under the leadership of the state sector of the economy, which is socialist in nature, the various components of the social economy should establish a division of labour and cooperation, facilitating the revival and development of the entire social economy. The view held by some people that it is possible to eliminate capitalism and introduce socialism at an early date is wrong; it is not adapted to conditions in our country.

VII · B 5 The question of agricultural cooperation[1]

A new upsurge in the socialist mass movement is in sight through-

1. Extracted from a speech delivered on 31 July 1955, published in October 1955, under the above title. (Mao Tse-tung. *Kuan-yü nung-yeh ho-tso-hua wen-t'i*, Peking, Jen-min Ch'u-pan-she, 1955, pp. 1, 18–28 *passim.*)

Available translations: Mao Tse-tung, *The Question of Agricultural Cooperation*, Foreign Languages Press, Peking, 1956.

out the Chinese countryside. But some of our comrades are tottering along like a woman with bound feet, always complaining that others are going too fast. They imagine that by picking on trifles, grumbling unnecessarily, worrying continuously, and putting up countless taboos and commandments they are guiding the socialist mass movement in the rural areas on sound lines.

No, this is not the right way at all; it is wrong.

The tide of social reform in the countryside – in the shape of cooperation – has already reached some places. Soon it will sweep the whole country. This is a huge socialist revolutionary movement, which involves a rural population more than 500 million strong, one which has very great world significance. We should guide this movement vigorously, warmly, and systematically, and not act as a drag on it . . .

It is wrong to say that the present pace of development of the agricultural producers' cooperatives has 'gone beyond practical possibilities' or 'gone beyond the consciousness of the masses'. The situation in China is like this: Its population is enormous, there is a shortage of cultivated land (only three *mou* of land per head taking the country as a whole; in many parts of the southern provinces the average is only one *mou* or less), natural catastrophes occur from time to time – every year large numbers of farms suffer more or less from flood, drought, gales, frost, hail, or insect pests – and methods of farming are backward. As a result, many peasants are still having difficulties or are not well off. The well-off ones are comparatively few, although since land reform the standard of living of the peasants as a whole has improved. For all these reasons there is an active desire among most peasants to take the socialist road . . .

It is quite true, the socialist revolution is a new revolution. In the past we only had experience with bourgeois-democratic revolution; we had no experience with socialist revolution. How can we get such experience? By sitting back and waiting for it, or by throwing ourselves into the struggle for the socialist revolution and learning in the process? How can we get experience in industrialization if we do not carry out the Five-Year Plan, if we do not engage in the work of socialist industrialization? Co-operation in agriculture is one of the integral parts of the Five-

Year Plan. If we do not guide the peasants in organizing one or several agricultural producers' cooperatives in every *hsiang* or village, where will the 'cadres' experience' come from, how will the level of that experience be raised? Clearly the idea that the present state of development reached by the agricultural producers' cooperatives has 'gone beyond the level of the cadres' experience' shows faulty thinking...

The Soviet Union's great historical experience in building socialism inspires our people and gives them full confidence that they can build socialism in their country.... Some comrades disapprove of the Party Central Committee's policy of keeping agricultural cooperation in step with socialist industrialization. ... That is to disregard the Soviet Union's experience. These comrades do not understand that socialist industrialization is not something that can be carried out in isolation, separate from agricultural cooperation. In the first place, as everyone knows, the level of production of marketable grain and industrial raw materials in our country is very low, whereas the state's demands for these items grow year by year. Therein lies a sharp contradiction. If, in a period of roughly three five-year plans, we cannot fundamentally solve the problem of agricultural cooperation, if we cannot jump from small-scale farming with animal-drawn farm implements to large-scale farming with machinery – which includes state-sponsored land reclamation carried out on a large scale by settlers using machinery ... we shall fail to resolve the contradiction between the ever-increasing demand for marketable grain and industrial raw materials and the present generally poor yield of staple crops. In that case our socialist industrialization will run into formidable difficulties: We shall not be able to complete socialist industrialization. The Soviet Union faced this problem in the course of building socialism. It solved it by systematically guiding and expanding agricultural cooperation. We, too, can solve this problem only by using the same method.

In the second place, some of our comrades do not think of linking up the following two factors: heavy industry, which is the most important branch in the work of socialist industrialization and produces the tractors and other agricultural machinery, the chemical fertilizers, modern means of transport, oil, electric power for the needs of agriculture and so on, and the fact that all these can be used on a big scale only on the basis of large-scale, cooperative farming. We are carrying out a revolution not only in the social system, changing from private ownership to common ownership, but also in technology, changing from handicraft production to mass production with up-to-date machinery. These two revolutions interlink. In agriculture, under the conditions prevailing in our country, the formation of cooperatives must precede the use of big machinery (in the capitalist countries, agriculture undergoes a capitalist transformation). ... What is more, there are two other things that some of our comrades do not think of linking up: the large sums needed to complete both national industrialization and the technical reconstruction of agriculture, and the fact that a considerable portion of these funds is derived from agriculture...

We have been taking steps to bring about a gradual advance in the socialist transformation of agriculture. The first step in the countryside is to call on the peasants, in accordance with the principles of voluntariness and mutual benefit, to organize agricultural producers' mutual-aid teams. Such teams contain only the rudiments of socialism. Each one draws in a few households, though some have ten or more. The second step is to call on the peasants, on the basis of these mutual-aid teams and still in accordance with the principles of voluntariness and mutual benefit, to organize small agricultural producers' cooperatives semi-socialist in nature, characterized by the pooling of land as shares and by single management. Not until we take the third step will the peasants be called upon, on the basis of these small, semi-socialist cooperatives and in accordance with the same principles of voluntariness and mutual benefit, to unite on a larger scale and organize large agricultural producers' cooperatives completely socialist in nature. These steps are designed to raise steadily the socialist consciousness of the peasants through their personal experience, to change their mode of life step by step, and so minimize any feeling that their mode of life is being changed all of a sudden...

VII · B 6 Maintaining the predominance of the poor peasants in the cooperatives[1]

The leading bodies in cooperatives must establish the dominant position of the poor peasants and the new lower middle peasants in these bodies, with the old lower middle peasants and the upper middle peasants – whether old or new – as the supplementary force. Only thus can unity between the poor and middle peasants be attained, the cooperatives be consolidated, production be expanded, and the socialist transformation of the entire countryside be correctly accomplished in accordance with the Party's policy. Otherwise, there can be no unity between the middle and poor peasants, the cooperatives cannot be consolidated, production cannot be increased, and the socialist transformation of the entire countryside cannot be achieved. Many comrades do not understand the reasoning behind this. They agree that it was necessary for the poor peasants to have been dominant during land reform because the poor peasants then constituted fifty, sixty, or even seventy per cent of the rural population and had not yet risen to the status of middle peasant, while the middle peasants at that time wavered in their attitude toward land reform. . . . But, say these comrades, now we are carrying out the socialist transformation of agriculture, most of the former poor peasants have already risen to the status of new middle peasants, and the old middle peasants own a good part of the means of production. Unless the old middle peasants take part, the problem of the cooperatives' shortage of the means of production cannot be solved. And so, these comrades believe, the slogan 'Rely on the poor peasants and establish their predominance!' should not be raised now, slogans of this type are disadvantageous to the formation of cooperatives. We consider these views to be erroneous. If the working class and the Communist Party want to use the spirit of socialism and the socialist system to transform thoroughly the system prevailing throughout the countryside of

1. Extracted from *Socialist Upsurge* . . . (see note to Text VI C 8), pp. 857–9 of the Chinese edition.

Available translations: pp. 236–8 of the English edition.

private ownership of the means of production in small peasant holdings, they can do so relatively easily only by relying on the broad masses of the former semi-proletarian poor peasants. Otherwise the transformation will be very difficult. For the rural semi-proletariat are not so insistent on private ownership of the means of production in small peasant holdings; they accept socialist transformation fairly readily. Most of them have already become new middle peasants; but compared with the old middle peasants, except for a few poor peasants who have become well-to-do middle peasants, the majority are of a relatively high level of political consciousness and often recall the hard life they led in the past. Furtheremore, the lower ranks of the old middle peasants are fairly close to the lower ranks of the new middle peasants, both in economic position and in political outlook; but they are different from both the upper ranks of the new and the upper ranks of the old middle peasants – that is, the well-to-do and comparatively well-to-do middle peasants. In the process of forming cooperatives, therefore, we must pay close attention to: (1) the poor peasants who are still in a difficult position, (2) the lower ranks of the new middle peasants, and (3) the lower ranks of the old middle peasants. . . . This does not mean that we will carry out once more the work of determining class status in the countryside. It is, rather, a statement of the principle which Party branches and comrades sent to guide the work of cooperation in the countryside should make sure to grasp, a principle which should be proclaimed publicly to the peasant masses. Nor are we saying that the well-to-do middle peasants may not join the cooperatives, only that we should wait until the level of their socialist consciousness has been raised, until they show a desire to join and are willing to accept the leadership of the poor peasants (including the present poor peasants and all the former poor peasants who have become lower middle peasants). It is then that we should allow them into the cooperatives. Don't force them to join before they are willing just for the sake of obtaining the use of their draught oxen and their farm implements. . . . People who are a little short on the means of production can organize cooperatives too. Many cooperatives formed by poor peasants and lower middle peasants have proved this.

VII · B 7 Let us create higher-stage cooperatives[1]

... Because ownership in the first-stage cooperatives remains of a semi-private nature, sooner or later it fetters the expansion of the forces of production, and people begin to demand that the form of ownership be changed to permit the cooperative to become a collectively-managed economic organization in which all means of production are owned jointly. When the ties hampering the forces of production are thus loosened, production will develop much more rapidly. Some places can make the change-over fairly quickly; others will probably have to go a bit slower. Most first-stage cooperatives that have been in existence about three years basically meet the requirements. The Party organizations in every province, city, and autonomous region should look into the situation and, with the agreement of the masses, arrange for the establishment of a number of experimental higher-stage cooperatives during 1956 and 1957.... When people see that large higher-stage cooperatives are better than small first-stage co-operatives, when people see that long-range planning brings them a life of a much higher material and cultural level, they will agree to combine their cooperatives and build higher-stage ones...

VII · B 8 Communes are better[2]

Chairman Mao emphasized particularly that arrangements for all types of work must be the subject of vigorous and uninhibited debate by the masses. He said that if plans and directions were not debated by the masses, the ideas would be yours [i.e., those of the cadres]. After such debates, the masses themselves became the masters, and were naturally prepared to work more energeti-

1. Extracted from *Socialist Upsurge* ... (see note to Text VI C 8), pp. 285–6 of the Chinese edition.
Available translations: pp. 477–8 of the English edition.

2. Extracted from the account of Mao's inspection tour in Shantung on 9 August 1958, as reported in *Jen-min jih-pao*, 13 August 1958.
Available translations: none.

cally. Chairman Mao emphasized once more that the leading cadres must go frequently to the lower levels to have a look, to aid the basic-level cadres in summing up their experience, and to give guidance on the spot. When T'an Ch'i-lung [Shantung provincial secretary] reported that Pei-yüan *hsiang* in Li-ch'en *hsien* was preparing to set up large [collective] farms, Chairman Mao said: 'It is better to set up people's communes. Their advantage lies in the fact that they combine industry, agriculture, commerce, education and military affairs. This is convenient for leadership.'

VII · C 1 Revolution can change everything[1]

... Of all things in the world, people are the most precious. As long as there are people, every kind of miracle can be performed under the leadership of the Communist Party. We are refuters of Acheson's counter-revolutionary theory. We believe that revolution can change everything, and that before long there will arise a new China with a big population and a great wealth of products, where life will be abundant and culture will flourish. All pessimistic views are utterly groundless ...

VII · C 2 Six hundred million paupers[2]

... Taking part in the cooperative movement in Tsunhua County is the Wang Kuo-fan cooperative, originally consisting of twenty-three poor peasant families and a three-quarter share in the ownership of a donkey [literally, 'three legs of a donkey']. It was nicknamed 'The Paupers' Co-op.' But within three years, relying on their own efforts, its members accumulated a large quantity of the means of production. They 'got it from the mountains',

1. Extracted from an editorial dated 16 September 1949 criticizing the American White Paper. Our source was *Jen-min jih-pao*, 17 September 1949.
Available translations: *Selected Works*, IV, p. 454.

2. Extracted from *Socialist Upsurge* ... (see note to Text VI C 8), pp. 5–6 of the Chinese edition.
Available translations: pp. 13–14 of the English edition.

they explained. Some of the people visiting the cooperative were moved to tears by this. I think the situation is the same as regards our whole nation. In a few decades, why can't 600 million paupers, by their own efforts, create a socialist country, rich and strong? The wealth of society is created by the workers, the peasants, and the working intellectuals. If only they take their destiny into their own hands, follow a Marxist-Leninist line, and energetically tackle problems instead of evading them, there is no difficulty in the world that they cannot resolve.

VII · C 3 China is poor and blank[1]

Throughout the country, the communist spirit is surging forward. The political consciousness of the masses is rising rapidly. Backward sections among the masses have roused themselves energetically to catch up with the more advanced, proving that China is forging ahead in her socialist economic revolution (where transformation of the relations of production has not yet been completed) as well as in her political, ideological, technical, and cultural revolutions. In view of this, our country may not need as much time as previously thought to catch up with the big capitalist countries in industrial and agricultural production. The decisive factor, apart from leadership by the Party, is our 600 million people. The more people the more views and suggestions, the more intense the fervour, and the greater the energy. Never before have the masses been so high in spirit, so strong in morale, and so firm in determination. The former exploiting classes are reduced to mere drops in the ocean of the working people; they must change whether they want to or not. There are undoubtedly some who will never change and would prefer to keep their heads as hard as rocks till their dying day, but this does not affect the general situation. All decadent modes of thought and other unsuitable parts of the superstructure are crumbling daily. It will still take time to clear this refuse away completely, but there can

1. Extracted from an article dated 15 April 1958, written for the first issue of the Party journal *Hung-ch'i*, 1 June 1958, pp. 3–4.

Available translations: *Peking Review*, no. 15, 10 June 1958, p. 6.

be no doubt that the influence of these things has disintegrated. Apart from their other characteristics, China's 600 million people have two remarkable peculiarities; they are, first of all, poor, and secondly, blank. That may seem like a bad thing, but it is really a good thing. Poor people want change, want to do things, want revolution. A clean sheet of paper has no blotches, and so the newest and most beautiful words can be written on it, the newest and most beautiful pictures can be painted on it. The *ta-tzu-pao* [big-character poster, later to figure so prominently in the Cultural Revolution of 1966–8] is a most useful new weapon. It can be used in cities, rural areas, factories, cooperatives, shops, government institutions, schools, army units, and streets – wherever the masses congregate. Where it has been used widely, people should go on using it. A poem written by Kung Tzu-chen of the Ch'ing dynasty reads:

> Let thunderbolts rouse the universe to life.
> Alas that ten thousand horses should stand mute!
> I urge Heaven to bestir itself anew
> And send down talented men of every kind.

The *ta-tzu-pao* have broken the dull air in which 'ten thousand horses stand mute'. . . . Do the working people of China still look like slaves as they did in the past? No, they have become the masters. The working people who live on the 9.6 million square kilometres of the People's Republic of China have really begun to rule this land.

VII · C 4 The masses can do anything[1]

During this trip, I have witnessed the tremendous energy of the masses. On this foundation it is possible to accomplish any task whatsoever. We must first complete the tasks on the iron and steel fronts. In these sectors, the masses have already been mobilized. Nevertheless, in the country as a whole, there are a few places, a

1. Extracted from a statement to a reporter of the Hsin Hua Agency, on 29 September 1958, following a tour of the country. (*Hung-ch'i*, no. 10, 1958, pp. 1–2.)

Available translations: S.C.M.P., no. 1871.

few enterprises, where the work of mobilizing the masses has still not been properly carried out, where mass meetings have not been held, and where the tasks, the reasons for them, and the methods have still not been made perfectly clear to the masses or discussed by the masses. There are still a few comrades who are unwilling to undertake a large-scale mass movement in the industrial sphere. They call the mass movement on the industrial front 'irregular' and disparage it as 'a rural style of work' and 'a guerrilla habit'. This is obviously incorrect.

However, while devoting ourselves to iron and steel production on a large scale, we must not sacrifice agriculture. ... The 1959 task in agriculture is to achieve a leap forward even greater than that of 1958. Consequently, we must organize the industrial and agricultural labour force effectively and extend the system of people's communes throughout the whole country ...

VII · D 1 Youth needs experience[1]

The young people – whether or not they be members of the Communist Party – who join the ranks of the revolutionary movement, bringing new blood and enthusiasm, are all very precious. Without them, the ranks of the revolution could not develop and the revolution could not triumph. But lack of experience is the natural failing of our young comrades. Now revolutionary experience comes from personal participation in revolutionary struggle. If one begins working at the grass roots, if, for several years, one does work that is genuine, not false, then experience will come to those who do not have it.

1. This is the complete text of a message dated 5 October 1939, published as an unnumbered page at the beginning of *Chung-kuo ch'ing-yün wen-hsüan*, Chung-kuo Ch'ing-nien She, 1940.
Available translations: none.

VII · D 2 The role of youth in the revolution[1]

... On this very day twenty years ago, a movement of great historical significance was begun in China – the May 4th Movement, in which the students participated. What role have the Chinese youth played since the May 4th Movement? They have played the role of the vanguard, and this is recognized by all the people of the country except the diehards. What is meant by the role of the vanguard? It is to take the lead, i.e., to stand at the head of the revolutionary ranks. The ranks of the anti-imperialist and anti-feudal people in China include a contingent composed of the country's young intellectuals and students. This contingent is of considerable size; not counting those who have died, it numbers several millions at present. This million-strong contingent is a front army in the fight against imperialism and feudalism, and an important front army too. But this front army is not enough; we cannot defeat the enemy by relying on it alone, because it is not yet the main force. Who then constitutes the main force? None other than the broad masses of workers and peasants. The young intellectuals and students of China must go into the midst of the masses of workers and peasants and mobilize and organize these broad masses who constitute ninety per cent of the country's population. Lacking this main force of the workers and peasants, and relying only on the contingent of the young intellectuals and students, we cannot achieve victory in the fight against imperialism and feudalism ...

The whole of the Chinese revolutionary movement found its origin in the action of young students and intellectuals. But every beginning must have a fulfilment. Thus, for example, when the students at Yenan break up virgin lands and plant grain, the breaking-up of the virgin lands is the beginning, but the fulfilment comes only with the harvest. The young students and intellectuals must unite with the broad masses of young workers and peasants. It

1. Extracted from a speech of 4 May 1939, at Yenan, on the occasion of the twentieth anniversary of the May 4th Movement. (*Chung-kuo ch'ing-yün wen-hsüan*, pp. 5–7.)

Available translations: *Selected Works*, II, pp. 245–6.

is only if the few millions of young students and the several tens of millions of young workers and peasants unite that they can become a powerful youth movement. Otherwise they cannot become a powerful movement. If the young people wish to achieve results they must also establish friendly relations with the adults; they must unite with the majority of the population, who are more than twenty-five years old. Do we also need the old people? Of course we need them. Old people have experience; one cannot neglect them because they are old. Consequently, the young people must unite with the old, even if they are a hundred, in order to struggle together against Japan. ... Old men carry out propaganda work very well; the common people love to listen to them. ... Comrades, the organization of children is also an important task in the framework of the youth movement. ... Out there, Japanese imperialism is busy training our children, to make of them little traitors to their country. How can we in our turn abstain from organizing the children? ... Once organized, children have many advantages. They can catch traitors, keep watch on the opium smokers, confiscate mah jong sets, and even serve as scouts to watch the roads. ... Thus we can see that the young people absolutely must unite with the adults, the old people, and the children. ... Let the young people go among the 450 millions of our people, let them organize them to make of them a great anti-Japanese revolutionary army. It is only if we have such a revolutionary army that we can overthrow Japanese imperialism. ... In the youth movement of several decades ago, a section of youth, unwilling to unite with the broad masses of workers and peasants, opposed their movement. ... Was such a tendency good? I think not, because in opposing the workers and peasants they were in fact opposing the revolution, and, as I say, constituted a countercurrent in the youth movement. *Such a youth movement was a narrow youth movement.* And a youth movement of this kind cannot bring about good results. *It is like planting a tree that gives no fruit or cereals that yield no crop. Can one say then that such a movement was truly revolutionary, anti-imperialist, and anti-feudal?* A few days ago I wrote a short article in which I made this remark: 'The ultimate line of demarcation between the revolutionary intellectuals on the one hand and the non-revolutionary and counter-revolutionary intellectuals on the other lies in whether they are willing to, and actually do, become one with the masses of workers and peasants.' There I proposed a criterion that I regard as the only criterion . . .

VII · D 3 Young people are less conservative[1]

. . . Youth is one of the most active and vital forces in society.[2] Young people are the most anxious to learn, they are the least conservative in their thinking. This is especially so in the era of socialism. We hope that the local Party organizations in various places will work with the Youth League organizations in studying attentively how to bring the power of our youth into the fullest possible play. We must not lump them together with everybody else and overlook their special characteristics. Of course, the young people must learn from the old people and adults, and should strive as much as possible to engage in all sorts of useful activities with their agreement. Old people and adults are relatively conservative in their thinking. They often retard the progressive activities of the young people. Only after the young people make a success of something are their elders willing to concede. ... Naturally, no compromise should be made with conservative ideas. All right, then, let's have a try. If we are successful, the conservatives will have to give in.

VII · E 1 Ancient culture and new culture[3]

New-democratic culture is national. It opposes imperialist op-

1. Extracted from *Socialist Upsurge* ... (see note to Text VI C 8), p. 959 of the Chinese edition.
Available translations: pp. 292–3 of the English edition.
2. Here the extract contained in *Quotations from Chairman Mao* (p. 166) is deliberately mistranslated to read 'Young people are *the* most active and vital force ...', no doubt under the influence of the idolization of the 'little generals' that characterized the cultural revolution at the time the book was first published.
3. Extracted from 'On new democracy', first published as an article in *Chieh-fang*, nos. 98–9, 20 February 1940, pp. 39–40.
Available translations: *Selected Works*, II, pp. 380–18.

pression and upholds the national dignity and independence of the Chinese people. It belongs to our own people and bears our national characteristics. It unites with the socialist and new-democratic cultures of all other peoples and establishes with them the relations whereby they can absorb something from each other and help each other to develop; like them, it constitutes a part of the new world culture,[1] but it can never unite with the reactionary imperialist culture of any country, for it is a revolutionary national culture. China should absorb on a large scale the progressive cultures of foreign countries as an ingredient for enriching her own culture. We must absorb whatever we find useful today, not only from the present socialist or new-democratic cultures of other nations, but also from the older cultures of foreign countries, such as those of the various capitalist countries in the age of enlightenment. ... However, we must treat these foreign materials as we do our food, which should be chewed in the mouth, submitted to the workings of the stomach and intestines, mixed with saliva, gastric juice, and intestinal secretions, and then separated into essence to be absorbed and waste matter to be discarded. Only thus can food benefit our body; we should never swallow anything raw or absorb uncritically. So-called 'wholesale Westernization' represents a mistaken viewpoint. China has suffered a great deal in the past from the formalist absorption of foreign things . . .

A splendid ancient culture was created during the long period of China's feudal society. To clarify the process of development of this ancient culture, to throw away its feudal dross, and to absorb its democratic essence is prerequisite for the development of our new national culture and for the increase of our national self-confidence; but we should not absorb anything and everything uncritically. We must separate all the rotten things of the ancient feudal ruling class from the fine ancient popular culture that is more or less democratic and revolutionary in character . . .

1. In the current edition, Mao modified this to read: 'They ... together form the new world culture,' implying that world culture is one, not divided into national compartments.

VII · E 2 The mastery of language is not easy[1]

... We are a revolutionary Party, acting for the masses, and if we do not learn the language of the masses, we cannot do our work well. At present many of our comrades doing propaganda work make no study of language. Their propagands is very dull, and few people care to read their articles or listen to their talk. Why do we need to study language and, what is more, spend much effort on it? Because the mastery of language is not easy and requires painstaking effort. First, let us study the *language of the masses.* The people's *language* is rich, vigorous, vivid and expressive of real life. A great many of our comrades have not studied this language, and consequently our articles and speeches contain few vigorous, vivid and effective expressions and resemble not a hale and healthy person, but an emaciated *pieh-san*,[2] a mere bag of bones. Secondly, let us study foreign languages. *The language of the people of foreign countries is not in the least foreign formalism; it is only when the Chinese copy them and import their expressions indiscriminately that they become lifeless foreign formalism.* We should not import foreign expressions indiscriminately, but should absorb what is good and suitable for our work. Our current language has already incorporated many foreign expressions, because the Chinese language is inadequate.[3] For instance, today we are holding a meeting of *kan-pu* (cadres), and the term *kan-pu* is derived from a foreign word. We should continue to absorb many fresh things from abroad, not only

1. Extracted from Mao's speech of 8 February 1942. (For source see note to Text VI C 2).

Available translations: Boyd Compton, *Mao's China*, pp. 42–3; *Selected Works*, III, pp. 59–60. Our translation owes something to both of these.

2. 'The people of Shanghai call *pieh-san* those lumpenproletarians (*yu-min*) in the city who have no regular employment and live by begging or thievery. Most of them are extremely scrawny.' (Note from the current Chinese edition of the *Selected Works*, which for some reason is not included in the English translation.)

3. In revising this text for the current edition Mao found that he had gone too far in depreciating the Chinese language, and re-wrote this sentence so that it is 'the old Chinese vocabulary' and not the Chinese language as such that is inadequate.

progressive ideas but new expressions as well. *For example, in his speech on the new Soviet constitution, Stalin spoke of the 'Alliance of Party and non-Party people'. We have absorbed this phrase into the administrative platform of the Shensi-Kansu-Ninghsia Border Region, calling it 'the carrying out of democratic cooperation between Communist Party members and non-Party people'. In a word, we cannot but absorb a great many good elements of this kind from foreign countries.* Thirdly, let us also study the language of the ancients. *A large part of the present-day popular language has been transmitted to us by the ancients, and the treasure-vault of the classical Chinese language can still be further excavated. Whatever is still alive in it, we should absorb in our articles, speeches and talks.* Of course, we are resolutely opposed to the use of obsolete allusions, and that is final; but what is good should be absorbed . . .

VII · E 3 Literature and art in the service of the people[1]

. . . So far as we are concerned, art and literature are . . . intended . . . for the people. . . . At the present stage China's new culture is an anti-feudal, anti-imperialist culture of the broad masses of the people under the leadership of the proletariat. Everything that truly belongs to the broad masses of the people must now of necessity be under the leadership of the proletariat. Nothing under the leadership of the bourgeoisie can possibly belong to the broad masses of the people . . .

Who, then, are the broad masses of the people? The broadest masses of the people, constituting more than ninety per cent of the total population, are the workers, peasants, soldiers, and petty

1. Extracted from two speeches before a conference on problems of literature and art, held in Yenan in May 1942. These have been frequently republished under the title 'Problems of Literature and Art'. With the exception of the paragraph on Mao's personal experience, which comes from his opening remarks, this extract is made up of passages from the second speech. (*Chieh-fang jih-pao*, 19 October 1943.)

Available translations: Mao Tse-tung, *On Literature and Art, The Chefoo News* (n.d.) *passim*. A revised text appears in the *Selected Works*, III, pp. 76–90 *passim*.

bourgeoisie. ... *We should also cooperate with those elements within the landlord and bourgeois classes who are still resisting the Japanese, but we must not forget that they oppose a broad-based democracy for the Chinese people. They have their own culture and ours is not meant for them, as they would only reject and repudiate it anyway.*

Our art and literature should be intended for the four groups of people mentioned above...

The question of 'whom to serve' having been solved, the question of 'how to serve' arises. To put it in the words of our comrades: Should we devote ourselves to elevation or to popularization?

In the past, some comrades rather, or even very much, despised and neglected popularization and stressed elevation unduly. Elevation should be stressed, but it is wrong to stress it lopsidedly and solely and excessively. ... Since our art and literature are basically intended for the workers, peasants, and soldiers, popularization means extending art and literature among these people, while elevation means raising their level of artistic and literary appreciation...

All revolutionary artists and writers of China, all artists and writers of high promise, must, for long periods of time, unreservedly and wholeheartedly go among the masses, the masses of workers, peasants, and soldiers; they must go into fiery struggles, go to the only, the broadest, the richest source to observe, learn, study, and analyse all men, all classes, all kinds of people, all the vivid patterns of life and struggle and *all the natural forms* of art and literature...

Although the natural state of literature and art is the only source for the conceptual form of literature and art, and although the former is incomparably more vivid and meaningful than the latter, still the people are not satisfied with the former and ask for the latter. What is the reason for this? This happens because, *while both are beautiful, created literature and art is more organized and concentrated, more typical and more idealized. It, therefore, offers more general application.*[1]

1. In the current version, this whole paragraph has been revised so that it now deals with the familiar problem of the relation between art and life. In

The living Lenin was incomparably more vigorous and meaningful than the Lenin of a novel, play or motion picture. But the living Lenin did so much work from morning to night, and his work was not much different from that of other people. Furthermore, only a few people have seen Lenin, and nobody could see him after his death. From this aspect, the Lenin of the novel, play, or motion picture is Lenin reinforced. The revolutionary novel, drama, motion picture, etc., can create all kinds of characters on the basis of actual life and help the masses to push history forward. For example, on the one hand there are people suffering from hunger, cold, and oppression; on the other hand there are men exploiting and oppressing men – a contrast that exists everywhere and seems quite commonplace to people; artists and writers, however, can take such daily occurrences and organize them, bring them to a focal point and make them more typical,[1] and so create art and literature that can awaken and arouse the masses and impel them to unite and struggle to change their environment...

The problem facing the workers, peasants and soldiers today is this: engaged in a ruthless and bloody struggle against the enemy, they remain illiterate, *ignorant*, and uncultured as a result of the prolonged rule of the feudal and bourgeois classes. Consequently, they are eager for a culture, knowledge, art, and literature that meet their immediate need...

But popularization and elevation cannot be sharply separated. ... The people need popularization, but along with it they need elevation too, elevation month by month and year by year...

Experienced writers should be respected; they are valuable to our cause. But we should also remind them that no revolutionary artist or writer can produce any work of significance unless he has

---

the original text given here, Mao contrasted literature and art in their natural form (*tzu-jan hsing-tai shang ti wen-hsüeh i-shu*) and literature and art as they are elaborated by the mind (literally 'conceptual art and literature' [*kuan-nien shang ti wen-hsüeh i-shu*]). Judging by the paragraph immediately following, it would appear that by 'literature and art in their natural form', Mao did not mean popular art. Rather, he saw life itself as a kind of living art. This concept, poetic rather than logical and rigorous, is obviously not incompatible with the image of Mao's personality that I have attempted to present.

1. In the current edition, Mao has inserted a reference to contradictions.

contact with the masses, gives expression to their thoughts and feelings, and becomes their loyal spokesman. Only by speaking for the masses can he educate them, and only by becoming their pupil can he become their teacher. If he regards himself as the master of the masses or as an aristocrat who lords it over the 'low people,' then no matter how great his talent, he will not be needed by the people and his work will have no future...

In this connexion I might mention the change in my own feelings. I began as a student and acquired the habits of a student; surrounded by students who could neither fetch nor carry for themselves, I used to consider it undignified to do any manual labour, such as shouldering my own luggage. At that time it seemed to me that the intellectuals were the only clean persons in the world; next to them, the workers and peasants seemed rather dirty. I would put on the clothes of other intellectuals, because I thought they were clean, but I would not put on clothes belonging to a worker or peasant, because I felt they were dirty. Having become a revolutionary I found myself in the ranks of the workers, peasants, and soldiers of the revolutionary army, and gradually I became familiar with them, and they with me. It was then and only then that a fundamental change occurred in the bourgeois and petty-bourgeois feelings implanted in me by the bourgeois schools. I came to feel that it was those unreconstructed intellectuals who were unclean as compared with the workers and peasants, while the workers and peasants are after all the cleanest persons, cleaner than both the bourgeois and the petty bourgeois, even though their hands are soiled and their feet smeared with cow dung. This is what is meant by having one's feelings transformed, changed from those of one class into those of another. If our artists and writers from the intelligentsia want their works to be welcomed by the masses, they must transform and remould their thoughts and feelings...

There is thus the political as well as the artistic criterion. How are the two related? ... All classes in all class societies place the political criterion first and the artistic criterion second. The bourgeoisie always rejects proletarian artistic and literary works, no matter how great. The proletariat must also reject the reactionary political essence of bourgeois literature and art, although their artistic quality may be acceptable. It is possible that completely reactionary literature and art, for instance *the creative work of fascists*, could have a certain degree of artistry. But the more artistic such a work, the greater the harm it will do to the people, and the more reason for us to reject it. The contradiction between reactionary political content and artistic form is a common characteristic of the art and literature of all exploiting classes in their decline. What we demand is unity of politics and art, of content and form, and of the revolutionary political content and the highest possible degree of perfection in artistic form. Works of art, however politically progressive, are powerless if they lack artistic quality. Therefore, we are equally opposed to works with harmful content and to the tendency toward the so-called poster-and-slogan style, which is concerned only with content and not with form. We must carry on a two-front struggle in art and literature...

VII · E 4 Down with the praise of reactionary feudal culture[1]

The questions raised by *The Life of Wu Hsün* are fundamental in character. Living in the era of the Chinese people's great struggle against foreign aggressors and the domestic reactionary feudal rulers towards the end of the Ching Dynasty, people like Wu Hsün did nothing whatever to disturb the tiniest fragment of the feudal economic base or its superstructure. On the contrary, they worked fanatically to spread feudal culture and, moreover, sedulously fawned upon the reactionary feudal rulers in order to acquire the status they themselves lacked for spreading feudal culture. Ought we to praise such vile conduct? Can we ever

1. Extracted from an anonymous editorial written by Mao for the 20 May 1951 issue of *Jen-min jih-pao*, under the title 'Give Serious Attention to the Discussion of the Film "The Life of Wu Hsün".' Our extract corresponds to that issued in May 1967, as one of the 'five militant documents' on art and literature. The portion omitted, indicated by the dots, consisted of a list of articles on Wu Hsün reflecting wrong viewpoints published in the Chinese press.

Available translations: *Peking Review*, no. 23, 1967, pp. 5–6.

tolerate singing the praises of such vile conduct to the popular masses, especially when such praise flaunts the revolutionary flag of 'serving the people', and the failure of the revolutionary peasant struggle is used to heighten the contrast? To approve or tolerate such praise means to approve or tolerate reactionary propaganda vilifying the revolutionary struggle of the peasants, the history of China and the Chinese nation, and to regard reactionary propaganda as justified.

The appearance of the film *The Life of Wu Hsün*, and particularly the praise lavished on Wu Hsün and the film, show the degree of ideological confusion reached in our country's cultural circles!...

In the view of many writers, history develops not by the replacement of the old by the new, but by the exertion of every effort to preserve the old from extinction; not by class struggle to overthrow the reactionary feudal rulers who had to be overthrown, but by the negation of the class struggle of the oppressed and their submission to the feudal rulers, in the manner of Wu Hsün. Our writers have not studied history to ascertain who were the enemies oppressing the Chinese people, and whether there is anything praiseworthy in those who submitted to these enemies and served them. Moreover, they have not tried to find out what new socio-economic forms, new class forces, new personalities and ideas have appeared in China and struggled against the old socio-economic forms and their superstructure (politics, culture, etc.) in the century and more since the Opium War of 1840, and they have accordingly failed to determine what is to be commended and praised, what is not to be commended and praised, and what is to be opposed.

Certain communists who have reputedly grasped Marxism warrant particular attention. They have learned the history of social development – historical materialism – but when they come across specific historical events, specific historical figures (like Wu Hsün), and specific ideas contrary to history (as in the film *The Life of Wu Hsün* and the writings about Wu Hsün), they lose their critical faculties, and some have even capitulated to these reactionary ideas. Is it not a fact that reactionary bourgeois ideas have found their way into the militant Communist

Party? What has become of the Marxism which certain communists claim to have grasped?

For the above reasons, there should be discussion on the film *The Life of Wu Hsün* and on other books and essays relating to Wu Hsün so as thoroughly to straighten out the confused thinking on this question.

VII · E 5 Party formalism gives the reader a headache[1]

The writer of this article understands the Party's line, and what he says is entirely correct. The article is moreover well-written and easily understandable, without a hint of Party formalism [*tang pa-ku*]. Here I should like to call the reader's attention to the fact that many of our comrades, when they write articles, are extremely fond of Party formalism. [Their writings are] without life or imagery, and give people a headache to read. Nor do they pay any attention to grammar or syntax; they are fond of a kind of semi-literary, semi-colloquial style, sometimes excessively verbose, sometimes excessively laconic in the manner of the classics. It is as though they were absolutely resolved to make the readers suffer. Of the hundred and seventy-odd articles included in this book, quite a few were thoroughly impregnated with Party formalism. It is only after they had been rewritten several times that they became fairly readable. Nevertheless, a minority of the pieces still contain some obscure and difficult passages. It is only because of the importance of their content that we have printed them here. When [literally 'in what year'] will the time at last come in which we shall see a bit less Party formalism that gives people a headache? This problem demands the attention of our comrades on the editorial staff of newspapers and periodicals, who must require of authors that they write lively and comprehensible articles, and also take a hand in helping authors to revise their articles.

1. Extracted from *Socialist Upsurge* . . . (see note to Text VI C 8), p. 1134 of the Chinese edition.

Available translations: *Mao Tse-tung on Literature and Art*, Third edition, Foreign Languages Press, Peking, 1967, pp. 132–3.

VII · E 6 Oppose spontaneous capitalist tendencies[1]

Political work is the life-blood of all economic work. This is particularly true at a time when the economic system of society is undergoing a fundamental transformation. From the very beginning, the movement to form agricultural cooperatives has been a severe ideological and political struggle. No cooperative can be established without going through such a struggle. Before a brand-new social system can be built on the site of the old, the site must first be swept clean. Remnants of old ideas reflecting the old system invariably remain in people's minds for a long time. They do not easily give way. After a cooperative is formed it must go through many more struggles before it becomes firmly established. Even then, the moment it relaxes its efforts it may collapse. ... Opposition to selfish, capitalistic spontaneous tendencies, and promotion of a socialist spirit which makes the principle of linking the collective interests with the interests of the individual the standard by which all words and deeds are judged – these are the ideological and political guarantees that the scattered, small-peasant economy will gradually be transformed into a large-scale cooperative economy. This is an arduous task. It must be based on the life and experience of the peasants and be conducted in a very practical manner, with careful attention to detail. Neither bluster nor over-simplification will do. It should be conducted not in isolation from our economic measures, but in conjunction with them.

VII · E 7 To overthrow a political power one must create public opinion[2]

1. Extracted from *Socialist Upsurge* ... (see note to Text VI C 8), pp. 123–4 of the Chinese edition.

Available translations: pp. 302–3 of the English edition.

2. Full text of a brief quotation attributed to Mao in the article 'Great truth, sharp weapon' published in *Hung-ch'i*, no. 9, 1967, p. 21. Mao is reported to have made these remarks in expounding his theories on never forgetting the class struggle at the Tenth Plenum of the Eighth Central Committee of the Chinese Communist Party in September 1962.

Available translations: *Peking Review*, no. 23, 1967, p. 17.

The use of the novel for anti-Party activities is a great invention. To overthrow a political power, it is always necessary, first of all, to create public opinion, to do work in the ideological sphere. This is true for the revolutionary class, and it is also true for the counter-revolutionary class.

VII · E 8 We must prevent China from changing colour[1]

Class struggle, the struggle for production, and scientific experiment are the three great revolutionary movements for building a mighty socialist country. These movements are a sure guarantee that communists will be free from bureaucracy and immune against revisionism and dogmatism, and will for ever remain invincible. They are a reliable guarantee that the proletariat will be able to unite with the broad working masses and realize a democratic dictatorship. If, in the absence of these movements, the landlords, rich peasants, counter-revolutionaries, bad elements and monsters of all kinds were allowed to crawl out, while our cadres were to shut their eyes to all this and in many cases fail even to differentiate between the enemy and ourselves but were to collaborate with the enemy and were corrupted, divided and demoralized by him, if our cadres were thus pulled out or the enemy were able to sneak in, and if many of our workers, peasants and intellectuals were left defenceless against both the soft and the hard tactics of the enemy, then it would not take long, perhaps only several years or a decade, or several decades at most, before a counter-revolutionary restoration on a national scale inevitably occurred, the Marxist-Leninist party would undoubtedly become a revisionist party or fascist party, and the whole of China would change its colour.

1. Complete text of a passage attributed to Mao in the Ninth Chinese Reply to the Soviet open letter of 14 July 1963, published on 14 July 1964, and there identified as a note on documents from Chekiang province regarding the participation of cadres in physical labour, dated 9 May 1963. (*Hung-ch'i*, no. 13, 1964, pp. 31–2.) This extract has now been included in Chapter III of *Quotations from Chairman Mao*.

Available translations: *Peking Review*, no. 29, 1964, p. 26. A longer passage from the Ninth Reply is included in *Marxism and Asia*.

VII · E 9 The dead still rule today[1]

There are quite a few problems in all forms of art such as the drama, ballads, music, the fine arts, the dance, the cinema, poetry and literature; the people engaged in them are numerous; and in many departments very little has been achieved so far in socialist transformation. The 'dead' still rule today in many departments. What has been achieved in the cinema, new poetry, folk songs, the fine arts and the novel should not be underestimated, but there, too, there are quite a few problems. As for such departments as the drama, the problems are even greater. The social and economic base has already changed, but the arts as part of the superstructure, which serve this base, still remain a great problem today. Hence we should proceed with investigation and study and attend to this matter in earnest.

Isn't it absurd that many communists are enthusiastic about promoting feudal and capitalist art, but not socialist art?

VII · E 10 Directives regarding the Cultural Revolution[2]

Overthrow the king of hell and set the little devils free. ('Battle cry' put forward in Shanghai, March 1966).

1. Full text of an instruction dated 12 December 1963, published in May 1967, as the fourth of the 'five militant documents'. (*Hung-ch'i*, no. 9, 1967 pp. 8–9). I have not found a contemporary text of this document.
Available translations: *Peking Review*, no. 23, 1967, p. 8.

2. These are the complete texts of a series of quotations attributed to Mao Tse-tung, published in the Chinese press between August 1966 and August 1968. The sources are, in the order in which the texts appear: Kang Sheng's speech of 11 October 1967, *Jen-min jih-pao*, 12 October 1967; *Hung-ch'i*, no. 11, 1966, p. 9; *Jen-min jih-pao*, 19 August 1966; ibid., 12 November 1966; ibid., 26 January 1967; ibid., 12 March 1967; ibid., 13 August 1967; ibid., 14 March 1967; ibid., 13 August 1967; ibid., 2 October 1967; *Hung-ch'i*, no. 15, 1967, p. 3; *Jen-min jih-pao*, 9 October 1967; ibid., 21 October 1967; *Hung-ch'i*, no. 16, 1967, p. 1; *Jen-min jih-pao*, 9 July 1968; ibid., 22 July 1968; ibid., 22 August 1968; ibid., 26 August 1968.
Available translations: All these directives are to be found in *Peking*

You should pay attention to state affairs and carry the Great Proletarian Cultural Revolution through to the end! (Statement to the crowd on 'meeting the masses' in Peking on 10 August 1966.)

This is a movement on a vast scale. It has indeed mobilized the masses. It is of very great significance to the revolutionization of the thinking of the people throughout the country. (Statement at first Red Guard rally, 18 August 1966.)

You should put politics in command, go to the masses and be one with them, and carry on the Great Proletarian Cultural Revolution even better. (Statement to 'some leading comrades' at seventh Red Guard rally, 10 November 1966.)

The People's Liberation Army should actively support the broad masses of the Left. (Published January 1967.)

Take hold of revolution and promote production. (Published in March 1967.)

In those places and organizations where power needs to be seized, the policy of the revolutionary 'three-in-one' combination must be carried out in establishing a provisional organ of power that is revolutionary and representative and has proletarian authority. This organ of power should preferably be called a revolutionary committee. (Published in March 1967; reprinted in quotation marks in August.)

There subsist various non-proletarian ideas in the Party. This is an extremely great obstacle to the application of the Party's correct line. (Published in March 1967.)

Review (I have modified some of the translations after comparison with the Chinese text). See *Peking Review*, no. 44, 1967, p. 26; no. 34, 1966, p. 9; no. 35, 1966, p. 3; no. 47, 1966, p. 5; no. 5, 1967, p. 10; no. 11, 1967, p. 10; no. 34, 1967, p. 24; no. 12, 1967, p. 18; no. 34, 1967, p. 26; no. 41, 1967, p. 10; no. 41, 1967, pp. 17–18; no. 43, 1967, p. 26; no. 44, 1967, p. 10; no. 47, 1967, p. 2; no. 45, 1968, p. 2; no. 37, 1968, n. 16; no. 35, 1968, p. 3; no. 35, 1968, p. 4.

The present Great Proletarian Cultural Revolution is only the first; there will inevitably be many more in the future. The issue of who will win in the revolution can only be settled over a long historical period. If things are not properly handled, it is possible for a capitalist restoration to take place at any time in the future. (Published in August 1967.)

We must combat selfishness and criticize and repudiate revisionism. (Quoted by Lin Piao in his speech of 1 October 1967, as a 'recent directive'.)

The revolutionary Red Guards and revolutionary student organizations should realize the revolutionary great alliance. So long as both sides are revolutionary mass organizations, they should realize the revolutionary great alliance in accordance with revolutionary principles. (Published on 1 October 1967.)

We must be good at guiding those people in our ranks with petty bourgeois ideas on to the path of the proletarian revolution. This is crucial to the success of the Great Proletarian Cultural Revolution. (Published in October 1967.)

Correct treatment of cadres is the key to creating the revolutionary 'three-in-one' combination, consolidating the revolutionary great alliance, and making a success of struggle-criticism-transformation in each unit. It must definitely be handled well. (Published in October 1967; attributed to Mao during his inspection trip, in September 1967.)

The situation in the Great Proletarian Cultural Revolution throughout the country is not just good but excellent. The entire situation is better than ever before. The important feature of this excellent situation is the full mobilization of the masses. Never before in any mass movement have the masses been mobilized so broadly and deeply as in this one. (Published in November 1967.)

The Great Proletarian Cultural Revolution is in essence a great political revolution under the conditions of socialism made by the proletariat against the bourgeoisie and all other exploiting classes; it is a continuation of the prolonged struggle waged by the Chinese Communist Party and the broad masses of revolutionary people under its leadership against the Kuomintang reactionaries, a continuation of the class struggle between the proletariat and the bourgeoisie. (Published in July 1968.)

It is still necessary to have universities; here I refer mainly to the need for colleges of science and engineering. However, it is essential to shorten the length of schooling, revolutionize education, put proletarian politics in command and take the road of the Shanghai Machine Tools Plant in training technicians from among the workers.[1] Students should be selected from among workers and peasants with practical experience, and they should return to practical work in production after a few years' study. (Published in July 1968.)

Our country has 700 million people, and the working class is the leading class. It is essential to bring into full play the leading role of the working class in the Great Cultural Revolution and in all fields of work. For its part, the working class should constantly raise its political consciousness in the course of struggle. (Published in August 1968).

In carrying out the Proletarian Revolution in education, it is essential to have working-class leadership; it is essential for the masses of workers to take part and, in cooperation with Liberation Army fighters, bring about a revolutionary 'three-in-one' combination, together with the activists among the students, teachers and workers in the schools who are determined to carry the Proletarian Revolution in education through to the end. The workers' propaganda teams should stay permanently in the schools and take part in fulfilling all the tasks of struggle-criticism-transformation in the schools; they should moreover lead the schools forever. In the countryside the schools should be managed by the poor and lower middle peasants – the most reliable ally of the working class. (Published in August 1968.)

1. Regarding this example of 'revolutionizing' education, see the article in *Peking Review*, no. 37, 1968, pp. 13-17.

VIII. China and the Non-European Countries

This chapter has a double theme: (1) Mao Tse-tung's ideas regarding the way in which revolution should be carried out in the countries of Asia, Africa, and Latin America; and (2) China's role in supporting the revolution in these areas, and more generally China's place in the world. Several of the ideas already formulated in previous chapters reappear here, such as the importance of armed struggle and the necessity of choosing between revolution and counter-revolution both within the country and on a world scale. Mao repeats in Text VIII B, written in 1939, what he had said in the previous several years in the military writings included in Chapter V, namely that guerrilla warfare is the key to the victory of the revolution in a backward country. And he reaffirms in Text VIII D what he had proclaimed in 1926 (Text III C): revolutionaries in Asia and Africa must choose between imperialism and reaction, for there is no third way. This intransigence underlies his condemnation of Nehru, in 1949, as a 'collaborator of imperialism' (Text VIII F).

In the domain dealt with in this chapter, one can once more clearly see the mixture of Marxism-Leninism and Chinese nationalism that characterizes Mao's thought. On the one hand, the enumeration of China's territorial losses in Text VIII C, taken from *The Chinese Revolution and the Chinese Communist Party*, displays the nostalgia for the grandeur of the past that inspired Mao Tse-tung when, as an adolescent, he was profoundly depressed by reading a pamphlet that spoke of the loss of Korea, Indochina and Burma.[1] And Text VIII D offers a curious illustration of the way in which Mao combines Marxist content with

1. Mao's feeling that Mongolia is in fact part of China likewise reflects these traditional attitudes. See below Text X A, and also *Mao Tse-tung*, p. 236 and footnote.

Chinese form. The term *hao han* ('hero' or 'brave fellow'), with its unmistakable evocation of the outlaw heroes of *All Men Are Brothers*, appeared entirely in its place in Text IV G; here, in the midst of a rather doctrinaire Leninist argument, it is nothing less than startling. But at the same time, it is clear that Mao does not reason primarily in traditional terms, but in terms of revolution and class struggle.

The problem is, of course, *what* revolution? In Text VIII D, written in 1940, Mao faithfully reproduced the Soviet position regarding leadership in the world revolution and the place of Europe and Asia in global revolutionary strategy. The oppressed peoples, he declared, were the 'allies' of the revolution; the proletariat of the capitalist countries was its 'main force'. But in 1949 he affirmed that if India followed China on the path toward socialism, this would in itself suffice to overthrow the world-wide domination of imperialism. (See Text VIII F.) And he soon went on to give the non-European countries priority in the overall strategy of revolution. In his declarations of 1960, extracted in Text VIII G, he proclaimed: 'What imperialism fears most is the awakening of the Asian, African and Latin American peoples. ...' Lenin and Stalin had already established that in striking blows against the 'safe rear' of imperialism in the colonies, one could facilitate the European revolution. Now Mao and his friends came to the conclusion that 'the rear has become the front'.[1]

The antecedents of this Asiocentric and Sinocentric vision are visible as early as 1936 in Text VIII A. Since the first edition of this book was prepared, this tendency has reached extremes that could hardly have been predicted five years ago. First Asia, Africa and Latin America were defined as the storm-centres of world revolution in our era; then China herself was openly proclaimed to be the leader and guide of the revolution. Simultaneously, the Soviet Union was first criticized for its half-hearted support of national liberation movements throughout the world, and then stigmatized as an enemy which should not even be allowed to participate in a united front. In the first text added to

1. Yu Ch'ao-li, 'Excellent situation in the struggle for peace', *Hung-ch'i* no. 1, 1960; English translation in *Peking Review*, no. 1, 1960, p. 15.

this chapter (Text VIII H, dating from 1963), Mao Tse-tung energetically denied that his criterion of revolutionary virtue was a racial criterion. And in Texts VIII I and VIII J, dating respectively from 1964 and 1967, he calls upon the 'people of the world' to unite and defeat U.S. imperialism. But it is clear to everyone that Mao's appeal is not merely to a union based upon revolutionary principles, but to the visceral solidarity of peoples long oppressed and humiliated by the white powers of Europe and America.

S.R.S.

VIII · A China is the key[1]

... Question: With the achievement of victory of a Red movement in China, do you think that revolution would occur quickly in other Asiatic colonial or semi-colonial countries, such as Korea, Indochina, the Philippines, and India? Is China at present the 'key' to the world revolution?

Answer: The Chinese revolution is a key factor in the world situation, and its victory is heartily anticipated by the people of every country, especially by the toiling masses of the colonial countries. When the Chinese revolution comes into full power, the masses of many colonial countries will follow the example of China and win a similar victory of their own ...

VIII · B Guerrilla warfare is the inevitable path[2]

... What is guerilla warfare? It is, in a backward country, in a big semi-colonial country, and for a long period of time, the

1. An extract from Edgar Snow's interview with Mao Tse-tung, 23 July 1936. My source was Mr Snow's typewritten manuscript in the 'Nym Wales Papers', at the Hoover Institution on War, Revolution, and Peace, Stanford, California. (The English text, from which the Chinese translations published later were made, is here taken as the original.) This text was published in the *Shanghai Evening Post and Mercury* of 3, 4 and 5 February 1937, a source which is not available at the time of writing.

2. Extracted from an editorial for the first issue of *The Communist*, an intra-Party journal, October 1939, *Hsüan-chi*, 1947, Supplement, pp. 47–8.

Available translations: *Selected Works*, II, pp. 291–2.

inevitable and therefore the best form of struggle for the people's armed forces to overcome the armed enemy and create their own strongholds. For eighteen years the political line and the building of our Party have been closely linked with this form of struggle. Apart from armed struggle, apart from guerrilla warfare, it is impossible to understand our political line and, consequently, to understand our Party-building. . . . We know that in China there would be no place for the proletariat, no place for the people, no place for the Communist Party, and no victory for the revolution without armed struggle. For eighteen years the development, consolidation, and Bolshevization of our Party have been undertaken in the midst of revolutionary wars *and have been inseparable from guerrilla warfare*. Without armed struggle, *without guerrilla warfare*, there would not have been such a Communist Party as exists today. Comrades throughout the Party must never forget this experience gained at the cost of blood.

VIII · C China's boundaries[1]

. . . After having inflicted military defeats on China, the imperialist countries forcibly took from her a large number of states tributary to China,[2] as well as a part of her own territory. Japan appropriated *Korea*, Taiwan, the *Ryukyu Islands*, the Pescadores, and Port Arthur; England took *Burma*, *Bhutan*, *Nepal*, and Hongkong; France *seized Annam*; *even a miserable little country like Portugal took Macao from us*. At the same time that they took away part of her territory, the imperialists obliged China to pay enormous indemnities. Thus heavy blows were struck against the vast feudal empire of China . . .

1. Extracted from 'The Chinese revolution and the Chinese Communist Party'. (See note to Text I B.)

2. In the current edition, Mao speaks more discreetly of states 'situated around China's border that were formerly under her dependence', avoiding the term 'tributary state'. In listing the territories taken by the imperialists, he now omits all the former dependent countries, which in 1939 he interspersed with portions of China's own territory. Lastly, the contemptuous reference to Portugal has been eliminated, and France is accused only of 'leasing' Kuangchou.

VIII · D There is no third way[1]

A change occurred in the Chinese bourgeois-democratic revolution after the outbreak of the first imperialist world war in 1914, and after the founding of a socialist state on one sixth of the globe through the Russian October Revolution in 1917.

Before these events, the Chinese bourgeois-democratic revolution belonged to the category of the old bourgeois-democratic world revolution and was part of that revolution. After these events, the Chinese bourgeois-democratic revolution changed its character and now belongs to the category of the new bourgeois-democratic revolution, and, so far as the revolutionary front is concerned, forms part of the proletarian-socialist world revolution . . .

In an era when the world capitalist front has collapsed in one corner of the globe (a corner that forms one-sixth of the world) and has fully revealed its decadence in other parts; when the remaining parts of capitalism cannot survive without relying more than ever on the colonies and semi-colonies; when a socialist state has been established and has declared that it is willing to fight in support of the liberation movement of all colonies and semi-colonies; when the proletariat of the capitalist countries is freeing itself day by day from the social-imperialist influence of the Social-Democratic Parties and has also declared itself in support of the liberation movement of the colonies and semi-colonies – in such an era, any anti-imperialist revolution in a colony or semi-colony, i.e., a revolution against the international bourgeoisie and international capitalism, no longer belongs to the old category of bourgeois-democratic world revolution, but to a new category, and is no longer part of the old bourgeois or capitalist world revolution, but part of the new world revolution, the proletarian-socialist world revolution. . . .

1. Extracted from 'On new democracy', published in *Chieh-fang*, nos. 98–9, 20 February 1940, pp. 24–30 *passim*. (For a longer extract of this passage, see *Marxism and Asia*, Text VIII 3.)

Available translations: *Selected Works*, II, pp. 343–56 *passim*.

This correct thesis propounded by the Chinese communists is based on Stalin's theory . . .

There are two kinds of world revolution. The first belongs to the bourgeois and capitalist categories. The era of this kind of world revolution is long past; it came to an end in 1914, when the first imperialist world war broke out, and especially in 1917, when the October Revolution occurred in Russia. Since then, the second kind, namely, the proletarian-socialist world revolution, has started. Such a revolution has the proletariat of the capitalist countries as its main force and the oppressed peoples of the colonies and semi-colonies as its allies. No matter what classes, parties or individuals in the oppressed nations join the revolution, and no matter whether they are conscious of the point mentioned above or whether they understand it subjectively, so long as they oppose imperialism, their revolution becomes part of the proletarian-socialist world revolution and they themselves become its allies . . .

Revolutions in different colonial and semi-colonial countries necessarily have certain different characteristics, but these constitute only the minor differences within the general framework of uniformity. So long as they are revolutions in colonies or semi-colonies, the state and political power will of necessity be basically the same in structure, i.e. a new-democratic state under the joint dictatorship of several anti-imperialist classes. In China today, this new-democratic form of state assumes the very form of the anti-Japanese united front . . .

. . . In the international situation of the 1940s and the 1950s, the heroes and brave fellows [*hao han*] in the colonies and semi-colonies must either support the imperialist front and become part of the force of world counter-revolution or support the anti-imperialist front and become part of the force of world revolution. They must support either one or the other, for there is no third way . . .

VIII · E China supports the Algerian people's struggle for liberation[1]

To Comrade Larbi Buhali and to all the comrades of the Central Committee of the Algerian Communist Party:

Permit me to express my profound gratitude for the message of congratulations of Comrade Larbi Buhali.

The Chinese people has obtained its liberation after a long period of aggression and oppression at the hands of imperialism. Consequently, it feels warm sympathy and resolute faith toward the struggles of all oppressed peoples for liberation. I am persuaded that the Algerian people, under the direction of the Algerian Communist Party and with the aid of the international camp of peace and democracy, will succeed in overthrowing the domination of imperialism.

Long live the victory of the struggle of the Algerian people for liberation!

Chairman of the Central Committee of the Chinese Communist Party

MAO TSE-TUNG
26 October 1949

VIII · F India's path is similar to that of China[2]

Dear Comrade Ranadive:

I have received your telegram of congratulations of 12 October,

1. The complete text of a telegram published in *Jen-min jih-pao*, 27 October 1949.

Available translations: none.

2. The complete text of a telegram sent to the Secretary-General of the Indian Communist Party, B. T. Ranadive; published in *Jen-min jih-pao*, 20 November 1949.

Available translations: *Communist*, Bombay, III, no. 1, January 1950, p. 110. (The above periodical not being available at the time of writing, I have taken the central portion of Mao's telegram from John H. Kautsky, *Moscow and the Communist Party of India*, published jointly by The Tech-

and I thank you very much for your warm good wishes addressed to the Chinese People's Republic and to the Chinese Communist Party. Your telegram expressing the fraternal friendship of the revolutionary Indian people filled the whole Chinese people with joy and pride. The Indian people is one of the great Asian people, with a long history and a vast population; in many respects, her past fate and her path to the future resemble those of China. I firmly believe that India, relying on the brave Communist Party of India and the unity and struggle of all Indian patriots, will certainly not remain long under the yoke of imperialism and its collaborators. Like free China, a free India will one day emerge in the socialist and people's democratic family; that day will end the imperialist reactionary era in the history of mankind. I wish you victory in the unity and struggle of the Indian people! Long live the fraternal unity between the Indian people and the Chinese people!

Chairman of the Central Committee of the Chinese Communist Party

MAO TSE-TUNG
19 November 1949

VIII · G The peoples of Asia, Africa, and Latin America should unite and drive American imperialism back to where it came from[1]

On 7 May, in Chengchow, Comrade Mao Tse-tung received public personages, workers for peace, trade union, youth, and student delegations, and delegates from twelve African countries and regions who were then visiting China . . .

---

nology Press of M.I.T., Cambridge, Mass., and John Wiley, New York, 1956, p. 80, supplying my own translation of the beginning and the end of the message, which are not cited by Mr Kautsky.)

1. Extracted from accounts published in the Chinese press in 1960. All the reports except that of 14 May can be found in *Hung-ch'i*, no. 10, 1960. The conversation of 14 May is reported in *Jen-min shou-ts'e*, 1960.

Available translations: *Chairman Mao Tse-tung's Important Talks with Guests from Asia, Africa, and Latin America*, Foreign Languages Press, Peking, 1960, pp. 2–8.

Comrade Mao Tse-tung, on behalf of the 650 million Chinese people, expressed full sympathy and support for the heroic struggle of the African people against imperialism and colonialism. He also expressed sympathy and support for the patriotic and just struggles of the South Korean people and the Turkish people against U.S. imperialism and its running dogs. He held that these struggles of the South Korean people and the Turkish people indicated that the storm of the struggles waged by the oppressed peoples of the various countries in Asia against imperialism and its running dogs will witness an even greater upsurge. These struggles will constitute a support to the just struggles of the African people, the Latin American people, and people the world over. The just struggles of the peoples of various countries in the world support each other, Comrade Mao Tse-tung said. He thanked the African friends for their profound friendship for the Chinese people, hailed the great unity of the Chinese and African peoples, and expressed firm confidence that ultimate victory will certainly be won in the common struggle against imperialism and colonialism.

On 8 May, in Chengchow, Comrade Mao Tse-tung received friends from eight Latin American countries then visiting China . . .

Comrade Mao Tse-tung thanked them for their friendship for the Chinese people. The Chinese people, he said, just like the Latin American people, had long suffered from imperialist oppression and exploitation. Relying on their own unity and support from the peoples of various countries, the Chinese people had carried on hard and prolonged struggles and ultimately had overthrown the rule of imperialism, feudalism, and bureaucrat-capitalism in China. They are now building their own country and changing its appearance of 'poverty and blankness'. The Chinese people are fully confident that they can build their country and therefore they need time, peace, and friends. The Cuban people, the people of Latin America, and the people of the whole world, he said, are all friends of the Chinese people; and imperialism and its running dogs are our common enemy, but they are a tiny minority. The winning of world peace, he said, depends primarily on the struggles of the peoples of the various countries. Comrade Mao Tse-tung expressed admiration for the heroic struggle of the Cuban people against U.S. imperialism. The struggles of the peoples of Cuba and other Latin American countries have helped the Chinese people, he said, and the struggle of the Chinese people has also helped the peoples of Cuba and other Latin American countries. The people are the decisive factor. Reliance on the unity and struggle of the people is bound to bring about the defeat of imperialism and its running dogs and achieve lasting world peace.

On 9 May, Chairman Mao Tse-tung received in Chengchow friends from the Iraqi Cultural Delegation, the Iraqi Workers Delegation, the Iranian Trade Union Delegation, and the Delegation of the Cyprus Confederation of Workers . . .

Comrade Mao Tse-tung said that U.S. imperialism is the biggest imperialism in the world today. It has its running dogs in many countries. Those backed by imperialism are precisely those discarded by the broad masses of the people. Chiang Kai-shek, Syngman Rhee, Kishi, Batista, Said, Menderes, and their ilk have either been overthrown or will be overthrown by the people. The risings of the people in these countries against the running dogs of U.S. and other imperialism are also fights against the reactionary rule of imperialism itself. The Japanese people are rising in action, Comrade Mao Tse-tung said. The broad masses of the Japanese people are now holding demonstrations on a bigger scale than ever to fight against the aggressive military-alliance treaty signed between the Kishi Government and U.S. imperialism. The Chinese people resolutely support this struggle waged by the Japanese people. The just struggles of the peoples of the various countries in the world, he said, have received and will continue to receive firm support from the 650 million people of China. The days of imperialism are numbered, he said. The imperialists have committed all manner of evils and all the oppressed peoples of the whole world will never forgive them. To defeat the reactionary rule of imperialism, Comrade Mao Tse-tung said, it is necessary to form a broad front and unite with all forces, except the enemy, and continue to wage arduous struggles . . .

On 14 May, in Wuhan, Comrade Mao Tse-tung received friends from Japan, Cuba, Brazil and Argentina . . .

Comrade Mao Tse-tung spoke of the ever-growing national and democratic movements in Asia, Africa and Latin America. He said that what imperialism fears most is the awakening of the Asian, African, and Latin American peoples, the awakening of the peoples of all countries. We should unite and drive U.S. imperialism from Asia, Africa, and Latin America back to where it came from ...

VIII · H The racial question is a class question[1]

Chairman Mao Tse-tung received visitors from Africa here this afternoon [8 August 1963]. During the reception, Chairman Mao Tse-tung made a statement calling upon the people of the world to unite against racial discrimination by U.S. imperialism and support the American Negroes in their just struggle against racial discrimination ...[2]

Chairman Mao Tse-tung had a very cordial, friendly talk with the friends from Africa. During the talk, he condemned the racial discrimination practised by U.S. imperialism, as well as that of the colonialist authorities of South Africa and in every part of the world. 'Racial discrimination', he said, 'is found in Africa, in Asia, and in other parts of the world. The racial question is in essence a class question. Our unity is not one of race; it is the unity of comrades and friends. We should strengthen our unity and wage a common struggle against imperialism, colonialism, and their running dogs, to attain complete and thorough national independence and liberation.'

After explaining how China's revolutionary struggle had won through to victory, Chairman Mao said: 'This proves that a revolution by the people can triumph and that imperialism and its running dogs can be defeated. The tide of anti-imperialism and anti-colonialism is sweeping through all Africa. All countries, whether or not they have already attained independence, will

1. This is the full text of Mao's remarks to his African visitors on this occasion, as reported in *Jen-min jih-pao* on 9 August 1963.
Available translations: *Peking Review*, no. 33, 1963, pp. 3–4.
2. For this statement, see below Text IX L.

sooner or later win complete and thorough independence and liberation. All the Chinese people support you. The people of Africa are awakening with each passing day; so are the people of the whole world. The workers, peasants, revolutionary intellectuals and all other revolutionary people, who constitute over ninety per cent of the world's population, can be united in the fight for the victory of the revolution.'

'In the fight for thorough emancipation,' Chairman Mao said, 'the oppressed peoples rely first of all on their own strength and then, and only then, on international assistance. The people who have already won victory in their revolution should help those who are still struggling for liberation. This is our internationalist duty.'

VIII · I American imperialism is closely surrounded by the peoples of the world[1]

The U.S. imperialist armed aggression against the Congo (Leopoldville) is a very grave matter.

The United States has all along attempted to control the Congo. It used the United Nations forces to carry out every sort of evil deed there. It murdered the Congolese national hero Lumumba, it subverted the lawful Congolese government. It imposed the puppet Tshombe on the Congolese people, and dispatched mercenary troops to suppress the Congolese national liberation movement. And now, it is carrying out direct armed intervention in the Congo in collusion with Belgium and Britain. In so doing, the purpose of U.S. imperialism is not only to control the Congo, but also to enmesh the whole of Africa, particularly the newly independent African countries, in the toils of U.S. neo-colonialism once again. U.S. aggression has encountered heroic resistance from the Congolese people and aroused the indignation of the people of Africa and of the whole world.

1. Full text of Mao's declaration of 28 November 1964 in support of the people of the Congo (Leopoldville).

Available translations: *Peking Review*, no. 49, 1964, p. 5. For the last paragraph, I have inserted the now classic and repeatedly cited version from Chapter VII of *Quotations from Chairman Mao*.

U.S. imperialism is the common enemy of the people of the whole world. It is engaged in aggression against South Vietnam, it is intervening in Laos, menacing Cambodia and blustering about extending the war in Indochina. It is trying everything to strangle the Cuban revolution. It wants to turn West Germany and Japan into two important nuclear bases of the United States. It ganged up with England in creating so-called Malaysia to menace Indonesia and other south-east Asian countries. It is occupying South Korea and China's Taiwan province. It is dominating all Latin America. It rides roughshod everywhere. U.S. imperialism has over-extended its reach. It adds a new noose around its neck every time it commits aggression anywhere. It is closely surrounded by the people of the whole world.

In their just struggle, the Congolese people are not alone. All the Chinese people support you. All the people throughout the world who oppose imperialism support you. U.S. imperialism and the reactionaries of all countries are paper tigers. The struggle of the Chinese people proved this. The struggle of the Vietnamese people is now proving it. The struggle of the Congolese people will certainly prove it too. Strengthening national unity and persevering in protracted struggle, the Congolese people will certainly be victorious, and U.S. imperialism will certainly be defeated.

People of the world, unite and defeat the U.S. aggressors and all their running dogs! People of the world, be courageous, dare to fight, defy difficulties and advance wave upon wave. Then the whole world will belong to the people. Monsters of all kinds shall be destroyed.

VIII · J The days of the U.S. aggressors in Vietnam are numbered[1]

On behalf of the Chinese people, I extend the warmest congratulations to the fighting people of southern Vietnam on the

1. Full text of Mao's message of 19 December 1967 to President Nguyen Huu Tho of the National Liberation Front (*Jen-min jih-pao*, 19 December). Available translations: *Peking Review*, no. 52, 1967, p. 5.

occasion of the seventh anniversary of the founding of the South Vietnam National Liberation Front.

You are putting up a good fight! Under exceptionally difficult conditions, you have, by relying on your own strength, battered U.S. imperialism, the most ferocious imperialism in the world, so that its forces are in disorder and it has no way out. This is a great victory. The Chinese people salute you.

Your victory manifests once again that a nation, big or small, can defeat any enemy, however powerful, provided only that it fully mobilizes its people, relies firmly on the people, and wages a people's war. By their war against U.S. aggression and for national salvation under the wise and able leadership of the great leader President Ho Chi Minh, the Vietnamese people have set a brilliant example for the oppressed peoples and oppressed nations the world over in their struggle for liberation.

The days of the U.S. aggressors in Vietnam are numbered. However, all reactionary forces on the verge of extinction invariably conduct desperate struggles. They are bound to resort to military adventure and political deception in all their forms in order to save themselves from extinction. And the revolutionary peoples are bound to meet with all kinds of difficulties before final victory. Nevertheless, all these difficulties can be surmounted, and no difficulty can ever obstruct the advance of the revolutionary people. Perseverance means victory. I am deeply convinced that, by persevering in protracted war, the Vietnamese people will certainly be able to drive the U.S. aggressors out of Vietnam.

We firmly support you. We are neighbouring countries as close as the lips and the teeth. Our two peoples are brothers sharing weal and woe. The fraternal people of southern Vietnam and the entire fraternal Vietnamese people can rest assured that your struggle is our struggle. The 700 million Chinese people are the powerful rearguard of the Vietnamese people; the vast expanse of China's territory is their reliable rear area. In the face of the solid fighting unity of our two peoples, all military adventures and political deceptions by U.S. imperialism will certainly fail.

Victory will definitely belong to the heroic Vietnamese people!

IX · Relations with the West

This chapter is concerned with relations with the capitalist countries of the West. Here the ideological hostility of the Leninist who sees in imperialism the cause of all the evils from which the world suffers and the xenophobia so common among Hunanese meet and reinforce one another.

The first two texts offer a few samples of this hostility, at once ideological and instinctive, directed against a variety of objects. The succeeding texts are of a more analytical character. In arranging these extracts, no attempt has been made to separate the analysis of concrete situations from more general reflections on the inevitability of war and the role of war in the progress of humanity. Mao Tse-tung, perhaps more than other Marxist authors, always remains very close to concrete reality. Thus Text IX C, dating from 1938, gives Mao's ideas regarding peaceful and warlike epochs in the history of humanity and his analysis of the conflict between the democracies and the fascist countries on the eve of Munich. In January 1939, he had lost hope in England and France, but still expected something from President Roosevelt. In September 1939, on the other hand, following the Nazi-Soviet Pact, he set forth the Soviet position according to which all the imperialist countries were equally guilty, England even a bit more so than Germany, in particularly violent terms. The same point of view is expressed in certain texts included in the current edition of the *Selected Works*, but Text IX E, which appears here in translation for the first time, is both more precise and more vehement. During the war, there was a time when Mao manifested respect and even gratitude toward the United States. But this friendly attitude, if not altogether meaningless and without foundation, was based on a certain number of ambiguities on both the Chinese and American side. In the spring of 1945, following the death of President Roosevelt, these ambiguities were beginning to be resolved in Washington in a manner that provoked a very violent reaction on Mao's part.

As will be seen from the variants in the first third of Text IX F, Mao at the time expressed himself in a more tactful manner than one would think in reading the rewritten version of the editorial in the *Selected Works*. Thus in particular he affirms that not only a *large* part of public opinion (today he speaks only of a part), but also quite a few politicians and military men were opposed to the policy of supporting Chiang Kai-shek, for which he attributes the initiative to Hurley and the 'imperialist elements' in Washington. But more curious than these variants is the second editorial, published one week later, which provides the remaining portion of Text IX F. In view of the importance of this document it seems appropriate to explain first of all why I attribute it to Mao Tse-tung, although he did not sign it. It is well known that Mao often wrote unsigned editorials and leading articles for the Yenan press. A considerable number of these were attributed to Mao by the editors of the *Selected Works* and may therefore be considered as unquestionably by Mao. Among these texts is the editorial of 12 July 1945, which constitutes the first third of Text IX F, and which, at the time of its publication, was attributed to 'a reporter from the Hsinhua Agency'. Now the editorial of 19 July begins as follows: 'The reporter from the Hsinhua Agency continued his criticism of Hurley's policy. . . .' Strictly speaking, one could also translate: 'A reporter from the Hsinhua agency [that is to say, another reporter] continued *the* criticism of Hurley's policy.' But the presentation of the article as a whole gives the impression that we are dealing with the same reporter; and since the reporter of 12 July turns out to have been Mao, I conclude that the reporter of 19 July was also Mao. This conclusion is supported by certain textual similarities.

Let us therefore assume that this text was written by Mao. If it was, it is extremely significant in two respects. On the one hand, the author proclaims three times in the space of a single paragraph that the Chinese people wants to follow Mao Tse-tung's way. Here we see Mao contributing to the cult of his own personality. On the other hand, he employs the term 'people's dictatorship', so far as I know for the first time. Hitherto, Leninists had spoken only of the dictatorship of one or several *classes.* To be sure, in this editorial of 1945 the reference is still to the 'joint democratic dictatorship of all the anti-imperialist and anti-feudal classes', but a few lines further on, in describing this dictatorship as the 'people's dictatorship of all the revolutionary classes', Mao appears to be groping toward the definitive term he was to employ in 1949, 'people's democratic dictatorship'. As already suggested, this term appears to express his profound conviction that in the black-and-white world of his imagination virtually the whole of the Chinese nation is on the side of the angels.

The last seven texts of this chapter are all variations on the same theme: the imperialists 'will never lay down their butcher knives', but at the same time they are only 'paper tigers'. It seems to me that there is here an echo of the conception of the hero that Mao Tse-tung has drawn from the Chinese tradition. When we read that the Manifesto of the Cominform 'has thrown world reaction into panic and confusion', we seem to see a character from the *Romance of the Three Kingdoms* or from *All Men Are Brothers* trembling with fright as he hears the terrible name of some celebrated captain or bandit.

In dealing with recent events and policies, it is impossible to separate Mao's attitude toward the United States, 'the most ferocious enemy of the world's peoples', from his ideas regarding the way in which this enemy can be resisted and vanquished with the aid of the peoples of the world, and (in the past at least) of the Soviet Union. Thus, the last few texts in this chapter should be read in connexion with Texts VIII G to J, which stress the methods by which, individually and collectively, the revolutionary peoples carry on their struggles, and in connexion with Texts X K, L and M, which deal with relations with other powers of the 'socialist camp', as it used to be called. As suggested in the introduction to Chapter VIII, there has been a constant evolution in Mao's thinking toward a strategic conception centred on the peoples of Asia and Africa rather than on the solidarity among all communist countries. He originally drew his famous conclusion that 'the East wind is prevailing over the West wind'

(Text IX J) from Soviet economic and technological might, and his reasoning in 1957 about the probable outcome of a nuclear war (Text IX K) was based squarely on Soviet support. As late as January 1964 (Text IX M), Mao still called for unity among the members of the socialist camp. (Text X M in the next chapter illustrates how far those days are now past.) But at the same time it was clear that the real force on which he was counting to put an end to American intervention in foreign countries was 'the raging tide of the people of the world'.

Like Text X E in the next chapter (see the introduction to Chapter X), Text IX L illustrates the limited character of Mao's knowledge of the United States. Much of his picture of the plight of the American Negro is, as we all know, only too accurate. But his conclusion that it is 'only the reactionary ruling clique among the whites' which supports racial discrimination is unfortunately unduly optimistic, and his tendency to lump together President Kennedy and Governor Wallace as allies of the Ku Klux Klan shows, to say the least, an imperfect understanding of the American federal system. But for all the crudeness of the picture he draws, the problem singled out by Mao of the link between race relations within and without the United States remains a real one, and we will ignore it at our peril.

S.R.S.

IX · A America, the most murderous of hangmen[1]

In the past, some merchants had a superstitious faith in America. They firmly believed that America was a good friend who helped China; they did not know that America is actually the most murderous of hangmen. Consider, for example, how America recently gave covert assistance to Ts'ao K'un, whom the merchants as well as the whole nation opposed, in his capture of political power; consider further how America exerted the greatest effort to obstruct the policy of prohibiting the export of cotton, which the merchants demanded. From these and many

1. Extracted from an article of July 1923, 'The Peking *coup d'état* and the merchants'. (See note to Text III A.)

other examples, we can see the error of superstitiously believing in America.

IX · B The League of Nations is a league of robbers![1]

Workers, peasants, and soldiers of all China! Exploited masses of the whole country!

The Provisional Central Government of the Chinese Soviet Republic long ago told the popular masses of the whole country that the League of Nations is a League of Robbers by which the various imperialisms are dismembering China. The principal task of the Lytton Commission of Enquiry sent to China by the League was to prepare the dismemberment of China and the repression of all the revolutionary movements that have raised the flag of the Chinese Soviets.

Now the Commission of Enquiry of the league of imperialist robbers – the Lytton Commission – has already published its report regarding the dismemberment of China. This report is an admirable document shown to the Chinese popular masses by the imperialists regarding the dismemberment they propose to inflict on China; and yet the Kuomintang, which is selling out and dishonouring the country, as well as the government which is the emanation of the Kuomintang, have accepted it completely! . . .

The Lytton Report is the bill of sale by which imperialism reduced the Chinese people to slavery! The Soviet Government calls on the popular masses of the whole country to participate in an armed uprising under the direction of the Soviet Government to wage a national revolutionary war in order to tear to shreds the Lytton Report, and to oppose all the new projects of the imperialists for dismembering China, repressing the Chinese revolution, and attacking the Soviet regions and the Soviet Union! Let us hurl out of China Japanese imperialism and all other

1. Extracted from a telegram of the Chinese Soviet Government, dated 6 October 1932, signed by Mao Tse-tung, Hsiang Ying, and Chang Kuo-t'ao. (*Su-wei-ai Chung-kuo*, pp. 86–8.)

Available translations: none.

imperialisms, in order to obtain the complete liberation and independence of the Chinese people! Let us defend the Soviet Union with arms in our hands, let us establish a close alliance between the toiling masses of China and of the Soviet Union.

The Soviet Government proclaims to the workers, peasants, and soldiers of the whole country, and to all the exploited popular masses, that if we really want to wage a national revolutionary war and oppose the dismemberment of China by the imperialists, we must first overthrow the reactionary domination of the Kuomintang, these scavengers who pick up the scraps of the imperialist dismemberment of China, and who are repressing the national war! . . .

IX · C A war for eternal peace[1]

The protracted nature of China's Anti-Japanese War cannot be separated from the fight for permanent peace for China and the world. In no historical epoch was war ever so near to permanent peace as it is today.

The life of humanity over the past several hundreds of thousands of years has already passed through two epochs: the epoch of the peaceful life of humanity and the epoch of the warlike life of humanity. The first of these epochs occupied the longest period in the history of humanity. In this epoch, the level of production was highly inadequate and men waged war only against nature. Wars between the groups composing humanity were neither necessary nor possible. The second epoch extends roughly from the end of clan society to our day. Because of the development of production and the appearance of social divisions, the epoch of warlike life of humanity began.[2] Although this second epoch is only a few thousand years old, nobody knows how many wars each nation has fought, either wars among groups within a nation or wars among groups of nations. In the imperialist epoch of capitalist society,

1. Extracted from *On Protracted War*, 1938. (See note to Text V H.)
2. In the current edition, this entire passage has been replaced by the following sentence: 'For several thousand years, ever since the emergence of classes, human history has been filled with interminable wars.'

wars are waged on a particularly extensive scale and with a peculiar ruthlessness. *The first great imperialist war* of twenty years ago, though unprecedented in history until then, *was not yet a war such as will not be known in all history, still less* the last of all wars. The war that has now begun is *without precedent in all history* and brings us close to the final war, that is to say, close to the permanent peace of mankind. At present, one third of the world's population has entered the war: just consider, Italy, then Japan, on the one hand, and Abyssinia, then Spain, then China, on the other. The population of the belligerent countries now amounts to almost 600 million, or at least one third of the total population of the world. The peculiar feature of the present war is its uninterruptedness and its nearness to permanent peace. Why is it uninterrupted? After engaging Abyssinia, Italy engaged Spain, with Germany contributing her share to the fight; then Japan engaged China. What next? No doubt Hitler will follow up and engage the great powers. 'Fascism Is War' – this is perfectly correct. *Although one cannot say that once victory has been decided in the war between anti-fascism and fascism there will be no more wars – on the contrary there certainly will be more – the fact remains that* there will be no interval between the present war and the great world war it will develop into. Mankind cannot escape the calamity of war. Why do we also say that the present war is near to permanent peace? The present war has resulted from the development of the general crisis of world capitalism, a crisis that is compelling the capitalist countries to enter into a new war, and above all the fascist countries to embark on new military adventures. In view of this crisis, we can foresee that this war will not result in the salvation of capitalism but in its collapse. This war will be bigger and more cruel than that of twenty years ago, inevitably involving all nations and dragging on for a very long time, and mankind will suffer greatly. But because of the existence of the Soviet Union and the heightened awareness of the peoples of the world, great revolutionary wars will undoubtedly emerge from this war to oppose all counter-revolutionary wars, thus giving this war as a whole the character of a war for permanent peace. Even if there should be another warring period after this, it will not be far from permanent world peace. Once man has reached[1] the age of permanent peace, he will never again desire war. Neither armies, nor warships, nor military planes, nor poison gas will then be needed. *At this moment will begin the third epoch in the history of humanity, the epoch of peaceful life during which there will never be war.* Throughout all eternity our sons and grandsons will never know war again. ... The war between China and Japan, two countries with a total population of over 500 million, will occupy an important place in this war for permanent peace ...

IX · D We are for Roosevelt and against Chamberlain[2]

... The great war of resistance now being waged by China is not merely the affair of China – it is also the affair of the world. In the democratic countries such as England, America, and France, there are broad popular masses including all the progressive people from the various social strata who sympathize with China's war of resistance and oppose the invasion of China by Japanese imperialism. It is only a reactionary faction that opposes China's war of resistance. ... In this great war of resistance we rely first of all on China's own strength to vanquish the enemy. ... But at the same time, we need outside aid. Our enemy is a world-wide enemy, and the war of resistance waged by China is a war of resistance of a world-wide character. History has already shown that a viewpoint attempting to isolate this war is erroneous. In all the democratic countries, such as England and America, there still exists an isolationist viewpoint whose adherents do not understand that if China is defeated, England, America, and the other countries will not be able to go on enjoying their own tranquillity. This erroneous viewpoint is not attuned to the needs of the times. For the others, to aid China is to aid themselves – this is the only concrete verity at the present time. ... China is pursu-

1. In the current edition, this has been changed to: 'Once man has lieminated capitalism, he will reach the age of permanent peace ...'

2. Extracted from Mao's Preface to the English edition of *On Protracted War*, dated 20 January 1939. My source was *Pa-lu-chün chün-cheng tsa-chih*, February 1939, pp. 8–9.

Available translations: none.

ing her war amidst many difficulties, but the flames of a war among the great powers of the world are coming closer every day and no country can remain aloof. We are in agreement with President Roosevelt's proclamation regarding the defence of democracy. We are, on the other hand, resolutely opposed to the policy of concessions to the fascist states in the West practised by Chamberlain. Up to this day, Chamberlain has also displayed a cowardly attitude toward Japan. I hope that the popular masses of England and America will arise and act positively to admonish their governments and make them adopt a new policy of resistance to wars of aggression – for the good of China and also for the good of England and America themselves.

IX · E The Second Imperialist War[1]

... The new world economic crisis, which began in 1937, has in recent years penetrated into so-called 'peaceful' states such as England, France, and America; it is also developing in Germany, Japan, and Italy. This economic crisis has also brought a grave political crisis in its wake. The people are discontented with capitalism and with the dictatorship of the bourgeoisie. Whether it be in the states that became fascist a long time ago, or in the states where they are taking advantage of the war to carry out fascization, this political crisis, this popular discontent, are daily becoming more acute. On the other hand, the socialist Soviet Union has been strengthened to the point where it can no longer be invaded. Under these conditions, the bourgeoisie of each of the imperialist states realizes that without a vast war, without transforming the limited war into a total war, without demolishing its imperialist friends, it cannot escape either the economic crisis or the political crisis, nor can it escape its own death.

These are the calculations of the bourgeoisie of all the countries of the world on the eve of its death. The authors of these calculations have no idea that in this way – by making use of a

1. Extracted from a lecture to the Party cadres in Yenan, 14 September 1939; reported in *Chieh-fang*, no. 85, 30 September 1939, pp. 1–6.
Available translations: none.

war to divide up the world anew in order to escape from the economic and political crisis and to avoid their own death – they cannot fail to create an even greater economic and political crisis and to hasten the day of their death. They are like a mad dog, they are already mad, the capitalist system has made them altogether mad, they cannot do otherwise than hurl themselves pell-mell against their enemies and against the walls of the world. Such is the reality of life today in all the capitalist countries of the world. A fight between mad dogs – such is the present imperialist war.

1. The aims of the war. 'War is the continuation of politics.' The nature of imperialism is predatory, and even in periods of 'peace' there is no instance when the policy of the imperialist states is not predatory. But when the predatory policy of certain imperialist states encounters the obstacle of certain other imperialist states and cannot break through this obstacle by peaceful means, then these states use warlike means to break through this obstacle so that they may pursue their predatory policies. . . . The aim of the Second Imperialist War is similar to that of the First Imperialist War. It consists in dividing up the world anew, that is to say, in dividing up anew the colonies, semi-colonies, and spheres of influence, in pillaging the peoples of the world, and in establishing their domination over the peoples of the world. . . . Apart from aims of this kind, are there any other aims? Are there any good aims? There are none whatever. Whether it be Germany, Italy, or Japan, whether it be England, America, or France, all the imperialist states participating directly or indirectly in the war have only a counter-revolutionary, an imperialist goal – pillaging the people. The 'lasting peace' of Japanese imperialism, the 'self-determination of peoples' of Hitler, the 'opposition to National Socialism' of Chamberlain, the 'aid to Poland' of Daladier – all this comes down to a single word: pillage. Merely because it sounds good and to fool the people, they order their secretaries to invent a few synonyms, that is all.

2. The nature of the war. The nature of the war is basically determined by the political aims of the war. All wars are divided into two categories. As Comrade Stalin has said, they are divided into (1) just wars the aim of which is not pillage but liberation, and (2) unjust wars of pillage. By its nature, the Second Imperialist War, like the First Imperialist War, belongs to the second category.... The two sides in the present war, in order to fool the people and mobilize public opinion, both proclaim with utter shamelessness that thev themselves are just and those on the other side unjust. In reality, all of this is nothing but a farce and a sham. Only wars of national liberation and wars of popular liberation, as well as wars undertaken by socialist countries to support these two kinds of liberation movements, are just wars. Many people are confused about the present war. According to them Germany is certainly unjust, whereas England and France are democratic and anti-fascist states, and Poland, for her part, is waging a national war of self-defence. They therefore believe that on the whole the Anglo-Franco-Polish side has after all a slightly progressive character. This is an altogether muddled conception, arising from the fact that people have not clearly understood either the aims of the war or the peculiarities that characterize the first and the second stages of the war.

3. The peculiarities of the first stage of the war. ... A portion of the imperialist states, the fascist states of Germany, Italy, and Japan, were waging wars of aggression like mad dogs, violating the interests of all small and weak peoples, violating the interests of all democratic countries, and unleashing a fascist menace within each democratic country. At this time the people of the whole world demanded that aggression be resisted and that democracy be defended; they demanded that another part of the imperialist states, the so-called democratic states of England, America, and France, intervene against these wars of aggression, and that they allow the people to retain a small residue of democracy. The Soviet Union made known many times that she was ready to establish a joint front against aggression with all the so-called democratic states. If these so-called democratic states had intervened at the time against the aggressors, if a war had broken out to prevent aggression, if for example it had been possible together with the Soviet Union to aid the armies of the Spanish

Government in their effort to stop the German and Italian aggressors, and to aid China in her effort to stop the Japanese aggressors, then such an action, such a war, would have been just, would have had a progressive character. But these so-called democratic states did not intervene; they adopted a policy of 'non-intervention'. Their aim was to bring about a situation in which the two sides – the side of the aggressors and the side of the victims of aggression – would be ravaged by war, after which they would intervene to fish in troubled waters. ... Nevertheless, at this time, apart from the circumstance that German, Italian, and Japanese imperialism were waging unjust wars of pillage, and that the so-called democratic states were allowing them to continue, there was another circumstance, there were also wars of national liberation ...

4. Our revolutionary policy during the first stage of the war. ... There is not the slightest doubt that the revolutionary policy of this stage has as its goal the organization of a united front against aggression of the people of the country that is the victim of aggression. ... At the same time, this policy does not ignore the organization by the Soviet Union and the governments of all the democratic countries of the struggle to prevent new aggression.... Even after Munich, because of the anger aroused among the broad masses of the English and French people and even among the left wing of the bourgeoisie by the defeat of Spain and the disappearance of Czechoslovakia, there was a possibility of compelling the Chamberlain and Daladier governments to abandon their policy of non-intervention and to organize, with the Soviet Union, a common front against aggression ...

5. The rupture of the Anglo-Franco-Soviet negotiations and the beginning of the second stage of the war. The bourgeoisies of the so-called democratic states fear on the one hand that the fascist states may violate their interests; but they fear the development of the revolutionary forces even more. They fear the Soviet Union, they fear the liberation movements of the peoples of their own countries, they fear the liberation movements in the colonies and semi-colonies. Consequently, they rejected a genuine united front against aggression and a genuine war against aggression involving the participation of the Soviet Union, and they organized by themselves a united counter-revolutionary front, they undertook by themselves a robbers' war of pillage.

The Anglo-Franco-Soviet negotiations lasted from 15 April to 23 August ... but from beginning to end, England and France refused to recognize the principle of equality and reciprocity. They wanted the Soviet Union to guarantee their security, but they were absolutely unwilling to guarantee the security of the Soviet Union or of the small countries of the Baltic.... In addition, they would not allow the Soviet Army to cross Poland to fight the aggressor. Naturally, the Soviet Union was not willing to conclude a treaty like that proposed by England and France, which would not have been adapted to revolutionary aims but only to counter-revolutionary aims.... This is the basic reason for the rupture of the Anglo-Franco-Soviet negotiations. At this point, Germany abandoned her anti-Soviet position and in fact was ready to abandon the so-called 'anti-Comintern Pact'; she recognized the inviolability of the Soviet frontier, and so the German-Soviet Non-aggression Treaty was concluded. The absolute lack of sincerity of England and France in their negotiations with the Soviet Union, their absolute refusal genuinely to oppose aggression, the way in which they decided to break off the Three Power Negotiations, proves nothing less than that Chamberlain had already decided on war. Consequently, if the great war broke out, it was not only Hitler but Chamberlain who wanted to fight, for if he had really wanted to avoid the war, he could have done so only with Soviet participation ...

6. The peculiarities of the second stage of the war. At the present time, now that war has broken out, the situation has undergone a fundamental change. The distinction that existed in the past between the fascist states and the democratic states has lost all meaning. At the present time, if one wishes to distinguish between things of different natures, there are only the following two categories: (1) all the countries that are waging an imperialist war of pillage as well as all the countries that are in reality supporting this war; and (2) those who are waging not wars of pillage but just wars of national liberation and popular liberation, as well as the countries that support these wars. . . .Today England has become the most reactionary country in the world, and the Number One anti-Soviet, anti-communist, anti-democratic, and anti-popular leader, the enemy of all small peoples, is none other than Chamberlain . . .

7. Our revolutionary policy during the second stage of the war. In conformity with the peculiarities of the second stage of the war, what should the revolutionary policy of the proletariat be, and especially of the Communist Party?

In my opinion, it should be the following:

1. In all the imperialist countries participating in the war, we must call on the people to oppose the imperialist war, make clear the imperialist nature of both warring camps, treat them all as the same kind of robbers. In particular, we must oppose English imperialism, this robber chief, incite the people not to allow themselves to be deceived by the imperialist robbers, carry out propaganda among the people, in order that they may transform the imperialist war into a revolutionary civil war, establish a united popular front against the imperialist war . . .

2. In all the neutral countries, such as America, the members of the Communist Party should reveal to the people the imperialist policy of the bourgeois government, which calls itself neutral, but in reality aids the war and seeks to enrich itself in the war . . .

3. In all the colonial and semi-colonial countries, the policy to follow is that of the national united front, either to resist the invader (as in China), or to oppose the mother country (as in the case of India), in order to attain national independence. . . . In all the colonies of countries participating in the war we must oppose the actions of the traitors to the nation who support the war waged by the mother country, oppose the mobilization of the people of the colony to participate in the war on the front of the mother country, remind the people of the colony of the misery

they suffered during the First Imperialist War. In the colonial and semi-colonial countries, if we do not oppose the traitors to the nation there is no hope for the movement of national liberation.

8. The perspectives of the war.... Wars between imperialisms and mutual weakening of imperialisms ... constitute a favourable condition for movements of popular liberation in all countries, for movements of national liberation in all countries, for China's war of resistance, for the building of communism in the Soviet Union. From this standpoint, the darkness that reigns in the world is only provisional and the future of the world is bright. Imperialism will surely perish, and the liberation of the oppressed people and of the oppressed nations will surely be achieved ...

IX · F Hurley, Chiang Kai-shek, and the *Reader's Digest* are a menace to world peace[1]

It becomes more and more obvious that the policy of the United States toward China as represented by its Ambassador Patrick J. Hurley *is creating a danger for both the Chinese and the American people. This danger can be surmounted only by taking into account the over-all interests of China and America for a long period.* This danger is that of a civil war in China. The Kuomintang Government, *sticking to its reactionary policies of neglecting the war against Japan and repressing the people's democratic movement*, has devoted itself to the making of civil war ever since its formation eighteen years ago. ... The late President Roosevelt did take this into account, and consequently in the interest of the United States he refrained from adopting the policy of helping

1. Extracted from two editorials, dated 12 and 19 July 1945, written for the Hsinhua News Agency. Both of these editorials were anonymous; for the reasons which justify attributing them to Mao, see the introduction to Chapter IX. The editorials appeared in *Chieh-fang jih-pao* on 13 and 20 July 1945.

Available translations: A translation of the first editorial (from which the first paragraph is taken) appears in *Selected Works*, III, pp. 335–6; there are no translations of the second.

one side in China against the other.[1] In November 1944, Hurley, visiting Yenan as Roosevelt's personal representative, adopted a favourable attitude toward the plans proposed by the Chinese Communist Party for the abolition of the Kuomintang's one-party dictatorship and the establishment of a democratic coalition government. *He had not yet repudiated President Roosevelt's wish of not supporting unilaterally the Kuomintang government.* Then, *unexpectedly*, Hurley changed his tune and went back on what he had said in Yenan. This change of tune was sharply indicated in the statement that he had made at Washington on 2 April, in which, from the lips of the self-same Hurley, the Kuomintang Government represented by Chiang Kai-shek suddenly became a beauty, while the Chinese Communist Party was a monster; he even bluntly declared that the United States would cooperate only with Chiang Kai-shek, not with the Chinese Communist Party. This, of course, is not only Hurley's personal opinion but that of a segment of the U.S. Government; it is however an erroneous and dangerous opinion, *contrary to Roosevelt's policy.* At this juncture Roosevelt died and Hurley, beside himself with joy, returned to the U.S. Embassy in Chungking. The danger of the U.S. policy toward China as represented by Hurley consists in its encouragement of the reactionary trend of the Kuomintang Government and the increased danger of civil war in China. *If this peril is not eliminated, the inevitable result will not only be a long period of misfortune for the people of China; by the same token, the American Government with its own hands will place a crushing burden on its own back.* That is to say, it will fall hopelessly into the deep, stinking cesspool of Chinese reaction; it will place itself in opposition to the hundreds of millions of awakened or awakening Chinese people, and become a hindrance to the Anti-Japanese War at present and to world peace in the future. ... On the question of China's future, a *large part* of American public opinion, *as well as quite a few politicians and military men*, have clearly perceived that the irresistible forces of the Chinese people who demand independence, freedom, *demo-*

1. In the current edition, the language is more precise: Mao speaks of 'a policy of aiding the Kuomintang in its armed struggle against the Communist Party'.

cracy, and unity, and *who want to make their country rich and powerful* [*fu ch'iang* – an ancient term meaning 'to enrich the country and make it strong militarily] will burst forth and supplant both foreign oppression and feudal oppression. They feel acutely worried about such a dangerous policy toward China as Hurley's, and demand that it be changed. Whether or when the policy of the United States will be changed we cannot say at present. But one thing is certain: If such a policy as Hurley's, a policy that aids and abets the anti-popular forces in China in opposition to the Chinese people whose number is so immense, is to continue, it will place a crushing burden on the government and people of the United States and plunge them into endless woes and troubles. This is a point that should be brought home to the people of the United States ...

Since 2 April, when Hurley set forth his erroneous policy of supporting Chiang and opposing the communists, the true face of a group of imperialist elements within the United States has become clearer. Recently the widely read American periodical *Reader's Digest* published in its June issue an article co-authored by [J.B.] Powell and [Max] Eastman entitled 'The Fate of the World Is at Stake in China' [Vol. 46, no. 278, pp. 12–22]. One can say that it is an open exposition of Hurley's policy. After emphasizing that China's weight 'may well be decisive in settling the fate of the world', Powell and Eastman affirm that 'the biggest political question of today' is 'whether China goes democratic or totalitarian'.... They say that the question whether China will go democratic or totalitarian 'is identical with the question whose leadership prevails – that of democratic America or of totalitarian Russia'. Chinese brethren, listen to these confessions from the very mouths of these imperialists themselves! In fact, their policy toward China consists in placing her under American 'leadership'. Needless to say, the meaning of this phrase is 'identical' with the following idea: to make China an American colony or semi-colony. Here every hypocritical mask is torn off and we see the motives of the imperialists in all their nakedness! ... The trickery of 'American democracy' and 'Russian totalitarianism' with which Powell and Eastman entertain themselves on several occasions in their article is altogether laughable and stupid.

Since they say that the way now followed by Chiang Kai-shek is 'the way of American democracy' it follows that in China 'the way of American democracy' is nothing else than the way of feudal fascism camouflaged as democracy. Moreover, since they say that the way now followed by Chiang Kai-shek is a way that can lead to giving America a position of 'leadership' in China, it follows that the 'way of American democracy' in China would also lead quite naturally to making China an American colony. ... Of course the people of China do not want to follow the way of colonization, which the American imperialist elements wish to impose on them. The way they wish to follow is that indicated by the leader of the Chinese Communist Party, Comrade Mao Tse-tung, which is the way of new democracy leading to independence, freedom, democracy, unity, wealth, and power [*fu ch'iang* – The repetition of this listing in the two editorials serves to strengthen my hypothesis that Mao is the author of both]! ... The new democracy that China wishes to practise is nothing else than the joint democratic dictatorship [*min-chu ti lien-ho chuan-cheng*] of all the anti-imperialist and all the anti-feudal classes; of course, it is neither American bourgeois dictatorship nor the proletarian dictatorship of the Soviet Union. If they like only the dictatorship of a minority of big landowners and big bourgeois, as it is practised by Chiang Kai-shek, and if they don't like the people's dictatorship of all the revolutionary classes [*ko ko-ming chieh-chi ti jen-min chuan-cheng*] of our Comrade Mao Tse-tung, and if they therefore absolutely insist on calling Chiang Kai-shek's feudal fascism 'democracy' and our new democracy 'totalitarianism', they naturally have that 'freedom'. But the people of China certainly wish to follow the new democratic way indicated by Mao Tse-tung, not the way of feudal fascism indicated by Chiang Kai-shek. ... In order that together we may triumph over the Japanese bandits and build world peace, we hope that all the upright elements among American public opinion and among American politicians and military men, all who are prepared to treat us on a basis of equality, will intervene actively to rectify Hurley's erroneous policy, for the final result of this policy can only be to delay victory over Japan and to destroy world peace.

IX · G Reactionaries and atom bombs are paper tigers[1]

... I do not mean to say that the U.S. reactionaries have no intention of attacking the Soviet Union. The Soviet Union is a defender of world peace and a powerful factor in preventing the domination of the world by U.S. reactionaries. ... That is why the U.S. reactionaries rabidly hate the Soviet Union and actually dream of destroying this socialist state. ... I think the American people and the peoples of all countries menaced by U.S. aggression should unite and struggle against the attacks of the U.S. reactionaries and their running dogs in these countries. Only by victory in this struggle can a third world war be avoided; otherwise it is unavoidable.

STRONG: That is well put. But suppose the United States uses the atom bomb? Suppose the United States bombs the Soviet Union from its bases in Iceland, Okinawa, and China?

MAO: The atom bomb is a paper tiger used by the U.S. reactionaries to scare people. It looks terrible, but in fact it isn't. Of course, the atom bomb is a weapon of mass slaughter, but the outcome of a war is decided by the people, not by one or two new types of weapon.

All reactionaries are paper tigers. In appearance, the reactionaries are terrifying, but in reality they are not so powerful. From a long-range point of view, it is not the reactionaries but the people who are really powerful. In Russia, before the February Revolution of 1917, which side was really strong? On the surface the Tsar seemed strong, but he was swept away by a single gust of wind in the February Revolution. In the final analysis, the strength in Russia was on the side of the Soviets of Workers, Peasants, and Soldiers. The Tsar was merely a paper tiger. Wasn't Hitler once considered very strong? But history proved

1. Extracts from Mao's interview with Anna Louise Strong, August 1946, *Hsüan-chi*, IV, pp. 1192–3.

Available translations: *Selected Works*, I, pp. 100–101.

that he was a paper tiger. So was Mussolini, so was Japanese imperialism. But the strength of the Soviet Union and of the people in all countries who loved democracy and freedom proved much greater than had been foreseen.

Chiang Kai-shek and his supporters, the U.S. reactionaries, are all paper tigers, too. Speaking of U.S. imperialism, people seem to feel that it is terrifically strong. . . . But it will be proved that the U.S. reactionaries, like all the reactionaries in history, do not have much strength. In the United States there are others who are really strong – the American people.

Take the case of China. We have only millet plus rifles to rely on, but ultimately history will prove that our millet plus rifles is more powerful than Chiang Kai-shek's aeroplanes plus tanks. Although the Chinese people still face many difficulties and will long suffer hardships from the joint attacks of U.S. imperialism and the Chinese reactionaries, the day will come when these reactionaries are defeated and we are victorious. The reason is simply this: The reactionaries represent reaction, we represent progress.

IX · H American imperialism is sitting on a volcano[1]

. . . America's strength is superficial and transient. The crisis[2] is like a volcano that menaces American imperialism every day. American imperialism is sitting on this volcano. This situation has driven the American imperialists to draw up a plan for enslaving the world; to run amuck like wild beasts in Europe, Asia, and other parts of the world; to muster the reactionary forces in all countries, the human dregs cast off by their peoples; to form an imperialist, anti-democratic camp against all the democratic forces headed by the Soviet Union; and to prepare for war in the hope that in the future at a distant time, some day, they can start a third world war to defeat the democratic forces. This is a pre-

1. Extracted from a report of 25 December 1947 (see note to Text VM). Available translations: *Selected Works*, IV, pp. 172–3.

2. Here Mao, in the current edition, inserted another reference to contradictions.

posterous plan. The democratic forces of the world must and certainly can defeat this plan. The strength of the world anti-imperialist camp has surpassed that of the imperialist camp. It is we, not the enemy, who are in the superior position. The anti-imperialist camp headed by the Soviet Union has already been formed. The socialist Soviet Union is free from crisis, in the ascendancy, and cherished by the world's broad masses: its strength has already surpassed that of the imperialist United States, which is seriously menaced by crises, on the decline, and opposed by the world's broad masses. The people's democracies in Europe are consolidating themselves internally and are uniting with each other. In the European capitalist countries the people's anti-imperialist forces are developing, with those in France and Italy taking the lead. Within the United States, there are people's democratic forces that are getting stronger every day. The peoples of Latin America are not slaves obedient to U.S. imperialism. In the whole of Asia a great national liberation movement has arisen. All the forces of the anti-imperialist camp are uniting and forging ahead. The communist and workers' parties of nine European countries have established their Information Bureau and issued a call to the people of the world to rise against the imperialist plan of enslavement. This call to battle has inspired the oppressed people of the world, charted the course of their struggle, and strengthened their confidence in victory. It has thrown world reaction into panic and confusion. All the anti-imperialist forces in the countries of the East, too, should unite, oppose oppression by imperialism and by their domestic reactionaries, and make the emancipation of the more than one billion oppressed people of the East the goal of their struggle. We must grasp our own destiny in our own hands. We should rid our ranks of all impotent thinking. All views that overestimate the strength of the enemy and underestimate the strength of the people are wrong. If everyone makes strenuous efforts, we, together with all the democratic forces of the world, can surely defeat the imperialist plan of enslavement, prevent the outbreak of a third world war, overthrow all reactionary regimes, and win lasting peace for mankind. . . . This is the historic epoch in which world capitalism and imperialism are going down to their doom and world socialism and democracy[1] are marching to victory. The dawn is in sight, we must exert ourselves.

IX · I Imperialists will never become Buddhas until their doom[2]

... How different is the logic of the imperialists from that of the people! Make trouble, fail, make trouble again, fail again, till their doom; that is the logic of the imperialists and all reactionaries the world over, and they will never go against this logic. This is a Marxist *truth*. When we say 'imperialism is ferocious', we mean that its nature will never change, that the imperialists will never lay down their butcher knives, that they will never become Buddhas till their doom. Fight, fail, fight again, fail again, fight again, till their victory; that is the logic of the people, and they too will never go against this logic. This is another Marxist *truth*. The Russian people's revolution proceeded according to this *truth*, and the Chinese people's revolution is proceeding according to it at the present time....

IX · J The East wind prevails over the West wind[3]

... Chairman Mao pointed out first of all that the October Socialist Revolution marks a turning point in world history; the appearance in the heavens of two artificial satellites and the coming to Moscow of delegates from the sixty-four communist and workers' parties to celebrate the holiday of the October Revolution mark a new turning point. The forces of socialism surpass the forces of imperialism. The imperialist forces have a leader, Amer-

1. In the current edition, this reads 'people's democracy'.

2. Extracted from an editorial written for the Hsinhua Agency, dated 14 August 1949, *Jen-min jih-pao*, 15 August 1949.

Available translations: Mao Tse-tung, *Selected Works*, IV, p. 428.

3. Extracted from Mao's remarks to Chinese students in Moscow, 17 November 1957. (*Mao Chu-hsi tsai Su-lien ti yen-lun*, pp. 14–15.)

Available translations: S.C.M.P., no. 1656. (This text differs considerably from the above, omitting certain important sentences.)

ica; our socialist camp must also have a leader, and that leader is the Soviet Union. If we do not have a leader our forces might disintegrate! Chairman Mao ... said it was an event of great significance that the communist and workers' parties of sixty-four countries attended the celebrations of the fortieth anniversary of the great October Socialist Revolution. It showed the solidarity of the socialist countries, led by the Soviet Union, it showed the solidarity of the communist and workers' parties the world over, with the Communist Party of the Soviet Union as their centre. Chairman Mao said that the direction of the wind in the world had changed. In the struggle between the socialist and capitalist camps, it was no longer the West wind that prevailed over the East wind, but the East wind that prevailed over the West wind. The whole world now has a population of 2.7 billion, of which the various socialist countries have nearly one billion, the independent, former colonial countries more than 700 million, the countries now struggling for independence or for complete independence plus the capitalist countries with neutralist tendencies 600 million, and the imperialist camp only about 400 million, besides which they are also divided internally. Earthquakes are likely to occur over there. At present, Chairman Mao said, it was not the West wind that was prevailing over the East wind, but the East wind prevailing over the West wind.

IX · K We must not fear nuclear war[1]

... In my opinion, the situation today is characterized by the fact that the East wind is prevailing over the West wind, in other words, by the fact that the forces of socialism are overwhelmingly superior to the forces of imperialism.

[Proceeding from that estimate, Comrade Mao Tse-tung pointed to the steadily growing possibility of preventing im-

1. The first sentence of this extract is part of the passage from Mao's remarks at the Moscow Conference of November 1957 published at the time. The paragraph following 'Comrade Mao Tse-tung then added' was released only six years later, in the Chinese Government statement of 1 September 1963 (published in the *Jen-min jih-pao* of the same date).

Available translations: *Peking Review*, no. 36, 1963, p. 10.

perialism from launching a new world war. Comrade Mao Tse-tung then added:]

At present another situation has to be taken into account, namely, that the war maniacs may drop atomic and hydrogen bombs everywhere. They drop them and we drop them too; thus there will be chaos and lives will be lost. The question has to be considered for the worst. The Political Bureau of our Party has held several sessions to discuss this question. If fighting breaks out now, China has got only hand grenades and not atomic bombs, but the Soviet Union has them. Let us imagine how many people will die if war should break out? Out of the world's population of 2,700 million, one third – or, putting the figure a bit higher, half – may be lost. It is they and not we who want to fight; when a fight starts, atomic and hydrogen bombs will be dropped. I debated this question with a foreign statesman.[1] He believed that if an atomic war was fought, the whole of mankind might be annihilated. I said that if the worst came to the worst and half of mankind died, the other half would remain while imperialism would be razed to the ground and the whole world would become socialist. In a certain number of years, there would be 2,700 million people again and definitely more. We Chinese have not yet completed our construction and we desire peace. However, if imperialism insists on fighting a war, we will have no alternative but to make up our minds and fight it, before going ahead with our construction. If every day you are afraid of war and war eventually comes, what will you do then? First I have said that the East wind prevails over the West wind and that war will not break out, and now I have added these explanations about the situation in case war should break out. In this way both possibilities have been taken into account.

IX · L Oppose racial discrimination by U.S. imperialism[2]

1. According to later Chinese and Soviet accounts, the statesman in question was Jawaharlal Nehru.

2. Full text of Mao's statement of 8 August 1963, *Hung-ch'i*, no. 16, 1963, pp. 1–2.

Available translations: *Peking Review*, no. 33, 1963, pp. 6–7.

An American Negro leader now taking refuge in Cuba, Mr Robert Williams, the former President of the Monroe, North Carolina, Chapter of the National Association for the Advancement of Coloured People, has twice this year asked me for a statement in support of the American Negroes' struggle against racial discrimination. I wish to take this opportunity, on behalf of the Chinese people, to express our resolute support for the American Negroes in their struggle against racial discrimination and for freedom and equal rights.

There are more than nineteen million Negroes in the United States, or about eleven per cent of the total population. Their position in society is one of enslavement, oppression and discrimination. The overwhelming majority of the Negroes are deprived of their right to vote. On the whole it is only the most back-breaking and most despised jobs that are open to them. Their average wages are only from a third to a half of those of the white people. The ratio of unemployment among them is the highest. In many states they cannot go to the same school, eat at the same table, or travel in the same section of a bus or train with the white people. Negroes are frequently and arbitrarily arrested, beaten up and murdered by U.S. authorities at various levels and members of the Ku Klux Klan and other racists. About half of the American Negroes are concentrated in eleven states in the south of the United States. There, the discrimination and persecution they suffer are especially startling.

The American Negroes are awakening, and their resistance is growing ever stronger. In recent years the mass struggle of the American Negroes against racial discrimination and for freedom and equal rights has been constantly developing.

In 1957 the Negro people in Little Rock, Arkansas, waged a fierce struggle against the barring of their children from public schools. The authorities used armed force against them, and there resulted the Little Rock incident which shocked the world.

In 1960 Negroes in more than twenty states held 'sit in' demonstrations in protest against racial segregation in local restaurants, shops and other public places.

In 1961 the Negroes launched a campaign of 'freedom riders'

to oppose racial segregation in transport, a campaign which rapidly extended to many states.

In 1962 the Negroes in Mississippi fought for the equal right to enrol in colleges and were greeted by the authorities with repression which culminated in a blood bath.

This year, the struggle of the American Negroes started in early April in Birmingham, Alabama. Unarmed, bare-handed Negro masses were subjected to wholesale arrests and the most barbarous repression merely because they were holding meetings and parades against racial discrimination. On 12 June, an extreme was reached with the cruel murder of Mr Medgar Evers, a leader of the Negro people in Mississippi. These Negro masses, aroused to indignation and undaunted by ruthless violence, carried on their struggles even more courageously and quickly won the support of Negroes and all strata of the people throughout the United States. A gigantic and vigorous nationwide struggle is going on in nearly every state and city in the United States, and the struggle keeps mounting. American Negro organizations have decided to start a 'freedom march' on Washington on 28 August, in which 250,000 people will take part.

The speedy development of the struggle of the American Negroes is a manifestation of the constant sharpening of class struggle and national struggle within the United States; it has been causing increasingly grave anxiety to the U.S. ruling clique. The Kennedy Administration has resorted to cunning two-faced tactics. On the one hand, it continues to connive at and take part in the discrimination against and persecution of Negroes; it even sends troops to repress them. On the other hand, it is parading as an advocate of the 'defence of human rights' and 'the protection of the civil rights of Negroes', is calling upon the Negro people to exercise 'restraint', and is proposing to Congress so-called 'civil rights legislation', in an attempt to numb the fighting will of the Negro people and deceive the masses throughout the country. However, these tactics of the Kennedy Administration are being seen through by more and more of the Negroes. The fascist atrocities committed by the U.S. imperialists against the Negro people have laid bare the true nature of the so-called democracy and freedom in the United States and revealed the inner link between the reactionary policies pursued by the U.S. Government at home and its policies of aggression abroad.

I call upon the workers, peasants, revolutionary intellectuals, enlightened elements of the bourgeoisie, and other enlightened personages of all colours in the world, white, black, yellow, brown, etc., to unite to oppose the racial discrimination practised by U.S. imperialism and to support the American Negroes in their struggle against racial discrimination. In the final analysis, a national struggle is a question of class struggle. In the United States, it is only the reactionary ruling clique among the whites which is oppressing the Negro people. They can in no way represent the workers, farmers, revolutionary intellectuals, and other enlightened persons who comprise the overwhelming majority of the white people. At present, it is the handful of imperialists, headed by the United States, and their supporters, the reactionaries in different countries, who are carrying out oppression, aggression and intimidation against the overwhelming majority of the nations and peoples of the world. They are the minority, and we are the majority. At most they make up less than ten per cent of the 3,000 million people of the world. I am deeply convinced that, with the support of more than ninety per cent of the people of the world, the just struggle of the American Negroes will certainly be victorious. The evil system of colonialism and imperialism grew up along with the enslavement of the Negroes and the trade in Negroes; it will surely come to its end with the thorough emancipation of the black people.

IX · M U.S. imperialism is the most ferocious enemy of the world's people[1]

The heroic struggle now being waged by the people of Panama against U.S. aggression and in defence of their national sovereignty is a great patriotic struggle. The Chinese people stand firmly on the side of the Panamanian people and fully support their just

1. Full text of Mao's statement of 12 January 1964 in support of the Panamanian people, *Hung-ch'i*, no. 2–3, 1964, pp. 2–3.
Available translations: *Peking Review*, no. 2, 1964.

action in opposing the U.S. aggressors and seeking to regain sovereignty over the Panama Canal Zone.

U.S. imperialism is the most ferocious enemy of the people of the entire world.

It has not only committed the grave crime of aggression against the Panamanian people, and painstakingly and stubbornly plotted against socialist Cuba, but has continuously been plundering and oppressing the people of the Latin American countries and suppressing the national-democratic revolutionary struggles there.

In Asia, U.S. imperialism has forcibly occupied China's Taiwan, turned the southern part of Korea and the southern part of Vietnam into its colonies, kept Japan under its control and semi-military occupation, sabotaged the peace, neutrality and independence of Laos, plotted to subvert the Royal Government of Cambodia, and committed intervention and aggression against other Asian countries. More recently, it has decided to send a U.S. fleet to the Indian Ocean, menacing the security of all the countries of south-east Asia.

In Africa, U.S. imperialism is feverishly pursuing its neo-colonialist policies, seeking vigorously to take the place of the old colonialists, to plunder and enslave the peoples of Africa, and to undermine and stamp out the national liberation movements.

The policies of aggression and war of U.S. imperialism also seriously threaten the Soviet Union, China, and the other socialist countries. Moreover, it is vigorously seeking to push its policy of 'peaceful evolution' in the socialist countries, in order to bring about the restoration of capitalism there and disintegrate the socialist camp.

Even toward its allies in Western Europe, North America and Oceania, U.S. imperialism is pursuing a policy of 'the law of the jungle',[1] trying hard to trample them underfoot.

The aggressive plans of U.S. imperialism to dominate the whole world run in a continuous line from Truman through Eisenhower and Kennedy to Johnson.

The people of the countries in the socialist camp should unite, the people of all the countries of Asia, Africa, and Latin America

1. Literally, 'the strong eat the flesh of the weak'.

should unite, the people of all the continents of the world should unite, all peace-loving countries and all countries that are subject to U.S. aggression, control, interference and bullying should unite, and so form the broadest united front to oppose the U.S. imperialist policies of aggression and war and to safeguard world peace.

Riding roughshod everywhere, U.S. imperialism has placed itself in the position of the enemy of the people the world over, and has increasingly isolated itself. The atom bombs and hydrogen bombs in the hands of the U.S. imperialists can never cow people not willing to be enslaved. The raging tide of the people of the world in opposition to the U.S. aggressors is irresistible. The struggle of the people the world over against U.S. imperialism and its running dogs will assuredly win still greater victories.

X. Relations with the Soviet Union and the Other Communist Parties

If communist and nationalist motives converged in the area covered by the previous chapter, they may easily conflict in the domain treated here. On the one hand, Mao Tse-tung long admired the Soviet leaders, particularly Stalin, and wanted to be their faithful disciple. On the other hand, he often observed that because of their distance from China and their ignorance of Chinese conditions, they gave very poor advice to the Chinese Communist Party. And in any case, he wanted to be the master in his own house.

The counterpoint between these two themes runs through the documents presented here regarding Mao's attitude toward the Soviet Union down to 1957. But in recent years, the problem has become more complex, for Mao has come to oppose Khrushchev and his successors not because of a pure conflict of national interest, but on the grounds that Soviet actions are harmful not merely to China but to the cause of world revolution. As suggested in the general introduction, how much Mao's proclamation that henceforth Peking constitutes the only genuine centre of Marxist-Leninist orthodoxy reflects a commitment to revolution for its own sake, and how much it betrays rather a concern for his own dignity and that of China, is one of the knottiest problems raised by the developments since 1963.

The first text, an extract from an interview with Edgar Snow in 1936, refers frankly to a possible conflict between the two imperatives of proletarian internationalism and Chinese nationalism. Regarding an eventual communist government in China, he says that it is only where the interests of the Chinese masses coincide with those of the Russian masses that such a government could be said to obey the will of Moscow. This clearly implies that in certain cases the interests of the Chinese masses and those of the Russian masses may diverge. To be sure, one must take account of Mao's purpose at the time, which was to appear as the leader of a truly national force in China. But there was very probably a large component of sincerity in these declarations.

Text X B, an extract from 'In memory of Norman Bethune', deals with the problem of internationalism and patriotism; since the first edition of this book was published, it has been singled out as one of the 'three constantly-read articles' by which Maoist morality is inculcated in China. Text X C, an extract from a speech to the cadres of the Communist Party, not an interview with a Western journalist, resembles Text X A in many ways. In particular, we find here the surprising affirmation that since 1935 the Comintern has not meddled (the Chinese term, *kan-she*, is not a particularly polite one) in the internal affairs of the Chinese Communist Party. One should also note Mao's affirmation that his and his comrades' task was even more complicated than that of the Soviet leaders. It is clear that in stating this, Mao wished to emphasize the ability of the Chinese leadership to deal with such difficult problems. Despite its contemporary ring, the statement that it is henceforth impossible to direct the world communist movement from a single centre is, on the contrary, not at all original, and was included in the official documents of the Comintern concerning its own dissolution.

Text X D shows that Mao long ago began to take an active interest in European politics and to attribute to himself responsibilities in this domain. The letter to Earl Browder, apart from the contrast it offers with the text following it, contains a curious manifestation of Mao's rather doctrinaire vision of the Western world. He appeared to believe that if revolution triumphed in China, Browder might replace Roosevelt in the White House. The original version of the telegram to William Z. Foster, which seemingly simply conveys the automatic approbation of a decision sanctioned by Moscow, contains a remarkable sentence deleted from the *Selected Works* thanking 'Comrade Browder', despite his disgrace, for his past services to China. This is another manifestation of Mao's independent attitude toward Moscow.

The three texts X G to X I show the evolution of Mao's

attitude toward Stalin. In the first of these, dating from 1939, Mao presents himself as the humble pupil of the Soviet dictator. In the present edition, Mao's article celebrating Stalin's sixtieth birthday, which originally constituted Text X G, has been replaced by his speech delivered on the same occasion. I hesitated between these two texts when compiling this anthology in the first place, and finally chose the article because a contemporary text was available, whereas the speech of 21 December is translated from the version published in 1949. The change has been made in the first instance because this speech is the *locus classicus* of Mao's famous statement, 'To rebel is justified', which provided the slogan for the all-out onslaught on the Party during the first phase of the Cultural Revolution. But it is also most interesting not only for the fulsomeness with which Stalin is praised, but for the limits of that praise. The Soviet leader is credited with developing and applying Marxism-Leninism, but not with making major theoretical contributions. And one cannot read Mao's justification of the need for a 'commander' who gives orders without finding in it a premonition of his own cult today.

Text X H, a eulogy of Stalin written immediately after the latter's death, represents the highpoint in Mao's praise of his 'great teacher'. Even as he wrote it, Mao must have been mindful of the 'mistakes' enumerated in Text X I, just as in this editorial of 1956 he stressed Stalin's achievements as well as his shortcomings.

Text X K, an extract from Mao's speech at Moscow airport in November 1957, and Text X M, a message to the Albanians written nine years later, illustrate the almost incredible distance travelled in the past decade. The Soviet leaders, who were hailed in 1957 for their contribution to the liberation of the oppressed peoples, have become in 1966 'slaves' who 'prostrate themselves before imperialism'. (As early as 1962, if the recently-published extract which appears as Text X L is authentic, Mao had in fact predicted that, as the Chinese press constantly clamours today, the Soviet people were about to rise up and overthrow their reactionary rulers.)

Text X J, dating from 1954, shows that cordial relations between Peking and Tirana are not merely of recent origin, but it would have been hard to predict that, as the Soviet leaders shrank in Mao's eyes to the dimensions of a 'dust heap', Enver Hoxha would become (in Text X M) 'a lofty mountain towering to the skies'. Particularly ironic is the denunciation of false friends and double dealers (obviously the Soviets) with 'honey dripping from their tongues and daggers concealed in their hearts' (*k'ou-mi fu-chien*), in exactly the same terms as Mao used in 1939, in celebrating Stalin's birthday, to characterize the imperialists. In Mao's eyes, Kosygin has succeeded Neville Chamberlain as a 'present-day Li Lin-fu'.

S.R.S.

X · A We are not going to turn the country over to Moscow![1]

Question: In actual practice, if the Chinese revolution were victorious, would the economic and political relationship between Soviet China and Soviet Russia be maintained within the Third International or a similar organization, or would there probably be some kind of actual merger of governments? Would the Chinese Soviet Government be comparable in its relation to Moscow to the present government of Outer Mongolia?

Answer: I assume this is a purely hypothetical question. As I have told you, the Red Army is not now seeking the hegemony of power, but a united China against Japanese imperialism.

The Third International is an organization in which the vanguard of the world proletariat brings together its collective experience for the benefit of all revolutionary peoples throughout the world. It is not an administrative organization nor has it any political power beyond that of an advisory capacity. Structurally it is not very different from the Second International, though in content it is vastly different. But just as no one would say that in a country where the Cabinet is organized by the social-democrats the Second International is dictator, so it is ridiculous to say that the Third International is dictator in countries where there are communist parties.

1. An extract from Edgar Snow's interview with Mao Tse-tung, 23 July 1936. (See note to Text VIII A.)

In the U.S.S.R., the Communist Party is in power, yet even there the Third International does not rule nor does it have any direct political power over the people at all. Similarly, it can be said that although the Communist Party of China is a member of the Comintern, still this in no sense means that Soviet China is ruled by Moscow or by the Comintern. We are certainly not fighting for an emancipated China in order to turn the country over to Moscow!

The Chinese Communist Party is only one party in China, and in its victory it will have to speak for the whole nation. It cannot speak for the Russian people or rule for the Third International, but only in the interests of the Chinese masses. Only where the interests of the Chinese masses coincide with the interests of the Russian masses can it be said to be 'obeying the will' of Moscow. But of course this basis of common benefit will be tremendously broadened, once the masses of China are in democratic power and socially and economically emancipated, like their brothers in Russia.

When Soviet governments have been established in many countries, the problem of an international union of soviets may arise, and it will be interesting to see how it will be solved. But today I cannot suggest the formula; it is a problem which has not been and cannot be solved in advance. In the world of today, with increasingly close economic and cultural intimacies between different states and peoples, such a union would seem to be highly desirable, if achieved on a voluntary basis.

Clearly, however, the last point is of utmost importance; such a world union could be successful only if every nation had the right to enter or leave the union according to the will of its people, and with its sovereignty intact, and certainly never at the 'command' of Moscow. No communist ever thought otherwise, and the myth of 'world domination from Moscow' is an invention of the fascists and counter-revolutionaries.

The relationship between Outer Mongolia and the Soviet Union, now and in the past, has always been based on the principle of complete equality. When the people's revolution has been victorious in China, the Outer Mongolian republic will automatically become a part of the Chinese federation, at its own will. The Mohammedan and Tibetan peoples, likewise, will form autonomous republics attached to the China federation.

X · B In memory of Norman Bethune[1]

A member of the Progressive Workers' Party of Canada, Comrade Norman Bethune was over fifty years of age when, sent by the Progressive Workers' Party of Canada and the Communist Party of the United States to help China in the Anti-Japanese War, he made light of a distance of thousands of miles and arrived in China. He came to Yenan last spring, went to work in the Wutai mountains, and unfortunately died a martyr to his duties. What kind of spirit is this that made a foreigner, without any selfish motive, regard the cause of the Chinese people's liberation as his own? It is the spirit of internationalism, the spirit of communism; and every Chinese communist must learn from this spirit. Leninism teaches that the world revolution can succeed only if the proletariat of the capitalist countries supports the struggle for liberation of the people of the colonies and semi-colonies, and the proletariat of the colonies and semi-colonies supports the struggle for liberation of the proletarians of the capitalist countries. Comrade Bethune put this Leninist line into practice. We Chinese communists must also carry out this line. We must unite with the proletarians of all the capitalist countries, with the proletarians of Japan, Britain, the United States, Germany, Italy, and all other capitalist countries; only then can we overthrow imperialism, and achieve the national and social liberation of our people and of all the peoples of the world. This is our internationalism, the internationalism with which we oppose both national chauvinism and narrow patriotism . . .

1. Extracted from Mao's eulogy, 21 December 1939, *Hsüan-chi*, II, p. 629.

Available translations: *Selected Works*, II, pp. 337–8.

X · C The Comintern has long ceased to meddle in our internal affairs[1]

... Comrade Mao Tse-tung first pointed out that the dissolution of the Communist International was, exactly as an American press agency had reported, 'a great event marking the dividing line between two epochs'...

Comrade Mao Tse-tung asked: 'Why should the Communist International be disbanded? Did it not devote all its efforts to the emancipation of the working class of the whole world and to the war against fascism?'

Comrade Mao Tse-tung said: 'It is true that the Communist International was created by Lenin himself. During its entire existence it has rendered the greatest services in helping each country to organize a truly revolutionary workers' party, and it has also contributed enormously to the great cause of organizing the anti-fascist war.' Comrade Mao Tse-tung pointed particularly to the great services of the Communist International in aiding the cause of the Chinese revolution...

Comrade Mao Tse-tung further pointed out: 'Revolutionary movements can be neither exported nor imported. Despite the fact that aid was accorded by the Communist International, the birth and development of the Chinese Communist Party resulted from the fact that China herself had a conscious working class. The Chinese working class created its own party – the Chinese Communist Party. The Chinese Communist Party, although it has a history of only twenty-two years, has already undertaken three great revolutionary movements.'...

Since the Communist International has rendered such great services to China and to various other countries, why should it be necessary to proclaim its dissolution? To this question Comrade Mao Tse-tung replied: 'It is a principle of Marxism-Leninism that

1. Extracted from a speech explaining the dissolution of the Communist International, delivered on 26 May 1943, to the cadres of the Chinese Communist Party, *Chieh-fang jih-pao*, 28 May 1943.

Available translations: Stuart Gelder, *The Chinese Communists*, Gollancz, 1946, pp. 169–71. (This translation is highly approximate, and omits some of the most important sentences and expressions.)

the forms of revolutionary organizations must be adapted to the necessities of the revolutionary struggle. If a form of organization is no longer adapted to the necessities of the struggle, then this form of organization must be abolished.'[1] Comrade Mao Tse-tung pointed out that at present the form of revolutionary organization known as the Communist International is no longer adapted to the necessities of the struggle. To continue this organizational form would, on the contrary, hinder the development of the revolutionary struggle in each country. What is needed now is the strengthening of the national Communist Party [*min-tsu Kung-ch'an-tang*] of each country, and we no longer need this international leading centre. There are three main reasons for this: (1) The internal situation in each country and the relations between the different countries are more complicated than they have been in the past and are changing more rapidly. It is no longer possible for a unified international organization to adapt itself to these extremely complicated and rapidly changing circumstances. Correct leadership must grow out of a detailed analysis of these conditions, and this makes it even more necessary for the Communist Party of each country to undertake this itself. The Communist International, which is far removed from the concrete struggle in each country, was adapted to the relatively simple conditions of the past, when changes took place rather slowly, but now it is no longer a suitable instrument. (2) . . . The anti-fascist states are of all kinds: socialist, capitalist, colonial, semi-colonial. Among the fascist states and their vassals there are also great differences; in addition, there are also the neutral countries, which find themselves in varying circumstances. For some time it has been felt that a centralized organization of an international character was not very appropriate for organizing rapidly and efficiently the anti-fascists of all these states, and this has become particularly obvious recently. (3) The leading cadres of the Communist Parties of the various countries have already grown up and attained political maturity. Comrade Mao Tse-tung explained this point by using the example of the Chinese Communist Party. The Chinese Communist Party has been through

1. This was quoted in October 1967 as an important teaching. See *Peking Review*, no. 44, 1967, p. 8.

three revolutionary movements. These revolutionary movements have been continuous and uninterrupted and extraordinarily complex, even more complex than the Russian Revolution. In the course of these revolutionary movements, the Chinese Communist Party has already acquired its own excellent cadres endowed with rich personal experience. Since the Seventh World Congress of the Communist International in 1935, the Communist International has not intervened in the internal affairs of the Chinese Communist Party. And yet, the Chinese Communist Party has done its work very well, throughout the whole Anti-Japanese War of National Liberation . . .

X · D Letter to the Spanish people[1]

People of Spain, Comrades in arms:

We, the Chinese Communist Party, the Chinese Red Army, and the Chinese Soviets, regard the war fought by the Spanish Republican Government as the most sacred war in the world. This war is being waged not only for the life of the Spanish people, but also for the oppressed peoples of the world, because the Spanish Government is resisting German and Italian fascism, which, with their Spanish accomplices, are destroying the culture, civilization, and justice of the world. The Spanish Government and the Spanish people are fighting the German and Italian fascists, who are in league with and giving support to the Japanese fascist invaders of China in the Far East. . . . Were it not for the support received from German and Italian fascism, Japanese fascism could not, as it is now doing, attack us like a mad dog . . .

We do not believe that the struggle of the Chinese people can be separated from your struggle in Spain. The Communist Party of China is supporting and encouraging you, the Spanish people, by struggling against Japanese fascism. The Communist Party of China, the Chinese Soviets, the Chinese Red Army, and the Chinese people are greatly moved by your defence of Madrid and

1. Extracted from a letter dated 15 May 1937, published in *Chieh-fang*, no. 4, June 1937, p. 3.

Available translations: *International Press Correspondence*, XVII, no. 26, p. 595.

by your victories on the northern and southern fronts. Each day our press here in the Soviet regions publishes reports and articles about your heroic struggle. . . . We firmly believe that the unity of your various parties in the People's Front is the basis for your final victory . . .

We know that your victory will directly aid us in our fight against Japanese fascism. Your cause is our cause. We read with emotion of the International Volunteers organized by people from every land, and we are glad that there are Chinese and Japanese in their ranks. Many comrades of the Chinese Red Army also wish to go to Spain to join you. . . . Were it not that we are face to face with the Japanese enemy, we would join you and take our place in your front ranks.

As many of you know, the Chinese Red Army has carried on a ceaseless and hard struggle for ten years. We fought without resources, through hunger and cold, with insufficient arms, ammunition, and medical supplies, until at last we won our victories. We know that you and your army are also passing through great hardships such as we also have passed through, and we are certain that you will be victorious. Our ten years' struggle has proved that if a revolutionary people and their revolutionary army are not afraid of suffering, but continue to fight heroically and unyieldingly against the enemy, they will be victorious . . .

X · E Letter to Comrade Browder[1]

Dear Comrade Browder:

Taking advantage of the visit of a comrade, I am sending this letter to you, honoured Comrade Browder, the good friend of the Chinese people and the leader of the American people . . .

We have heard from several American comrades and from other quarters that the American Communist Party and the great mass of the American people are profoundly concerned about China's anti-Japanese struggle, and they have already aided us in several ways. This gives us the feeling that our struggle is not an isolated

1. Extracted from *Mao Tse-tung lun-wen-chi*, pp. 156–7.
Available translations: none.

one, that we are receiving heroic assistance from abroad; at the same time, we have the feeling that, when we obtain victory, this victory will be of great assistance to the struggle of the American people for liberation.

Today's world is on the eve of a great explosion, and the working class of the whole world, as well as all the peoples seeking liberation, must certainly unite and carry on a common struggle.

Revolutionary greetings!

MAO TSE-TUNG

24 June [1937]

X · F Telegram to Comrade Foster[1]

To Comrade Foster and to the Central Committee of the American Communist Party:

We are happy to hear that the extraordinary conference of the Communist Political Association of the United States has decided to reject the revisionist and capitulationist line of *Comrade* Browder and to re-establish a Marxist leadership, and that it has reconstituted the American Communist Party. We congratulate you warmly on this great victory of the American working class and of the Marxist movement. *In his past activity, Comrade Browder has rendered many services to the struggle of the Chinese people, which deserve our gratitude.* But his whole revisionist and capitulationist line (which found its full expression in *Comrade* Browder's book *Teheran*), essentially reflected the influence of the reactionary capitalist clique in the United States within the American workers' movement. This reactionary capitalist clique is now attempting to extend its influence in China, too, and is supporting the erroneous, anti-national, anti-popular, and anti-democratic policy of the reactionary clique within the Kuomintang, putting the Chinese people in a grave danger of civil war, and causing prejudice to the interests of *the two great peoples, Chinese and American, during and after the war*. The victory of the

1. This is the full text of the missive as it appeared in *Chieh-fang jih-pao* 31 July 1945.

Available translation: *Selected Works*, III, p. 337.

American working class and of its vanguard, the American Communists, over the revisionist and capitulationist line of *Comrade* Browder will undoubtedly represent a great contribution to the war against Japan actually being waged by the American and Chinese peoples, and to the great cause of the edification of a peaceful and democratic world after the war.

Chairman of the Central Committee of the Chinese Communist Party:
MAO TSE-TUNG
29 July [*1945*]

X · G Stalin is our commander[1]

Today we are holding a meeting to congratulate Stalin on his sixtieth birthday. 'From ancient times, few men have reached the age of seventy,' and to live to the age of sixty is also rare. But why is it that we celebrate only Stalin's birthday? And why is it, moreover, that such celebrations are taking place not only in Yenan, but in the whole country and in the whole world? Provided only that they know who the man is who was born this day, provided they know what manner of man he is, then all those who suffer oppression will congratulate him. For Stalin is the saviour of all the oppressed. What kind of people are opposed to congratulating him, and do not like to congratulate him? Only those who do not suffer oppression, but on the contrary oppress other people, first of all the imperialists.

Comrades! A foreigner, who is separated from us by thousands of miles, and whose birthday is yet celebrated by everyone – is this not an unprecedented event?

This is because he is leading the great Soviet Union, because he is leading the great Communist International, because he is leading the cause of the liberation of all mankind, and is helping China to fight Japan.

At the present time, the whole world is divided into two fronts

1. Full text of Mao's speech at a meeting in Yenan on 21 December 1939, as printed in *Jen-min jih-pao*, 20 December 1949.
Available translations: none.

struggling against one another. On the one side is imperialism, which represents the front of the oppressors. On the other side is socialism, which represents the front of resistance to oppression. Some people imagine that the national-revolutionary front in the colonies and semi-colonies occupies an intermediate position, but its enemy is imperialism, and hence it cannot do otherwise than call upon the friendship of socialism, and it cannot but belong to the revolutionary front of resistance to the oppressors. China's diehards imagine that they can play the harlot and at the same time set up arches in honour of their own virtue, fighting communism with one hand and resisting Japan with the other. They call themselves the middle-of-the-road faction, but they will never achieve their aims. If they do not repent, they will certainly end by going over to the side of counter-revolution. Both the revolutionary and the counter-revolutionary fronts must have someone to act as their leader, someone to serve as their commander. Who is the commander of the counter-revolutionary front? It is imperialism, it is Chamberlain. Who is the commander of the revolutionary front? It is socialism, it is Stalin. Comrade Stalin is the leader of the world revolution. Because he is there, it is easier to get things done. As you know, Marx is dead, and Engels and Lenin too are dead. If we did not have a Stalin, who would give the orders? This is indeed a fortunate circumstance. Because there is in the world today a Soviet Union, a Communist Party, and a Stalin, the affairs of this world can be more easily dealt with. What does a revolutionary commander do? He sees to it that everyone has food to eat, clothes to wear, a place to live, and books to read. And in order to attain these objectives, he must lead a thousand-odd million men in struggle against the oppressors, and bring them to final victory. This is precisely what Stalin will do. Since this is the case, should not all those who suffer oppression congratulate Stalin? I think they should, I think they must. We should congratulate him, support him, and study him.

The two aspects of Stalin which we want to study are the doctrinal and practical aspect.

There are innumerable principles of Marxism, but in the last analysis they can all be summed up in one sentence: 'To rebel is justified.' For thousands of years everyone said: 'Oppression is justified, exploitation is justified, rebellion is not justified.' From the time when Marxism appeared on the scene, this old judgement was turned upside down, and this is a great contribution. This principle was derived by the proletariat from its struggles, but Marx drew the conclusion. In accordance with this principle, there was then resistance, there was struggle, and socialism was realized. What is Comrade Stalin's contribution? He developed this principle, he developed Marxism-Leninism, and produced a very clear, concrete and living doctrine for the oppressed people of the whole world. This is the complete doctrine of establishing a revolutionary front, overthrowing imperialism, overthrowing capitalism, and establishing a socialist society.

The practical aspect consists in turning doctrine into reality. Neither Marx, Engels, nor Lenin carried to completion the cause of the establishment of socialism, but Stalin did so. This is a great and unprecedented exploit. Before the Soviet Union's two five-year plans, the capitalist newspapers of various countries proclaimed daily that the Soviet Union was in desperate straits, that socialism could not be relied upon, but what do we see today? Stalin has stopped Chamberlain's mouth, and also the mouth of those Chinese diehards. They all recognize that the Soviet Union has triumphed.

Stalin has helped us from the doctrinal standpoint in our war of resistance against Japan. Apart from this, he has given us material and practical aid. Since the victory of Stalin's cause, he has aided us with many airplanes, cannons, aviators, and military advisers in every domain, as well as lending us money. What other country in the world has helped us in this way? What country in the world, led by what class, party, and individual, has helped us in this way? Who is there, apart from the Soviet Union, the proletariat, the Communist Party, and Stalin?

At the present time there are people who call themselves our friends, but in fact they can only be classed with Li Lin-fu of the Tang Dynasty. This Mr Li Lin-fu was a man who had 'honey dripping from his tongue and daggers concealed in his heart'. The imperialists all have honey dripping from their tongues and daggers concealed in their hearts, and Chamberlain is a present-day Li Lin-fu. What imperialist country has abolished the special privileges enjoyed by many countries in China such as the right to station troops, consular jurisdiction, extra-territoriality and so on? Not a single one. Only the Soviet Union has abolished them.

In the past, Marxism-Leninism provided theoretical guidance to the world revolution. Today something has been added: it is possible to give material aid to the world revolution. This is Stalin's great contribution.

After we have celebrated Stalin's birthday, we must continue to carry out propaganda among the people of the whole country to make these facts known. We must explain things clearly to the 450 million Chinese, so that our whole people understands: only the socialist Soviet Union, only Stalin, are the good friends of China.

X · H The greatest friendship[1]

Joseph Vissarionovich Stalin, the greatest genius of the present age, the great teacher of the world communist movement, the comrade-in-arms of the immortal Lenin, has departed from the world.

Comrade Stalin's contribution to our era through his theoretical and practical work is beyond estimation. Comrade Stalin is representative of the whole of this new era of ours. His activities have led the Soviet people and the working people of all countries to transform the whole world situation, which means that the cause of justice, of people's democracy and socialism, has attained victory over an immense sector in the world, a sector embracing 800 million people – more than one third of the earth's population . . .

Comrade Stalin was responsible for over-all, epoch-making

1. Extracted from a tribute written on the occasion of Stalin's death in March 1953, published under the above title. (*Tsui wei-ta-ti yu-i*, Peking, 1953, *passim*.)

Available translations: *Daily News Release*, Hsinhua Agency, no. 1265, 10 March 1953, pp. 1–2.

developments in the theories of Marxism-Leninism and impelled Marxism forward to a new stage. Comrade Stalin creatively developed Lenin's theory on the law of uneven development of capitalism and the theory that socialism can first be victorious in one country; Comrade Stalin creatively contributed the theory of the general crisis of the capitalist system, contributed the theory of building communism in the Soviet Union, contributed the theory of the fundamental economic laws of present-day capitalism and socialism, contributed the theory of the revolution in colonial and semi-colonial countries. Comrade Stalin also creatively developed Lenin's theory on Party-building. All these creative theories of Comrade Stalin further united the workers throughout the world, further united the oppressed classes and the oppressed peoples throughout the world, thereby enabling the struggle for liberation and happiness on the part of the world working class and all oppressed people and the victory of this struggle to attain unprecedented scope.

All the writings of Comrade Stalin are immortal Marxist documents. His works, *The Foundations of Leninism*, *The History of the C.P.S.U. (Bolsheviks)*, and his last great work, *Economic Problems of Socialism in the U.S.S.R.*, are an encyclopedia of Marxism-Leninism, the summation of the experience of the world communist movement in the past hundred years. . . . We Chinese communists, like the communists of all countries of the world, sought our own road to victory in the great works of Comrade Stalin.

Since the passing of Lenin, Comrade Stalin has always been the central figure in the world communist movement. We rallied around him, ceaselessly asked his advice, and constantly drew ideological strength from his works. Comrade Stalin was full of warm love for the oppressed people of the East. 'Do not forget the East' was Comrade Stalin's great call before and after the October Revolution. Everyone knows that Comrade Stalin had an ardent love for the Chinese people and believed the might of the Chinese revolution to be immeasurable. To the problems of the Chinese revolution he contributed his sublime wisdom. And it was by following the theories of Lenin and Stalin and with the support of the great Soviet Union and all the revolutionary forces of all other countries that the Chinese Communist Party and the Chinese people a few years ago won their historic victory.

Now we have lost our great teacher and most sincere friend – Comrade Stalin. What a calamity this is! No words exist to express the sorrow that this misfortune has brought us.

Our task is to transform sorrow into strength. In memory of our great teacher Stalin, the great friendship that exists in the name of Stalin between the Communist Party of China and the Chinese people and the Communist Party of the Soviet Union and the Soviet people will be boundlessly strengthened . . .

The Communist Party of the Soviet Union is a party personally nurtured by Lenin and Stalin; it is the most advanced, the most experienced, and the most theoretically cultivated Party in the world. This Party has been and is our model both in the past and at present and will still be our model in the future. We fully believe the Central Committee of the Communist Party of the Soviet Union and the Soviet Government, headed by Comrade Malenkov, will definitely be able to follow Comrade Stalin's behest to drive forward the great cause of communism and carry it to further glorious fruition . . .

The reason why the friendship between the great peoples of China and the Soviet Union is unbreakable is that our friendship has been built up on the great principles of internationalism of Marx, Engels, Lenin, and Stalin . . .

Manifestly, the strength created by this kind of friendship of ours is infinite and truly invincible.

Let all imperialist aggressors and warmongers tremble before our great friendship!

Long live the theories of Marx, Engels, Lenin, and Stalin!

Eternal glory to the heroic name of the great Stalin!

X · I Stalin's place in history[1]

. . . After Lenin's death, Stalin, as the chief leader of the Party and the state, creatively applied and developed Marxism-

1. Extracted from the *Jen-min jih-pao* editorial of 5 April 1956. (See note to Text VI B 2.)

Leninism. In the struggle to defend the legacy of Leninism against its enemies – the Trotskyites, Zinovievites, and other bourgeois agents – Stalin expressed the will and wishes of the people and proved himself to be an outstanding Marxist-Leninist fighter. The reason Stalin won the support of the Soviet people and played an important role in history was primarily that he, together with the other leaders of the Communist Party of the Soviet Union, brought about the triumph of socialism in the Soviet Union and created the conditions for the victory of the Soviet Union in the war against Hitler; these victories of the Soviet people conformed to the interests of the working class of the world and all progressive mankind. It was therefore quite natural for the name of Stalin to be greatly honoured throughout the world. But, having won such high honour among the people both at home and abroad by his correct application of the Leninist line, Stalin erroneously exaggerated his own role and counterposed his individual authority to the collective leadership, and as a result certain of his actions were opposed to certain fundamental Marxist-Leninist concepts he himself had propagated . . .

Marxist-Leninists hold that leaders play a big role in history. The people and their parties need forerunners who are able to represent the interests and will of the people, stand in the forefront of their historic struggles, and serve as their leaders. . . . But when any leader of the Party or the state places himself over and above the Party and the masses instead of in their midst, when he alienates himself from the masses, he ceases to have an all-round, penetrating insight into the affairs of the state. As long as this was the case, even so outstanding a personality as Stalin could not avoid making unrealistic and erroneous decisions on certain important matters. . . . During the latter part of his life, Stalin took more and more pleasure in this cult of the individual and violated the Party's system of democratic centralism and the principle of combining collective leadership with individual responsibility. As a result, he made some serious mistakes: for example, he broadened the scope of the suppression of counter-revolution; he lacked the necessary vigilance on the eve of the anti-fascist war; he failed to pay proper attention to the further development of agriculture and the material welfare of the peasantry; he gave certain wrong advice on the international communist movement, and, in particular, made a wrong decision on the question of Yugoslavia. On these issues, Stalin fell victim to subjectivism and one-sidedness and divorced himself from objective reality and from the masses.

The cult of the individual is a rotten carry-over from the long history of mankind. The cult of the individual is rooted not only in the exploiting classes but also in the small producers. As is well known, patriarchism is a product of small-producer economy . . .

The struggle against the cult of the individual, which was launched by the Twentieth Congress, is a great and courageous fight by the communists and the people of the Soviet Union to clear away the ideological obstacles blocking their advance . . .

It must be pointed out that Stalin's works should, as before, still be seriously studied and that we should accept all that is of value in them, as an important historical legacy, especially those many works in which he defended Leninism and correctly summarized the experience of building up the Soviet Union. . . . But there are two ways of studying them – the Marxist way and the doctrinaire way. Some people treat Stalin's writings in a doctrinaire manner and therefore cannot analyse and see what is correct and what is not – and everything that is correct they consider a panacea and apply indiscriminately, and thus inevitably they make mistakes. For instance, Stalin put forward a formula that in different revolutionary periods the main blow should be so directed as to isolate the middle-of-the-road social and political forces of the time. This formula of Stalin's should be treated according to circumstances and from a critical, Marxist point of view. In certain circumstances it may be correct to isolate the middle forces, but it is not correct to isolate them under all circumstances. Our experience teaches us that the main blow of the revolution should be directed at the chief enemy and to isolate him, whereas with the middle forces, a policy of both uniting with them and struggling against them should be adopted, so that they are at least neutralized; and, as circumstances permit, efforts should be made to shift them from their position of neutrality to one of alliance with us in order to facilitate the development of the revolution. But there was a time – the ten years of civil war from 1927 to 1936 – when some of our comrades crudely applied this formula of Stalin's to China's revolution by turning their main attack on the middle forces, singling them out as the most dangerous enemy; the result was that, instead of isolating the real enemy, we isolated ourselves and suffered losses to the advantage of the real enemy. In the light of this doctrinaire error, the Central Committee of the Communist Party of China during the period of the anti-Japanese war formulated a policy of 'developing the progressive forces, winning over the middle-of-the-roaders, and isolating the diehards' for the purpose of defeating the Japanese aggressors. . . .

Some people consider that Stalin was wrong in everything. This is a grave misconception. Stalin was a great Marxist-Leninist, yet at the same time a Marxist-Leninist who committed several gross errors without realizing that they were errors. We should view Stalin from a historical standpoint, make a proper and all-round analysis to see where he was right and where he was wrong, and draw useful lessons therefrom. Both the things he did right and the things he did wrong were phenomena of the international communist movement and bore the imprint of the times. Taken as a whole, the international communist movement is only a little over a hundred years old and it is only thirty-nine years since the victory of the October Revolution; experience in many fields of revolutionary work is still inadequate. Great achievements have been made, but there are still shortcomings and mistakes . . .

Reactionary forces the world over are pouring ridicule on this event; they jeer at the fact that we are overcoming mistakes in our camp. But what will come of all this ridicule? There is not the slightest doubt that these scoffers will find themselves facing a still more powerful, forever invincible, great camp of peace and socialism, headed by the Soviet Union, while the murderous, bloodsucking enterprises of these scoffers will be in a pretty fix.

X · J The Albanian people has a glorious revolutionary tradition[1]

... The Albanian people is a hard-working and courageous people with a glorious and historic revolutionary tradition. In the ten years since its liberation, the Albanian people, under the leadership of the Albanian Labour Party, has smashed all the plots and attempts at sabotage of internal and external enemies. It is now engaged in building a beautiful life for itself with complete confidence, and it has obtained brilliant successes. In the struggle to build socialism and to defend the independence and the security of its fatherland, the Albanian people has displayed a patriotic spirit and an incomparable enthusiasm for work that have aroused the admiration of the Chinese people . . .

During the past five years, our two peoples have already established a fraternal friendship. I am profoundly convinced that, following the exchange of ambassadors, the sincere and friendly collaboration between our two countries will not fail to develop further. This will not only contribute to the happiness of the peoples of our two countries, but will also help to strengthen the world forces for peace and democracy, headed by the Soviet Union.

X · K No power on earth can separate us[2]

Dear Comrades Khrushchev, Voroshilov, and Bulganin:
Dear Comrades and Friends:

... The anniversary of the October Revolution is a great festival of victory for the Soviet people and for the proletariat, the labouring masses, and all oppressed peoples of the world. The

1. Extracted from Mao's reply to the speech of the Albanian ambassador, on the occasion of the ambassador's presentation of credentials, 13 September 1954; published in *Hsin-hua yüeh-pao*, no. 10, 1954, pp. 189.

Available translations: none.

2. Extracted from Mao's speech at the Moscow airport, 2 November 1957. (*Mao Chu-hsi tsai Su-lien-ti yen-lun*, pp. 1–2.)

Available translations: S.C.M.P., no. 1646.

victory won by the Soviet people under the leadership of the great Lenin and the great Communist Party of the Soviet Union forty years ago initiated a new epoch in human history. In the process of forty years of construction, the Soviet Union has made brilliant achievements at an extraordinary speed and in many fields has advanced to the forefront of the countries of the world, thus setting an outstanding example for the peoples who are striving for progress and happiness. The launching of the first man-made earth satellite by the Soviet Union is no simple feat. It marks the beginning of a new era of man's further conquest of nature.

The socialist camp headed by the Soviet Union is a strong bulwark ensuring world peace and a faithful friend to all peoples who refuse to suffer imperialist oppression and enslavement . . .

The October Revolution enabled the Chinese people to find the way to emancipation, prosperity, wealth, and power [*fu ch'iang*]. In their own cause, the Chinese people have received tremendous sympathy and generous assistance from the people of the Soviet Union. The peoples of our two countries have already formed a fraternal alliance in their common struggles, and there is no force on earth which can separate us.

Comrades, we will stand together forever, fighting for world peace and for the victory of our common cause!

Glory to the great October Socialist Revolution!

Glory to the great Soviet people and to the great Communist Party of the Soviet Union!

Long live the great friendship between the Chinese and Soviet peoples!

Long live world peace!

X · L Revisionist rule will not last long[1]

The Soviet Union was the first socialist state, and the Communist

1. Full text of a statement reputedly made in 1962, attributed to Mao and quoted in a joint *People's Daily – Red Flag – Liberation Army Daily* editorial of 6 November 1967, on the occasion of the fiftieth anniversary of the October Revolution, *Hung-ch'i*, no. 16, 1967, p. 17.
Available translations: *Peking Review*, no. 46, 1967, p. 16.

Party of the Soviet Union was founded by Lenin. Although the leadership of the Soviet Party and state has now been usurped by the revisionists, I would urge comrades to remain firm in the conviction that the broad masses of the Soviet people, Party members, and cadres are good, that they want revolution, and that revisionist rule will not last long.

10 · M The Soviet leading clique is a mere dust heap[1]

To the Fifth Congress of the Albanian Party of Labour
Dear Comrades:

The Communist Party of China and the Chinese people send their warmest congratulations to the Fifth Congress of the Albanian Party of Labour.

We wish your congress every success!

The glorious Albanian Party of Labour, headed by Comrade Enver Hoxha, is firmly holding aloft the revolutionary red banner of Marxism-Leninism while encircled ring upon ring by the imperialists and the modern revisionists.

Heroic people's Albania has become a great beacon of socialism in Europe.

The revisionist leading clique of the Soviet Union, the Tito clique of Yugoslavia, and all the other cliques of renegades and scabs of various shades are mere dust heaps in comparison, while you, a lofty mountain, tower to the skies. They are slaves and accomplices of imperialism, before which they prostrate themselves, while you are dauntless proletarian revolutionaries who dare to fight imperialism and its running dogs, fight the world's tyrannical enemies.

The Soviet Union, Yugoslavia, and all those countries where the modern revisionist clique is in power have either changed colour or are in the process of doing so. Capitalism has been or is being restored there, and the dictatorship of the proletariat has been or

1. Full text of Mao's message of greetings to the Fifth Congress of the Albanian Party of Labour, dated 25 October 1966, *Hung-ch'i*, no. 15, 1966, pp. 1–2.

Available translations: *Peking Review*, no. 46, 1966, p. 5.

is being transformed into the dictatorship of the bourgeoisie. Against this adverse current of counter-revolutionary revisionism, heroic socialist Albania has stood firm. Persevering in the Marxist-Leninist revolutionary line, you have adopted a series of measures of revolutionization and consolidated the dictatorship of the proletariat. Taking the path of socialism, you are building your country independently and have won brilliant victories. You have contributed precious experience to the history of the dictatorship of the proletariat.

'A bosom friend afar brings a distant land near.' China and Albania are separated by thousands of mountains and rivers but our hearts are closely linked. We are your true friends and comrades. And you are ours. We are not like those false friends and double-dealers who have honey dripping from their tongues and daggers concealed in their hearts, and neither are you. Our militant revolutionary friendship has stood the test of violent storms.

The truth of Marxism-Leninism is on our side. The international proletariat is on our side. The oppressed nations and oppressed peoples are on our side. The masses of people who constitute over ninety per cent of the world's population are on our side. We have friends all over the world. We are not afraid of being isolated, and we most certainly can never be isolated. We are invincible. The handful of pitiful insects who oppose China and Albania are doomed to failure.

We are now in a great new era of world revolution. The revolutionary storms in Asia, Africa and Latin America are sure to deal the whole of the old world a decisive and crushing blow. The great victories of the Vietnamese people's war against U.S. aggression and for national salvation are convincing proof of this. The proletariat and working people of Europe, North America and Oceania are in the midst of a new awakening. The U.S. imperialists and all other such harmful insects have already created their own grave-diggers; the day of their burial cannot be far off.

Naturally, the road of our advance is by no means straight and smooth. Comrades, please rest assured that whatever may happen in the world, our two Parties and our two peoples will always be united, will always fight together and be victorious together.

Let the Parties and peoples of China and Albania unite, let the Marxist-Leninists of the whole world unite, let the revolutionary people of the whole world unite and overthrow imperialism, modern revisionism, and the reactionaries of every country! A new world without imperialism, without capitalism, and without any system of exploitation is certain to be built.

A Brief Chronology

1893 December: Mao is born in the village of Shao Shan, Hunan Province.

1895 China, defeated by Japan, is forced to recognize the independence of Korea and to cede Taiwan and the Pescadores to Japan.

1898 Failure of the reform attempted by K'ang Yu-wei, Liang Ch'i-ch'ao, and T'an Ssu-t'ung.

1900 Boxer uprising is quelled.

1911 October: Outbreak of the revolution. Mao joins the anti-imperial army and remains in it for six months.

1913 Mao becomes a student of the Fourth Normal School in Changsha, and then is transferred to the First Normal School when the two schools amalgamate.

1915 *Hsin ch'ing-nien* is founded by Ch'en Tu-hsiu. Mao becomes a faithful reader.

1917 *Hsin ch'ing-nien* publishes 'A study of physical culture' by Erh-shih-pa-hua Sheng (Mao Tse-tung).

1918 Spring: Mao graduates from the First Normal School.
Formation of the first Marxist study groups at Peking University, under the leadership of Li Ta-chao and others.
Autumn: Mao goes to Peking and becomes a librarian's assistant at the University. The head librarian is Li Ta-chao.

1919 April: Mao goes to Shanghai with some friends who are going to France, and then returns to Changsha.
4 May: Beginning of the celebrated protest movement of the students against the decision of the Paris Peace Conference giving Shantung to Japan.
July: Mao Tse-tung founds *Hsiang-chiang p'ing-lun*, a review propagating the ideas of the May 4th Movement. He organizes protest movements of the students against the local warlord and against Japan and participates in a variety of other literary and political enterprises.

1920 Mao Tse-tung organizes a communist group in Hunan and works in the labour movement.

1921 July: Mao is one of the participants in the First Congress of the Chinese Communist Party in Shanghai.
October: Mao becomes Secretary of the Chinese Communist Party for Hunan Province.

1922 August: The Central Committee of the Chinese Communist Party, urged on by the emissary of the International, adopts the policy by which communists will join the Kuomintang as individual members.

1923 June: Mao is elected to the Central Committee of the Chinese Communist Party by the Third Congress of the Party.

1924 January: The First National Congress of the Kuomintang approves the reorganization of the Party and the admission of communists as members. The policy adopted by the Chinese Communist Party in August 1922 can thus be put into practice on a large scale. Mao Tse-tung participates in the Congress, and is elected an alternate member of the Kuomintang Central Executive Committee.
February: Mao assumes important functions in the Shanghai Bureau of the Kuomintang, under Wang Ching-wei and Hu Han-min.
Autumn: Mao, under attack from his comrades in the Chinese Communist Party for his excessive zeal in cooperating with the Kuomintang, retires to his native village for a rest.

1925 May: Mao Tse-tung leaves Shao Shan and undertakes to organize the peasant movement in Hunan.
30 May: The police of the British concession in Shanghai open fire on a demonstration of students and workers, killing several persons. During the succeeding weeks, a vast strike movement gets under way in Shanghai and Canton, accompanied by a boycott of Hong Kong.
October: Threatened with arrest as a result of his work in organizing peasant associations in Hunan, Mao flees to Canton, where he works in the Peasant Bureau of the Kuomintang.
December: Mao Tse-tung becomes editor of a new Kuomintang organ, *Cheng-chih chou-pao* (*The Political Weekly*).

1926 January: Mao participates in the Second Congress of the Kuomintang, where he advocates leniency toward the extreme right wing of the party.
20 March: First incident between Chiang Kai-shek and the communists.
May: Mao becomes principal of the Kuomintang Peasant

Movement Training Institute for the Sixth Session, from May to October.

June: Beginning of the Northern Expedition against the warlords and their government in Peking.

1927 January–February: Mao visits Hunan once more and writes his 'Report on an Investigation of the Peasant Movement in Hunan.'

March: Chiang Kai-shek occupies Shanghai and Nanking.

March: Mao Tse-tung participates in the Third Plenum of the Kuomintang Central Executive Committee in Wuhan.

April: Raid on the Soviet Embassy in Peking. Li Ta-chao is arrested and strangled. Chiang Kai-shek decimates the workers' organizations in Shanghai and consolidates his power by mass executions.

April: Mao drafts a resolution on the agrarian question for the Kuomintang Land Committee, and advocates the confiscation of the rich peasants' land.

June: On orders from Stalin, Mao helps restrain 'peasant excesses' in his capacity as a member of the Executive Committee of the All-China Peasant Association.

August: Uprising at Nanchang by troops under the command of Yeh T'ing and Ho Lung. Mao is sent to Changsha to lead an uprising during the autumn harvest.

September: After the failure of the Autumn Harvest Uprising, Mao takes refuge with the remnants of his forces in the Chingkang Mountains and establishes a revolutionary base there.

November: P'eng P'ai, who has been organizing the peasants for several years, founds the first Chinese Soviet government in Hailufeng; this government survives until February 1928.

November: The Central Committee of the Chinese Communist Party censors Mao Tse-tung for his 'military opportunism' and removes him from all his posts in the Party hierarchy.

December: On orders from Stalin, the Chinese Communists undertake the uprising known as the 'Canton Commune', which is rapidly repressed.

1928 April: Junction of Mao's forces with those of Chu Te in the Chingkang Mountains, and creation of the Fourth Army of the Chinese Workers' and Peasants' Red Army. Chu Te becomes military commander, Mao Tse-tung political commissar.

1929 August: Mao and Chu establish a Soviet regime in Kiangsi.

1930 July: Failure of the attempt to take and hold Changsha, ordered by Li Li-san.

November: Chiang Kai-shek launches his first 'campaign of encirclement' against the Soviet areas in Kiangsi.
The Communist International condemns the 'adventurist' line of Li Li-san.

1931 May: Chiang Kai-shek launches his second encirclement campaign.
July: Chiang Kai-shek launches his third encirclement campaign.
September: Japanese attack against Mukden.
Autumn: Pursued by the police, the principal leaders of the Chinese Communist Party, who had hitherto been living underground in Shanghai, begin to take refuge in the Soviet base in Kiangsi.
November: The first All-Chinese Congress of Soviets, at Juichin, proclaims the establishment of the Chinese Soviet Republic and elects Mao chairman.

1932 April: The Provisional Central Government of the Chinese Soviet Republic declares war on Japan.
May: Conclusion of an armistice between the Nationalist Government and Japan.
June: Chiang Kai-shek launches his fourth encirclement campaign.

1933 January: The Chinese communists offer to conclude an alliance with 'any armed force' which is prepared to wage a joint struggle against Japan.
October: Chiang Kai-shek launches his fifth encirclement campaign.
November–December: The Chinese communists fail to come to the aid of the Fukien rebels, led by Ts'ai T'ing-k'ai, with whom they had concluded an 'anti-Chiang agreement' on 26 October.

1934 January: Second All-Chinese Congress of Soviets.
October: Beginning of the 'Long March'.

1935 January: A special conference of the Politburo of the Chinese Communist Party at last puts Mao Tse-tung in effective control of the Party.
Autumn: Arrival of the first elements of the Red Army, led by Mao, in the north-west.

1936 August: Letter of the Central Committee of the Chinese Communist Party to the Kuomintang proposing collaboration against Japan.
December: Following the Sian incident, Chiang Kai-shek

modifies his attitude toward cooperation with the communists.

1937 July: Beginning of Japanese war of aggression against China.
15 July: Agreement between the Chinese communists and Chiang Kai-shek.
August–October: The Chinese Communist Party announces the transformation of the Chinese Soviet Republic into a regional authority; the Red Army becomes the Eighth Route Army and the New Fourth Army.

1938 October: In his report entitled 'On the new stage', Mao Tse-tung gives a theoretical justification for the policy of collaboration with the Kuomintang.

1939–1940 December–January: In two important writings, entitled 'The Chinese revolution and the Chinese Communist Party' and 'On new democracy', Mao Tse-tung formulates a line involving fewer concessions to the Kuomintang.

1941 January: Attack of Nationalist troops against the New Fourth Army.

1942 February: Mao launches the 'rectification' (*cheng-feng*) movement for the ideological remoulding of the Chinese Communist Party.

1945 April: Mao delivers a report 'On coalition government' to the Seventh Congress of the Chinese Communist Party.
August: Mao flies to Chungking to negotiate with Chiang Kai-shek.
10 October: Agreement between the Chinese Communist Party and the Kuomintang, followed almost immediately by the outbreak of new hostilities.

1946 January: Cease-fire agreement, negotiated by General Marshall.
July: Beginning of large-scale civil war.

1947 December: In his report 'The present situation and our tasks', Mao Tse-tung announces an offensive on all fronts.

1949 January: Peking is occupied by the communists.
April: Following the collapse of the efforts for a negotiated peace with the Kuomintang, Mao Tse-tung orders the People's Liberation Army to cross the Yangtse and to pursue the conquest of China.
June: Mao Tse-tung writes 'On people's democratic dictatorship'.
October: Mao Tse-tung proclaims the establishment of the Chinese People's Republic.
November: The Nationalist Government moves to Taiwan.
December: Arrival of Mao in Moscow.

1950 February: Conclusion of a Sino–Soviet treaty of friendship and alliance.
June: Mao Tse-tung and Liu Shao-ch'i advocate carrying out land reform with moderation, and 'preserving a rich-peasant economy' in order to promote production.
October: Intervention of Chinese 'volunteers' in Korea.

1951 Mao launches a series of campaigns – 'thought reform' of the intellectuals, the campaign against counter-revolutionaries, the 'Three-Antis' and 'Five-Antis' – in order to re-shape Chinese society and the thinking of the Chinese people.

1953 January: *Jen-min jih-pao* announces the beginning of the first Five-Year Plan.
August: Signature of the armistice in Korea.

1955 July: Mao's report 'On the question of agricultural co-operation' marks a brisk acceleration of agricultural collectivization.

1956 April: Mao's viewpoint on 'de-Stalinization' is given in a *Jen-min jih-pao* editorial entitled 'On the historical experience of the dictatorship of the proletariat'.

1957 February: Mao's speech 'On the correct way of handling contradictions among the people'.
November: Mao Tse-tung, in Moscow, proclaims that henceforth the East wind will prevail over the West wind.

1958 May: Liu Shao-ch'i, at the second session of the Eighth Congress of the Chinese Communist Party, launches the policy of the 'Great Leap Forward' and the theory of the 'permanent revolution'.
September: Mao Tse-tung advocates the creation of People's Communes throughout China and the mobilization of the masses for the production of steel.
December: Mao announces his decision not to stand for another term as Chairman of the Chinese People's Republic.

1959 July: At the Lushan Plenum of the Central Committee of the Chinese Communist Party, P'eng Te-huai violently attacks Mao's radical policies; he is subsequently removed from his post as Minister of Defence.
September: Publication of a Tass statement on the Sino–Indian border conflict which marked the first public expression of foreign policy divergences between Moscow and Peking.

1960 April: Withdrawal of Soviet technicians from China.
November: At the second Moscow meeting of communist and

workers' parties, the Chinese and Soviet delegations clash sharply on the 'peaceful road to socialism'.

1961 October: Chou En-lai, Chinese delegate to the Twenty-second Congress of the Communist Party of the Soviet Union, lays a wreath on Stalin's tomb and then leaves abruptly for home.

1962 September: At the Tenth Plenum of the Central Committee of the Chinese Communist Party, Mao Tse-tung puts forward the call: 'Never forget the class struggle'.

October: Sino–Indian border war.

1963 May: In a note on materials regarding the participation of cadres in productive labour Mao Tse-tung calls for the 'three great revolutionary movements' of class struggle, the struggle for production, and scientific experiment as the only method for preventing a 'change of colour' in China.

June: In a letter to the Soviet Communist Party the Chinese Communist Party declares for the first time that henceforth Africa, Asia, and Latin America constitute the 'storm centres' of world revolution.

October: In an attack on the Soviets entitled 'Apologists for neo-colonialism' the Chinese elaborate on the idea that henceforth the centre of the world revolution has shifted from Europe to Asia.

1964 February: In China a campaign is launched to 'learn from the People's Liberation Army'.

February: In the Soviet Union a plenum of the Central Committee of the Communist Party of the Soviet Union launches a full-scale ideological counter-attack against the Chinese and denounces for the first time the 'personal dictatorship' of Mao Tse-tung.

May: Publication by the General Political Department of the People's Liberation Army of the first edition of *Quotations from Chairman Mao*.

July: An editorial entitled 'Khrushchev's phoney communism and its lessons for the world' quotes Mao as calling for bringing up 'millions of successors' for the revolutionary cause in order to give the lie to imperialist prophecies regarding 'a peaceful evolution' towards capitalism in China such as has taken place in the Soviet Union.

1965 January: The 'twenty-three-article directive' attributed to Mao launches the 'four clean-ups' movement in the countryside.

February: Beginning of American bombardment of North Vietnam.

September: Lin Piao, in an article 'Long live the victory of the People's War', calls for the encirclement of the 'cities' from the 'countryside' on a world scale.
November: Attacks on Wu Han, the Vice Mayor of Peking, give the first warning signals of the coming 'Cultural Revolution'.

1966 May: Mao denounces in a directive on the Cultural Revolution 'persons like Khrushchev nestling beside us'.
August: Mao writes his big-character poster entitled 'Bombard the headquarters'. The Eleventh Plenum of the Central Committee of the Chinese Communist Party adopts the 'sixteen-point decision' regarding the Cultural Revolution.
August–November: Mao reviews millions of Red Guards at mass rallies in Peking.

1967 January: Mao launches a new phase of the Cultural Revolution in which revolutionary committees based on the 'triple union' endeavour to take over all power from the state and Party authorities.
April: Beginning of a campaign of denunciation directed against Liu Shao-ch'i, designated by the epithet 'China's Khrushchev', and against his ideological influence.

1968 August: An editorial hailing the second anniversary of Mao's big-character poster 'Bombard the headquarters' emphasizes that 'Chairman Mao's proletarian headquarters' is the 'one and only leading centre' and that 'we must carry out every one of Chairman Mao's instructions ... even when we do not understand it'.
September: Revolutionary committees have at last been set up in all provinces of China except Taiwan.
October: The Twelfth Plenum of the Central Committee of the Chinese Communist Party officially denounces Liu Shao-ch'i as a scab, renegade and traitor, and approves as a basis for discussion a new draft Party constitution proposed by Mao Tse-tung.

Bibliography

In the absence of any more serious study of Mao Tse-tung's thought, this book, although originally planned for students of history and politics, may also be of interest to those with a knowledge of China and Chinese. Therefore, this bibliography has been compiled for this dual audience. The first part lists supplementary readings on Mao and contemporary China in Western languages. The second part gives the principal Chinese-language sources used in the compilation of this anthology.

Part 1: Suggested Readings

Modern China. A good general history of China is L. C. Goodrich's *A Short History of the Chinese People* (third revised edition), Allen & Unwin, 1958; Harper & Row, New York, 1959. An intellectual history emphasizing political as well as narrowly philosophical problems is that of H. G. Creel, *Chinese Thought from Confucius to Mao Tse-tung*, University of Chicago, 1953.

On the more recent period an excellent survey is H. McAleavy's *A Modern History of China*, Weidenfeld & Nicolson, and Frederick A. Praeger, New York, 1967. Regarding the political aspects of China's evolution since the Opium War, which marks the beginning of a period of increasingly rapid change under the impact of the Occident, see Li Chien-nung, *The Political History of China 1840–1928*, Van Nostrand, Princeton, N.J., 1956. A Chinese view of these problems is given in Hu Sheng, *Imperialism and Chinese Politics*, Foreign Languages Press, Peking, 1957.

Regarding the intellectual revolution which is one of the most important aspects of this process of transformation, see J. K. Fairbank and S. Y. Teng, *China's Response to the West*, Harvard University, Cambridge, Mass., 1954, containing a selection of very interesting texts in English translation with commentaries, and also Joseph Levenson, *Confucian China and Its Modern Fate* (three volumes), University of California, Berkeley, Calif., and Routledge, 1958–65. On the most dramatic period of this intellectual upheaval, which is also the period during which Mao Tse-tung began his adult life, see Chow Tse-tsung, *The May Fourth Movement*, Harvard University, Cambridge, Mass., 1960.

The Chinese Revolution Since the Foundation of the Chinese Communist Party. The only full-scale study of Chinese communism both before and after the conquest of power is that of Peter Tang, *Communist China Today* (two volumes), Research Institute on the Sino–Soviet Bloc, Washington, 1961–2. The author is extremely partisan and not particularly imaginative, but he has produced a useful description of the structures of the regime as well as an extensive chronology. An official viewpoint, no longer orthodox in the context of the Cultural Revolution, was set forth by Ho Kan-chih in *A History of the Modern Chinese Revolution*, Foreign Languages Press, Peking, 1959.

On the period prior to the conquest of power, *A Documentary History of Chinese Communism* by Conrad Brandt, Benjamin Schwartz, and John Fairbank, Harvard University, Cambridge, Mass., 1952, remains a basic reference work, although written at a time when many sources had not yet been unearthed and despite the criticisms to which, like all pioneer efforts, it has been exposed.

Of the works devoted to narrower periods, the most important on the years of collaboration between the Kuomintang and the communists, 1923–7, are Conrad Brandt's *Stalin's Failure in China*, Harvard University, Cambridge, Mass., 1958, and Harold Isaacs's *The Tragedy of the Chinese Revolution* (third edition), Stanford University, Stanford, Calif., 1961. The first edition of Isaacs's book contained a preface by Trotsky and corresponded closely to Trotsky's viewpoint; the author has changed his position since. An important documentary source recently published is Robert C. North and Xenia Eudin's *M. N. Roy's Mission to China*, University of California, Berkeley, Calif., 1963.

In dealing with the following period, that of the Kiangsi Soviet Government, Hsiao Tso-liang has attempted, in *Power Relations within the Chinese Communist Movement 1930–1934*, University of Washington, Seattle, Wash., 1961, to demolish the thesis of the *Documentary History* regarding the originality and the independence of the Chinese communist movement, and to prove that Mao was really Moscow's man. Although the position of Brandt, Schwartz, and Fairbank may be somewhat overstated, I remain unconvinced that Hsiao's thesis is closer to the truth. Two more recent studies written from viewpoints sympathetic to Mao are Shanti Swarup's *A Study of the Chinese Communist Movement*, Oxford University, 1966, and John E. Rue's *Mao*

Tse-tung in Opposition, 1927–1935, Stanford University, Stanford, Calif., 1966.

Robert C. North has written in *Moscow and Chinese Communists*, Stanford University, Stanford, Calif., second edition, 1963, the history of the Chinese communist movement in the perspective of relations with the Soviet Union. The relations with Moscow have also been studied by Charles B. McLane in *Soviet Policy and the Chinese Communists, 1931–1946*, Columbia University, New York, 1958.

On the period 1935–49 a most important and original contribution has been made by Chalmers A. Johnson, who has put forward in *Peasant Nationalism and Communist Power*, Stanford University, Stanford, Calif., 1962, the thesis that the Chinese communist movement, during the Yenan period, was basically a species of nationalism. Lyman P. van Slyke in *Enemies and Friends: The United Front in Chinese Communist History*, Stanford University, Stanford, Calif., 1967, has also made a useful contribution to our knowledge of the ideological framework during this period. Finally, Tang Tsou in *America's Failure in China, 1941–1950*, University of Chicago, 1963, throws a great deal of light, not only on the foreign policy problems which are his primary theme, but also on the struggle for power between the communists and the nationalists within China.

The basic documents of the first great rectification campaign, during World War II, have been translated and provided with a very useful commentary by Boyd Compton in *Mao's China: Party Reform Documents 1942–1944*, University of Washington, Seattle, Wash., 1952. (This volume was republished in paperback in 1967.)

The Evolution of the Chinese People's Republic since 1949. By all odds the most important study of China since 1949, and one which deals in depth, not only with the concrete changes in Chinese social and political organization, but with the ideological problems which are the subject of the present volume, is Franz Schurmann's *Ideology and Organization in Communist China*, University of California, Berkeley, Calif., 1966, revised 1968. Light is also thrown on both orders of problems by John Wilson Lewis's *Leadership in Communist China*, Cornell University, Ithaca, New York, 1963. The Chinese army, which is somewhat neglected, both by Schurmann and by Lewis, has been the subject of two useful studies: John Gittings's *The Role of the Chinese Army*, Oxford, 1967, and Samuel B. Griffith's *The Chinese People's Liberation Army*, McGraw-Hill, New York, 1967.

A solid documentary basis for the first great upsurge of revolutionary extremism is supplied by *Communist China, 1955–1959: Policy Docu-*

ments with Analysis, edited by R. R. Bowie and J. K. Fairbank, Harvard University, Cambridge, Mass., 1962, which contains the complete text of nearly all the most important materials, including many of Mao's writings and speeches. On the episode of the Hundred Flowers, see Roderick Macfarquhar, *The Hundred Flowers Campaign and the Chinese Intellectuals*, Frederick A. Praeger, New York, 1960.

In more specialized domains, a good general picture of the development of the Chinese economy at an early stage is to be found in Yüan-li Wu's *An Economic Survey of Communist China*, Bookman Associates, New York, 1956. The first Five-Year Plan is evaluated by Li Choh-ming in *Economic Development of Communist China. An Appraisal of the First Five Years of Industrialization*, University of California, Berkeley, Calif., 1959. The most complete and authoritative account of China's economic policies and their results, as seen from the perspective of the present day, is to be found in Galenson, Liu and Eckstein (editors), *Economic Trends in Communist China*, to be published shortly by The Aldine Press. In the field of agriculture, Chao Kuo-chün has traced the evolution of policy from the origins to the communes in *Agrarian Policy of the Chinese Communist Party*, Asia Publishing House, Bombay, 1960.

The most convenient general survey of China's foreign policy is Vidya Prakash Dutt's *China and the World*, Frederick A. Praeger, New York, 1966. Another important study is that of A. Doak Barnett on relations with Peking's Asian neighbours – *Communist China and Asia*, Harper, New York, 1960.

Regarding the relations between Moscow and Peking, Donald Zagoria's pathbreaking study on the conflict with Moscow – *The Sino-Soviet Conflict, 1956–1961*, Princeton University, Princeton, New Jersey, 1962 – is brought up to date in William E. Griffith's *The Sino-Soviet Rift*, M.I.T., Cambridge, Mass., 1967.

Although a large number of books regarding the Cultural Revolution have been written, and some have already come off the press, it is obviously too early for any definitive study of the subject. One of the most serious of those which have so far appeared is Jack Gray and Patrick Cavendish's *Chinese Communism in Crisis: Maoism and the Cultural Revolution*, Pall Mall Press, and Frederix A. Praeger, New York, 1968.

The Biography of Mao Tse-tung. Among the sources on Mao's life available in translation, the only ones that deserve mention here are Mao's autobiography, as told by him to Edgar Snow in 1936, and the testimony of the two Hsiao brothers, his boyhood friends. Although the autobiography obviously cannot be regarded as an objective source, it is a highly interesting document, and although he observes certain conventions of the time, such as throwing all the blame for the failure of 1927 on Ch'en Tu-hsiu, Mao expresses himself with a certain freedom, recognizing, for example, the great influence of Ch'en on his own development. In any case, it is the single most important and instructive document we possess. Edgar Snow published the complete text as he took it down at the time in *Red Star over China*, Random House, New York, 1938.

As for the two Hsiao brothers (the name is usually transcribed as Siao by these men themselves), the pro-communist brother, Hsiao San or Emi Siao, in his biography of the young Mao (English translation: *Mao Tse-tung, His Childhood and Youth*, People's Publishing House, Bombay, 1953), follows Mao's own autobiography fairly closely, but adds a certain number of details. The anti-communist brother, Hsiao Hsü-tung or Siao-Yü, has published a volume of souvenirs called *Mao Tse-tung and I Were Beggars*, Syracuse University, Syracuse, New York, 1959. Although his dates are inaccurate, and although his present hostile attitude obviously colours the picture he draws of his former friend, some of the conversations he has reconstructed from memory conform to the views expressed by Mao in the article of 1917, which appears at the beginning of this volume.

The situation as regards biographies of Mao Tse-tung has improved substantially since the publication of the first edition of this book five years ago. This is due in particular to the publication of Jerome Ch'en's *Mao and the Chinese Revolution*, Oxford University, 1965. The serious, objective and well documented character of Ch'en's study highlights the weaknesses of such book as G. Paloczi-Horvath's *Mao Tse-tung, Emperor of the Blue Ants*, Secker & Warburg, 1962; Doubleday, New York, 1963; and Robert Payne's *Portrait of a Revolutionary: Mao Tse-tung*, Abelard-Schuman, New York, 1961. Ch'en's biography takes the story of Mao's life only down to the conquest of power in 1949. I have given my own version of Mao's life in *Mao Tse-tung*, Penguin Books, 1967, revised edition, 1969; also being published in 1969 in hardback by Allen Lane, The Penguin Press and Simon & Schuster, New York.

The Ideas of Mao Tse-tung. Benjamin Schwartz, in *Chinese Communism and the Rise of Mao* (third edition), Harvard University, Cambridge, Mass., 1958, though dealing to a considerable extent with the events of the years 1930–35, which brought Mao to a dominant position in the Chinese Communist Party, constantly emphasizes problems of theory and tactics. His final chapter, 'The Maoist Strategy', remains the most concise and striking presentation of the thesis according to which 'Maoism' represents a new stage in the degeneration of Marxism. The idea of Mao's originality has been violently attacked by Karl A. Wittfogel, who sees in him merely a faithful disciple of Stalin. Professor Wittfogel has not yet set forth his views in a full-scale work, but he has summarized them in various articles: 'The legend of "Maoism"', *China Quarterly*, nos. 1 and 2, 1960; 'Mao: doctrine et stratégie', *Le Contrat social*, V, no. 3, May–June 1961.

Among the official interpretations of Mao's thought, the one that received the widest distribution prior to the Cultural Revolution was that of Ch'en Po-ta, set forth in such writings as *Mao Tse-tung's Theory of the Chinese Revolution*, *On Reading Mao Tse-tung's 'Report on the Peasant Movement in Hunan'*, and various other pamphlets published by the Foreign Languages Press, Peking. Ch'en's productions are of the most extreme mediocrity, but they did at one time express the official position. Using countless citations, he endeavoured to show that Mao is both a faithful disciple of Stalin and an innovator who has opened the way to revolution in the underdeveloped countries.

As for the current interpretation of 'Mao Tse-tung's thought', it varies from day to day. The various key texts, as they appear, are published in generally very accurate English translations in the weekly *Peking Review*.

For the period of 1926–49, a complete English translation of the current Chinese version of Mao's writings is available in the four-volume edition of the *Selected Works*, brought out by the Foreign Languages Press in Peking. This replaces the five-volume edition published earlier by International Publishers, New York, and by Lawrence & Wishart, which has now been repudiated by the Chinese. However, texts not included in the *Selected Works* are to be found in *Selected Writings from the Works of Mao Tse-tung*, Foreign Languages Press, Peking, 1967.

The following is a list, in chronological order, of some of the most important of Mao's writings:

The only item written before 1926 translated in its entirety into a Western language is the 1917 article on physical culture, which I have published as a separate volume: Mao Ze-dong, *Une Étude de l'éducation physique*, Mouton, Paris, 1962.

Among the writings included in the *Selected Works* (excluding military writings, which will be dealt with in a separate paragraph) the following should be mentioned:

VOLUME 1

'Report of an investigation of the peasant movement in Hunan' (1927); 'The struggle in the Chingkang Mountains' (1928). These two very important texts are among those that have undergone the most extensive modifications in the current edition, but no complete translation of either in the original form is available.

'On correcting mistaken ideas in the Party' (1929). This text, which has received considerable attention during the Cultural Revolution, is in fact only the first chapter of a much longer resolution. There are no translations of the remainder of the resolution.

'The tactics of the struggle against Japanese imperialism' (1935); 'On practice' (1937); 'On contradiction' (1937).

VOLUME 2

'Against liberalism' (1938); 'The role of the Chinese Communist Party in the national war' (1938). As indicated at the beginning of Text II A, 'The role of the Chinese Communist Party', presented in the *Selected Works* as the whole of Mao's report to the Sixth Plenum of the Central Committee, is only an extract. The full report is available in a very bad translation, also cited in the note to Text II A, which is to be found in a few American libraries.

'The Chinese revolution and the Chinese Communist Party' (1939). This very important text has also undergone many modifications. A good translation of the original text appeared in *Current Background*, no. 135, issued by the U.S. Consulate General, Hong Kong. It is available in many university libraries. One can therefore dispense with the *Selected Works* version.

'On new democracy' (1940). This text has also been substantially modified. Some extracts, as originally written, are translated in *Marxism and Asia*.

VOLUME 3

'Let us reform our style of work' (1 February 1942); 'Against Party eight-legged essays' (8 February 1942). These two very important speeches have been completely rewritten in the current version of Mao's writings. As the authentic text is easily available in Boyd Compton, *Mao's China*, one can dispense with the *Selected Works* version completely.

'Interventions at the conference on art and literature' (May 1942). Here, too, the changes are very extensive; two translations of the original text are available – the one cited at the beginning of Text VI B 2 and one issued by International Publishers in 1950 in a separate pamphlet. One can therefore dispense with the *Selected Works* text.

'On coalition government' (1945). This text, too, has been completely rewritten, since it dates from a soft-line period in relations with the Kuomintang. The translation cited at the beginning of Text VI A 4 therefore is preferable.

VOLUME 4

'The present situation and our tasks' (1947); 'On people's democratic dictatorship' (1949).

The *Selected Works* neglects almost completely the period of the Kiangsi Soviet Republic (1931–4), which is also sparsely represented in this anthology. The lengthiest text of this period is Mao's report to the Second Congress of Soviets, in January 1934, which is available in a complete Russian translation: *Vtoroi S'ezd Kitaiskikh Sovetov* (Moscow, 1934). Extracts from this text in English translation appear in the *Documentary History* by Brandt, Schwarz and Fairbank. One can also find a few texts signed by Mao and his colleagues of the Kiangsi Soviet in *Fundamental Laws of the Chinese Soviet Republic*, with a preface by Bela Kun, International Publishers, New York, 1934.

Mao's post-1949 writings have not yet been collected into one volume, even in Chinese. The following texts are among the few accessible ones: Speech of 21 September 1949 (see Text I D for the source); Speech of 6 June 1950, in *New China's Economic Achievements*, China Committee for the Promotion of International Trade, Peking, 1952, pp. 1–9; Speech of July 1955 on agricultural collectivization, available in Bowie and Fairbank's *Communist China, 1955–1959*; introduction and notes to *Socialist Upsurge in China's Countryside* (see Text VI B 3 for the reference); speeches of 27 February and 6 November 1957 (also in *Communist China, 1955–1959*).

Since 1958, as I have already emphasized, Mao has been remarkably discreet in his utterances on Chinese internal affairs. In the course of the Cultural Revolution a large number of directives attributed to him have been published, some of which are included in Chapters VI and VII of this anthology. Others are to be found from time to time in *Peking Review*. On the other hand, since 1963 Mao has published increasing numbers of statements regarding problems of foreign affairs; a number of the most important of these have been added to Chapters VIII, IX and X of this volume.

As for Mao's poetry, so important for the understanding of his personality, a complete translation of the thirty-eight poems now available is included as an appendix in Jerome Ch'en's biography of Mao. Another version complete with the Chinese text has been published in *Poems of Mao Tse-tung translated and annotated by Wong Man* and *Ten More Poems of Mao Tse-tung*, Eastern Horizon Press, Hong Kong, 1966 and 1967. I have also given my own version of a certain number of poems in my biography of Mao.

The problem of Mao's originality as a military strategist in the narrow sense is a very controversial one. J. E. Garvey, in *Marxist-Leninist China: Military and Social Doctrine*, Exposition Press, New York, 1960, concludes that the Chinese communists are orthodox Leninists who are distinguished from the Soviets primarily by the fact that they are more intelligent, and also by an ingrained xenophobia. Samuel B. Griffith, in *Mao Tse-tung on Guerrilla Warfare*, Frederick A. Praeger, New York, 1961, has written the most concise and elegant account of the essence of guerrilla warfare as practised by Mao. (The text he has translated, of which the original has been lost, was published in 1937 under the title *Yu-chi chan* (*Guerrilla Warfare*). This appears to be an earlier version of a volume published in 1938 by Chieh-fang She, the publishing house of the Chinese communists, entitled *K'ang-Jih yu-chi chan-cheng ti i-pan wen-t'i* (*All the Problems of the Anti-Japanese Guerrilla War*). In this volume, only Chapter VII, which is identical with 'Strategic problems of the anti-Japanese guerrilla war' in Volume 2 of the *Selected Works*, with the usual variants, is attributed to Mao. However, it is indicated in the preface to this 1938 edition that Mao went over the whole volume, and there is no doubt that the book reflects his views. A review article summing up the literature on the subject is Howard L. and Scott A. Boorman's 'Chinese communist insurgent warfare 1939–45', *Political Science Quarterly*, vol. 81, no. 2, June 1966, pp. 171–95. I have given my own succinct account of the development of Mao's military thinking in my introduction to Mao Tse-tung's *Basic Tactics*, Frederick A. Praeger, New York, 1966.

Other pertinent readings on the originality of Mao's military thought include Harold C. Hinton, 'Political aspects of military power and policy in Communist China', in Harry L. Coles (editor), *Total War and Cold War*, Ohio State University, Columbus, Ohio, 1962, pp. 266–92; Raymond L. Garthoff, 'Unconventional warfare in communist strategy', *Foreign Affairs*, July 1962, pp. 566–75; and E. L. Katzenbach and G. Z. Hanrahan, 'The revolutionary strategy of Mao Tse-tung', *Political Science Quarterly*, September 1955, pp. 321–40.

Part 2: Sources

A. Periodicals

The dates below are those for which the periodical in question was examined in the course of preparing this anthology and do not necessarily indicate the total period of its publication. *Chieh-fang* (Yenan), 1937–41; *Chieh-fang jih-pao* (Yenan), 1941–6; *Ch'ün-chung* (Shanghai), 1938–47; *Ch'ün-chung* (Hong Kong), 1948; *Chung-kuo nung-min*, 1926; *Hsiang-tao*, 1922–7; *Hsin-hua yüeh-pao* (later *Hsin-hua pan-yüeh-k'an*), 1949–60; *Hsin ch'ing-nien*, 1917; *Hu-nan li-shih tzu-liao*, 1958–60; *Hung-ch'i*, 1958–68; *Jen-min jih-pao*, 1950–68; *K'ang-chan ta-hsüeh* (Canton), 1938; *Min-tsu chan-hsien* (Tientsin), 1935; *Tou-cheng* (For a description of the various series of *Tou-cheng*, see Chün-tu Hsüeh, *The Chinese Communist Movement, 1921–37. An Annotated Bibliography of Selected Materials in the Chinese Collection of the Hoover Institution on War, Revolution and Peace*, Hoover Institution, Stanford, Calif., 1960).

B. Books and Pamphlets

Mao Tse-tung, *Chi-ch'u chan-shu*, Tzu-ch'iang Ch'u-pan-she, Hankow, 1938.

——, *Ching-chi wen-t'i yü ts'ai-cheng wen-t'i*, Chieh-fang She, Yenan, 1944.

——, *Chung-kuo Kung-ch'an-tang Hung-chün ti-ssu-chün ti-chiu-tz'u tai-piao ta-hui chüeh-i-an*, Hsin-min-chu Ch'u-pan-she, Hongkong, 1949.

——, *Hsüan-chi*, Chin-ch'a-chi Hsin-hua Shu-tien, 1947, six volumes and supplement. Of this edition I have used only the supplement (*hsü-pien*), dated December 1947.

——, *Hsüan-chi*, Jen-min Ch'u-pan-she, Peking, 1951–60 (four volumes). The current official edition, designated throughout this anthology by the words *Hsüan-chi*, followed by the number of the volume in Roman numerals.

——, *Kuan-yü cheng-ch'üeh ch'u-li jen-min nei-pu ti mao-tun*, Peking, 1960.

——, *Kuan-yü nung-yeh ho-tso-hua wen-t'i*, Jen-min Ch'u-pan-she, Peking, 1955.

——, *Lun hsin chieh-tuan*, Chieh-fang She, Yenan, 1939.

——, *Lun lien-ho cheng-fu*, Chieh-fang She, Yenan, 1945.

——, *Mao chu-hsi shih-tz'u san-shih-ch'i shou*, Peking, 1965.

——, *Mao chu-hsi tsai Su-lien ti yen-lun*, Peking, 1957.
——, *Mao Tse-tung lun-wen-chi*, Ta-chung Ch'u-pan-she, Shanghai, 1937.
——, *Mu-ch'ien hsing-shih ho wo-men ti jen-wu*, Chieh-fang She, Yenan, 1948.
——, *Tsui wei-ta-ti yu-i*, Jen-min Ch'u-pan-she, Peking, 1953.
Mao Tse-tung and others, *Chung-kuo ch'ing-yün wen-hsüan*, Hsin-hua Shu-tien, Yenan, 1940.
——, *Chung-kuo ko-ming yü Chung-kuo Kung-ch'an-tang*, Chieh-fang She, Yenan [1940?].
——, *Chung-kuo nung-ts'un ti she-hui-chu-i kao-ch'ao*, Jen-min Ch'u-pan-she, Peking, 1956 (three volumes).
——, *Su-wei-ai Chung-kuo*, Izdatel'stvo Inostrannykh Rabochikh, Moscow, 1934.

Special note on the sources for 'The great union of the popular masses'

The review edited by Mao in July and August 1919, *Hsiang-chiang p'ing-lun*, is not available outside China, nor are any of the other periodicals in which he wrote during the May Fourth period. At the same time, Mao's writings at this time represent such an important stage in his evolution that I have thought it indispensable to include a few extracts, even if it was necessary to base them on secondary sources. Two of these texts (VI A 1 and VII A 1) are simply translated from passages published in the review *Hu-nan li-shih tzu-liao*, which appeared in Changsha in 1958–60, and in which various materials on the history of Hunan were reprinted. It is, of course, possible that these texts have been tampered with by the editors of this journal, but on the whole I believe that these recent versions give a reasonably adequate idea of the original writings.

The articles published by Mao in *Hsiang-chiang p'ing-lun*, from which I have taken Texts I A and IV A, raise much more difficult questions. On the one hand, they were rather long ('The great union of the popular masses' is said to have had 5,000 characters), and no source gives an adequate picture of the whole, so that the text must be reconstructed from a patchwork of sources. On the other hand, 'The great union of the popular masses' plays a crucial role in the attempts of certain authors writing in Peking to rewrite Mao's intellectual biography so as to prove that in 1919 he had already formulated – at least in embryonic form – all the theses he was to put forward twenty years later. It is therefore necessary to be particularly skeptical about the authenticity of the citations and especially of the summaries of this text published since 1949 in China.

At the same time, it should be pointed out that some Chinese historians have shown themselves to be much more scrupulous than others in their methods of handling sources. (This can be checked to a certain extent because passages of the article have been published in facsimile and are thus somewhat more reliable.) Thus, Li Jui, who wrote what was at one time an authorized biography of the young Mao, using many manuscript sources (LI JUI, *Mao Tse-tung t'ung-chih ti ch'u-ch'i ko-ming huo-tung* [Chung-kuo Ch'ing-nien Ch'u-pan-she, Peking, 1957]), attributes to Mao the statement that the present deplorable conditions of humanity have caused the outbreak of 'revolution' (*ko-ming*), whereas the original text, available in facsimile, speaks of 'reform' (*kai-ke*). (See the third paragraph of Text IV A.) Other sources recently published in China faithfully reproduce the language of the original on this point.

It is obviously out of the question, in a book of this kind, to analyse the various versions of this text paragraph by paragraph. I therefore limit myself to listing a few of the most important sources, for those who might wish to go more deeply into the matter. First of all, two works containing facsimiles:

Wu-ssu yün-tung tsai Shang-hai shih-liao hsüan-chi, Shanghai, 1960. (Contains a facsimile of some of the introductory paragraphs of 'The great union of the popular masses'. Paragraphs 1, 2, 4, and 5 of Text IV A, with the exception of the words in square brackets at the beginning of paragraph 4, have been checked against this source.)
Wu-ssu shih-ch'i ch'i-k'an chieh-shao, Jen-min Ch'u-pan-she, Vol. I., Peking, 1958. (Contains a facsimile of the manifesto from the first issue of *Hsiang-chiang p'ing-lun*, against which the first two paragraphs of Text I A were checked.)

The second of the above volumes also contains citations of numerous passages from 'The great union of the popular masses'. Among the other principal sources for my extracts from this text are the following:

An article in *Hsin chien-she*, May 1959, especially pp. 7–8; an article in *Hu-nan li-shih tzu-liao*, no. 7, 1959, of which the second part, in no. 8 of the same journal, provided the source for Texts VI A 1 and VII A1; *Hu-nan chin pai-nien ta-shih chi-shu* probably published in Changsha. The preface is dated 20 December 1958).

Although the citations in these sources are obviously less convincing than the facsimiles mentioned above (though it is possible to modify a facsimile), and although I have some doubts, expressed in the general introduction and in the introduction to Chapter IV, regarding the manner in which these authors interpret Mao's thought of 1919, I think that Texts I A and IV A probably convey enough of the style and substance of the original version to be of interest.

Comparative Table of the Texts included in the Original and Revised Editions

Number in present edition	*Number in original edition*
Prologue	Prologue
I A	I A
I B	I B
I C	I C
I D	I D
II A	II A
II B	II B
II C (expanded in this edition)	II C
II D	II D
II E	II E
III A	III A
III B	III B
III C	III C
III D	III D
III E	III E
III F	III F
III G	III G
III H	III H
III I	III I
III J	III J
III K	III K
III L	III L
IV A	IV A
IV B	IV B
IV C	IV C
IV D	IV D
IV E	IV E
IV F	IV F
IV G	IV G
IV H	IV H

V A	V A
V B	V B
V C	V C
V D	V D
V E	V E
V F	not included
V G	V F
V H	V G
V I	not included
V J (with new last paragraph)	V H
V K	not included
V L	V H (last paragraph)
V M	V I
VI A 1	VI A 1
VI A 2	VI A 4
VI A 3	VI A 6
VI B 1	VII A 1
VI B 2	VII A 2
VI B 3	VII A 3
VI C 1	not included
VI C 2	VI A 2
VI C 3	not included
VI C 4	VI A 3
VI C 5	not included
VI C 6	VI A 5
VI C 7	VII C 1
VI C 8	not included
VI C 9 (expanded in this edition)	VII C 3 (first half)
VI C 10	not included
VI C 11	not included
VI C 12	not included
VI C 13	not included
VII A 1	VI C 1
VII A 2	VI C 2
VII A 3	not included
VII A 4	replaces previous Text VI C 3
VII B 1	VII B 1
VII B 2	VII B 2
VII B 3	VII B 3
VII B 4	not included

VII B 5	VII B 4
VII B 6	not included
VII B 7	VII B 5
VII B 8	not included
VII C 1	VII C 2
VII C 2 (expanded in this edition)	VII C 3 (second part)
VII C 3	VII C 4
VII C 4	VII C 5
VII D 1	VI D 1
VII D 2	VI D 2
VII D 3	not included
VII E 1	VI B 1
VII E 2	not included
VII E 3	VI B 2
VII E 4	not included
VII E 5	not included
VII E 6	not included
VII E 7	not included
VII E 8	not included
VII E 9	not included
VII E 10	not included
VIII A	VIII A
VIII B	VIII B
VIII C	VIII C
VIII D	VIII D
VIII E	VIII E
VIII F	VIII F
VIII G	VIII G
VIII H	not included
VIII I	not included
VIII J	not included
IX A	IX A
IX B	IX B
IX C	IX C
IX D	IX D
IX E	IX E
IX F	IX F
IX G	IX G
IX H	IX H
IX I	IX I

IX J	IX K
IX K	replaces previous Text IX J
IX L	not included
IX M	not included
X A	X A
X B	X B
X C	X C
X D	X D
X E	X E
X F	X F
X G	replaces previous Text X G
X H	X H
X I	X I
X J	X J
X K	X K
X L	not included
X M	not included

Index

Also by Stuart Schram, in the Pelican series,
'Political Leaders of the Twentieth Century'

Mao Tse-tung

By any reckoning Mao Tse-tung must be regarded as one of the greatest and most remarkable statesmen of modern times. As a poet of distinction, as a political philosopher of major importance, and as a strategist whose 6000-mile trek across China has become a legend, Mao has devoted his life to China and the Chinese peasants. Indeed the Chinese People's Republic has shaped a whole pattern of revolution for poor peasant societies. In this biography Stuart Schram sifts fact from fiction in the long story of Mao's struggle to free the greatness of China and to give a new meaning to Marxism.